MARKETING FINANCIAL SERVICES
Second Edition

Hooman Estelami
Fordham University

MARKETING FINANCIAL SERVICES

Hooman Estelami
Fordham University

Editor: Stewart Skrondal
Production Manager: Matthew Murry

First published by Dog Ear Publishing 4010 W.
86th Street, Ste H
Indianapolis, IN 46268
www.dogearpublishing.net

ISBN: 978-145750-774-8

This book is printed on acid-free paper.

Printed in the United States of America

To the Memory of My Mother ... Parvin Anvar-Estelami

TABLE OF CONTENTS

DETAILED TABLE OF CONTENTS

PREFACE

Since the writing of the first edition of this book, the global financial services marketing landscape has dramatically changed. At the time of writing the first edition, bank failures were an unheard of phenomenon in the United States. Since then hundreds of banks have failed, account delinquency for credit products skyrocketed, and consumer bankruptcy rates have reached record levels. Larger financial institutions in the U.S. had to be protected from failure by the federal government and new regulations motivated by these dramatic changes have since been introduced. These changes were universal, experienced not only in the United States but worldwide, and mandated the writing of a new edition of *Marketing Financial Services*.

The writing of this edition was also motivated by the absence of a formal textbook on the marketing of financial services. The books available, while useful in their own specific contexts, have limited applicability to the rigorous training of professionals in the field. While many how-to cookbooks with hands-on flavors exist, they fail to provide a solid and coherent structure for the reader, and miss out on much of the important practical details that are essential to disciplined management of marketing activities in today's financial services organizations. This book therefore attempts to train the reader on the practical aspects of financial services marketing in a well-organized and structured manner.

The marketing of financial services is a topic that has fascinated practitioners and academicians for decades. Scientific research and market evidence on the behavior of decision makers in financial markets has resulted in the accumulation of a wealth of knowledge with great practical applications. Scientific studies, many of which have been published in the past decade, have documented the predictable manner in which consumers make financial decisions, which at times defies rational thinking. Decisions that relate to some of the most significant human tasks, such as investing one's life savings, planning for children's education, and protecting oneself against financial risks, have often been found to be made in ways that challenge rational economic prescriptions. The pattern of consumer decisions in financial services has heightened the importance of establishing a universal framework for financial services marketing, and is one of the basic reasons for the existence this book.

The writing of the book has also been motivated by my own experiences as a consultant to the industry for over two decades. These experiences have not only helped shape the applied aspects of the book, but have also given me an appreciation for the complexity of issues that financial services marketers face on a daily basis. One of the challenges I have observed many marketing managers in financial services organizations face has been the lack of consistent, coherent, and disciplined approaches towards the practice of marketing. This book is an attempt to address this issue by providing a rigorous and applied framework for both practitioners and business students.

The framework has been extensively tested in my own teaching of the topic to both seasoned executives and business students at various skill levels.

This book has been structured to facilitate both the independent study of the topic by the reader, and formal classroom approaches to learning. The first three chapters outline the trends in the marketplace for financial services and provide the framework for typical mental strategies that consumers utilize when evaluating financial services offers. By focusing on these issues, this book takes on a consumer-based perspective on what constitutes effective marketing practice. Individual chapters have been dedicated to pricing, advertising, distribution, and product development in financial services. The unique aspects of these marketing activities within the context of financial services are discussed in considerable detail in order to help readers gain the depth of knowledge necessary for managing these activities. Two additional chapters of this book discuss segmentation techniques and customer relationship management practices that have become the cornerstones for effective marketing in an increasingly fragmented marketplace. Regulatory forces that influence financial services markets are also discussed in a stand-alone chapter, and the book concludes with a framework for identifying successful financial services marketing strategies. In addition, a series of cases are presented in the final chapter of the book.

The general style of the book has been developed to ensure relevance to practitioners eager to gain formal training on the marketing of financial services and to business students both at the undergraduate and graduate levels. The material presented has been extensively used, tested, and refined with these groups. Where trends, statistics, and research findings are presented, the information sources have been cited in the text in order to assist readers to conduct further examination of topics of interest to them. Each chapter not only contains a list of all references related to factual information presented, but is also supplemented with relevant practical questions and topics that tap into the knowledge developed in the chapter. Instructors in academic institutions interested in adopting the book for classroom use may find it helpful to utilize the supplemental *Instructor's Manual, Instructional Presentation Slides*, the *BancSim2* computer simulation, the multimedia resources available for online teaching of the course, and instructor webinars focused on coaching faculty through the teaching process. Instructors can contact me directly at *estelami@MarketingFinancialServices.net* in order to obtain access to the relevant content, and can also consult *MarketingFinancialServcies.net* for additional resources.

It is important to acknowledge all the special people who have helped make the second edition of this book possible. I owe many thanks to Stewart Skrondal for his editorial guidance throughout the revision process. The helpful comments of Matt Murry and Ray Robinson and two manuscript reviewers is also much appreciated. In addition, I owe a great deal to my wife, Nazanin, who has supported me every step of the way, and our two children Neema and Nikki who tolerated my limited availability while I was working on the manuscript revisions. I also have much to thank my father, Dr. Mohammad Estelami. He has set very high standards for me to reach as a researcher, writer, teacher and above all as a father. I also owe a great deal to my mother, Parvin Anvar-Estelami, who unfortunately passed away while I was working on the manuscript revisions. She helped guide much of my thinking through the years and had it not been for her encouraging me to follow an academic career path, this book would have most likely never come to life. Her constant inquiry and encouragement on my research and writing helped shape a great deal of my intellectual life, including the development of this book. Above that, she was a most supportive mother, and the love and care that she showed me and the countless sacrifices that she made are more than any child could ask for. Her many sacrifices as a mother, her kindness, warmth, passion for knowledge, and her high moral standards have been a guiding light. I hope to pass on some of her contribution to my thinking through this book to readers, and for this reason the book is dedicated to her memory.

CHAPTER ONE

The Challenges of Marketing Financial Services

The marketing of financial services is a unique and highly specialized branch of marketing. The practice of advertising, promoting, and selling financial products and services is in many ways far more complex than the selling of consumer packaged goods, automobiles, electronics, or other forms of goods or services. The environment in which financial services are marketed is becoming more competitive, making the marketing of financial services an increasingly unique discipline. Financial services marketers are challenged every day by the unique characteristics of the products they market. For example, often financial services cannot be visually communicated in advertisements as easily as consumer goods can. Furthermore, the relatively unexciting nature of financial services makes the task of attracting consumer attention and inspiring consumer desire a difficult one. However, the study of financial services marketing is in many ways far more fascinating than other areas of marketing. There are many predictable behaviors that consumers often exhibit in their dealings with financial services providers. The predictability of these behaviors and the abundance of data on existing and potential customers enable a uniquely scientific approach to developing and executing successful strategies for the marketing of financial services, much more so than in other markets.

EVIDENCE OF A QUICKLY CHANGING MARKET ENVIRONMENT

The collapse of the U.S. financial markets in 2008 and a series of subsequent regulations put in place to prevent similar future events testified to the degree of volatility by which financial markets operate. The economic climate resulting from the

2008 collapse was directly comparable to the collapse of the financial markets in the 1930s leading to the Great Depression. In the early 1930s, a series of bank failures had resulted in the heavy regulation of the financial services sector in the United States. These bank failures forced legislators to implement stringent regulations that prohibited commercial banks from participating in investment banking activities. Regulations such as the Glass-Steagall Act of 1933 and the Bank Holding Act of 1956 limited the types of products and services that financial institutions could offer their customers. As a result, for decades many financial services organizations were limited to a narrow range of markets in which they could legally operate. In 1999 the *Financial Services Modernization Act* reversed many of these regulations opening the doors for more competition in financial services markets. However, the increased competition, poor financial decisions by some of the largest financial institutions, and increasing levels of consumer debt contributed to the financial collapse of 2008. As a result, a series of new regulations such as the *Credit Card Accountability, Responsibility and Disclosure Act of 2009* and the *Dodd-Frank Wall Street Reform and Consumer Protection Act of 2010* were eventually signed into law. Since then, as shown in Exhibit 1.1, the financial services market environment has significantly changed. Below, we will discuss some of the evidence to illustrate the notable changes that characterize financial services markets.

Industry Consolidation and Concentration

Over the last decade, the level and complexity of marketing activities undertaken by financial services organizations, and the resulting competitive intensity, has increased significantly.[1] Deregulatory measures which went into effect at the start of the previous decade allowed financial services marketers to cross product market boundaries which had partitioned the market for decades. For example, prior to 1999 banks were allowed to sell insurance products but were limited in their ability to underwrite them themselves. Insurance agencies were allowed to sell insurance products but not to provide banking services such as deposit accounts. The regulatory environment following the *Bank Modernization Act of 1999* removed many of the barriers between the various financial institutions. This also contributed to increased degrees of industry concentration, consolidations, and mergers among financial services providers. For example, the number of commercial banks operating in the United States has experienced a significant and consistent decline since the mid 1990s. Similarly, in the online securities trading business only a handful of brokers now manage the majority of online trades.[2] These trends suggest that marketing power is being concentrated in many financial services categories, and thus there is a need for focused and well-calculated marketing strategies to ensure long-term success.

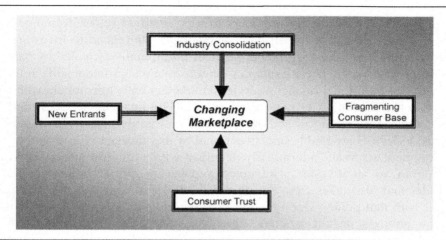

Exhibit 1.1 Evidence of Change in Financial Services Markets

In addition to the changing market conditions, the process and technologies for providing financial services is undergoing revolutionary change. The practice of offshore outsourcing (whereby a service organization utilizes a workforce outside of the country to provide customer service or other forms of service activities) has grown steadily in the financial services sector. This shift has and will continue to affect an array of jobs and will influence the future of the financial services marketing profession. The process of marketing of financial services is also changing due to emerging regulations enforced by regulatory bodies that control the nature and extent of marketing activities of financial services providers. As a result of these changes, competition is increasingly intense and it has become more challenging to achieve marketing success. In such an environment, the optimization of marketing capabilities in a financial services organization is even more critical for the long-term health and survival of the organization.

Emergence of New Entrants in the Marketplace

The traditional boundaries of financial services marketing have in recent years been challenged by the emergence of new competitors from both within and outside of the financial services sector. For example, some automobile manufacturers have begun to provide home equity loans, mortgages and other credit products to the public. Customers who use these financial products would gain credit towards the purchase of a new vehicle made by the manufacturer. Similarly, in contrast to the environment prior to the enactment of the *Bank Modernization Act*, when property and casualty insurance agents were primarily providers of a pre-defined set of insurance products, today's agents are equipped to sell their clients products related to investments, time deposits, retirement planning, and other services traditionally provided by banking and investment professionals. These examples demonstrate a significant shift in the type of competitors that traditional financial services marketers have to compete with today. In addition to the introduction of new competitors in the financial services marketplace, the array of financial products and services has noticeably expanded. Some of these products and services are highly unconventional by any measure. For example, through a "life settlement contract," a terminally ill person with a life insurance policy is able to sell the policy to an investor. The investor pays an upfront dollar amount to the policyholder and also takes over the responsibility of making the monthly payments associated with that policy. Upon the death of the policyholder, the investor is able to collect the policy's payout amount. Essentially, in a life settlement contract, the investor is betting on the policyholder's death and using the financial product (life insurance policy) as the means to facilitate this bet. The existence of such unconventional financial transactions and the entrance of new competitors from outside the financial services sector are changing the shape of financial services markets.

Fragmenting Consumer Base

There is also mounting evidence that financial services markets are challenged by a consumer base that is becoming highly fragmented. For example, despite the fact that the banking industry in the United States has been functioning in one form or another for centuries, there are millions of households in the United States who have no bank account.[3] Growing levels of consumer debt, rising bankruptcy rates and an increase in delinquency rates for both credit cards and mortgages over the past two decades have indicated a marketplace where portions of the population are struggling for their financial survival.[4] While groups of consumers are increasingly experiencing economic hardship, the picture in other segments of society seems to be much more positive. For example, the number of high net worth American households has risen to record levels, while specific indicators of household hardship have also grown for segments of the population.[5] These facts indicate that the consumer base is becoming more partitioned, and as a result, financial services designed to serve these consumers may need to become more diverse in order to keep up with the market's increased fragmentation.

Demographic shifts in the United States are also influencing the way in which financial services marketers operate. Data from the *U.S. Census Bureau* indicates an aging U.S. population. For example, in the 1990 census, the percentage of the population over the age of 40 was 38.1%. In the 2000 census this figure had grown to

43.3%, and in the 2010 census it was found to be 54.7%. In this 20-year time period, the median age in the United States grew by 4 years. An aging population implies an increase in the demand for those financial services that are most relevant to consumers in higher age brackets. These may include products and services related to retirement planning, life insurance, and reverse mortgages. Income data also suggests that the U.S. population is becoming more diverse in terms of its income and wealth distribution. While the average income has steadily grown since the 1970s, the disparity among household incomes has also grown. As a result, the population is fragmenting into two distinct groups, one getting wealthier and the other getting poorer. The notion of "two-tier marketing" – that of focusing on the lower class and the upper class – has become an accepted principle in segment-based consumer marketing activities.[6] This principle suggests that the marketplace, which traditionally consisted of the lower, middle, and upper-classes, is transitioning into only two classes of upper and lower-class consumers. The potential effects of a polarizing population on successful positioning strategies of financial services providers may only become clear as the demographics of the U.S. population further evolve.

In addition, the consumer base seems to be challenged by the accumulation of household debt. The volume of consumer installment credit has witnessed a consistent and notable growth over the past two decades, as evident in growth of both revolving credit (for example, credit card debt), and non-revolving credit (for example, home mortgages). This increase is attributed to two major factors. The first reason is the increasing value of real estate during this time period coupled with the public's desire for home ownership. This combination resulted in heavy borrowing in order to facilitate the purchase of real estate. The trends in the U.S. real estate market therefore helped determine the extent by which non-revolving consumer debt grew. A second factor that accounts for the growth in consumer debt is increased credit card borrowing and a lack of consumer discipline in controlling discretionary spending. Credit card companies and other providers of short-term revolving credit successfully attracted large numbers of consumers through aggressive marketing campaigns. These campaigns, combined with a low interest rate environment, encouraged many individuals to take on considerable amounts of debt, resulting in the expansion of consumer debt.

Consumer Trust

Securing a sense of mutual trust between the consumer and the financial institution has at times been a challenge in financial services markets. Distrust affects both the consumer and the company, as both may feel uncertain about the underlying intentions of the other party. Studies show that a significant portion of consumers will not hesitate to cheat their insurance company, if they have a chance to do so.[7] These consumers may, for example, choose to misinform their insurance company about their individual risk characteristics when applying for an insurance policy, misrepresent to the insurer the sequence of events that resulted in an insurance claim, or neglect to disclose relevant information that may invalidate the insurance policy or the claim.

Similar issues of distrust can be found in consumers' and regulators' opinions about financial services providers' underlying intentions in a variety of marketing contexts in categories ranging from credit cards and home mortgages to securities brokerage services and insurance. The growing number of law suits and punitive measures imposed by the *Securities and Exchange Commission* and various other regulatory bodies over the past decade against major investment and insurance companies, combined with the aftermath of the financial crisis of 2008 has helped further strengthen public distrust of the financial services community. Research on consumer sentiment towards various professions indicates that in general consumers have a mixed view of financial services professionals.[8] Lack of trust therefore seems to be an inherent characteristic of many financial services transactions and a continuing challenge to the practice of marketing financial services.

SOURCES OF CHANGE IN FINANCIAL SERVICES MARKETS

The manifestation of the changes outlined above can be attributed to specific factors that have transformed the competitive landscape in the financial services arena. These factors are summarized in Exhibit 1.2. One such factor is the deregulation of the industry which took place at the turn of the century and has resulted in the removal of barriers that had for decades insulated financial services providers from directly competing with each other. Deregulation enabled the entrance of new players into the industry and changed the rules of competition. However, it eventually also resulted in the enactment of new regulations put in place at the end of the last decade to reverse some of the effects of deregulation. Furthermore, the changing economic landscape and the introduction of technological innovations to financial services markets have had a dramatic impact on the successful implementation of marketing strategies.

Regulations

A significant overhaul of financial services marketing regulations took place at the end of the previous decade. The *Dodd-Frank Wall Street Reform and Consumer Protection Act of 2010* was in response to many of the changes that the U.S. financial markets had experienced following the economic collapse of 2008. This act helped establish new guidelines for

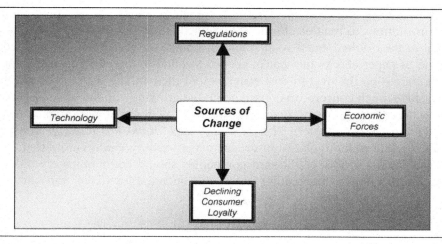

Exhibit 1.2: Sources of Change in Financial Services Markets

financial institutions in a broad range of financial product categories, and established new regulatory bodies that have a tighter grip on the marketing activities of financial services providers. To some extent these regulations limit the flexibility that the industry had hoped for following deregulatory measures which were originally put in place in 1999, through the *Financial Services Modernization Act*. While the Financial Services Modernization Act of 1999 (also referred to as the *Gramm-Leach-Bliley Act*), had created an environment that encouraged intense competition, the reduced regulatory constraints had resulted in the injection of increased risk into the financial system and had made the oversight tasks of regulators more difficult. The challenge to the industry and its regulators has since been to enable fair competition while protecting consumers from making uninformed decisions. Several additional regulations which limit or control the marketing activities of financial services organizations have contributed to this goal and were put in place during the previous decade. For example, the *Telemarketing Act of 2003* limits a marketer's ability to call consumers, especially those who have requested to be on a national "do not call" list. Other regulations have been implemented in the past decade that address how information about consumers can be shared across financial institutions. For example, the *Fair and Accurate Credit Transactions Act of 2003* requires credit bureaus to allow individuals to control the amount of their credit history that is publicly made available. In addition, the 2003 act required credit bureaus to notify consumers of any negative information that may have an adverse effect on their credit history, and since 2005, customers have been entitled to one free credit report every year. Another regulation which significantly boosted the operational efficiency of the banking sector was the *Check Clearing Act for the 21st Century,* otherwise known as *Check 21*. This regulation enabled financial institutions to treat electronically scanned copies of a written check as the legal equivalent to the original, hand-written check. The result was a monumental reduction in the volume of paper checks that banks needed to handle, thereby decreasing processing time, and increasing the overall cost efficiency of the banking sector. Toward the end of the past decade much concern was raised about the growing volume of consumer debt and potentially deceptive marketing practices associated with credit card marketing activities. The *Credit Card Accountability, Responsibility and Disclosure (CARD) Act* signed into law in 2009 required more clarity in the language used by credit card issuers. It created specific standards for how credit card companies should communicate with consumers with the specific aim of preventing unfair rate increases and fee traps in credit card markets.

Consumer Loyalty

It has been well established that in the majority of financial services categories, customer defection rates are significantly lower than they are in most other markets. The tendency of customers to remain with their current financial services provider has traditionally been quite strong. It is important to note though that defection patterns vary significantly across various categories of financial services. For example, life insurance policyholders have an intrinsic interest in staying with the same insurance provider, since changing insurance carriers may result in the reassessment of the application, a need for new health exams, and possibly higher rates and lower coverage levels. On the other hand, credit card accountholders may feel less obligated to stay with the same company because the negative impact of switching is limited, and changing credit card companies may in fact considerably lower borrowing costs. The incentives offered by competitors in the credit card markets often outweigh potential switching costs, resulting in higher rates of customer defection.

Despite the benefits that low customer defection rates present to financial services marketers, they are not necessarily reflective of customers' true preferences for their current financial services provider. Nevertheless, this pattern of behavior may limit financial services providers' desire to improve their offerings and to be competitive. Customer retention in financial services may often be indicative of the fact that, many customers lack initiative to find the most competitive offerings, are not necessarily attracted to the very best deal, and may in fact fail to consider all possible competing options available to them. Even with the knowledge of competing offers, a customer may still choose to remain with the current financial services provider once considering the possible inconveniences associated with switching. Inconveniences in switching may be reflected in the elaborate transactions that often have to take place, billing arrangements that may have to be rearranged, and contracts and paperwork that would have to be redrafted, negotiated, and signed.

The traditional resistance that consumers have towards switching financial services providers has for decades created a sub-optimal, non-competitive environment. Since customers tend to remain with their current provider, they may seek very little information on competing offers and the chances of them terminating their relationship with their current financial services provider has been minimal. The end-result is that financial services organizations may lack motivation for self-improvement, offering their customers sub-standard products and services. However the ability to sustain such a mode of operation may be limited due to social media and the use of the Internet for the exchange of service experience information among consumer groups. Consumers' growing level of education on financial decision making and a marketplace that is becoming increasingly fragmented will therefore require thoughtful approaches to the marketing practice.

Economic Forces

One of the factors that makes the marketing of financial services unique is the fact that most financial services have to be judged by consumers within the context of the current economic environment in which they are offered. The attractiveness of a savings product, for example, might be a function of the interest rates and expected rates of inflation. Similarly, investment options may largely relate to one's expectations of how the stock market might behave in the near and distant future. Other factors, such as the cost of energy, expectations of unemployment, exchange rate fluctuations, and general trends in the economy might encourage or discourage consumers from purchasing particular financial products and services. The overwhelming influence that economic forces have on the attractiveness of financial products and services greatly impacts their marketing.

The economic environment as characterized by measures such as interest rates, the cost of energy and economic growth rates can significantly influence the volume of activity in financial services markets. For example, low interest rates contribute to high levels of consumer borrowing. Furthermore, leading economic indicators, such as the price of crude oil, may signal economic cycles where increased production costs due to high energy prices may limit economic activity. Increases in the cost of energy often have an impact on consumers' budgets and reduce overall consumer spending. Therefore, subsequent effects on financial services which support such spending, for example by providing consumers with credit, would be affected.

Technology

The nature of how financial services are marketed is directly affected by the emergence of revolutionary data-exchange technologies. This is due to the fact that financial services are largely information based. For example, rarely does a consumer come in contact with the actual currency that represents his or her financial assets. These assets are in fact stored in the form of data in a bank's databases. Therefore, the functioning of many financial services can often be best characterized as bits and bytes of data transformed on electronic networks of data exchange, rather than physical currency or paper contracts stored in bank vaults and filing cabinets. As a result, technologies that facilitate information flow often transition into the world of financial services marketing.

Technology also influences the nature of interactions between the customer and the financial services provider. Many customer service contacts are increasingly automated through online means, banking-by-phone, or the use of automated teller machines (ATMs). The emerging generation of ATM devices are able to conduct transactions beyond the simple disbursement of cash or taking of deposits. ATM technology capable of electronically scanning in paper checks that can be immediately deposited to a customer's bank account and reflected in the accountholder's balance significantly reduce costs and accelerate transaction processing. ATM devices are also equipped with technologies to conduct biometric identification of the customer, by for example, conducting a retina eye scan to secure access to one's bank account.[9] In addition, voice recognition technologies have been deployed in telephone customer service operations to conduct voice-stress analysis on customers and help detect cases of insurance fraud.[10] The automobile insurance industry has also deployed black-box devices on cars in order to better understand a policyholder's driving habits and to assist insurance adjusters and accident investigators in determining the causes of accidents.[11] Technology, in one form or another greatly influences the way we as consumers interact with financial services organizations. The emergence of new technologies presents financial services providers with the possibility to create new markets for their services and the ability to increase marketing efficiency in serving existing markets.

The shift towards technology brings about significant profit advantages to financial services marketers. For example, it is estimated that the average cost of a customer transaction at a commercial bank is approximately one dollar. A shift to phone banking reduces the cost by almost half. Using an ATM machine brings down the cost to about a quarter, and online banking has an average transaction cost of only a few pennies. These cost differences have resulted in an accelerated cost-driven push towards the use of new technologies.[12] These cost differences are simply too difficult to ignore by the average financial services organization seeking to maximize profits. It is important to acknowledge though that such a shift towards new technologies may lead to the gradual elimination of human contact with customers. Encouraging customers to use an ATM device or to conduct their banking online, while cost-effective, eliminates the personal contact and human interactions that traditionally characterize many encounters with financial services institutions. Therefore, for example, the old-fashioned notion of the retail bank clerk who is intimately knowledgeable about a customer's banking needs and who personally knows the customer is a vanishing phenomenon in today's banking experience. In such an environment, it is imperative that financial services marketers find innovative ways to secure the loyalty and trust of their customers, and to provide the personal touch that may be needed to retain customers.

THE FORMAL STUDY OF FINANCIAL SERVICES MARKETING

The objective of this book is to help the reader develop a thorough understanding of the marketing practice in financial services. With that in mind, one has to take into account the underlying cognitive processes which guide consumers' financial decisions. We will therefore study how consumers decide to purchase financial services and contrast this process with how non-financial services and goods are purchased. The differentiating aspects of marketing financial services versus other marketing contexts are also highlighted throughout the book. This book will also detail the elements of what constitutes successful marketing practice, as it relates to pricing, advertising, and selling of financial services.

Unique Aspects of Financial Services

Subjective Perceptions of Quality: A unique aspect of financial services marketing which differentiates it from other marketing practices is the illusive notion of quality. In the traditional context of marketing manufactured goods, quality is typically objectively measured utilizing standard quality assessment methods and by assessing product defect rates on the production line. However, in the context of financial services, the notion of quality is a highly subjective phenomenon. For example, while the objective quality of an insurance company might be reflected by the willingness of the company to pay out customer claims, this measure is rarely known by the average customer. In the insurance business, the majority of policyholders do not utilize their policy benefits since the events being insured typically have low probabilities of occurrence. As a result, most policyholders never experience the process of filing a claim, and for those that do, the outcome of their experience may not be captured or recorded anywhere for others to examine and learn from. The net effect is that the most objective aspect of the quality of an insurance company, which is the protection it offers its policyholders in case of losses, may never be determined by the majority of consumers. Quality assessments in such a context are therefore not objective and largely based on subjective factors such as the customer's recognition of the name of the company or suggestions and advice provided by friends or insurance brokers. Similarly, in the context of securities brokerage services, customers may not necessarily be able to determine whether the broker is providing them with the most objective and informed advice. The objective quality of a broker-recommended investment portfolio may not be evident for many years until the securities within that portfolio have exhibited their long-term characteristics. A similar issue can be identified in the context of tax returns. While a tax accountant's ability to secure the highest tax refund is probably the most objective aspect of quality, a client may never be certain of having received the highest possible refund. Such an inquiry would require one to file taxes with multiple accountants as a means of "testing," which is a highly impractical exercise. In all these contexts, despite the important role that the financial services provider plays in securing the financial well-being of the customer, quality assessments by the customer may be driven by highly subjective aspects of the service experience such as the friendliness of the service providers or perceptions of the level of expertise portrayed in the service process.

Price Complexity: The prices of financial services are intrinsically complex. For example, the lease price of an automobile might consist of monthly payments, the number of payments and a down payment, rather than the single sticker price used when purchasing the vehicle with cash. Often the price consists of multiple numbers, some of which the consumer may not even completely understand. This not only makes the task of understanding the various prices available in the marketplace difficult for the consumer, but it also creates scenarios that may lead to deceptive and, in some cases, unethical practices by marketers.

Regulations: The practice of marketing financial services is significantly different from other marketing practices due to the many regulations that rule the industry. For example, the type of content included in a financial service advertisement may be controlled and closely monitored by regulatory bodies, such as the *Securities and Exchange Commission*, the *Federal Trade Commission,* and the departments of insurance in individual states.

Market Clustering: One of the other unique aspects of financial services marketing is the fact that consumers' needs for financial services vary significantly from one customer to the other. As a result, the types of services that a financial services organization introduces to the marketplace may be best suited for specific groups of consumers rather than for the mass markets. Recognizing and identifying individuals that a particular financial service is best suited for is the task of the financial services marketer. Therefore, it is important to not only understand the underlying technology that is used for segmenting and grouping customers based on their needs, but also to have an accurate understanding of consumer segments that are most relevant to a given financial service. This is especially true in light of the abundance of customer data available for segmentation analysis. For example, most financially active individuals in the United States have credit history records that can be purchased and used by marketers as the basis for understanding each person's credit behavior and financial needs. Financial institutions also possess large amounts of transaction-based data on their existing customers that can be effectively used to target them with relevant financial services.

Consumer Protection: Any informed discussion of financial services marketing must also include issues related to consumer protection and conflicts of interest, which have historically characterized the industry. The human inability to make rational financial decisions has fascinated researchers in psychology, economics, finance and marketing for decades. Consumers can often make catastrophic decisions related to financial services. Research in psychology has for example established an array of human judgment errors that are persistent and highly influential in consumers' financial decisions. It appears that the human brain is simply not hardwired to respond rationally to financial stimuli. This issue is further complicated by the fact that most financial service offers are so complex that by making minor changes in the presentation of the offer, one could make many otherwise unattractive products look highly attractive. This can be a highly problematic concern from both ethical and regulatory perspectives.

THE STRUCTURE OF THIS BOOK

This book has been developed based on my experiences as an educator, consultant, and researcher in financial services marketing. This book is different from other books on financial services marketing in several distinct ways. It examines the marketing of financial services from a consumer decision-making perspective. There is extensive discussion about the psychology of decision making in financial services. The book adapts a highly practical approach to financial services marketing, making it relevant to marketing practitioners, executives and business students. In order to provide the psychological foundation for financial decision making, Chapter 2 will expose the reader to the principles of consumer information processing in financial services. These principles are used to help explain the decision patterns of consumers when choosing among financial services providers. Chapter 3 will provide a detailed view of the wide range of financial products and services available in the marketplace. This chapter addresses the essential need for financial services marketers to have a thorough understanding of the range of offerings which they can present to consumers. An appropriate discussion of effective marketing in financial services would also need to examine the most effective implementation strategies proven to work in the marketplace. Chapters 4 through 7 will therefore provide the basis for optimal pricing, advertising and distribution strategies for financial services, and discuss how new forms of financial services are introduced to the marketplace.

As outlined earlier, the marketing of financial services is a unique practice due to the abundance of data on individual consumers. This enables financial services organizations to use market segmentation technologies for matching the most relevant products to individual consumers. This book will therefore provide the framework for the use of segmentation in financial services markets, and builds on this approach by discussing customer satisfaction and customer relationship management in Chapters 8 and 9. No discussion of marketing financial services would be complete without recognizing the impact of regulations. Chapter 10 will profile the major regulations that influence financial services marketing practice in the United States. Chapter 11 provides a perspective on the future of the financial services industry, and establishes a framework for building successful marketing strategies. Chapter 12 will conclude the book by providing a series of case studies on the marketing of financial services.

The practice of financial services marketing is a scientific and methodical discipline. The increased level of competition, revolutionary use of new technologies, and increasing regulatory forces have in recent years raised the importance of developing and implementing formal marketing plans for financial institutions. Financial organizations that may in the past have had no formalized marketing planning processes in place will not only have to rigorously develop such processes but also execute the resulting plans and evaluate their own performance according to their pre-determined objectives. Therefore, many readers of this book will at some point in time be involved in mobilizing financial services organizations, through the development of well-informed marketing strategies. It is hoped that this book will provide the methodical framework needed for such mobilization.

ENDNOTES

1 A. Roy (2011), "Strategic Positioning and Capacity Utilization: Factors in Planning for Profitable Growth in Banking," *Journal of Performance Management*, Vol. 23, Iss.3, pp. 23-58; J. Keay (2010), "The Price of Stability," *Global Finance*, Vol. 24, Iss. 8, pp. 18-21; R. Macey (2006), "Commercial Banking and Democracy: The Illusive Quest for Deregulation," *Yale Journal on Regulation*, Vol. 23, Iss. 1, pp. 1-26.

2 *Market Share Reporter* (2011). Robert S. Lazich (editor). Farmington Hills, MI: Thomas Gale Research Inc.

3 G. Platt, A. Guerrero, A. Hawser and D. Bedell (2011), "Growth Returns and Questions Linger for Banks," *Global Finance*, Vol. 25, Iss. 5, pp. 52-99; S. Rhine, W. Greene, and M. Toussaint-Comeau (2006), "The Importance of Check-Cashing Businesses to the Unbanked: Racial/Ethnic Differences," *The Review of Economics and Statistics*, Vol.

88, Iss. 1, pp.146-159; Sally Law (2006), "Attracting the Non-Customer," *US Banker*, Vol. 116, Iss. 2, p. 36.

4 M. Taylor (2011), "Measuring Financial Capability and its Determinants Using Survey Data," *Social Indicators Research*, Vol. 102, Iss. 2, pp. 297-314; H. Yu-An, I. Phau and C. Lin (2010), "Consumer Animosity, Economic Hardship, and Normative Influence: How Do they Affect Consumers' Purchase Intentions?" *European Journal of Marketing*, Vol. 44, Iss. 4/7, pp. 909-937.

5 T. Hintermaier and W. Koeniger (2011), "On the Evolution of US Consumer Wealth Distribution," *Review of Economic Dynamics* Vol. 14, Iss. 2, pp. 317-328.

6 D. Leonhardt (1997), "Two Tier Marketing: Companies are Tailoring their Products and Pitches to Two Different Americas," *Business Week*, March 17, Iss. 3518, pp. 82-91; J. Hilsenrath and S. Freeman (2004), "Affluent Advantage: So Far Economic Recovery Tilts to Highest-Income Americans," *Wall Street Journal*, June 20, p. A1.

7 S. Fullerton and L. Neale (2010), "An Assessment of the Acceptability of an Array of Perceived Consumer Transgressions in the American Marketplace," *Journal of Leadership, Accountability and Ethics*, Vol. 8, Iss. 2, pp. 17-27; "More than Half of U.S. Consumers Say Poor Service Leads to Fraudulent Insurance Claims, Accenture Study Finds," *Business Wire*, 9/22/2010.

8 Susan Berfield (2005), "Thirty and Broke," *Business Week*, Nov. 14, Iss. 3959, pp. 76-83, citing credit card debt figures reported by *Cardweb.com*; Interested readers should also consult: Terry Burnham (2005), *Mean Markets and Lizard Brains*. John Wiley & Sons: New York, for a review of other documented consumer vulnerabilities in financial services markets.

9 C. Campbell, P. Maglio and M. Davis (2011), "From Self-service to Super-service: A Resource Mapping Framework for Co-Creating Value by Shifting the Boundary Between Provider and Customer," *Information Systems and eBusiness Management*, Vol. 9, Iss. 2, pp. 173-191; R. Sausner (2010), "Iris Scans: Coming to an ATM Near You?" *Carline*, Vol. 10, Iss. 40, p. 5.

10 C. Fleming (2004), "Insurers Employ Voice-Analysis Software to Detect Fraud," *Wall Street Journal*, May 17, p. B1.

11 C. O'Malley (2008), "Black-box Bill Seeks Full Disclosure," *Indianapolis Business Journal*, Vol. 28, Iss. 48, p. 1; I. Ayres and B. Nalebuff (2003), "Black Boxes for Cars," *Forbes*, Volume 172, Iss. 3, p. 84; "Better Drivers Pay Less for Car Insurance with Pay As You Drive Program from Progressive," *Business Wire*, 5/23/2011.

12 A. Roy (2011), "Strategic Positioning and Capacity Utilization: Factors in Planning for Profitable Growth in Banking," *Journal of Performance Management*, Vol. 23, Iss.3, pp. 23-58; *Functional Cost Analysis*. The Federal Reserve Board: Washington; K. Furst, W. Lang, and D. Nolle (2002), "Internet Banking," *Journal of Financial Services Marketing*, August/October, Vol. 22, Iss. 1/2, pg. 95; J. Kolodinsky, J. Hogarth, and M. Hilgert (2011), "The Adoption of Electronic Banking Technologies by U.S. Consumers," *The International Journal of Bank Marketing*, Vol. 22, Iss. 4/5, p. 238.

CHAPTER TWO

The Consumer Decision Process in Financial Services

In this chapter, we will discuss the consumer decision process for financial services. We will first explore theories that outline how a rational, well-informed consumer should decide among a set of financial services offers presented in the marketplace. We will then examine evidence that suggests that consumers may not necessarily be fully informed and rational when making decisions about financial services and products. Consumers' use of simplifying decision rules, and the resulting impact on the marketing of financial services will be discussed in detail.

There are several facts that are unique to the consumer decision process in financial services. The first is the very nature of financial services, which is typically unimaginative and unexciting. A simple examination of advertisements for financial services would reveal that financial services advertising is often lame and less inspirational than the types of advertising and communications one may attribute to other kinds of services or goods. For example, financial products and services often cannot be visualized, making it more difficult for the marketer to communicate their benefits using imagery. The benefits gained from an investment option, the stability of an insurance company, or the accuracy of financial transaction records at a commercial bank can rarely be visually communicated in the context of an advertisement, especially in an exciting and attention-grabbing manner.

Furthermore, the complexity of financial services makes the task of evaluating a financial service difficult for the average person. Financial services possess a large number of attributes, many of which might be unfamiliar to consumers who have to make decisions based on these attributes. For example, a typical home mortgage might have well over a dozen attributes, and even a standardized service such as a checking account may have a sufficiently large number of attributes, such that the average consumer might be unable to fully appreciate the differences between offers by competing banks. This may translate into opportunities for financial services companies to creatively attract and educate consumers about the benefits of their own products and services. However, opportunities for deceptive marketing, violation of corporate principles and established regulations may also exist. The complexity of financial services often leads to an array of largely predictable consumer decision patterns that are a result of consumers' use of simplifying rules, called "heuristics." Heuristics enable consumers to cope with the challenging task of evaluating complex decisions by for example, focusing only on a subset of the available information. While such an approach may not result in the best decision, it results in patterns of consumer behavior observed across a wide array of decision contexts. The nature and magnitude of these patterns of behavior is a core topic of discussion in this chapter.

WHAT IS A FINANCIAL SERVICE?

When attempting to understand consumer behavior in financial services, it is important to have a good understanding of the underlying components that exist in most financial services and products. In the discussion that follows and in the remainder of this book, the terms "financial service" and "financial product" will be used interchangeably. The term "financial product" is often used in the context of commoditized financial transactions that involve standardized features such as property and casualty insurance and residential mortgages. For example, the basic dimensions of an automobile insurance policy are typically well-defined and standardized across competitors. On the other hand, the term "financial service" is often used in the context of customized transactions such as brokerage services and financial advice, which are often catered to individualized customer needs and require a great deal of individualized attention from the service provider. Nevertheless, the two terms are widely used interchangeably in a variety of marketing contexts, and will be accordingly treated in this book.

In general, almost every financial service has a series of inputs and at least one core output. The three inputs that are consistently present in the majority of financial services include *(1) time frame, (2) risk,* and *(3) monetary inputs.* The output of a financial service is often, but not always, a monetary outcome (Exhibit 2.1). To gain an understanding of the input/output framework, imagine a typical term life insurance policy. In term life insurance, a prospective policyholder is seeking to secure a particular level of monetary benefits to be paid to one's beneficiaries or dependants in the event of the policyholder's death. The inputs to this transaction include the policyholder's health risks as measured by factors such as smoking habits, blood pressure, cholesterol levels, and high-risk sporting activities (such as sky diving, riding motorcycles, and rock climbing.) In addition, the policy needs to be specific in terms of the length of time for which it is valid. Life insurance contracts with long time frames (for example, 20 years) are often associated with higher premiums as the risk of death during the policy time frame increases, and the chances of medical problems developing in the later stages of the policy is higher due to the aging of the policyholder. Therefore, the first two elements of risk and time frame can easily be visualized in the context of term life insurance policies. The final input to this particular form of financial service is the premiums that the policyholder has to pay. Higher benefits justify higher premiums. Therefore, a policyholder purchasing a $1 million policy (monetary output) is expected to pay higher premiums (monetary input) than one subscribing to a $500,000 policy. The relationship between premiums, time frame, risk levels, and the policy benefit level is an area of specialization in pricing and actuarial science, which will be further discussed in Chapter 4.

A similar input/output framework can be visualized in the context of home mortgages. In a home mortgage contract, the term (time frame) of the mortgage has to be clearly stated(for example, a 30 year mortgage). Mortgage terms can range from a few years to decades. The element of risk in mortgage contracts is established by examining the mortgage applicant's credit score. Several credit bureaus in the United States are specialized in compiling background financial information on all individuals with a credit history. An individual's credit history is then translated into a numeric figure referred to as the credit score. The score reflects the individual's risk level in future credit transactions. The final input to a mortgage arrangement is the monthly payments (monetary input), which in combination with the term of the mortgage (time frame) and the credit risk of the mortgage holder (the credit score) will determine the total mortgage amount that the mortgage applicant would be able to secure (monetary output).

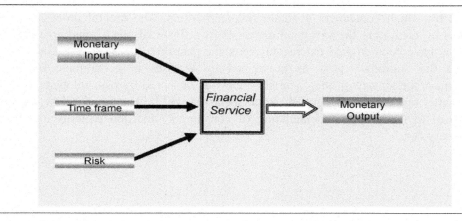

Exhibit 2.1 Basic Input/Output Dimensions of a Financial Service

It is important to note that, in many financial services transactions, the monetary input and the monetary output may be perceived in reverse by the consumer. For example, when purchasing a term life insurance policy, the consumer may approach an insurance agent in order to inquire about a specific benefit level (monetary output) and to ask what the associated premiums (monetary input) would be. Similarly, a prospective homeowner seeking a specific mortgage amount may approach a mortgage broker or a bank to shop for the lowest monthly payments. Nevertheless, in both of these transactions, the individual's monetary input will determine the monetary output that would be made available through the financial services provider. As can be seen in Exhibit 2.2, the input/output framework can be applied to a variety of financial services. However, depending on the service, some of the dimensions of the transaction may have a greater role in the consumer decision process.

It is important to acknowledge that the various input/output dimensions of a financial product or service may not be evident at all times, and certain dimensions may dominate the input/output framework. Nevertheless, in most financial transactions, these dimensions exist in one form or another. For example, in a fund transfer service, the monetary input consists of the dollar amount being transferred plus any additional administrative fees that apply. The monetary output is the transferred amount paid to the recipient, and the time frame is the length of time it will take the funds to be made available to the recipient. Similarly, in the context of financial advisory services, the monetary inputs to the process are the advisory fees and invested funds, and the monetary output is the financial returns eventually realized from the investments recommended by the advisor.

The input/output framework for financial services will be used shortly to describe the dynamics by which consumers evaluate financial offers. The mental processes used by consumers in integrating the various dimensions of a financial service and arriving at their evaluations have been studied extensively over the past three decades. These studies have contrasted the "rational" view as prescribed by theories in economics, finance, and information processing, with the "heuristic" view as observed by psychologists, marketers, and consumer researchers. Both of these perspectives will be examined below, as they are both critical to the proper understanding of consumers' decision patterns in regards to financial services.

Financial Product/Service	Monetary Input	Risk	Time frame	Monetary Output
Auto Insurance	Yearly premiums	Driving record of applicant	Policy length	Policy Coverage
Home Mortgage	Monthly payments	Credit score of applicant	Length of mortgage	Mortgage amount
Mutual Fund	Investment dollars	Fund strategy	Length of investment	Investment $\times$ $(1+i)^{time}$ +f (risk)
Certificate of Deposit	Deposit dollars	Insured by the FDIC for up to $100,000	CD length	Investment $\times$ $(1+i)^{time}$ (Note: for defined returns CDs)
Money Transfer	Dollar amount + transaction fees	Likelihood of funds not being received by the recipient	Speed of fund transfer	Dollar amount transferred to the recipient

Exhibit 2.2 Dimensions of Several Financial Services

RATIONAL CONSUMER DECISION MAKING

The Rational Decision Process

It is essential to understand the process by which a rational consumer should evaluate financial service offers in the marketplace. The discussion of the "rational" consumer is essential since it allows us to contrast the processes that should theoretically be true with what in fact consumers tend to follow in their decision making. Both of these decision approaches will be discussed. The framework for the rational consumer's decision process is based on theories of information processing and human problem-solving adapted by Blackwell, Minard, and Engel and by Bettman in the consumer behavior literature.[1] The traditional model of rational consumer decision making is a step-by-step process and consists of the following general steps:

- Need Recognition
- Information Search
- Pre-purchase Evaluation
- Purchase
- Consumption
- Post-purchase Evaluation

The first step in the consumer decision process is referred to as *need recognition.* In this step, the consumer recognizes that the existing state of his or her own experience, often referred to as the *actual state,* does not meet certain expectations, norms, or ideals often referred to as the *ideal state.* This triggers a need in the consumer and initiates the decision process for finding a solution that would help remedy the discrepancy between one's actual experience and one's ideals. The need recognition step therefore helps trigger the consumer's decision process. In the context of financial services, need recognition might for example include the recognition by the head of a household that he or she needs to protect his or her family against financial losses resulting from the unlikely event of his or her death. The individual may recognize the discrepancy between the actual state of having no current coverage and the ideal state of having adequate term life insurance protection. To create this contrast and to trigger need recognition, the marketer of term-life insurance policies may choose to focus on helping consumers appreciate the financial needs of their dependants, through print or broadcast advertising or through individualized communications.

The next phase in the consumer's decision process is *information search.* Information search relates to the consumer's collection of relevant information on competing products and services in order to facilitate an informed decision. In the context of a term life insurance policy, information search may entail using the Internet to locate term life insurance providers, talking to friends who currently have term life insurance coverage, or paying additional attention to advertisements by life insurance companies in the mass media. The information search process is critical to consumer decision making in financial services; research that will be discussed in this chapter has established that consumers do considerably less information gathering than what is optimally required of them. This step is especially important in the financial services domain because it highlights the strategic importance of advertising as a means for being taken into consideration by the consumer. If a financial services company fails to advertise sufficiently to create a recognized identity in the consumers' minds, it will most likely not be part of the information search process, and may be subsequently overlooked as an option by a great majority of consumers.

The third step in the consumer's decision process is *pre-purchase evaluation.* In this phase, the consumer considers all the information collected in the information search phase and decides which of the various alternatives fits his or her needs best. In the context of a term life insurance policy, this phase may require the consumer to examine the prices (premiums) as well as the features (policy benefits, restrictions, etc.) of the various policies for which information has been collected in order to decide which single policy to proceed with. Alternatively, in the context of a home mortgage, the consumer may have to examine a variety of factors, such as the mortgage rates offered by different companies, the complexity of their application process, and the speed by which they are able to process the mortgage application, in order to form an evaluation of which one mortgage company is the best to proceed with.

The pre-purchase evaluation step is uniquely complex in financial service markets because there are established mathematical formulas that can determine what the "correct" choice should be for the consumer. This is because probability and finance theory can assist in objectively assessing the best available option. This often requires an understanding by the consumer of the underlining mathematical relationships that exist between the inputs and the output of a financial service. For example, in an insurance arrangement, the insurance company accepts the responsibility to pay benefits to the policyholder (or the policyholder's beneficiaries) for claims that may be a result of an uncertain event such as an accident or death. From a consumer perspective, the relationship between the payout amount (monetary output) and the premiums paid (monetary input) needs to take into account the probability that the event could take place in a given time frame. The functional relationship can therefore be captured as:[2]

Output = Input × probability of event occurrence

Similarly, in the case of risk-free investment the correct mathematical relationship between the input (investment amount) and the output (expected investment returns) is depicted by the following formula:[3]

Output = Input × (1 + interest rate) time frame

Alternatively, in a risky investment scenario such as a securities purchase, the relationship may become more complex as components of risk begin to play a role in what one expects to be the output of the investment process, as shown below:[4]

Output = Input × ₁*(1 + interest rate)* time frame *+ f (risk)*ᵢ

In the above equation, *f* is a function which takes into account the monetary impact of risk as reflected by stock price volatility and uncertainty in the future potential of the stock. Frameworks such as the *Capital Asset Pricing Model (CAPM)* can be used to establish the appropriate mathematical relationship that captures the nature and impact of risk on expected investment returns.[5] As will be discussed shortly, what is fascinating about the consumer evaluation process for financial services is that the "rational" consumer is expected to be capable of accurately conducting the elaborate mathematics required. Furthermore, the consumer is expected to have all the necessary inputs associated with the required mathematics (for example, the probability of an event taking place) readily available. We will examine the validity of these core assumptions later in this chapter. Due to the great complexity of many financial services and the fact that their inputs are often numeric in nature, considerable mathematical effort may need to be undertaken, in order for the consumer to correctly determine the best available offer. Consumer research evidence, which will be subsequently reviewed, consistently suggests that most consumers fail to do a good job of carrying out these relatively complex mathematical tasks and typically utilize heuristics to simplify their decisions, even in the case of high-valued financial decisions.

The fourth step in the consumer's decision process is *purchase*. In the context of a term life insurance policy this step involves the customer's commitment to the term life insurance contract either through an agent, broker, or through direct contact with the financial institution. In most financial services, the purchase step is often associated with the signing of a contract between the consumer and the financial institution. For example, the "purchase" of a credit card would consist of the customer agreeing to the terms and conditions that enable the issuance of a credit card account in the customer's name. In the case of a checking account, the purchase would consist of the customer depositing an opening balance into the account and agreeing to the terms and conditions of the checking account service.

The next step in the consumer's decision process is *consumption*. In this phase, the consumer will begin to use the financial service. For example, an accountholder in a retail bank may utilize the bank's ATM service or use the bank facilities to transfer funds. Alternatively, the client at a brokerage house may seek investment advice from the broker. These experiences will form the basis for the next step in the consumer decision process which is *post-purchase evaluation*. In this final step, the consumer will make a determination as to whether the decision to use the chosen financial services provider was a good one. The consumer's actual experiences will therefore guide this assessment. What is interesting is that for many financial services post-purchase evaluations are difficult to arrive at. For example, in the context of a term life insurance policy, the policyholder will never personally see the benefits of the policy. By definition, term life insurance benefits are only activated when the policyholder dies (except for specific forms of life insurance with "living benefits"). Similarly, the long-term returns on a mutual fund may not be recognized for years, and the quality of all the various services offered by a commercial bank may not be experienced by all customers. However, there may be specific aspects of quality that can still be assessed by a customer. For example, the accessibility of customer service personnel, the accuracy of the financial statements, and the cleanliness of retail facilities may provide cues for the customer on the overall quality of a financial service. While these cues may or may not be accurate indicators of the true quality of the most

Decision Step	Checking Account	Mutual Fund
Need Recognition	Customer need for access to banking services	Client's asset growth goals
Information Search	Location of the bank's branch	Recognition of the fund company's name based on prior ad exposure
Pre-purchase Evaluation	Recommendations by neighbors and friends	Fund performance data based on third party rankings
Purchase	Opening an account	Purchasing shares of the fund
Consumption	Using checking, ATM, and other banking services	Observing growth of the fund's value
Post-Purchase Evaluation	Satisfaction with statement accuracy, check processing speed, customer service, ATMs, etc.	Assessment of whether the fund has grown at the expected rate

Exhibit 2.3 Decision Steps for Two Different Types of Financial Services

important attributes of a financial service (e.g., payout behavior of an insurance company, investment returns of a mutual fund), they may have a great impact on the overall post-purchase perceptions that customers might develop with respect to the financial services organization.

Exhibit 2.3 shows how the different steps of the consumer decision process may materialize within other financial services contexts. The two services exhibited in Exhibit 2.3 are checking accounts and mutual funds. As one might see, the process may be significantly different for one type of financial service than for another. For example, in the need recognition phase, the triggering point that helps the customer recognize the need is significantly different for a checking account (which is a necessity) than, for a mutual fund, which is an investment product with long-term growth objectives. Furthermore, in the information search and pre-purchase evaluation phases, a mutual fund is likely to benefit greatly from mass-media advertising and image-building activities, as well as favorable fund performance data. In contrast, the choice of a checking account might be much more influenced by the logistics of where the bank branches are located as well as recommendations made by one's friends, family, and colleagues. Understanding these influences is critical to successful allocation of resources when building an effective financial services marketing strategy.

However, as also shown in Exhibit 2.3, post-purchase evaluations may be difficult for the consumer to conduct. In the context of a mutual fund, the performance of the fund may not be realized for years because mutual funds are generally long-term investment instruments. In the context of a checking account, the customer's interactions with the bank clerks and customer service staff may take place over an extended period of time and may also be biased by specific scenarios or experiences that may have been either delightful or disappointing. This makes the post-purchase evaluation of a financial services provider difficult for consumers. Similarly, a customer's experiences with a credit card company may be difficult for the customer to assess unless scenarios requiring elaborate contact with the company have taken place. As a result, no immediate post-purchase assessments may occur in the short-term, and those that are formed may be highly inaccurate and biased by individual interactions with the service provider.

The Rational Framework and Financial Services Marketing

While the rational framework discussed above has a highly intuitive appeal, consumers may not necessarily carry out all the steps involved in the decision process. Nevertheless, understanding the model is critical in order to appreciate how actual decisions are made by consumers. Moreover, the framework provides the means by which financial services marketers can determine how to promote their services. This is especially true of the first three steps of the decision process – need recognition, information search, and pre-purchase evaluations – in which the dynamics are relatively predictable and consistent for most consumers and across a variety of financial services categories.

Typically, the need recognition phase is the most crucial phase in the consumer's decision process. Many consumers may not fully recognize why they may need a particular financial service. Therefore, it is the job of the financial services marketer to help them recognize their financial needs. In addition to need recognition, financial services marketers may choose to focus their marketing efforts on the information search step of the decision process. This is often achieved through mass-media advertising and aggressive promotion campaigns. By doing so, a financial services organization would ensure that its brand is familiar to the consumer. Massive advertising campaigns aimed at increasing a financial service brand's exposure in the market and advertising execution styles that create memorable messages are critical to attracting consumers in this step of the decision process. Additionally, financial services organizations may expend considerable effort to ensure that pre-purchase evaluations are favorable towards their specific services. This is especially important given the complexity of financial services and consumers' general inability to process complex information. Advertisements describing the benefits of a particular financial service or the weaknesses of competing services would help achieve this. However, care must be taken in this phase to ensure that the contents of the ad comply with regulations enforced by regulatory bodies such as the *Securities and Exchange Commission*, the *National Association of Securities Dealers*, the *Federal Reserve*, state insurance regulators and others. Some of these restrictions will be discussed in Chapter 10.

HEURISTIC DECISION MAKING

Challenges to the Traditional Theories of "Rationality"

Traditional theories of finance and economics that are used to describe rational consumers' actions in the marketplace often assume that consumers make their decisions about financial matters in a highly informed and logical manner. For example, the *Capital Asset Pricing Model (CAPM)*, which is a widely accepted framework in finance for the pricing of securities, assumes a certain level of systematic market volatility in the prices of a security.[6] These systematic variations in the prices of a security are then used to determine its market price. According to CAPM, individual decision makers who evaluate these prices have a clear picture of the systematic risk associated with each security, resulting in equilibrium prices in the marketplace. The *Black and Scholes* model, which is also a widely accepted framework for securities pricing assumes that consumers are well-informed decision makers, and that capital markets are "efficient" in that new information about an investment option is quickly disseminated among decision makers in the marketplace.[7] *Arbitrage Pricing Theory (APT),* which provides a framework for the construction of hedge portfolios, also assumes similar information efficiencies in the marketplace. APT, capitalizes on arbitrage opportunities across securities markets, to develop optimal investment portfolios and at its core assumes well-informed and rational decision makers operating within the marketplace.[8]

The commonality among the theories mentioned above is that the decision maker is assumed to possess an ability to obtain, process, retain, and, if necessary, disseminate complex information about financial products and services and be able to carry out the elaborate mathematics required in order to evaluate financial offers. While these conditions may be true for many institutional investors and professional investment decision makers in financial services organizations, they are far less true in the context of most day-to-day consumer decisions related to financial services. Moreover, there is mounting evidence of consumers' lack of rationality in decision making. The accumulating evidence suggests that poor decision making is not only restricted to average consumers, but is also exhibited by professional and well-trained investors such as fund managers and stock brokers, thereby hinting at fundamental handicaps in human decision making and predictable errors in judgment.[9]

In contrast to the rational and well-informed framework of what a consumer should do when deciding between financial services, research evidence suggests that most consumers are far less perfect and educated in their decision process. Consumers tend to use simplifying rules ("heuristics") to cope with the complexity of decisions facing them on a daily basis. Evidence for heuristic decision making can be found in recent trends in consumers' use of various financial products and services. For example, the amount of consumer spending utilizing debit cards has steadily grown over the years and now exceeds the amount of spending for credit cards.[10] In other words, consumers spend more money using debit cards than they do using credit cards. This pattern of behavior defies rational decision making. When purchasing products, a consumer is far better protected and financially secure using a credit card than a debit card. This is because using a debit card involves the immediate withdrawal of funds from one's bank account. In contrast, using a credit card involves delayed disbursement of funds during which time the consumer could be earning interest from the funds in his or her bank account. In addition, many credit cards offer loyalty programs that provide additional benefits for the consumer who uses a credit card instead of a debit card. Furthermore, regulations that have been in place for almost two decades provide additional protections against fraudulent charges for consumers using credit cards, while such regulations for debit cards are less protective of consumers.[11] The higher use of debit cards therefore represents an irrational and suboptimal decision on behalf of the consumer, and questions the basic notions of informed and rational decision making.

However, this seemingly irrational behavior can be explained by theories of self-regulation.[12] According to self-regulation theory, humans seek mechanisms that will help them regulate and control their actions and consumption behavior, and will undertake additional expenses to ensure that their behaviors are not harmful to them in the long run. For example, an overweight individual may choose to pay to enroll in a diet program. The additional cost of enrolling in this program is necessary for the individual to ensure that he or she is able to control his or her own food consumption. While from an economic point of view paying extra to consume less appears irrational, from a self-discipline perspective it makes perfect sense. The credit card scenario is in this way very similar to that of a diet plan. Despite the many benefits represented by using credit cards, most consumers are weary of excessively utilizing their credit card because they feel uncertain about their own ability to control their spending. Credit cards enable consumers to spend freely (subject to their credit limit, of course), while the amount of spending on a debit card is strictly limited by one's available bank balance. Debit card use will therefore provide a self-regulating mechanism by ensuring that one does not spend beyond one's means. The consumer may therefore forgo the numerous benefits of a credit card in order to avoid the pain that accompanies subsequent financial hardship associated with the repayment of high credit card bills and accompanying interest charges.

A similar self-regulating scenario can be found in the popular product offered by retail banks referred to as "Christmas clubs." As a member of a Christmas club, the bank customer deposits funds in his or her Christmas club account on a regular basis throughout the year. However, the customer gains no interest on the deposited balance and is unable to withdraw the funds until the end of the year for the purpose of Christmas gift shopping. Theoretically, this type of product should not survive in a market full of rational consumers.[13] The Christmas club concept may be viewed as economically unsound because one gives up access to one's own deposited funds and earns no interest from these deposits. Placing these funds elsewhere, for example by depositing them in a savings account or purchasing a certificate of deposit, may provide the customer with more access to the funds as well as earned interest income. However, these options do not protect one from the temptation to withdraw the funds for other uses, and may not provide the self-regulation and protection features that Christmas clubs offer. Again, this economically irrational behavior can best be described by consumers' own inability to trust their own judgments, and lack of discipline when it comes to their own day-to-day spending behavior throughout the year.

Other examples in which heuristic, sub-optimal, and seemingly irrational consumer decisions have been documented include the low level of savings exhibited by consumers in retirement funds. Consumers seem to be discounting the importance of saving for the future and incorrectly overestimate their ability to catch up with the financial requirements of retirement. This is further compounded by the historically low household savings rate in the United States and concerns over the future of the Social Security system. Despite these concerns, consumers continue to accumulate debt at unprecedented levels and fail to recognize and plan for their retirement needs.[14] These patterns of behavior therefore suggest that financially important decisions may in fact be far less carefully handled by consumers than what is prescribed by rational economic thinking.

UNDERSTANDING CONSUMERS' FINANCIAL DECISIONS

The rational framework for consumer decision making in financial services is challenged by findings in behavioral economics and cognitive psychology that have established that consumers are generally not well-informed decision makers. The assumptions that consumers carry out the necessary levels of information search to identify their best options and that they are rational and non-emotional in their decisions have consistently been disproved in empirical research.[15] Furthermore, the evidence seriously questions consumers' ability to carry out even the minimal level of mathematical computations required to evaluate a simple financial product objectively. In addition, despite the fact that risk and uncertainty are fundamental characteristics of the majority of financial services, research has established that consumers are quite ignorant about the true probability of many events (risk) for which they purchase financial products and services.[16] For example, the probability of getting in a car accident, the chances of dying due to a health problem, and the likelihood that a particular stock will turn around, should all have an influence on one's decisions to purchase insurance coverage at various prices or the decision to invest or divest in specific securities. Nevertheless, these probabilities are unknown to the majority of consumers, making their decision process far less accurate than any means of rationality would prescribe.

Selective Processing of Financial Service Offers

It is critical that marketers of financial services have an accurate understanding of how consumers make their decisions related to financial services. This requires one to understand how the various attributes of a financial service or product are interpreted by the consumer in order to form some overall impression or evaluation of the offered service. In general, two distinct stages are used by consumers in their evaluation and decision process for offers that they may be presented with in the marketplace.[17] The first stage is referred to as *discriminatory prescreening* and the second stage is referred to as *compensatory decision making*, both of which are described below.

Discriminatory prescreening reflects a mental strategy used to minimize the stressful task of examining a large number of financial services offers. In discriminatory pre-screening, the consumer discriminates among the various financial services available by narrowing down the choices to a subset and then eliminating services that do not possess certain desired attributes. As a result, weaknesses in an important service attribute may result in the total elimination of a financial services provider from consideration by the consumer.[18] For example, a consumer may be unwilling to purchase an insurance policy from a company which she has never heard of. She may feel that unknown insurance companies may be risky choices, and it might be better to only consider well-recognized insurance companies. Similarly, a consumer that is thinking of opening a bank account may limit his choices to banks with branches within the geographical vicinity of his place of residence.

The discriminatory prescreening stage is therefore a selective and at times intolerant approach to decision making. A financial service's weakness in an important attribute (for example, a well recognized company name or convenient branch location) may therefore not be compensated by strengths in other attributes of the service, resulting in its total elimination from consideration by the consumer. Because of this service evaluation strategy, it is critical for a financial services company to ensure that it is not eliminated from consideration by the consumer due to weaknesses in a specific attribute of importance. If the financial service possesses a weak attribute that consumers consider critical, it will most likely be eliminated from consideration. The financial services marketer would therefore need to ensure that that particular attribute is improved upon and made less salient in marketing communications.

The discriminatory prescreening process is intrinsically hardwired into the human neurological system. It reflects the brain's limited information processing ability and its strategy for coping with the large amount of information that it must process on a daily basis.[19] The complexity of financial services and the abundance of choices available to consumers forces them to simplify the decision process by focusing only on a subset of the available service attributes. A financial services provider can therefore be vulnerable to being eliminated from consideration by consumers' selective information processes. This may also present potential difficulties for the consumer who, due to the use of this approach, may choose to ignore financial services that may in fact represent much better value but unfortunately have been eliminated due to the use of discriminatory prescreening.

Once a consumer has utilized discriminatory prescreening to narrow down the range of choices, an approach referred to as *compensatory decision making* is then used.[20] In compensatory decision making, the set of choices that have made it through the discriminatory prescreening phase are carefully considered and studied by the consumer and a decision as to which one particular option is the best choice is made. The fundamental idea behind compensatory decision making is that, in contrast to the discriminatory prescreening phase during which weaknesses in an important attribute result in the omission of a product from the consumers' consideration, in the compensatory decision phase, weakness that a particular service attribute might have may be compensated for by strengths in other service attributes.

For example, a consumer who is considering automotive leases might be willing to accept a high monthly payment in return for a low down payment. Similarly, an insurance policy with a high deductible amount can still be attractive to a consumer since the premiums are low. Compensatory decision making therefore provides the financial services marketer with a certain level of flexibility around the performance of the various service attributes. It also reduces the chances of the consumer discriminating against a specific service provider solely due to poor performance on only a single attribute. Compensatory decision making requires the consumer to examine all the presented attributes and to form an overall judgment based on the values of these attributes. In this stage, a well-informed consumer may in certain financial services contexts be required to utilize a mathematical approach to evaluating a financial offer. For example, once a consumer has narrowed down his choices based on brand name to three different insurance policies, the attractiveness of each policy would have to be determined based on what is covered by each policy, the probability of occurrence for the events covered, and the dollar amount of offered coverage. As stated earlier in this chapter, elaborate computations would be needed to determine the optimal choice.

Consumer research evidence points to three general categories of behaviors that consumers seem to use in order to simplify their decisions in the compensatory decision phase (Exhibit 2.4). These simplifying rules or heuristics have a profound impact on the patterns of decisions made by consumers and the quality of these decisions. The first category of heuristics is driven by the fundamental limitations of the human brain in conducting numeric computations: consumers are rarely able to conduct elaborate mathematical computations, use the appropriate interest rates in evaluating financing offers, or conduct accurate comparisons between various financial services offers. Research consistently points out that in most cases, consumers simplify their decision making by focusing on only a subset of the attributes of financial services while ignoring the remaining attributes and may fail to carry out many of the necessary computations.[21]

The second category of heuristic decision behaviors in financial services relates to the emotional and non-objective manner in which financial decisions are often made. For example, consumers often label money depending on where they receive it from, and their decisions to spend the received money may be a function of how it was received in the first place. This fact defies the basic notions of rational budgetary discipline. Furthermore, consumers tend to treat their investment and divestment decisions based on biased reference points such as how much they paid for the investments rather than the future potential of the investment. They also tend to commit to financial investments beyond levels merited by sound investment advice and often tend to be overconfident in the quality of decisions they make. The final category of behavioral patterns that consumers exhibit in financial services decisions is the largely uninformed state in which these decisions are made. Consumers' lack of knowledge about the probabilities of some of the most important life events for which they purchase financial products such as insurance, and a lack of motivation in conducting the required amount of information search to find their best options, translate into highly uninformed and often poor decisions.

As a result, these patterns of behavior challenge the basic notion of a well-informed consumer, which is the foundation for much of traditional thinking in economics and finance.[22] In the sections below, each of these behavioral patterns will be discussed in considerable detail. It is important to note and re-emphasize that, despite their established effects, these patterns of behavior point to critical consumer vulnerabilities, and misuse of their knowledge may not only be ethically problematic but it may also be challenged by company policies, legal constraints, and emerging regulations.

Source of the Heuristics	Types of Heuristics Used
Limitations in Human Cognitive Circuitry	*1. The Magical Number 7* *2. Asymmetric Discounting* *3. The Attraction Effect* *4. Anchoring and Adjustment*
Emotions	*5. Mental Budgeting of Funds* *6. Belief in Eventual Turnarounds* *7. Reversing Risk Preferences* *8. Non-rational Escalation of Commitment*
Insufficient Consumer Knowledge	*9. Underperformance of Information Search* *10. Poor Knowledge of Risk* *11. Decision Arrogance* *12. Proxy Decision Making*

Exhibit 2.4: Sources of Heuristics Used to Evaluate Financial Services

CONSUMER DECISION PATTERNS RELATED TO HUMAN COGNITIVE CIRCUITRY

We will discuss four patterns of behavior in this section, all of which relate to the limited ability of the human brain to process complex financial services offers. These decision patterns are a result of the fact that evaluating financial offers is often complicated by the need to process numeric attributes or a large number of attributes, and therefore consumers tend to rely on simplification strategies in order to cope with the complexity of scenarios facing them.

1. The Magical Number 7

Research in cognitive psychology has established that the human memory system consists of two memory banks: short-term memory and long-term memory.[23] Long-term memory is where one's general knowledge of life's events and facts such as one's name, address, friends' names, and other important factual information is stored. Short-term memory, on the other hand, is used to process information that is in transition and therefore does not need to be stored for the long-term. For example, when doing arithmetic in one's head, short-term memory can be used to store the intermediate results of the computations, such as the results of an addition task or the carrying over of a digit.[24] The distinction between short-term and long-term memory is similar to the difference between a computer's random access memory (RAM) and its hard drive. The hard drive is similar to long-term memory where important information is stored in a relatively permanent form. In contrast, the contents of the RAM constantly change, are deleted, and updated, and will vanish if the computer is turned off for even a few seconds.

The human short-term memory is extensively used in the evaluation of complex objects, and this is especially true when elaborate evaluations or computations are needed. However, the short-term memory system is able to capture only about seven pieces of information at any one point in time. This principle is often referred to as the "magical number seven" in cognitive psychology and is the driving force for some of the limitations in human ability to process complex stimuli such as financial offers.[25]

The result of this limitation is that many of the computations that are necessary for objectively evaluating a financial product or service may become impossible for consumers to carry out. For example, when offered an automobile lease such as "$289 a month for 24 months," in order to carry out the required arithmetic (multiplication) to estimate the total dollar layout associated with the lease, a considerable amount of mental computations would have to be carried out. To appreciate the amount of work that is required, recall your elementary school days when you had to hand-calculate such multiplications. Storing the intermediate results of the arithmetic (e.g., results of an addition or the carrying over of a digit) presents considerable demands on one's short-term memory, when conducting the computations without access to pencil and paper. Research on physiological stress effects of mental arithmetic has established that such computational tasks exert a considerable amount of stress, as measured by factors such as increases in blood pressure and the pulse rate.[26] The net effect is that most consumers abandon the numeric processing of even moderately complex tasks and seek ways to simplify their decision making. For example, the consumer may choose to focus only on a single dimension of an automobile lease, such as the monthly payments, and make the decision purely based on whether he is able to afford the monthly layout of cash, thereby paying less attention to the total number of payments or other relevant dimensions of the lease offer.[27]

In addition, the fact that the human brain is limited to processing only about seven pieces of information at any one point in time implies that products that are complex and have many attributes would become very difficult for the average consumer to evaluate. This is especially important in the context of financial services that often have a large number of attributes associated with them. For example, in considering home mortgages, the typical attributes involved include the interest rate, whether the interest rates are fixed or adjustable, the lock-in period, mortgage origination fees, processing fees, escrow account requirements, late payment penalties, and the name of the company extending the mortgage, as well as other applicable attributes. As shown in Exhibit 2.5, in other financial services, the number of attributes that the consumer has to consider may easily reach and often exceeds the number seven. It is important to recognize that, when the consumer is presented with multiple financial services to evaluate (for example several different mortgage offers), the number of individual pieces of information that have to be simultaneously considered also multiplies, most likely exceeding the number seven, thereby further complicating the consumer's evaluation task. For example, assuming that a mortgage product has 10 different attributes, a consumer comparing 3 different companies has a total of 30 items of information to simultaneously process.

An additional side effect of this limitation in the human cognitive system is that, in situations where the individual service attributes influence one another, the consumer is further handicapped in conducting the appropriate evaluation of the offer. For example, in certain financial services, the total value of the package offered by the financial service may be a function of the combined effects of two or more specific product attributes. Automobile leases are a good example in which the total dollar layout associated with a lease is a function of the combined effects of the monthly payments and

Financial Service	Attributes
Home Mortgage	Interest rate, variable vs. fixed rate, lock-in period, origination fee, processing fees, escrow accounting, property assessment fees, penalties, brand name, etc.
Auto Loan	Interest rate, origination fee, down payment, conditions for use of vehicle, late payment penalties, wear-and-tear charges, excess mileage fees, end-of-lease balloon payment, etc.
Home Equity Line of Credit	Fixed vs. variable rates, interest rate, origination fee, late payment penalties, amount of the credit line, repayment conditions, etc.
Credit Card	Interest rate, introductory APR, minimum monthly payments, annual fees, length of introductory rate, late payment penalties, loyalty program, processing fees, etc.

Exhibit 2.5: Examples of Financial Services Attributes

the number of payments. Higher monthly payments combined with a large number of payments imply a large total cash layout. Another example is property and casualty insurance for which the expected payout is a function of the combined effects of the probability of an event taking place (for example, a fire or an automobile accident) and the total benefit payout associated with the purchased policy as dictated by the policy limit (for example, an automobile insurance policy with a coverage limit of $100,000 for liabilities resulting from accidents). Low probability events with little benefit coverage imply very low expected payouts and should accordingly be priced low while the opposite should be true for high probability events with large expected payouts. Nevertheless, evidence in consumer behavior indicates that consumers are limited in their ability to evaluate the combined effects of such factors and are therefore biased in their perceptions of offers in the marketplace. They may for example pay more than they should for an insurance policy that provides little coverage for rare events, or may fail to recognize the total cash layout associated with an automobile lease that has a large number of payments and high monthly payments.[28]

Furthermore, the limitations in consumers' ability to process a large number of attributes result in the simplification of the decision process by encouraging the typical consumer to focus only on a subset of the product attributes and ignore the rest. For example, in securing a home mortgage, the consumer may focus on the interest rate, the name of the mortgage company, and the location of branches in which she could apply. However, other aspects of the mortgage contract such as the closing costs, escrow account requirements, late payment penalties, or the interest rate paid on the escrow account balance may be completely ignored. As a result, the consumer's decision may be less informed than what sound economic thinking would prescribe, as the other aspects of the mortgage contract may weigh heavily in the consumers' overall perceptions.

2. Asymmetric Discounting

A second principle that has been established concerning consumers' evaluation of financial transactions relates to the time value of money. The time value of money refers to the fact that the value of either the receipt or payment of cash at future points in time is a function of the length of time before the transaction takes place. Rational thinking would suggest that payments that are more distant in time are less valued and a discount (interest) rate is applied to determine their value. Consumer research indicates that the discount rates that consumers use to conduct trade-offs between present payments and future returns are systematically different from the discount rates used on the financial markets. An example of this is a financial service that many tax accounting firms have begun offering in recent years, for accelerating the receipt of clients' refunds. In such a service, an individual taxpayer that has just had his taxes filed by the accountant is offered immediate access to the tax return amounts instead of the usual waiting period of four to eight weeks. However, a processing fee is charged for this service reducing the amount of the tax return from its original amount. For example, the consumer may have a $2,500 tax refund that the Internal Revenue Service (IRS) would process in six weeks, but is offered a $2,400 check ($100 fee) which he could deposit in a bank account and use immediately. This seems like a reasonable and even highly attractive offer to many consumers. However, if one were to calculate the rate of interest associated with this transaction, it would be computed to be extremely high, as in the example given above in which the interest rate charged by the accounting firm for accelerating the tax return is over 35%. This is a very high interest rate since even if the individual had been desperately in need of cash the same amount of funds could have most likely been accessed through a credit card, possibly at lower interest rates. Nevertheless, thousands of taxpayers each year opt for such transactions, causing one to question consumers' ability to appreciate the time value of money objectively.[29]

The pattern of behavior discussed above indicates that consumers are somewhat impatient to gain immediate access to cash. They may therefore tolerate higher than normal interest rates in return for gaining immediate access to funds rather than tolerate a delay in receiving payment at some point in time in the near future. The opposite of this phenomenon occurs in the context of financial events that are very distant in time. For example it is well established that the U.S. population has underinvested in its own retirement. Most individuals are known to save less than the prescribed amount into their retirement funds and generally underestimate the importance of retirement savings.[30] For many consumers, retirement is perceived to be so far away that its importance and significance may be perceived as irrelevant. These patterns of behavior suggest that consumers use very high discount rates for immediate events and very low discount rates for events that are distant in time.

Theories of self-regulation that focus on consumers' immediate consumption desires have been used to explain this pattern of behavior. According to these theories, the human neurological system responds to immediate gratification much more strongly than distant rewards, and as a result associates great pleasure with immediate access to consumption. As a result, the tradeoffs that consumers are willing to undertake to accelerate immediate consumption may reflect discount rates that far exceed the interest rates observed in the financial markets. Interestingly, this pattern of behavior seems to be hardwired into the neurological system and has been replicated in studies of animal psychology with pigeons and monkeys.[31] As a result the discount rates that consumers use to evaluate future transactions are asymmetric, such that rates used by consumers are higher than the prevailing rates in financial markets (for example, bank interest rates for credit products) for immediate transactions, and lower than financial market rates for distant events.

The implication of asymmetric discounting is that consumer decisions for financial services that have time as a core attribute may be highly irrational. Immediate consumption would therefore be preferred to future savings by a degree in excess of the time value of money determined by the application of financial market interest rates. Evidence on the growth of consumer debt through credit card use testifies to this. For example, it is estimated that the average household has over $10,000 of non-mortgage debt, which includes credit card debt, short-term loans, auto loans, and other forms of credit.[32] Additional evidence is found in consumer research findings with respect to household energy consumption behavior. Researchers in the energy sector have for decades studied consumer preferences for upgrading energy consuming appliances such as heating equipment, air conditioning, and kitchen appliances. These studies have shown that most consumers undervalue the benefits of energy-saving appliances.[33] Therefore, they often choose not to replace their old energy consuming appliances with upgraded appliances that significantly reduce their energy bills in the long run. This behavior occurs despite the fact that the cost of replacing the old appliance with a newer, more efficient one will quickly be recovered in the cost-savings associated with lower utility bills. Consumers are therefore reluctant to conduct the immediate investment needed for such upgrades, since the discount rate that they apply for the immediate cash layout is considerably higher than what is applied to the stream of cost savings they could experience in perpetuity. As a result, they mistakenly undervalue the infinite stream of savings that they will experience from such upgrades.

	Price	Liability Coverage
Policy A	$1,275	$150,000
Policy B	$1,569	$200,000

Exhibit 2.6: Choice Between Two Insurance Policies

	Price	Liability Coverage
Policy A	$1,275	$150,000
Policy B	$1,569	$200,000
Policy C	$1,725	$175,000

Exhibit 2.7 Use of Attraction Effect to Influence Consumer Choice

3. The Attraction Effect

The attraction effect is a principle that explains biases that can be introduced to consumer decision outcomes when consumers are presented with a choice set consisting of a large number of products or services. Simply stated, the attraction effect postulates that the attractiveness of a specific product increases when new products dominated by that original product are introduced to the set of choices facing the consumer.[34] For example, Exhibit 2.6 shows two different insurance policies with different annual premium levels and coverage amounts. Policy A has a lower premium but offers lower liability coverage, while policy B offers higher coverage with a higher premium level. The attraction effect suggests that consumers' choice between policy A and policy B can be systematically shifted by introducing a new policy that is dominated by one of the original policies. Exhibit 2.7 shows an example of how this might be accomplished. The introduction of Policy C with the highest annual premium of $1,725 and a liability coverage that is below the coverage offered by policy B makes policy B a considerably more attractive option than before (Fig 6). As a result, consumer preferences may shift in favor of policy B, by simply having a dominated alternative (policy C) introduced to their set of available choices. Note that the newly introduced policy is only dominated by policy B, and that policy A is not dominating it; therefore, the share gains would be experienced by policy B rather than policy A.

The attraction effect principle is used sometimes in sales scenarios where a salesperson, broker, or agent has some control over the set of choices presented to the consumer. For example, in real estate, an agent may choose to show the prospective homebuyers a series of homes, but selectively presents a dominated alternative (for example a home that is priced high, rundown, and poorly maintained) in order to shift the homebuyers' preference towards a specific home that dominates the rundown, overpriced house. This same pattern of behavior may be exhibited in the brokerage business for mortgages and insurance products. Brokers have the ability to choose what is presented to the client and can therefore influence the client's choice through the attraction effect. It is critical to appreciate that such practices may be highly unethical and in many cases are prohibited not only by company policies but also by regulations. In fact, these practices have often resulted in legal challenges by regulatory bodies such as the *NASD*, the *SEC*, state insurance departments, or other consumer protection bodies.[35] The persistent impact of the attraction effect in financial services markets is that brokers, agents, salespeople, and marketers can influence consumer decision outcomes by modifying the decision context. This fact highlights the ethical obligations that these intermediaries have on consumer welfare.

4. Anchoring and Adjustment

In their seminal research studies published in the 1970s, psychologists Amos Tversky and Daniel Kahneman helped establish some of the underlying principles that guide human perception and resulting biases.[36] Their work has had a profound effect on our understanding of consumer behavior both within and outside financial services markets. One of their most robust and widely validated principles was the principle of *anchoring and adjustment*. The anchoring and adjustment principle relates to consumers' thought strategies used to cope with their limited ability to process large volumes of information. According to this principle, in order for consumers to cope with the level of information overflow that characterizes their decision environment, they may choose to simplify their task by focusing on one product attribute and forming an initial judgment (anchoring). They then proceed to examine the remaining attributes and adjust their original judgment (adjustment). This strategy helps the average consumer significantly reduce cognitive stress.

For example, in evaluating a financing arrangement for an automobile, the consumer may not be able to carry out the multiplication of the monthly payments and the number of payments. As discussed earlier in relation to the "magical number 7" principle, consumers often find the arithmetical task required for such computations to be cognitively stressful. They therefore seek alternative approaches to evaluating the presented offer in a simpler manner. According to the anchoring-and-adjustment principle, the consumer will most likely focus on the most important attribute, which is the monthly payments,[37] in order to form an overall assessment of whether he or she could afford those payments (anchoring). The individual will then proceed to examine other attributes of the lease such as the number of payments or the down payment, and modify his or her original evaluation (adjustment).[38]

What is uniquely important about the anchoring and adjustment principle is that the adjustment that is made by the consumer to the original evaluation that had been made using the anchor is typically far below the levels required by rational decision making. As a result of the original anchor, for example, the monthly payments dominate one's overall evaluation of an automobile lease, but the number of payments may have much lower diagnostic value for the consumer. Research has established that, when evaluating payments extended over multiple periods of time, consumer sensitivity to the number of periods is considerably lower than the periodic payment amount.[39]

The anchoring and adjustment principle would therefore suggest that the most favorable presentation of a financial offer needs to take into account which financial product attribute is most likely to be used by the consumer as an "anchor" for forming the initial judgments. In a mortgage contract for example, the anchor may be the interest rate, and the adjustment variables might be the number of years, the points charged upfront, and the brand name. These remaining "adjustment" attributes of the mortgage may have very little impact on the changes consumer make to their overall evaluations. Therefore, the anchor may dominate the overall evaluation made by the consumer. Similarly, in an automobile insurance policy, the consumer may be focused primarily on the premium levels and use this attribute as an anchor. Subsequent adjustments might be made based on the amount of coverage provided, dollar level of policy deductibles, and excluded items from the policy. However, these adjustments are typically less than they should be, and consumer judgments may largely ignore these and other remaining policy attributes.

Clearly, ethical and legal issues need to be considered when deciding what the most favorable presentation of a financial services offer to the consumer might be. Due to the large number of product attributes in financial services, the likelihood of consumers simplifying their decision process by utilizing an anchoring and adjustment process is very high. This not only implies that financial services marketers need to empirically determine which attribute is used as the anchor by the typical consumer, but must also ensure that the products and services that they present to the marketplace have attractive values for the anchoring attribute. Financial offers that fail to have a favorable "anchor" attribute are most likely to be rejected by consumers.

BEHAVIORAL PATTERNS RELATED TO EMOTIONS

The next set of principles that we will discuss relates to the overwhelming effects that emotions have on consumer decision making, especially in financial services. For example, consumers view each dollar at hand in the context of the source from which they have received it, and their choice of where to spend the money is often affected by where the money came from in the first place. This defies rational economic thinking in which money has no labels and is simply part of an objective budgetary process.[40] Furthermore, other emotions may affect consumers' financial decisions. For example, consumers' perceptions of risk are known to be highly inaccurate and biased. In other words, the general knowledge that consumers have about the probability of certain important events taking place is very poor. Consumers also have a tendency to engage in long sequences of risky losses despite conflicting rational prescriptions. They may for example, continue to participate in a losing investment, when in fact they should be pulling out. The effects of these principles on consumer purchases of financial services will be discussed below.

5. Mental Budgeting of Financial Decisions

Despite the fact that the spending of money represents an outlay of cash, studies of consumer spending psychology have established that consumers often categorize different forms of spending into different types of budgets in their minds referred to as "mental accounts."[41] For example, consumers have a mental account for daily expenditures such as meals, transportation, and newspapers. They also have a similar account related to monthly expenditures such as rent and utilities. Additionally, mental accounts related to yearly events such as tax returns and large durable purchases might exist. Furthermore, different accounts might exist for windfall gains and unforeseen losses. To appreciate this, imagine how charities often seek donations. Most charities would ask the public to donate funds and proceed to phrase the donation amount on a daily expenditure basis. Promotional material from a charity might for example state that that you would save the life of a third-world child by donating the equivalent of what you spend for a cup of coffee every day. Rarely would such a charity phrase the donation amount on what the total cost of the donation might be on a yearly basis, which may easily be equivalent to several hundred dollars a year. By phrasing the donation amount as a daily expenditure the charity has prompted the consumer to unconsciously process the requested donation as a daily budget item rather than a yearly item, the latter of which typically exhibits higher levels of resistance and price sensitivity.[42]

While the existence of mental budgeting process helps us cope with the complexity of our expenditure decisions, research has shown that by encouraging a consumer to reexamine a given expenditure and associate it with a different type of mental account (for example by treating a large yearly expenditure as a small daily expenditure), one could change the consumer's willingness to spend. A typical example of this is the practice of financing high-end appliances, consumer durables, and luxury goods. Sellers are often aware of the unattractive impact of the high sticker prices for these items and opt to frame the price using financial products such as leases and consumer loans in ways that do not highlight the total cash layout. In the financial services sector, a similar approach is taken in marketing term life insurance policies. A life insurance marketer may for example, advertise a policy using words such as: "for 50 cents a day you too can have term life insurance coverage." In general, consumers are less resistant toward spending when such expenditures are framed in terms of short-term budgets (such as a daily expenditure) rather than long-term budgets (such as a yearly expenditure).

Research has established that in addition to mental budgets which are a function of time frame (for example, daily versus yearly budgets), additional accounts related to unexpected financial gains or losses might also exist. Examples might be an unexpectedly high tax return, or the winning of a lottery. In general, consumer behavior with respect to windfall gains is found to be highly irrational. The higher than expected tax return may for example result in the purchasing of non-necessity goods which the consumer may have never even considered purchasing before and has no immediate use for. Instead of treating the unexpected incoming funds as cash assets, consumers tend to be less sensitive to spending the money, and may accordingly use these funds in ways that challenge disciplined budgetary planning. What is unique about mental accounting and its relationship to financial services marketing is the fact that many financial services such as credit and savings products and long-term insurance policies have a time-dependent component related to how the payments are made. For example, the payments for a car loan take place over years on a regular monthly basis. Similarly, the premiums for an insurance policy may be collected at regular intervals throughout a year. Financial services marketers therefore have the option of presenting such premiums in the context of different time frames, and understanding which time frame would produce the most attractive results in the consumer's mind is critical to creating an effective marketing pitch. For example, an automobile lease, an insurance policy, or short-term consumer loan may be perceived to be more attractive if it is communicated in terms of daily expenditures rather than equivalent yearly amounts. It is important to note, however, that regulations prohibit the framing of certain financial services using specific time frames that may make the financial service or product appear excessively attractive, and it is therefore important for one to consult related advertising regulations and to obtain the necessary legal advice to ensure compliance with existing laws.

6. Believing in Eventual Turnarounds

In the context of investment products, it has been shown that investor behavior is at times characterized by a sense of long-term optimism for investments that have long lost significant value. Similarly, investors tend to exhibit a sense of doubt for investments that have gained value, and this principle, which, is often referred to as "selling winners, keeping the losers", was derived from research observations on investors' buy and sell decisions on the stock market.[43] For example, research has shown that investors typically have a tendency not to sell stocks in their portfolio that are selling below the price they had originally paid for the stock ("kept losers"). Instead, they tend to sell those stocks that have grown in value beyond the price that they had originally paid ("sold winners"). While this pattern of behavior might seem reasonable, what is disturbing about the empirical findings is the fact that the sold winners, after having been sold, were found to outperform the kept losers – a pattern which should not exist in a marketplace with well-informed rational consumers.[44]

In other words, while educated and informed investors should take into account the future potential of a stock, they instead allow their own purchase price to bias their buy and sell decisions. When a stock is selling at a price below the price that the investor had paid for it, the rational investor's decision should not be influenced by how much she had paid for it. Instead, the decision should take into account the future expected price for the stock and whether the price will move up or down. However, investors typically place excessive attention on the price that they had themselves paid for the stock and use this figure as a reference point in their buying and selling decisions. Therefore, when a stock is trading above the price that one had purchased it for, a sense of doubt over the continuation of this pattern and a belief in a downward turnaround may result in one deciding to sell the stock. Similarly, when a stock is trading below one's purchased price, investors tend to believe that the price will eventually turnaround to regain the original price paid for it. By doing so, investors fail to act quickly in selling off stocks that may further deplete in value, thereby creating a pattern of keeping losing stocks.

One underlying investor belief that motivates this behavior is that the stock price will eventually turn around and reach values equivalent to what was originally paid for it. Similarly, when making selling decisions on a stock, the investor may heavily depend on the purchase price of the stock. Therefore, when a stock gains in value (is selling above the purchase price) the investor may seek to capitalize on the gain, believing that the stock price will eventually have a downward turnaround towards his purchase price. By doing this, the investor may be ignoring the future potential of the stock, which may constitute further growth and value creation. This would result in the investor deciding to realize the immediate gains associated with the selling of the stock over the purchase price, resulting in a portfolio that has a low share of winning (growing) stocks.

Consumers' beliefs in such eventual turnarounds have a profound impact on their investment behavior. This is especially true in the context of selling decisions and long-term management of investment portfolios. It is important to note, however, that despite the sub-optimal effects that the turnaround beliefs might have in investment decisions, there may be tax benefits to making decisions that may on the surface appear to be the selling of winners or the keeping of losers. For example, Internal Revenue Service code allows an individual tax payer to obtain tax deductions for capital losses resulting from the selling of securities below their purchased price.[45] As a result, an investor who may have a losing position with respect to an individual stock may decide to keep the stock due to the tax benefits which may be gained in the future by eventually selling it. These tax benefits therefore make the selling of a losing stock a less urgent matter. Nevertheless, brokers, investment advisors, and other financial professionals must take great care to ensure that their clients are making sound economic decisions and are not guided by irrational decisions, processes, and biased perceptions. The opportunities for poor consumer decisions as a result of the "turnaround" bias are unfortunately abundant, especially in the context of investment products.

7. Shifting Risk Preferences

As discussed earlier, a fundamental dimension of many financial services is risk and uncertainty. A driving force in consumers' decisions with respect to the purchasing of financial services therefore relates to their perceptions of risk. Research has established that consumer preference for risk may be a function of whether the risk is framed in terms of gains or losses. Gains may for example, be cases in which investments of different risk levels and profit gain expectations are being considered. Losses may on the other hand, relate to scenarios where consumers may choose to purchase insurance by paying insurance premiums in order to remove the risk of possibly much greater monetary losses. Research has shown that depending on whether the decision scenario is framed as a gain or a loss, consumers' risk tolerance may significantly shift.[46] To appreciate the nature of this shift, consider the choice between two different forms of investment (gains) described in the following scenario:[47]

> *Choice 1: Receive $100.*
> *Choice 2: Take a 10% chance of getting $1,000 but a 90% chance*
> *of getting $0.*

When consumers are asked to decide which one of the above two options they would prefer most state that they prefer choice 1. The difference between choices 1 and 2 is that the second choice represents a risky scenario. The intrinsic risk associated with the second choice is that one is uncertain about the outcome of the investment, in that while it is possible for one to gain a significant amount of cash ($1,000), it is also more likely that no returns would come from such a decision ($0). In contrast, the first choice represents a financial gain ($100) with absolute certainty (no risk). The nature of preferences between the choices above indicates that we are generally risk-averse for scenarios framed as gains (for example, investments and savings products), choosing the less risky option.

However, risk preference patterns seem to reverse when losses are being considered, and as described below, the pattern of consumer preferences may shift towards risk-seeking choices. Consider the following scenario:

> *Choice 1: Pay $100 to the insurance company*
> *Choice 2: Take a 90% change of not paying anything, and a 10%*
> *chance of paying $1,000.*

When asked to choose between the above two options, many consumers would prefer the second option. In other words, they would rather not have to pay $100 and take the chance of paying nothing. Similar to the scenario described earlier, the first choice is a risk-free option whereby no probabilities are involved and one is certain of the outcome (having to pay the insurance company a specific amount of money). The second choice, on the other hand, reflects a risky scenario as the outcome cannot be predicted with certainty. While the expected dollar value of all the choices is identical in both the gain and loss scenarios (for example, when multiplying the probabilities by the dollar outcomes), a reversal in consumer preferences for risk is evident in the second scenario. The fact that most consumers select the second choice in the above scenario implies that they have a preference for the risky choice. This is the reverse of the preference pattern which had been exhibited in the choice scenario preceding the above, where the risk-free (certain) scenario was preferred.

From the above example, it may be clear that generally, consumers tend to be more tolerant of risk in situations where losses are involved. Conversely, in situations where gains are involved, a preference for certain (risk-free) outcomes is revealed. This reversal of human behavior as a function of losses or gains has been attributed by some psychologists as an underlying neurological phenomenon that guides not only human but also animal behavior. It is a reflection of the survival instincts of living organisms, which, when faced with threats of losses, are more willing to take on risk.[48] Alternatively, scenarios that involve gains focus decision makers on the utility of the gains, resulting in the adoption of a conservative tone to decision making. As a result, in scenarios where gains are involved outcomes that are certain tend to be preferred to risky options. It is important to note that the shift in risk preferences is also a function of the extent of risk involved as reflected in the probabilities associated with a loss or a gain. For example, if the likelihood of a negative outcome is high in a risky scenario, decision makers may opt to proceed with the risk-free alternative.

The significance of the risk preference reversal patterns discussed above in the context of financial services is especially notable for insurance and long-term investment and savings products. For example, it has been well recognized by many state transportation authorities that a sizable segment of drivers often chooses to take the risk of not having purchased automobile insurance. Needless to say, these individuals present themselves and others on the road with significant financial risks in cases of accidents. As a result, the Department of Motor Vehicles in all states now mandates that all drivers must be insured, and no vehicle registrations are issued without the presentation of valid insurance documentation.[49] Similarly, many employers require their employees to regularly contribute to their pension funds. This is in recognition of the fact that individuals in general underestimate the financial risks that they cause themselves and their families to face by not investing sufficiently into their retirement funds. Therefore, unless employers mandate regular contributions to retirement funds, many employees might choose to take on the risk of not investing in a pension fund altogether.[50]

8. Non-rational Escalation of Commitment

Human decisions that involve long-term commitments to a particular plan of action have at times been subject to a form of judgment error referred to as "non-rational escalation of commitment."[51] This phenomenon reflects a decision maker's desire to continue the course of action that has originally been committed to despite the fact that emerging evidence may suggest that the chosen line of action may not be as profitable as originally expected. A simple example of this may occur in the context of phone calls to customer service lines.[52] For example imagine that you have called the customer service line for your bank and you have been waiting for over 15 minutes to talk to somebody. At that point in time you have to make a decision as to whether you will continue on waiting, or will instead redial the number hoping to be queued to a different customer service queue. Studies on customer service and call center operations have shown that the waiting time of the customer service call in a queue will influence the caller's desire to continue waiting for a customer service person to respond.[53] The longer one waits, the more one may be committed to remaining on hold in hopes that eventually someone will pick up the phone at the other end. While this pattern of behavior may be attributed to the belief that having waited so long, the likelihood of someone responding should have increased, it also is driven by the belief that the amount of time spent waiting needs to be rewarded, and that by holding on to the phone, one will eventually be rewarded for the long wait. This latter motivation is reflective of individuals' desire to maintain a course of action, despite conflicting evidence (for example, a customer service phone queue that simply does not respond to the customer's call in a timely manner).

The underlying psychological principle that helps explain non-rational escalation of commitment in financial services has to do with the tendency for consumers to focus their attention on the past performance of a financial product and to ignore future expectations. Furthermore, as Bazerman and others note, one's excessive commitment to a given plan of action may be a result of social pressure and a decision maker's desire not to appear inconsistent and indecisive within her social group.[54] This pattern of behavior is further amplified by the competitive nature in which decisions are often made. For example, a consumer's desire to stick with a stock that is losing value may be a function of his peer group's decisions. Clearly, peer pressure, the desire for social consistency, and a lack of attention to future prospects do not reflect rational and good financial decisions, but are commonly observed in financial services markets. Needless to say, non-rational escalation of commitment can severely harm the consumer, especially in investment products. Financial advisors and investment professionals should therefore take great care to ensure that the decisions made by their clients, as well as their own recommendations to these clients, are not biased by such a phenomenon.

BEHAVIORAL PATTENS RELATED TO INSUFFICIENT CONSUMER KNOWLEDGE

A driving force in consumer decisions in financial services markets is their level of knowledge (or lack thereof) about the financial products and services available in the marketplace. Generally, consumers seem to lack the necessary amount of information about the features of financial services, appropriate prices, and the variety of services available to them. Moreover, for financial services that involve elements of risk such as insurance and investment products, consumers have highly inaccurate knowledge of the risks involved and the associated probabilities. Interestingly, however, they tend to overestimate their own knowledge and decision making abilities far beyond their true skill levels or decision making capabilities. We will discuss the impact of these patterns of behavior on the marketing of financial services below.

9. Underperformance of Information Search

Consumer research has established that, in most consumer decisions both financial and non-financial, there is a tendency for consumers not to conduct the necessary amount of information gathering that is needed to fully understand the various available alternatives prior to making important decisions. For example, a consumer deciding which university to attend for graduate studies may limit her choices to a handful of schools and to not take into account all possible schools which may have similar programs and be equally relevant to her educational objectives. Similarly, a consumer examining various models of automobiles may limit his search to a small number of dealers and not shop around sufficiently to get the best possible price or find the most appropriate model.

A low degree of information search is equally evident in consumer purchases of financial services. For example, when choosing between term life insurance providers, a consumer may only limit her choice to companies with established names. Similarly, when choosing among a series of mutual funds, a consumer may use the fund company name and the investment style as screening variables and limit the funds considered only to those that fit these criteria. By doing so, consumers would ignore many other options that may be available to them which may possibly be far more attractive. Studies of consumer decisions have generally shown that consumers typically conduct only a fraction of the amount of information search that is optimal and required in order to identify the best available choice in the marketplace.[55]

Various causes have been associated with the underperformance of information search. One contributor is the fact that consumers overestimate the value of their own time. As a result, they are unwilling to make the required sacrifice of their own leisure time in order to conduct the hard work of researching required to locate their best option in the marketplace.[56] In addition, it has been established that the cognitive limitations associated with detailed decisions create a stressful experience for many consumers and, as a result, consumers have a tendency to want to terminate the decision process sooner rather than later.[57] This behavior is further amplified in the context of financial services that typically are intrinsically unexciting, highly technical, and numerical in nature. While shopping around between different car dealerships and test driving different cars may have an intrinsic level of entertainment value, shopping around between mutual funds, insurance brokers, or retail banks does not carry nearly the same amount of consumer excitement and involvement. As a result, consumers may terminate information search in financial services decisions before they would do so in other purchase contexts.

The tendency for consumers not to undertake the necessary amount of information search has significant implications on the marketing of financial services. For example, one of the underlying principles behind the notion of "one-stop shopping," which has characterized much of the merger activity in the financial services sector is driven by this very principle. One-stop shopping in the commercial banking sector implies that consumers would be able to satisfy all their financial needs by using a single commercial bank branch. Therefore, a bank customer who usually conducts his banking at the local bank branch can also now purchase his automobile insurance and obtain a mortgage from the same bank location. This clearly presents significant conveniences for consumers who would have otherwise needed to visit an insurance agent and a mortgage broker at different locations.[58] The resulting convenience for the consumer reduces the desire to conduct information search by examining other competing insurance or mortgage offers available from brokers or banks elsewhere. The lower amount of information search may therefore reduce consumers' price sensitivity, while increasing the volume of sales associated with the bank branch's multiple financial product lines. The underperformance of information search also helps provide one explanation for the critical role that brokers play in the marketing of financial services such as mortgages and insurance products. Brokers have the responsibility of seeking and identifying financial services providers that may best fit their client's unique needs. By doing so, the broker removes the burden of information search from the client while taking on the responsibility of making informed and educated recommendations that should be in the best interest of the client.

10. Poor Knowledge of Risk

Risk is a fundamental characteristic of many financial services and products. For example, when purchasing insurance, a well-informed rational consumer must have an assessment of the risk (probability) of the events being insured. If an insured event has a very high probability of occurrence the consumer's willingness to purchase an insurance policy must be great, and the opposite should be true if the event is highly unlikely. Nevertheless, research indicates that consumers generally have very little knowledge about the probability of many of life's important events.[59] For example, surveys of consumers on their estimates of the frequency by which deaths occur due to various causes show that the estimated rates provided by consumers systematically vary from the actual rates. While this is not an unexpected result, it is especially problematic within the context of insurance products. When purchasing a life insurance policy, for example, one's knowledge of the actual mortality rate associated with one's age is important in order to determine what a fair premium would be. Nevertheless, an individual would rarely be aware of the mortality rate associated with his age bracket. Therefore, the likelihood of using this diagnostic information to assess prices of term life policies is minimal.

What is also interesting about studies of consumers' perceptions of risk is the systematic biases that exist in these perceptions. In general, consumers underestimate the likelihood of events that are high in probability and overestimate events that are very unlikely to occur. The consumer tendency to overestimate rare events can be attributed to the fact that rare events are often more memorable.[60] The unique circumstances and extreme nature of a rare event cause a disproportionate amount of attention to be given to it by consumers. This is further compounded by the fact that the news media often chooses rare events as the focus of their coverage. As a result, the population's exposure to news of rare events is disproportionate to the true frequency by which these events take place. Rare events therefore become more memorable and consumers may overestimate their incidence. As Bazerman argues, consumers can also underestimate frequent events due to denial or attribution strategies. For example, the death of an individual due to heart disease (which is a high frequency event) might be attributed by the average person to the deceased person's smoking habits, when in fact the root cause may have simply been genetics or chance. Consumers may therefore seek reasons other than randomness in explaining the occurrence of frequent events, thereby discounting their importance and denying their own vulnerabilities.

Consumers' lack of knowledge of risk has a significant impact on financial services marketing. It suggests that consumers can be sold financial products associated with low risk events at prices above their fair economic value. For example, tire stores often sell additional insurance coverage with their tires, which covers the cost of repairs or replacement of the tire in case of severe punctures due to road debris. Such events are sufficiently rare that the rational consumer will unlikely need to utilize such a policy especially considering the prices that are charged for such policies. Nevertheless, a notable proportion of consumers purchasing new tires proceed to purchase such policies. A similar product is the extended warranty sold by electronics stores, which covers repairs to the product beyond the time period covered by the manufacturer's warranty. While there are some clear benefits to having extended warranties for many durable goods, the prices of these warranties often far outweigh the expected failure rates and associated replacement costs of the products to which they apply. As a result, retailers have found the sale of extended warranties to be one of the most profitable lines of their business, questioning the true benefit of this form of financial product to the consumer.

Clearly, consumers seem to overestimate the likelihood of product failures to the extent that they may be willing to pay for some of the over-priced extended warranties and tire protection plans on the market. The flipside of this bias is that consumers often underestimate the value of many other insurance products that could help protect them against catastrophic losses resulting from environmental and safety hazards. The very presence of an underestimation/overestimation bias creates opportunities for deceptive or overpriced insurance products, and at the same time causes the average consumer to have a less-than-required level of appreciation for insurance products that they may very well need. Flood and automotive insurance fall into this latter category of financial services. It is therefore no surprise that the purchase of automobile insurance is mandated by law and in the case of flood insurance, required by mortgage companies in flood zones. Consumers' underestimation of the risks of automobile accidents or floods mandates the forceful requirement of insurance coverage, in order to ensure that individuals are not exposed to unnecessary financial risks.

11. Decision Arrogance

Another bias that is attributed to consumer decisions is a general sense of optimism about one's own ability to make good decisions or one's general knowledge of a topic area. Such optimism often translates into an arrogant sense of confidence, which can eventually hinder the quality of financial decisions made. Interestingly, this phenomenon, which Bazerman and others refer to as "overconfidence," has been shown to be especially true for events or facts for which the individual has little, if any, objective information.[61] The result of this is that, for many critical decisions, consumers may in fact confidently make assessments and decisions that are uneducated and inaccurate, leading to catastrophic outcomes.

It is also important to note that this phenomenon is true not only for the average consumer, but it has also been documented for well-trained and highly responsible decision makers. For example, a study conducted by Morningstar examined the performance of the top 10 mutual funds in the United States in a 5 year time span. The study found that, had the fund managers for the top ten mutual funds at the start of this time period decided not to change the portfolio mix of their funds during the five years, these funds would have significantly outperformed their actual experienced performance level by the end of this time period.[62] This pattern is partially a result of the fund manager's overconfidence in their own ability to make quality decisions. A similar study conducted by Barber and Odean and examined the investment behavior of individual investors. The study found that those investors who were the most active traders and conducted the highest amount of buying and selling of securities (those in the top 20% of trading activity) exhibited significantly poorer results than the remaining group of consumers surveyed. [63] Furthermore, the study showed that, despite the investment activity exhibited by all investors, the average portfolio gain was below what the market indices had achieved. As a result, the average investor would have been better off investing his or her funds in an index fund (which tracks the overall stock market), rather than actively buying and selling individual securities in hope of beating the market. Again, this pattern of behavior may reflect consumers' overconfidence in their own ability to buy and sell the right securities. The result is that they may choose to be active participants in securities markets for which they may have little knowledge or decision making ability.

12. Proxy Decision Making

In contrast to the bias resulting from decision arrogance, some consumers may view their own ability to make good decisions as inadequate, and instead rely on the decisions of others. By doing so, other individuals' decisions may be considered as proxies for good decisions in the specific financial contexts facing the consumer.[64] For example, a consumer may rely on buy-and-sell decisions of a friend to determine his own stock portfolio decisions. Alternatively, a consumer may rely on social media as a source of information on her financial decisions. The main limitation of this form of decision making is that the individuals chosen as sources for good decisions may in fact be uninformed or poor decision makers. In addition, research specifically focusing on social media suggests that at times those claiming to be experts may in fact be biased participants in the medium with hidden motives to boost or harm the image of a company or an investment instrument. [65] Research also suggests that consumers may choose to rely on proxy-based financial decisions simply to relieve themselves of the burden of elaborate information processing associated with financial matters.[66] The net effect is likely to be a risky and uninformed decision.

ETHICAL IMPLICATIONS OF THE CONSUMER DECISION PROCESS

The startling contrast between what a rational consumer should do and what is often done by the average consumer faced with choices in the financial services marketplace is alarming. While theories of rationality and educated decision making may be true for a small proportion of the population, research suggests that the majority of consumers suffer from fundamental limitations in human cognitive abilities that restrict their ability to fully understand the financial services being presented to them. As a result, the decisions made by most consumers may not match predictions that assume rational and logical decision making. It is important to note that the phenomenon highlighted in this chapter are not limited only to the context of individual consumers making specific financial decisions. In fact most of the biases discussed in this chapter have been widely observed among corporate financial decision makers within the context of business-to-business environments. While this may at first seem surprising, this observation emphasizes the fact that at the heart of every financial decision, regardless of the context or scale, there is a human decision maker at work who has to process the presented financial offering in order to make a choice. Therefore, the biases that influence an individual consumer are likely to have similar effects among decision makers in business settings, and for this reason many of the phenomenon discussed in this chapter have direct equivalents in the corporate world.[67]

When developing financial services marketing strategies, it is essential to appreciate some of the limitations cited in this chapter. However, it is equally important to appreciate the ethical dilemmas that these limitations present to the financial services marketer. The abuse of consumers' inability to process the necessary information when evaluating a financial service is not only unethical, but in certain cases it may violate regulations and result in legal repercussions. It is therefore essential for a financial services marketer not only to be aware of regulations that govern and restrict their marketing activities, but also to be fully aware of company policies that may constrain the scope of activities one could engage in. Even when complying with regulations and company policy, one needs to have comfort in the types of marketing activities undertaken from a personal ethical perspective. The ultimate test for this may be for one to ask oneself whether the marketing actions and communications would be perceived as deceptive and misleading if the marketer himself, or family members and loved ones were the target of the marketing campaign.

It is also noteworthy that despite the many efforts made by regulators through the years to improve and increase the level of consumer protection, millions of consumers are subjected to deceptive and questionable marketing practices every year. The extent to which regulations may have helped protect consumers in this process is in fact unclear. Regulations that have focused on improving the nature of communications in the market-place by increasing the amount of information disclosed to the consumer may have in some cases hindered consumers' ability to process the necessary information. For example, the Truth in Lending Act requires lenders to disclose the details of a credit arrangement such as the APR (annual percentage rate) and financing fees related to the offer. As a consequence, advertisers are mandated by law to provide detailed information, often in the form of fine print disclosures in their advertisements. While the Truth in Lending Act has been a positive force in certain consumer interactions, its effect in broadcast advertising has been questioned.[68] Some critics argue that the act creates conditions of information overflow that may in fact hinder consumers' ability to fully grasp the essential dimensions of the presented offer. For example, the regulation's requirements mandate the advertiser to communicate items of information that may easily exceed consumers' ability to process them (e.g., magical number 7). In a typical lease advertisement broadcast on television, for example, the disclosure requirements result in advertisements that have fine print that may not even be observable due to the poor resolution level of some television sets, and the communicated information may only be on the screen for a brief time (often only a few seconds), not allowing the consumer to fully read the text displayed on the screen.

Under these conditions, regulations cannot be the only solution to protecting consumers from misinformed decision making, and much research by regulators, academics, and financial services organizations may be needed to identify how best to help consumers make informed decisions. Knowledge of the patterns of consumer behavior related to financial decisions should only be utilized in legal and ethical ways by marketers, and misuse of this information may place the marketer at great risk of failing regulatory compliance, and lead to legal challenges by regulators and consumer protection bodies. Misuse of consumers' limited ability to process the complexities of financial offers in the marketplace may also lead to the loss of trust by consumers and permanently damage the company's brand image in the marketplace. At the same time the principles of consumer decision making in financial services can be used to educate consumers and to promote financial products and services that best serve untapped consumer needs. For example, investment professionals, recognizing consumers' tendency to use asymmetric discounting, could educate consumers on the necessity for retirement planning and saving for the future. Similarly, the fact that consumers underestimate the probabilities of high frequency events may provide insurance companies with the opportunity to communicate the importance of insurance protection for specific classes of risk. Such an approach would not only help provide consumers with relevant products, but would also create new marketing opportunities for financial services organizations in a saturated marketplace. Financial services marketers have the ability to develop and to market products and services which may greatly benefit consumers, and an understanding of the consumer decision process is essential to this endeavor.

CHAPTER QUESTIONS

1. What possible relationships do you see in relating the following pairs of principles discussed in this chapter
   (a) Magical number 7 and underperformance of information search
   (b) The attraction effect and magical number 7
   (c) Mental budgeting and anchoring-and-adjustment
   (d) Decision arrogance and eventual turnaround beliefs
   (e) Magical number 7 and proxy decision making

2. Considering the biases discussed in this chapter, which one do you think creates a context in which regulators must ensure consumer protection against possibly deceptive marketing practices?

3. What potential actions could financial services marketers take in order to avoid the harmful effects of discriminatory pre-screening on their brands?

4. Choose three of the principles below and identify examples in which financial services marketers have utilized these principles in their marketing practices:
    (a) Magical number 7
    (b) Asymmetric discounting
    (c) The Attraction effect
    (d) Anchoring and adjustment
    (e) Mental budgeting
    (f) Eventual turnaround beliefs
    (g) Reversing risk preferences
    (h) Non-rational escalation of commitment
    (i) Underperformance of information search
    (j) Poor knowledge of risk
    (k) Decision arrogance
    (l) Proxy decision making

5. In your observations, what non-rational consumer behaviors have you witnessed relating to financial services decisions, other than the categories discussed in this chapter?

6. What are the implications of each of the principles discussed in this chapter on the most effective marketing practices for financial services providers?

ENDNOTES

1 Roger Blackwell, Paul Minard, and James Engel (2005), *Consumer Behavior.* Mason, OH: South-Western College Publishing.; L. Schiffman and L. Kanuk (2006), *Consumer Behavior.* New York: Prentice-Hall; J. Hammond, R. Keeney, and H. Raffia (1999), *Smart Choices.* Harvard Business School Press: Cambridge, MA; Newell, A. and H.A. Simon (1972), *Human Problem Solving.* Englewood Cliffs, NJ: Prentice Hall. Bettman, J.R. (1979), *An Information Processing Theory of Consumer Behavior.* Reading, MA: Addison-Wesley.

2 S. Klugman (2011), *Bayesian Statistics in Actuarial Science.* Springer ; E. Ohlsson and B. Johansson (2010), *Non-Life Insurance Pricing with General Linear Models.* Springer. J. Kimball Dietrich (1996), *Financial Services and Financial Institutions.* Prentice Hall: Upper Saddle River, NJ. pp. 335-3452; G. Michael Moebs (1986), *Pricing Financial Services.* Dow Jones-Irwin: Homewood, IL.

3 Scott Besley and Eugene Brigham (2008), *Principles of Finance.* South Western College Publishing.

4 William E. Sharpe (1964), "Capital Asset Pricing: A Theory of Market Equilibrium Under Conditions of Risk," *Journal of Finance,* Vol. 19, pp. 425-442; Robert B. Litterman (2003), *Modern Investment Management: An Equilibrium Approach.* John Wiley and Sons: New York; Shannon P. Pratt (2002), *Cost of Capital: Estimation and Application.* John Wiley and Sons: New York

5 F. Fabozzi, S. Focardi and P. Kolm (2010), *Quantitative Equity Investing: Techniques and Strategies.* New York: Wiley. Robert B. Litterman (2003), *Modern Investment Management: An Equilibrium Approach.* John Wiley and Sons:

New York; Shannon P. Pratt (2002), *Cost of Capital: Estimation and Application.* John Wiley and Sons: New York.

6 William E. Sharpe (1964), "Capital Asset Pricing: A Theory of Market Equilibrium Under Conditions of Risk," *Journal of Finance,* Vol. 19, pp. 425-442; John Lintner (1965), "The Valuation of Risk Assets and the Selection of Risky Investment in Stock Portfolios and Capital Budgets," *Review of Economics and Statistics,* Vol. 47, pp. 13-37

7 Fischer Black and Myron Scholes (1973), "The Pricing of Options and Corporate Liabilities," *Journal of Political Economy,* Vol. 81, Iss. 3, pp. 637-654.

8 Stephen Ross (1976), "Arbitrage Theory of Capital Asset Pricing," *Journal of Economic Theory,* Vol. 13, pp. 341-360.

9 Ian McDonald (2004), "Professional Help Can Prove to Be a Hindrance," *Wall Street Journal,* August 5, p. C3., citing study conducted by Morningstar. Max H. Bazerman (2002), *Judgment in Managerial Decision Making.* John Wiley and Sons: New York.

10 D. Wolman (2012), *The End of Money: Counterfeiters, Preachers, Techies, Dreamers, and the Coming Cashless Society.* De Capo Press.

11 Christopher Conley (2004), "Holiday Shoppers Should Rethink How They Pay," *Wall Street Journal,* Dec 22, p. D3

12 George Ainslee (1975), "Specious Rewards: A Behavioral Theory of Impulsiveness and Impulse Control," *Psychological Bulletin,* 82 (July), 463-496; Thomas Schelling (1978), "Egonoics, or the At of Self-Management," *A.E.R. Papers and Proceedings,* Vol. 68 (May), pp. 290-294.

13 Richard Thaler and H. Shefrin (1981), "An Economic Theory of Self Control," *Journal of Political Economy,* Vol. 89, Iss. 2, pp. 392-406.

14 Jonathan Clements (2009), "If You Didn't Save 10% of Your Income This Year, You're Spending Too Much," *Wall Street Journal,* Dec 22, p. D1; Kris Maher (2005), "US Retirement Security Improves: Most Developed Countries Have Higher Savings Rates But Lag in 401(k)s," *Wall Street Journal,* June 22, p. D2, citing Hewitt Associates.

15 Daniel Kahneman and Amos Tversky (1979), "Prospect Theory: An Analysis of Decision Under Risk," *Econometrica,* Vol. 47, pp. 263-291; Amos Tversky and Daniel Kahneman (1974), "Judgment Under Uncertainty: Heuristics and Biases, *Science,"* Vol. 185, pp. 1124-1131; Amos Tversky and Daniel Kahneman (1981), "The Framing of Decisions and the Psychology of Choice," *Science,* Vol. 211, pp. 453-463.

16 Daniel Kahneman and Amos Tversky (1973), "On the Psychology of Prediction," *Psychological Review,* Vol. 80, pp. 237-251; P. Slovic and B. Fischhoff (1977), "On the Psychology of Experimental Surprises," *Journal of Experimental Psychology: Human Perception and Performance,* Vol. 3, pp. 544-551.

17 Amos Tversky (1972), "Elimination by Aspects: A Theory of Choice," *Psychological Review,* Vol. 79 (July), pp. 281-299; Amos Tversky and Shmuel Sattah (1979), "Preference Trees," *Psychological Review,* Vol. 86, Iss. 6, pp. 542-573.

18 Hillel J. Einhorn (1970), "Use of Nonlinear, Noncompensatory Models in Decision Making," *Psychological Bulletin,* Vol. 73, pp. 221-230; Allen Newell and Herbert A. Simon (1972), *Human Problem Solving.* Englewood Cliffs, NJ: Prentice Hall.

19 J. Hammond, R. Keeney, and H. Raffia (1999), *Smart Choices.* Harvard Business School Press: Boston, MA; Newell, A. and H.A. Simon (1972), *Human Problem Solving.* Englewood Cliffs, NJ: Prentice Hall.

20 Robin Dawes and Bernard Corrigan (1974), "Linear Models of Decision Making," *Psychological Bulletin,* Vol. 81 (March), pp. 95-106; Norman Anderson (1996), *A Functional Theory of Cognition.* Mahwah, NJ: Erlbaum; Norman Anderson (1981), *Foundations of Information Integration Theory.* New York: Academic Press.

21 Daniel Kahneman and Amos Tversky (1979), "Prospect Theory: An Analysis of Decision under Risk," *Econometrica,* Vol. 47, pp. 263-291; Amos Tversky and Daniel Kahneman (1974), "Judgment under Uncertainty: Heuristics and Biases, *Science,"* Vol. 185, pp. 1124-1131; Amos Tversky and Daniel Kahneman (1981), "The Framing of Decisions and the Psychology of Choice," *Science,* Vol. 211, pp. 453-463. Bettman, J.R. (1979), *An Information Processing Theory of Consumer Behavior.* Reading, MA: Addison-Wesley. Kortney Stringer (2003), "The Weird Science of Getting a Car Rental Deal," *Wall Street Journal,* Dec 30, p. D1. Christopher Windham (2004), "Catastrophic Health-Care Policies Catch On," *Wall Street Journal,* Oct 26, p. D4.

22 Scott Besley and Eugene Brigham (2011), *Principles of Finance.* South Western College Publishing. Ariel Rubinstein (2004), *Theory of Games and Economic Behavior.* Princeton University Press: Princeton, NJ.

23 Ian Neath and Aimee Suprenant (2012), *Human Memory*. Belmont, CA: Wadsworth Publishing; Roger Blackwell, Paul Minard, and James Engel (2005), *Consumer Behavior*. Mason, OH: South-Western College Publishing.

24 Hitch, G. (1978), "The Role of Short-term Memory in Mental Arithmetic," *Cognitive Psychology*, 10, 302-323.

25 Miller, G.A (1956), "The Magical Number Seven, Plus or Minus Two: Some Limits on Our Capacity for Processing Information", *Psychological Review*, 63 (March), 81-97.

26 G. Wolters, M. Beishuizen, G. Broers, and W. Knoppert (1990), "Mental Arithmetic Effects on Calculation Procedure and Problem Difficulty on Solution Latency," *Journal of Experimental Child Psychology*, Vol. 49, No 1, pp. 20-30; S. Dehaene (1992), "Varieties of Numerical Abilities," *Psychonomic Science*, Vol. 6, No. 2, pp. 71-92; M.H. Aschcraft (1992), "Cognitive Arithmetic: A Review of Data and Theory," *Cognition*, Vol. 44, August, pp. 75-106.

27 H. Estelami (2009), "Cognitive Drivers of Suboptimal Financial Decisions: Implications for Financial Literacy Campaigns," *Journal of Financial Services Marketing*, Vol. 13, Iss. 4, pp. 273-283

28 Hooman Estelami (1999), "The Computational Effect of Price Ending in Multi-Dimensional Price Advertising," *Journal of Product and Brand Management*, Vol. 8, Iss. 3, pp. 244-256.

29 Kelley K. Spors (2004), "Instant Loan, Endless Headaches," *Wall Street Journal*, March 28, p. 4

30 Jonathan Clements (2004), "If You Didn't Save 10% of Your Income This Year, You're Spending Too Much," *Wall Street Journal*, Dec 22, p. D1. Kris Maher (2005), "US Retirement Security Improves: Most Develop Countries Have Higher Savings Rates But Lag in 401(k)s," *Wall Street Journal*, June 22, p. D2, citing Hewitt Associates.

31 G. Ainslie and R. Hernstein (1981), "Preference Reversal and Delayed Reinforcement," *Animal Learning and Behavior*, Vol. 9, pp. 476-482; J.E. Mazur (1987), "An Adjusting Procedure for Studying Delayed Reinforcement," in M.L. Commons et al., eds., *Quantitative Analysis of Behavior: The Effects of Delay and of Intervening Events on Reinforcement Value*. Hillsdale: Erlbaum; N. Henderson and I. Langford (1998), "Cross-Disciplinary Evidence for Hyperbolic Social Discount Rules," *Psycological Bulletin*, Vol. 44, Iss. 11, pp. 1493-1500.

32 Jane Kim (2009), "If Your Credit Use Tops 50% of Limit, Rating May Suffer," *Wall Street Journal*, March 4, p. D4, citing report by Experian Consumer Credit

33 Jerry A. Hausman (1979), "Individual Discount Rates and the Purchase and Utilization of Energy-Using Durables," *Bell Journal of Economics*, 10 (Spring), pp. 33-54.

34 J. Payne (1982), "Contingent Decision Behavior," *Psychological Bulletin*, 92 (September), 223-230; J. Huber, J. Payne, and C. Puto (1982), "Adding Asymmetrically Dominated Alternatives: Violations of Regularity and Similarity Hypotheses," *Journal of Consumer Research*, Vol. 9 (June), pp. 90-98.

35 "Why Insurance Needs a Cleanup", *Business Week*, Nov 1, 2004, Issue 3906, p. 128. Paula Dwyer (2003), "Mutual Funds: Is Your Broker Ripping You Off?" *Business Week*, June 9, Issue 3836, p. 114. Daisy Maxey (2004), "Monthly Mutual Funds Review, The Year of Living Scandalously," *Wall Street Journal*, Sept 3, p. R.1.

36 Daniel Kahneman and Amos Tversky (1979), "Prospect Theory: An Analysis of Decision Under Risk," *Econometrica*, Vol. 47, pp. 263-291; Amos Tversky and Daniel Kahneman (1974), "Judgment Under Uncertainty: Heuristics and Biases, *Science*," Vol. 185, pp. 1124-1131; Amos Tversky and Daniel Kahneman (1981), "The Framing of Decisions and the Psychology of Choice," *Science*, Vol. 211, pp. 453-463.

37 H. Estelami and P. DeMaeyer (2010), "An Exploratory Study of Divided Pricing Effects on Financial Services Quality Expectations," *Journal of Financial Services Marketing*, Vol. 15, Iss. 2, pp. 19-31; Hooman Estelami (1997), "Consumer Perceptions of Multi-Dimensional Prices", in Merrie Brucks and Deborah J. MacInnis (Eds.), *Advances in Consumer Research*, Vol. 24, Association for Consumer Research, Provo, UT, pp. 392-399; Hooman Estelami (1999), "The Computational Effect of Price Ending in Multi-Dimensional Price Advertising," *Journal of Product and Brand Management*, 8(3), 244-256.

38 Morwitz, V.G., E.A. Greenleaf, and E.J. Johnson (1998), "Divide and Prosper: Consumers' Reaction so Partitioned Prices", *Journal of Marketing Research*, 35 (November), 453-463.

39 John T. Gourville (1998), "Pennies-a-Day: The Effect of Temporal Reframing on Transaction Evaluation", *Journal of Consumer Research*, 24 (March), 395-408. Hooman Estelami (1999), "The Computational Effect of Price Ending in Multi-Dimensional Price Advertising," *Journal of Product and Brand Management*, 8(3), 244-256. Morwitz, V.G., E.A. Greenleaf, and E.J. Johnson (1998), "Divide and Prosper: Consumers' Reaction so Partitioned Prices", *Journal of Marketing Research*, 35 (November), 453-463.

40 Scott Besley and Eugene Brigham (2011), *Principles of Finance*. South Western College Publishing; Ariel Rubinstein (2004), *Theory of Games and Economic Behavior*. Princeton University Press: Princeton, NJ.

41 Richard Thaler (1985), "Mental Accounting and Consumer Choice," *Marketing Science*, Vol. 4, No. 3, pp. 199-214.

42 John T. Gourville (1998), "Pennies-a-Day: The Effect of Temporal Reframing on Transaction Evaluation", *Journal of Consumer Research*, 24 (March), 395-408.

43 H. Shefrin and M. Statman (1985), "The Disposition to Sell Winners Too Early and Ride Losers Too Long: Theory and Evidence," *Journal of Finance*, Vol. 40, pp. 777-790; Max H. Bazerman (2002), *Judgment in Managerial Decision Making*. John Wiley and Sons: New York, pp. 105-106.

44 M. Bazerman and D. Moore (2008), *Judgment in Managerial Decision Making* New York: Wiley; B. Barber and T. Odean (2000), "Trading is Hazardous to Your Wealth: The Common Stock Investment Performance of Individual Investors," *Journal of Finance*, Vol. 55, pp. 773-806.

45 William Raabe, Gerald Whittenburg, and Debra Sanders (2005), *Federal Tax Research*. South-Western College Publications.

46 Amos Tversky and Richard Thaler (1990), "Anomalies: Preference Reversals," *The Journal of Economic Perspectives*, Vol. 4, Iss. 2, pp. 201-211; M. Bazerman and D. Moore (2008), *Judgment in Managerial Decision Making* New York: Wiley..

47 M. Bazerman and D. Moore (2008), *Judgment in Managerial Decision Making* New York: Wiley. Amos Tversky and Richard Thaler (1990), "Anomalies: Preference Reversals," *The Journal of Economic Perspectives*, Vol. 4, Iss. 2, pp. 201-211. Daniel Kahneman and Amos Tversky (1979), "Prospect Theory: An Analysis of Decision Under Risk," *Econometrica*, Vol. 47, pp. 263-291; Amos Tversky and Daniel Kahneman (1974), "Judgment Under Uncertainty: Heuristics and Biases, *Science,"* Vol. 185, pp. 1124-1131; Amos Tversky and Daniel Kahneman (1981), "The Framing of Decisions and the Psychology of Choice," *Science*, Vol. 211, pp. 453-463.

48 J. March (1988), "Variable Risk Preferences and Adaptive Aspirations," *Journal of Economic Behavior and Organization*, Vol. 9, Iss. 1, pp. 5-24.; Catrin Rode and Xt Wang (2000), "Risk-Sensitive Decision Making Examined Within An Evolutionary Framework," *The American Behavioral Scientist*, Vol. 43, Iss. 6, pp. 926-939.

49 *Insurance Operations and Regulations* (2002), Insurance Institute of America.

50 Kris Maher (2005), "US Retirement Security Improves: Most Developed Countries Have Higher Savings Rates But Lag in 401(k)s," *Wall Street Journal*, June 22, p. D2, citing Hewitt Associates.

51 Max H.Bazerman and Margaret Neale (1992), "Nonrational Escalation of Commitment in Negotiation," *European Management Journal*, Vol. 10, Iss. 2, pp.163-168.

52 Max H. Bazerman (2002), *Judgment in Managerial Decision Making*. John Wiley and Sons: New York, chapter 5 provides several interesting examples of the non-rational escalation of commitment phenomenon.

53 Dyan Haugen and Arthur Hill (1999), "Scheduling to Improve Field Service Quality," *Decision Sciences*, Vol. 30, Iss. 3, pp. 783-804; A. Pramar (2003), "Can't Get No (Customer) Satisfaction," *Marketing News*, April 14, 2003, p. 15; Robert Ford, Cherrill Heaton, and Stephen Brown (2010), "Delivering Excellent Service: Lessons From the Best Firms," *California Management Review*, Vol. 44, Iss. 1, pp. 39-56; Shirley Taylor (1994), "Waiting for Service: The Relationship Between Delays and Evaluations of Service," *Journal of Marketing*, Vol. 58 (April), pp. 56-69.

54 Max H. Bazerman (2008), *Judgment in Managerial Decision Making*. John Wiley and Sons: New York; Max H.Bazerman and Margaret Neale (1992), "Nonrational Escalation of Commitment in Negotiation," *European Management Journal*, Vol. 10, Iss. 2, pp.163-168.

55 George Stigler (1961), "The Economics of Information," *Journal of Political Economy*, Vol. 59 (June), pp. 213-225; Blackwell, Paul Minard, and James Engel (2005), *Consumer Behavior*. Mason, OH: South-Western College Publishing.

56 S. Gupta and H. Kim (2011), *Online Customers' Purchase Decision: A Mental Accounting Theory*. Brussels: Verlag; Dilip Soman (2001), "The Mental Accounting of Sunk Time Costs: Why Time Is Not Like Money," *Journal of Behavioral Decision Making*, Vol. 14 (July), pp. 169-185; Erica Mina Okada and Stephen Hoch (2004), "Spending Time Versus Spending Money," *Journal of Consumer Research*, Vol. 31, Iss. 2, pp. 313-323.

57 Richard Larrick, James Morgan, and Richard Nisbett (1990), "Teaching the Use of Cost-Benefit Reasoning in Everyday Life," *Psychological Science*, Vol. 1 (November), pp. 362-370; T. Scitovsky (1976), *The Joyless Economy*. New York: Oxford University Press.

58 Randall Smith and Deborah Lohse (1999), "Banks are Likely to Pursue Mergers With Insurers After Overhaul of Rules," *Wall Street Journal,* Oct 25, p. A.2

59 Jeff D. Opdyke (2004), "Underwater With No Insurance," *Wall Street Journal,* Nov 16, p. D2. David Wessel (2004), "How Not to Outlive Your Savings," *Wall Street Journal,* Sep 30, p. D1. Max H. Bazerman (2002), *Judgment in Managerial Decision Making.* John Wiley and Sons: New York, pp. 43-46; Charles Clotfelter and Philip Cook (1989), *Selling Hope: State Lotteries in America.* Cambridge MA: Harvard University Press

60 Max H. Bazerman (2002), *Judgment in Managerial Decision Making.* John Wiley and Sons: New York, pp. 45-51, provides several possible explanations for the bias in consumer perceptions of risk.

61 Max H. Bazerman (2002), *Judgment in Managerial Decision Making.* John Wiley and Sons: New York, pp. 31-33

62 Ian McDonald (2004), "Professional Help Can Prove to Be a Hindrance," *Wall Street Journal,* August 5, p. C3, citing study conducted by Morningstar.

63 B. Barber and T. Odean (2000), "Trading is Hazardous to Your Wealth: The Common Stock Investment Performance of Individual Investors," *Journal of Finance,* Vol. 55, pp. 773-806. Max H. Bazerman (2002), *Judgment in Managerial Decision Making.* John Wiley and Sons: New York.

64 J. Escalas and J. Bettman (2005), "Self-Construal, Reference Groups and Brand Meaning," *Journal of Consumer Research,* Vol. 32, Iss. 3, pp. 378-389.

65 T. Goldsmith (2011), "The Invisible Hand and the Wisdom of the Hive: Social Lives, Self-interest, and Self-deception," *Society,* Vol. 48, Iss. 1, pp. 4-11; B. J. Logsdon and K. Patterson (2009), "Deception in Business Networks: Is it Easier to Lie Online?" *Journal of Business Ethics,* Vol. 90, pp. 537-549;

66 M. Bazerman and D. Moore (2008), *Judgment in Managerial Decision Making* New York: Wiley.

67 R. Hastie and R. Dawes (2009), *Rational Choice in an Uncertain World: The Psychology of Judgment and Decision Making.* New York: Sage.

68 G. Brenkert (2008), *Marketing Ethics.* New York: Wiley-Blackwell. Paul Hancock (2005), "Unfair or Deceptive Acts or Practices: Would You Recognize Them if You Saw Them?" *ABA Bank Compliance,* Vol. 26, Iss. 5, pp. 6-15; Glenn Canner, Gregory Elliehausen and Fred Ruckdeschel (1983), "The Sellers Points Problems for Truth in Lending," *Journal of Retail Banking,* Vol. 5. Iss. 3, p. 25; Carl Felesenfeld (1978), "Consumer Credit Regulation: Illusion or Reality?" *The Business Lawyer,* Vol. 33, p. 1145.

CHAPTER THREE

Categories of Financial Products and Services

In this chapter, we will describe the various types of financial products and services available in the marketplace. The categories that will be discussed include savings products such as savings accounts, certificates of deposit, and pension plans, which allow consumers to save their funds in order to accumulate financial assets for possible use and withdrawal at a future point in time. We will also discuss credit products such as mortgages, home equity lines of credit, and credit cards, which enable consumers to borrow funds in order to purchase goods and services. This chapter will also focus on insurance products, which provide consumers with financial protection against risks resulting from various life events. In addition, transaction processing services such as debit cards and checking accounts as well as financial advisory and brokerage services will be discussed.

It is important to recognize that the grouping of financial products and services presented here does not necessarily match the industry categories as specified by the U.S. Department of Commerce, Standard & Poor's, and others. Instead, the category structure utilized reflects consumers' interaction processes with financial services, and not the underlying structure of organizations serving them. This is done in order to better reflect the decision process from a consumer perspective. In addition, it is important to recognize that due to space limitations, not all financial services have been profiled, and attention has been given to the most popular forms of financial services used by consumers.

SAVINGS PRODUCTS

Five different types of savings products will be discussed. The first is savings accounts, which are typically provided by commercial banks, savings and loans institutions, and credit unions. The second savings product discussed is certificates of deposit (CDs), which provide a unique form of savings for individuals who are willing to accept restricted access to their funds, in return for potentially higher interest earnings. Stocks and mutual funds, which are popular investment products that are associated with higher levels of risk and returns, will also be discussed. Finally, we conclude with pension plans, which are long-term saving instruments that facilitate the accumulation of savings for retirement while providing unique tax benefits. Exhibit 3.1 provides an overview of these products.

Savings Accounts

Savings accounts are offered by commercial banks, savings and loans institutions, credit unions and most other financial services providers that offer deposit accounts. Savings accounts are the first formal means by which individuals and household form financial reserves for a variety of purposes. Often a savings account is linked to a customer's checking account in order to facilitate the flow of funds between the two types of accounts. In contrast to checking accounts, which may receive little or no interest depending on the bank, savings accounts deposits typically earn some form of interest.

The primary distinction between checking and savings accounts is that, for a savings account, the bank could require the accountholder to provide advanced notice on the intent to withdraw funds, although most financial institutions rarely exercise this right. Savings accounts are categorized as "time deposits" as it is assumed that the deposited amounts will be held in the account for certain length of time prior to being withdrawn. This is a critical feature of these accounts as it enables the banking system to rely on such deposits as a basis for lending activities (subject to specific reserve requirements that banks must hold, based on guidelines set by the Federal Reserve). Checking account deposits, on the other hand, can be withdrawn without advanced notice, and the customer can demand the withdrawal of the full amount at any time, and are therefore referred to as "demand deposits." Due to the competitive nature of commercial banking, the distinction between checking and savings accounts in terms of the advanced notice requirements prior to fund withdrawal has blurred, and many checking accounts also provide interest earnings to the accountholders.

Exhibit 3.1: Savings Products

Financial Product / Service	Typical Risk Determinants	Input	Output	Time frame
Savings Accounts	Interest rate variability. FDIC insured up to $100,000.	Deposits into the account.	Withdrawal of funds and earned interest	Immediate withdrawal (subject to advanced notice requirements, if applicable)
Certificates of Deposit	Penalties for early withdrawal. Variability in underlying rates (if applicable). FDIC insured up to $100,000.	Purchase cost of the CD, plus any transaction fees that may apply.	Withdrawal of funds and earned interest.	Depending on the term of the CD, may range from months to years. Early withdrawals may result in loss of interest earned or other penalties.
Stocks	Lower future stock price and unpredictable dividends.	Purchase price of stock and brokerage fees	Selling price of the stock, earned dividends.	Can often be sold at any time.
Mutual Funds	Fund share price volatility and unpredictable fund dividends	Purchase price of fund shares and brokerage fees, management fees, and applicable early selling penalties	Selling price of the fund shares, earned dividends	Typically long-term. Some funds may apply penalties for early sale of shares.
Pension Plans	Volatility of pension plan's investment value and returns	Employees contributions, employer contributions (if applicable)	Retirement benefits upon reaching retirement age	Withdrawals prior to retirement age are restricted by penalties and may be taxed

The deposits placed by customers in a savings account form the foundation of the modern banking system. These deposits are used by a bank to issue loans to other customers, who then proceed to pay the bank interest on outstanding loans. The interest earned not only becomes a revenue source for the bank, but it also is partially passed on to the customers who have deposited funds at the bank. The banks' lending process helps the economic system achieve liquidity, and enable borrowing and subsequent investment to support economic development and productive activity. The interest rate paid on balances in a savings account is closely related to short-term interest rates such as the federal funds rate and the prime rate. Most banks that provide savings accounts are required by regulation to be insured by the *Federal Deposit Insurance Corporation* (FDIC). The FDIC, which was formed in 1933 in response to a series of catastrophic bank failures, provides insurance coverage to participating banks in order to protect them against similar catastrophes. For the customer depositing funds in a bank, this translates to guaranteed coverage of all amounts deposited up to $250,000.[1] This means that, in the remote case that the bank fails or goes bankrupt, the FDIC will ensure that customers do not lose their original deposits in the bank (up to $250,000).

Savings accounts are a mass-market product. A savings account is often used as a financial deposit bucket to earn a higher interest rate than one could earn from deposits in a checking account. They provide customers with relatively immediate access to funds, while earning interest. Other forms of savings accounts are *Passbook Savings Accounts* (PSAs), which were more popular decades ago, but still continue to be offered by a select group of banks. In contrast to the modern savings account, for which monthly statements are mailed out to customers, PSAs require customers to visit the bank in order to obtain updated account balance information. The balances are recorded by the bank teller in the pass book, which the customer keeps. Due to the high cost of personnel and staffing needs to update customers' PSA passbooks at bank branches and the inconvenience to customers in having to visit a bank branch to update the passbook, PSAs have, for the most part, given way to the modern savings account.

Another form of savings account is what is often referred to as a "Christmas club" account. Customers enrolled in a Christmas club deposit funds in this unique form of savings account throughout the year. The unique aspect of these accounts is that the customer is unable to withdraw funds from the account until the Christmas shopping season begins (early December). While this may seem to be an odd product feature, it is a result of customers' own lack of discipline, and their desire for a financial service that prevents them from withdrawing funds unless it is for the purposes of Christmas shopping. Christmas club accounts therefore relate to customer's lack of self-control in controlling their spending behavior, as also discussed in the context of self-regulation theory in Chapter 2. As a result, a customer may seek a self-regulation mechanism that would prevent her from making undisciplined purchases using the saved amounts. Withdrawals from Christmas club accounts are therefore only allowed in the immediate period prior to Christmas, during which funds are needed for Christmas gift purchases. The four basic dimensions of savings accounts as they relate to the framework presented in Chapter 2 are as follows:

- *Risk*: The risk that the customer might potentially face is not having access to his or her funds when needed. While this would only be a possibility in the event of a bank failure, as mentioned earlier, the first $250,000 of a customer's bank deposits are insured by the FDIC, for deposits made in member banks. Therefore, the risk of losing one's deposits is considerably reduced for the majority of savings accounts. The variability in the interest rate earned, however, can be a potential risk factor as the rate variations are often correlated with short-term interest rates. A downward movement in the interest rates associated with a savings account would translate into lower interest earnings.
- *Input*: The input that the customer provides to a savings account is the total amount of deposits placed in the account. Banks may choose to charge administrative

fees for the maintenance of the account, or may charge nothing. Banks are able to use the deposited funds for their own lending activities which are an additional source of revenue for them.

- *Output*: The output of a savings account is accessibility to the original deposits plus any additional interest earned on those deposits.
- *Time Frame*: Savings accounts are classified as time deposits, which technically require customers to provide advanced notice of their intent to withdraw funds. However, in the modern practice of banking, this is not a widely applicable feature, as most banks would allow their accountholders to withdraw their savings deposits with little or no advanced notice.

Savings accounts and other time deposit products are primarily provided by commercial banks, savings and loans institutions, and credit unions, which vary in their market dominance from region to region. There are less than 10,000 commercial banks operating in the United States. In addition, since the deregulation of the financial services industry in the late 90s, other financial services providers such as insurance companies and brokerage firms are providing their customers with services similar to savings accounts.[2] Nevertheless, the main providers of savings accounts continue to be commercial banks that continuously consolidate and merge, resulting in a smaller number of institutions, each with a larger share of the market. The merger of financial institutions and the blurring of traditional lines drawn between savings and investment products has enabled customers in some institutions to benefit from linking their savings accounts with investment instruments such as mutual funds and stocks in a convenient and easy-to-transact interface.

Certificates of Deposit

A Certificate of Deposit (CD) is a relatively stable form of savings product. When purchasing a CD, the customer deposits a lump sum amount and promises not to withdraw the amount until a pre-specified time period has passed. The interest rate on a CD could be pre-determined or linked to returns on specific financial instruments such as U.S. Treasury bills, which may be higher than the rates received on savings accounts. However, the customer is trading off the potential for a higher rate of return against limited access to the deposited funds for the duration of the deposit contract. Nevertheless, the fact that the deposits may be insured by the FDIC makes the CD a conservative savings product, attractive to specific segments of the market and applicable to unique financing scenarios. In terms of the four basic dimensions of financial products outlined earlier, the following is how they apply to CDs:

- *Risk:* Choosing to withdraw the deposited funds prior to the maturation of the CD would result in the application of pre-determined penalties. In addition, depending on what financial instrument the CD is linked to, the variability in the earned rates might be a potential source of risk. Since the deposited funds are insured by the FIDC for up to $100,000 of deposits, CDs provide downward protection against asset value volatility.
- *Input:* Customer deposits into a Certificate of Deposit are typically made in denominations of $1,000 or $10,000, but may also be negotiable for other amounts.
- *Output:* Deposited amount plus interest earned, upon reaching maturation date.
- *Time Frame:* Can vary from several months to several years. Longer time frames are typically associated with higher interest rates.

Customers attracted to certificates of deposit typically require a conservative investment product that provides for relatively short-term, yet restricted, access to funds. The CD is especially attractive to those individuals who are willing to part with their funds for a short time period and do not desire liquidity with the deposited funds. Therefore, CDs may serve as a valuable part of a diversified portfolio of financial instruments.

Stocks

In contrast to CDs, stocks are one of the most volatile forms of savings and investment products. Consumers can purchase stocks, which are simply partial ownership certificates for publicly traded companies. The shareholder of a company's stock is then entitled to his or her share of dividends paid out by the company. In addition, the consumer as the shareholder is able to sell the stock at a future point in time and realize the profits or losses associated with changes in the stock's price. With respect to the four basic dimensions of financial products, the following is how they apply to stocks:

- *Risk:* The future potential for a stock as it relates to dividend payouts and the stock price itself is highly volatile. Therefore, stocks represent a high-risk savings option.
- *Input:* Purchase price of the stock and the brokerage fees for buying and selling the stock.

- *Output:* Selling price of the stock and any dividends earned while holding the stock.
- *Time Frame:* Most stocks can be bought and sold at any time, and as such time limits typically do not apply to them. However, depending on the nature of the investment and the investment portfolio objectives, stocks may be treated as longterm financial instruments, which require investors to hold onto them for long periods of time. Also short-term stock trading strategies are often used by those investors who seek to utilize speculative economics to profit from short-term stock price fluctuations.

Typically, stocks attract individuals that are tolerant of high risk levels. The volatility associated with stock prices is considerably high. Stock ownership not only requires one to have tolerance for the fluctuations associated with the ups and downs of stock prices, but also to be well-informed about the fundamentals of the companies being invested in. Stocks are typically traded using brokers who act on behalf of the customer to buy and sell shares on the main stock exchanges. Some of the main exchanges which account for the trading of stocks in the United States are the New York Stock Exchange (NYSE), the NASDAQ, and the American Stock Exchange. Since the 1990s with the explosive growth of the Internet, a notable shift away from tradition brick-and-mortar brokers toward the use of online brokerage services took place, and for the mass market, online trading is the most active means of buying and selling stocks.

Mutual Funds

In contrast to stocks, which are relatively high-risk financial products, mutual funds provide for a more stable form of investment and long-term savings. This is because mutual funds consist of not just one stock, which may fluctuate greatly in value, but rather a portfolio of stocks. Therefore, mutual funds typically experience lower levels of volatility than any individual stock. As a result of the relatively diversified nature of mutual funds, they provide a more stable investment picture for consumers. In addition, mutual funds have the benefit of being managed by professional investment managers who are typically better informed about market trends and company profiles than the average investor.

Mutual funds also enable consumers to choose the nature of their investments by providing funds that are focused on specific types of companies or industries. For example, certain mutual funds might focus on high technology companies or on health care companies, while other mutual funds might focus on international or defense stocks.

Therefore, consumers are able to exercise some degree of speculative investing while limiting volatility in investment value. The typical purchasers of mutual funds are long-term investors who seek the more stable investment picture of mutual funds and do not seek to reap any immediate benefits from short-term market fluctuations of individual stocks. In addition, these investors value the added benefit of having a professional investment manager looking after the fund. With respect to the four basic elements of financial products, the following is how they apply to mutual funds:

- *Risk:* Since mutual funds are based on a portfolio of company stocks, they exhibit return volatility that is significantly higher than what one would experience with savings accounts, CDs, or money market funds. However, mutual fund share values are considerably more stable than any individual company's stock. The primary risk presented to a consumer investing in a mutual fund is in the loss of the value of the fund and uncertainty about dividend payouts by companies included in the fund.
- *Input:* The input associated with the purchase of a mutual fund is the price of the shares of the fund. No-load mutual funds have no additional charges associated with such a purchase. However, mutual funds with loads might have additional fees associated with the purchase of the fund. In addition, transaction fees might be charged by brokerage firms that facilitate the purchase of the fund shares. Mutual funds also have management fees, which are typically charged as a percentage of the total dollar amount invested.
- *Output:* The selling price of mutual fund shares and any dividend paid by the fund.
- *Time Frame*: Depending on the fund structure, no time limits may apply. However, certain funds require shares to be held for a minimum time period, for example 3 months or 6 months, prior to the sale of the shares. In such cases, early selling of the shares might be associated with penalties, often in the form of a percentage of the dollar value of the sold shares.

There are thousands of mutual funds available to consumers, each with their own investment flavor designed to match the preferences of specific groups of consumers. The trends in the mutual fund business include the introduction in recent years of new funds that have a predetermined retirement date. These funds are designed for investors who do not seek to be overly involved in managing and changing their mix of mutual funds as they get closer to retirement age. Financial advisors suggest that an individual's savings and investments must become more conservative as one gets closer to retirement age. This would mean that the types of mutual funds held should become less risky with time. However, most investors do not actively change the mix of funds to follow this rule. In fact, a classic study conducted by Teachers Insurance and Annuity Association (TIAA) of college professors' investment strategies showed that most professors maintain their original mix of funds (typically half stocks, half bonds) throughout their working life, and fail to adjust the mix as they get closer to retirement age.[3] The new breeds of mutual funds help remedy the problem by automatically adjusting the mix. These funds, therefore, adjust the portfolio mix to become less risky as they approach the target retirement year.

In addition, new breeds of mutual funds have emerged that focus on specific ethical dimensions of investing. There are, for example, funds that avoid investing in companies that conduct medical research using animal experiments, or that are active in countries which are considered to be in violation of human rights laws. These funds, therefore, introduce a new ethical dimension to consumers' investment experiences and target those individuals who not only value investment returns, but also care about the underlying principles behind the companies the funds are invested in [4]. An interesting trend related to mutual funds shows that a significant amount of mutual funds are sold through third-party companies and not by the fund management companies themselves. This puts a great deal of power in the hands of brokerage firms, financial planners, and commercial banks who have direct contact with the consumer and exercise a significant amount of influence on consumers' financial decisions. This trend is likely to increase in the near future due to deregulation and the emergence and involvement of multiple competitors in the investment arena resulting from the fragmentation of the distribution process in financial services.

Pension Plans

Pension plans require consumers to contribute on a regular periodic basis to a retirement fund in order to receive benefits upon reaching retirement age. Sometimes, pension plan contributions are supplemented or matched by one's employer. What is unique about pension plans is that they are the dominant form of untaxed savings. Contributions made to a pension plan are made on a pre-tax basis, and the investment earnings are not taxed. Taxes are only applied at the time of withdrawing funds from the pension plan, which in most cases would only occur after retirement age has been reached. This is a unique benefit compared to other forms of savings since, during the retirement age, the tax brackets of most individuals is considerably lower than their tax bracket at younger ages. The fact that the interest earned is also tax free, allows the faster accumulation of savings for retirement purposes.

The other unique aspect of pension plans is somewhat of a shortcoming compared to other means of savings, and it relates to the individual's uncertainty about retirement needs. Since the contributions made to a pension plan are not readily retrievable until retirement age has been reached, retrieving the funds is typically only possible in an emergency in which one may borrow against the fund balance. The inflexibility associated with retrieving deposited funds makes the consumer's job of predicting future needs and balancing them against present finances and cash flows a challenging task. It has been shown that consumers typically under invest into their retirement funds, perhaps for this reason. In terms of the four basic dimensions of financial products, the following is how they apply to pension plans:

- *Risk:* Depending on the types of funds available from a pension plan company, the risk characteristics of investments in which pension savings are placed might vary. Pension fund contributors may be able to control the risk characteristics associated with their deposits by selecting from a combination of funds managed by the pension company. This could be done by investing in different types of pension funds that focus on different forms of investment options such as real estate, securities, and bonds, with varying risk and return levels.
- *Input:* The input into a pension plan consists of the employee's periodic and year-end contributions, which may or may not be matched by his or her employer.
- *Output:* Retirement benefits are only available after retirement age has been reached. The benefits could be made in a variety of forms, such as a lump-sum payment or monthly payments, until the policyholder has died. Inheritance benefits may also exist for the beneficiaries of a deceased pensioner. Defined-benefit pension plans are those for which the retirement benefits are pre-specified at the time of contributing to the plan, while defined-contribution plans do not make such specifications.
- *Time Frame:* Pension plan contributions are to be made until retirement age has been reached, and penalties apply for early withdrawal of funds.

The *Internal Revenue Service* (IRS) imposes maximum limits on how much one can contribute to a pension plan during any one-year time period. In addition, pension benefits may be supplemented by Social Security benefits upon reaching the retirement age as specified by the *Social Security Administration*. This age may vary depending on the individual's date of birth. The currently questionable state of the Social Security system in the United States has given an increased level of importance to pension planning for most individuals and is likely to help increase the flow of funds into pension funds in the coming years. Typically, most financial advisers suggest that individuals save at least 10% of their annual income every year in order to accumulate sufficient savings for their retirement years.[5]

Other Savings Products

Two other popular savings products will be discussed here in general terms. *Individual Retirement Accounts* (IRAs) are retirement funds that can be set up by an individual at a commercial bank, a broker's office, or other financial institutions. IRAs may be self-managed by a consumer and independent of an employer's financial benefits programs. Individuals are able to contribute to their IRA account on a pre-tax basis up to specific amounts. Depending on the financial services provider that manages the IRA account, the individual consumer can choose from a portfolio of investment options ranging in risk and return characteristics. In most cases, IRA interest income is tax-exempt and taxes are only applied upon withdrawal of the funds.

The second savings product which has received considerable interest in recent years is *College Savings Funds*. These funds allow parents to save over an extended period of time in order to pay for their children's college education. Contributions made to these funds are tax-exempt (up to a limit), and so is the interest earned on the accounts. Taxes only apply at the time of withdrawals, which is when the child enters college. Yearly contributions are, however, limited by the tax code, and exceeding these limits would cause taxes to be applied to the excess amounts. Some of these funds are operated by state governments and others are managed by financial institutions such as mutual fund companies and commercial banks.

Financial Product / Service	Typical Risk Determinants	Input	Output	Time frame
Home Mortgages	Interest rate fluctuations for ARMs, mortgage company's tolerance of poor payment history	Monthly mortgage payments, mortgage application and processing fees, late payment penalties	Access to funds for purchase of real estate property	Can vary from a few years to several decades
Collateralized Loans	Repossession of the asset purchased through the loan by the lender in case of poor payment history	Monthly payments, application and financing fees	Repossession of the asset financed by the loan	Variable from several months to several years depending on the type of asset and its life expectancy
Credit Cards	Rise in interest rates charged, poor customer service of the credit card issuer	Interest charges, monthly payments, late payment fees, transaction processing fees	Enabling the purchase of goods and services, ability to borrow funds towards a purchase	Short-term (rates can be adjusted with short notice by the credit card issuer)

Exhibit 3.2 Credit Products

CREDIT PRODUCTS

Credit products facilitate consumer borrowing of funds. These products are generally of two different forms: collateralized and non-collateralized. Collateralized credit refers to credit in which the lender, such as the bank, has the ability to gain possession of an asset that is used as collateral in case the borrower fails to make the scheduled payments. For example, a mortgage company may be able to gain possession of a purchased house in case the homeowner fails to make the monthly mortgage payments for an extended period of time. Non-collateralized credit, on the other hand, has no assets that are linked to it, and is therefore riskier from the lender's perspective. As a result, non-collateralized credit products, such as credit cards, typically charge the consumer considerably higher interest rates than collateralized credit products. We will first discuss three collateralized products: home mortgages, home-equity loans, and collateralized loans. We will then discuss the most popular form of non-collateralized credit, which is the credit card. Exhibit 3.2 provides an overview of these products.

Home Mortgages

A home mortgage enables a consumer to borrow money in order to purchase a home. The consumer and the mortgage company, in essence, jointly own the home. Typically, home buyers are required to put down 20% of the purchase price of the property in order to qualify for a mortgage, although lower down payments are also possible with the purchase of primary mortgage insurance (PMI). Mortgages are a mass-market product, which means that many consumers would, at some point in time, need to utilize them in order to purchase a house. It is estimated that about 65% of Americans own their homes.[6] In terms of the four basic dimensions of financial products, the following is how they apply to mortgages:

- *Risk:* As in most credit products, the element of risk is most relevant to the lender who is making the mortgage amount available to the customer. Risk is assessed by the mortgage applicant's credit history, often captured in the primary borrower's credit score. Credit scores typically range between a low of 350 and a high of 850. Mortgage applicants with credit scores below 600 are often considered as high risk, resulting in higher interest rates for them. From a consumer perspective, risk might be related to fluctuations in the interest rate charged for adjustable rate mortgages (ARMs). In addition, the homebuyer's inability to make the regular payments may translate into the loss of possession of the property.

- *Input:* The primary input into a mortgage by the customer is the monthly mortgage payments. In addition, a down payment of 20% is typically required to obtain a mortgage, otherwise the mortgage applicant is required to purchase primary mortgage insurance (PMI). PMI is an insurance policy designed to ensure that the mortgage company will be able to receive payment in case the mortgage holder defaults. The mortgage application process may also have additional fees associated with it, such as an application fee, an assessment fee, and closing costs.
- *Output:* The output of the mortgage contract is the total amount of funds needed to purchase the property, less the down payment made to the seller of the property by the homebuyer.
- *Time Frame:* The time frames for most residential mortgages range between a few years to 30 years, although 40-year mortgages have also been introduced in recent years.

Monthly mortgage payments are a function of the total mortgage amount and the interest rate charged. The charged interest rate itself can be fixed or adjustable. Monthly payments for fixed mortgages are set at the time of the signing of the mortgage contract and remain the same during the entire term of the mortgage. These rates are typically linked to the 10-year treasury rates at the time of signing the mortgage agreement. However, the monthly payments for adjustable rate mortgages (ARMs) change with interest rates after a specified initial period. ARMs may apply a low interest rate for an initial length of time, and then adjust according to their rate adjustment specifications and what the interest rates are after the initial time period. Therefore, the monthly payments for an ARM mortgage can fluctuate greatly between the beginning of the mortgage term and the end. Because ARM mortgages can feature lower payments in the first few years of the mortgage contract, homebuyers who may choose to sell the property in a short number of years are attracted to them.[7]

Innovative products have over the years emerged in the mortgage marketplace. For example, mortgage companies have introduced 40-year mortgages that allow for lower monthly payments in return for a longer commitment period. In addition, a breed of ARM mortgages known as *Flex-ARMs* became popular during the real estate boom of the previous decade. These mortgages provided the mortgage holder with the flexibility of changing payment options in the midst of the mortgage cycle, for example by allowing the homeowner to move from a 15-year mortgage to a 20-year mortgage. The mortgage company would automatically adjust the mortgage contract and the associated payments for the balance of the mortgage period. Some mortgages also enable mortgage holders to skip payments, if needed. This type of mortgage is obviously more relevant to homeowners who may anticipate uncertainty in their future finances and in their ability to make regular monthly mortgage payments. However, they have been harshly criticized over the years by public policy advocates as enablers for undisciplined consumption behavior by households and have been attributed to household bankruptcy incidents.[8]

It is estimated that mortgage payments account for about a fifth of the gross income of the average homeowner[9]. In order to secure a mortgage, mortgage applicants must meet certain minimum requirements. Depending on the mortgage company's standards, for example, a minimum credit score must be exceeded. In addition, many banks require that the amount of debt payments and financial obligations of the applicant (for example yearly payments for the mortgage, car loans, property taxes, etc.) are not to exceed a certain percentage of their pretax annual income. Typically, this percentage is 35 to 40%, and exceeding it might represent financial risk to the mortgage company as well as to the mortgage applicant[10]. There is a growing trend toward using the Internet to obtain information on mortgages and to shop for mortgage rates. The majority of new homebuyers shop for mortgage rates using the Internet. However only a fraction secure their mortgages directly on the Internet.[11] Mortgages are a collateralized form of credit. Therefore, if the homeowner does not make the regular monthly payments, the mortgage company may be entitled to seek possession of the property and to place it on the market in order to recover its own investment into the property. Mortgage companies are also able to charge late fees and additional penalties for delinquent accounts and may protest the use of the property for non-residential or rental use.

Home Equity Loans and Lines of Credit

Homeowners use home equity loans and lines of credit in order to borrow funds against the equity owned in a real estate property. Through these financial products, a homeowner is able to borrow funds that use the property as collateral. The homeowner can use the home equity funds for a variety of needs: to pay off and consolidate credit card debt, undertake home improvements, to purchase a car, or pay for a child's college education. Since this is a collateralized form of credit, the applied interest rates are typically lower than other sources of credit, such as credit cards and non-collateralized bank loans. The types of individuals most attracted to home equity loans and home equity lines of credit are typically homeowners in the later stages of life with dependants and high monthly expenditures. These individuals use the equity built into their home through years of mortgage payments and rising property values as a means for obtaining access to funds that will help them manage their short-term cash flow shortfalls. Parents of children who are about to attend college or households who have incurred large medical expenses traditionally have great need for such financial products. Home equity loans can also be used for less pressing needs, such as the purchase of high-end durable consumer goods, automobiles, or vacations. The four basic elements of financial products that apply to home-equity loans and lines of credit are as follows:

- *Risk*: The primary element of risk is presented to the lender, since the lender is making the funds available to the homeowner. Risk is assessed in a similar way as in mortgages. Typically, the associated risk with home equity products is higher, however, since the applicant might be experiencing financial distress from factors such as accumulating credit card debt and unpaid medical or college bills. To the homeowner, the risk presented is in the form of possible actions the lender might take if regular monthly payments are not made.
- *Input:* The monthly payment amount associated with a home equity loan or line of credit is determined based on the interest rate, as well as the total amount borrowed. There may also be closing costs and additional fees charged by the financial institution providing the home equity loan or line of credit.
- *Output*: For a home equity loan, a lump-sum payment is made to the homeowner. The amount is a function of the credit worthiness of the homeowner as well as the value of equity built into the home. For home equity loans, the interest rate that is charged is typically fixed and determined at the time of signing the home equity contract. For home equity lines of credit, the interest rate fluctuates from month to month, depending on short-term interest rates. However, the homeowner is typically not obligated to take out the entire line of credit amount and may have the option of not using any of the available credit.
- *Time Frame:* Home equity loans are a non-revolving form of credit and typically have a fixed repayment period. Home equity lines of credit are typically considered revolving credit. Similar to credit cards, they often do not have a predetermined maturation date for the repayment of the borrowed amount. However, changes in the customer's finances and credit worthiness might influence the willingness of the lending bank to continue access to the line of credit.

Home equity loans and home equity lines of credit have a unique tax benefit. Internal Revenue Service code may allow the interest paid on these forms of credit to be tax deductible, making them a highly attractive credit option for a large number of homeowners. The volume of home equity financing has significantly grown in recent years due to this tax benefit, and the rise in property values has allowed for larger home equity amounts to be made available to homeowners. In addition, consumers' use of home equity financing has increased in recent years due to the high level of credit card borrowing, which is often associated with much higher interest rates. This has given consumers the incentive to consolidate their credit card debt and to reduce interest payments by transferring these debts into home equity loans or lines of credit that, due to their collateralized nature, typically have lower interest charges than credit cards. A related credit product is reverse mortgages. This product is most relevant for older consumers who have a significant amount of equity in their home. Through a reverse mortgage a homeowner is able to borrow against the equity in their home and obtain access to a stream of incoming cash flow or related line of credit. The amount of funds accessible depends on a variety of factors such as the amount of equity in the property, the age of the homeowner (or the younger spouse in case of joint ownership), and market interest rates.

Collateralized Loans

Collateralized loans represent borrowing initiated by consumers in order to purchase large ticket items such as automobiles, home appliances and furniture, or to facilitate transactions such as the payment of college tuition. These loans are collateralized because the lender has the ability to repossess the purchased items or any other assets, such as a home, placed as collateral in case the borrower fails to make the regular loan payments. Typically, consumers who take on collateralized loans seek immediate financing for large expenditures for which they currently lack funds. The four basic dimensions of financial products that apply to collateralized loans are as follows:

- *Risk:* The element of risk is most relevant to the lender and is assessed by the credit history of the borrower, typically captured through a credit profile and credit score reported by the major credit rating agencies. In addition, the type of assets financed by the loan may influence the risk levels associated with the lending process. For example, an automobile that is tracked by the Department of Motor Vehicles and may be located by law enforcement agencies for repossession is considered a less risky asset than home furnishings or electronics, which are more difficult to track.
- *Input:* The consumer's input into a collateralized loan is captured by the monthly payments, which are primarily based on the total loan amount and the interest rate that is applied. In addition, the consumer may be required to pay a down payment as well as a balloon payment at the end of the time frame. Additional financing and application fees may also apply.
- *Output:* Access to funds for purchasing the product or service being financed.
- *Time Frame:* The time frame for collateralized loans typically relates to the useful

life of the product being financed. For example, the time frame for auto loans is typically in the range of three to five years, while for home furnishings and electronics it tends to be shorter (e.g., 12 to 24 months).

The major players in the collateralized loan business are commercial banks, which operate retail branches where consumers can apply for such loans. In addition, financing companies that specialize in specific retail markets and are associated with retailers, distributors and dealerships of products such as appliances, electronics, and automobiles are the primary providers of collateralized loans in these markets. A lease is a unique form of collateralized loan in which the customer does not gain ownership of the product. Instead, the customer would have to return the product to the financing company at the end of the lease. Certain forms of leases allow for full possession of the product at the end of the lease by the customer contingent upon specific conditions being met, such as the payment of a large end-of-lease balloon payment. Other leases may restrict the uses of the product. For example, many automobile leases limit the number of miles the vehicle can be driven during the leasing period and impose penalties for mileage above the allowed amount or abusive use of the vehicle beyond its normal wear and tear.

Credit Cards

The first credit cards were introduced in the 1950s by gas stations, hotels, and automobile rental companies, who provided the cards to their regular customers as an added service. The credit card also allowed these establishments to provide a mechanism for creating loyalty in their customers by easing repeat purchases. Shortly thereafter, the cards began to be more aggressively marketed to the public by companies such as Diners Club, American Express and Bank of America. In 1958, Bank of America introduced the Banc America Card, which was subsequently renamed Visa. By using the credit card, the cardholder is able to purchase goods and services at participating retailers. Retailers that participate in a credit card network such as that of Visa, MasterCard, American Express, or Diners Club, utilize the credit card data network associated with these companies to process consumer payments. These companies' data networks enable one to check the credit card account of the consumer to ensure a sufficient credit line exists to complete the retail transaction and then adjust the credit card account to record the purchase made. A payment is subsequently made to the retailer for the purchased amount, less an administrative fee (typically from 1% to 5% of the transaction amount). The four basic elements of financial product as they relate to credit cards are as follows:

- *Risk:* As in other credit products, risk is primarily a concern to the lender, which is the credit card issuing bank. This risk is assessed, as in the case of most other credit products, through the cardholder's credit score and credit history, which is obtained from the major credit bureaus. If the cardholder fails to make payments, then the credit card issuing bank may use specialized collection agencies to recover the funds. To the consumer (cardholder) the risks associated with the credit card would be in rising interest rates charged by the credit card company as well as the potential actions of the credit card company in case of delayed payments or delinquency. Delayed payments of credit card balances can also negatively affect one's credit score.

- *Input:* The input that the customer provides are the monthly payments, annual membership fees (if applicable), interest paid on carried-over monthly balances, and any transaction or late-payment fees that might apply.
- *Output:* The primary output of a credit card is the ability for the cardholder not to have to carry cash or to use personal checks in the process of purchasing goods and services. In addition, credit cards enable the cardholder to borrow funds for purchases or cash-advances, and stretch the repayment of the borrowed amount over an extended period of time. Cards may also have loyalty and reward programs associated with them. These programs provide incentives for cardholders to utilize the card more frequently. The incentives could be in the form of refunds that are applied as a percentage of the transaction amounts, or in the form of reward benefits that can be redeemed for the purchase of goods and services at participating providers.

- *Time Frame:* Credit cards provide a short-term financial service. In some cases, interest rates that apply to credit card balances may fluctuate with time. These fluctuations often correlate with short-term interest rates. Credit card companies have the ability to change the interest rate they charge on an account with little advanced notice[12], and they can also choose to terminate a customer's account. Despite their short-term nature, it is important to note that cardholders who choose to make the minimum monthly payments on a credit card balance may find their debt obligation to be of a long-term nature. For example, with an interest rate of 15% and a balance of $1,000, it would take a cardholder who only pays the minimum monthly payment of 2%, nearly two decades to repay the balance.

From a marketing perspective, it is important to distinguish between credit card brands and credit card issuing banks. The leading credit card brands in the United States are Visa, MasterCard, American Express, Discover, and Diners Club. These credit card companies provide their brands as well as access to their data network to individual banks that choose to issue credit cards using these brand names. In addition, the data network is made available to retailers in order to enable credit card transactions. The result is that the credit cards issued by the banks to their customers can be accepted and processed at all retail locations that have access to the network of the credit card company. The credit card brands facilitate transaction processing, but they do not hold funds or conduct any of the fund-based banking that is needed. This is conducted by the issuing banks that use the credit card brand as a way to market their services to their customers, retailers, and the public.

The pattern of growth in the use of credit cards is noteworthy. Over the past two decades, the amount of consumer debt associated with credit card use has consistently grown.[13] The increased growth in the use of credit cards has resulted in a corresponding increase in consumer debt accumulation and complications associated with it. The rate of account delinquencies on credit card accounts has generally reflected a similar pattern of growth.[14] Certain segments of the population seem to be highly dependent on credit cards as a means for borrowed spending. Two of the most affected groups have traditionally been college students and senior citizens, many of whom are experiencing what is referred to as "debt hardship" (formally defined as an individual or a household that spends over 40% of its income on debt payments).[15] Regulations put in place at the end of the last decade, such as the *Credit Card Accountability, Responsibility and Disclosure (CARD) Act of 2009* were partially motivated by the desire to protect these population groups, and to prevent the general population from accumulating excessive amounts of credit card debt.

The practice of marketing credit cards has evolved over the years. In the 1980s and prior to that, most credit cards charged their accountholders an annual fee. However, during the second half of the 1980s, the industry was deregulated and competition for customers significantly increased. In the 1990s, the notion of charging cardholders an annual fee disappeared for most credit card issuers, and a tendency to focus on market share through new customer acquisitions was exhibited by most credit card issuing banks. As a result, the standards used to determine a credit card applicant's creditworthiness were relaxed. This, combined with the low interest rate environment of the 1990s, resulted in an explosive growth in the number of credit cards issued. Due to the less restrictive standards applied to the issuing of credit cards, not all of the new customer accounts generated during this time were customers who were able to manage their credit responsibly. Since the beginning of the current decade, credit card companies have become less tolerant of customers who are not disciplined in managing their credit card debt. This is partially due in part to the unattractive portfolio of customers accumulated in the 1990s. As a result, the penalties which customers have to pay for late payments have significantly increased in recent years, and for some credit card issuers they have become one of their primary sources of revenues.[16]

In recent years, the credit card industry has experienced a high degree of consolidation and mergers. Credit card issuing banks may for example, sell their portfolio of customer accounts to other banks or financial institutions that are interested in expanding their own customer base.[17] The motivating philosophy for acquirers of these accounts is to gain economies of scale, believing that by maintaining a larger portfolio of accounts, one would perform more efficiently and increase profitability by operating on a larger scale. In addition, these acquisitions may facilitate better access to retail customers, and enable the cross-selling of products to these customers.[18] For institutions that sell their portfolio of accounts, the motivation is often to purify their mix of accounts by focusing only on specific segments of the market or by selling off high-risk accounts to banks that for example may have the specialization needed to deal with the collection process for slow-paying accounts.

The concentration of the credit card business has helped the industry gain operational efficiencies. However, it has also been associated with consumer difficulties. For example, the amount of late payment penalty fees charged by credit card companies has significantly grown over time.[19] During this time period, the available time for cardholders to pay the credit card bill, as measured by the number of days between the statement issuing date and the payment due date has decreased. This clearly makes it more challenging for customers to make payments in a timely manner and increases the chances of late payment fees being applied to their accounts. Furthermore, while interest rates have been at historically low levels in the past decade, the rates charged on most credit card accounts continue to be high. In addition, credit card companies are allowed to change their rates with very short notice. It is therefore no surprise that, of all the financial services, credit cards have the highest rate of consumer complaints.[20] Such trends were a driving force behind some of the regulatory measures put in place through the Credit Card Accountability, Responsibility and Disclosure Act of 2009. Increased competition in the industry is likely to improve the offers available to consumers. For example, the anti-competitive restrictions that had for decades been placed by MasterCard and Visa on their member banks were lifted by law during the last decade. These restrictions had prohibited a member bank to issue credit cards with any competing brands. The removal of this restriction paved the way for increased competition within the industry and encouraged the development of more competitive credit card packages for consumers.[21]

INSURANCE PRODUCTS

Insurance is among the oldest financial products and has been available in most civilized societies in one form or another for centuries. It is formally defined as a contract that provides the policyholder with pre-defined benefits in cases of specified losses. In this section, we will discuss several commonly used insurance products: homeowners insurance, automobile insurance, life insurance, and specialized insurance products.

These insurance policies provide consumers with financial protection and peace of mind in a variety of settings specific to their unique applications. Exhibit 3.3 provides an overview of these products.

Homeowners Insurance

A homeowners insurance policy provides the owner of a residential property with protection against losses incurred due to major accidents such as fire, vandalism, and, in some cases, specific natural disasters. Homeowners insurance is a mass-market product, as most homeowners are required by their mortgage company to have insurance coverage in order to qualify for the mortgage. The four basic elements of financial products that relate to homeowners insurance are as follows:

- *Risk:* The risks associated with homeowners insurance policies are relevant to both the insurance company and the policyholder. From the perspective of the insurance company, risks might be a function of the type of property, its age, location, and the age and condition of the major appliances and the heating and cooling systems. From the policyholder's perspective, as in all insurance products, the primary risk is in the insurance company's unwillingness to pay for claims. Unfortunately, this is a relatively unknown variable to most consumers who do not have access to payout data or do not know how to locate complaint reports filed with the Department of Insurance in their state. Furthermore, the financial strength of the insurance company, as reflected by its financial rating reflects the company's ability to pay out claims to its policyholders.

Financial Product / Service	Typical Risk Determinants	Input	Output	Time frame
Homeowners Insurance	Insurance company not paying claims in case of property damage	Premiums, deductibles in case of a claim	Financial coverage for claims made up to the maximum policy coverage, subject to coverage limits	Yearly, biannually
Automobile Insurance	Insurance company not paying claims in case of an accident	Premiums, deductibles in case of a claim	Financial coverage for claims made related to an accident	Yearly, biannually
Life Insurance	Insurance company not paying in case of policyholder's death	Premiums, application fees, medical examination fees	Face value of policy in case of the death of policyholder	Typically 10-30 year for term life policies, or for the entire life of the policyholder for whole life and universal policies

Exhibit 3.3 Insurance Products

- *Input:* The input to a homeowners insurance policy is the regular premiums paid. In addition, deductibles may apply depending on the form of the policy and the type of claim.
- *Output:* This is the total dollar amount of coverage purchased. Depending on the policy, different levels of covered benefits may exist. For example, basic policies may cover damage caused by fire and smoke, but not cover damage resulting from floods. More expensive policies may cover such expenses as damage caused by frozen pipes, electric currents, and in some cases certain natural disasters. The provided coverage varies from company to company and may also vary from state to state.
- *Time Frame:* Homeowners policies are typically renewed on a yearly basis and insurance companies may have the right to discontinue the policy if they can reasonably justify such a decision.

One of the concerns in the homeowners insurance market has been the fluctuation in property values as real estate markets fluctuate. As a result, homeowners who originally purchased their policies many years earlier may be over- or under-insured depending on the current value of their property.

Automobile Insurance

Automobile insurance provides coverage for the policyholder for vehicles and occupants involved in accidents. Additional coverage for theft, vandalism, and other forms of losses can also be obtained. In most states, automobile insurance coverage is required by the state's Department of Motor Vehicles for a driver to operate the vehicle. The four basic elements of a financial product that relate to automobile insurance policies are as follows:

- *Risk:* Similar to homeowners insurance, risk is relevant to both the insurance provider and the policyholder. From the perspective of the insurance company, risk is assessed by examining the age and driving history of the policyholder. Certain aspects of the driving history such as driving under the influence of alcohol or excessive speeding will result in significantly higher risk levels being associated with the driver. From the perspective of the policyholder, risk is primarily an issue of the insurance company's willingness to payout claims and its financial ratings.
- *Input:* The inputs provided by a policyholder to an insurance contract are the premiums paid, as well deductibles that may apply in cases of claims.

- *Output:* The outcome of an automobile insurance policy is the financial coverage provided as well as other related benefits. Depending on the insurance contract, the policy may cover the costs of damages made to the other vehicles involved in the accident, the policyholder's own vehicle, and other property damage up to certain limits. In addition, benefits such as access to a rental car while the vehicle is being repaired, coverage for medical expenses for the vehicles' occupants, and for damages resulting from vandalism may apply. The extent of coverage varies from policy to policy and is typically positively correlated with the premiums charged.

- *Time Frame:* Most automobile insurance policies are renewed on an annual or semi-annual basis. The insurance company typically has the right to raise premiums, in case the driving history of the driver has deteriorated during the term of the contract.

Factors such as age and occupation are known to correlate with driving risk and the resulting premiums that a driver has to pay. For example, it is estimated that the likelihood of a college student getting into an automobile accident is over three times that of a farmer and over twice that of a fireman.[22]

Life Insurance

Life insurance provides benefits to the beneficiaries of the policyholder in the case of the policyholder's death. Life insurance premiums are based on mortality tables, which estimate a person's likelihood of death depending on his or her age. In addition to age, mortality tables take into account other factors that may contribute to an individual's likelihood of death, such as risky sporting activities, smoking, obesity, specific medical conditions, and gender. What is unique about life insurance compared to other forms of insurance is that it is the type of insurance for which the probability of a claim being made (in other words, the policyholder dying) is predictable with relative accuracy using mortality tables. In contrast, for automobile insurance, the likelihood of an accident or the timing and amount of the claim might be highly unpredictable. While the benefit payout of a term life insurance policy is determined by the full coverage amount of the policy, the total cost of an automobile accident which would have to be covered by an automobile insurance policy is a highly variable figure. In addition, an automobile insurance company (and its policyholder) may be held accountable for losses incurred during a policy term, years after the term has expired. In contrast, the payout of life insurance claims is determined by the face value of the policy, which is fixed and is only valid during the term of the life insurance policy. The four basic elements of financial products that apply to life insurance are as follows:

- *Risk:* To the insurance company, risk is assessed by assessing the applicant's health history, lifestyle, and profession, the presence of high-risk activities such as skydiving and motorcycle riding, and other relevant information. To the policyholder, risk is assessed by the willingness of the insurance company to pay claims to the beneficiaries of a deceased policyholder. Furthermore, the financial strength of the insurance company, as reflected by its financial rating reflects the company's ability to pay out claims to its policyholders and represents an additional element of risk from the policyholder's perspective.
- *Input:* The input to a life insurance policy are the yearly premiums charged, as well as any policy signing fees and commissions that may be charged by an insurance broker or an agent.
- *Output:* The total amount of coverage provided by the policy is the primary output of the policy.
- *Time Frame:* Depending on the type of life insurance policy purchased, a pre-determined time frame for the policy may or may not exist. The time frame could range from one year to life.

The primary customers for life insurance policies are individuals who have dependants that might suffer from financial hardship in case of the policyholder's death. The benefits of a life insurance policy provide the policy beneficiaries with the ability to replace part or all of the revenue-earning potential that the deceased policyholder would have had. The life insurance benefits would help the beneficiaries of the policy to handle ongoing household expenditures, pay off credit card debt, and other financial obligations that the policyholder would have otherwise been partially or fully responsible for. Policies are typically sold through insurance brokers, employers, or directly through the insurance companies themselves, and are fixed in their dollar amount (e.g., $100,000, $500,000, $1,000,000, etc.)

The most popular types of life insurance policies are "term life," "whole life," and "universal life." Term life policies pay out a predetermined dollar amount in the case of the policyholder's death during the term of the policy (hence "term" life). Whole life policies provide similar death benefits as term life policies but may also cover costs associated with medical bills and burial expenses. Whole life policies also tend not to be bound by a pre-specified time period, the way term life policies are, and may provide coverage for the entire length of the policyholder's life (hence "whole" life). Universal life policies provide similar benefits as whole life policies but also serve as a savings and investment instrument and may also have specific tax benefits. The premiums paid earn interest, and the income earned may accumulate at a tax-free rate unless the earned interest is withdrawn by the policyholder prior to retirement age. Typically, these policies are more flexible and can be more easily adjusted in terms of the coverage amount than term life or whole life policies. However, they may have a surrender charge associated with them if the policyholder chooses to discontinue the life insurance policy.[23]

In order to obtain life insurance coverage, an individual would have to undergo a thorough medical examination. Factors such as smoking, high blood pressure, and other medical conditions and health concerns would result in higher premiums. Nevertheless, life insurance rates have generally declined over time. This trend is partially due to the fact that average life expectancy has increased due to medical advances that have reduced individuals' probability of death at all age levels. The decline in prices is also attributed to an increase in the level of competition and the commoditization of the life insurance category. Consumer perceptions of differences across life insurance companies are diluting, and a greater focus on competitive prices has begun to affect consumer decision making.

The life insurance industry is a rather intriguing one in that some of the associated services and transactions available to consumers may be perceived to be rather unconventional by most people. For example, life insurance policies are available for parents of newborn children. While it may sound absurd for one to purchase a life insurance policy for a child that has just been born, the objective of these policies is primarily to serve as an investment tool for the parents to save for their child's future. The regular premiums paid not only provide for life insurance benefits in case the child dies, but also accumulate interest in a similar way to a universal life policy. After reaching a target age, the child would then be able to withdraw funds from the policy or borrow money against the existing balance. Another intriguing product in the life insurance business is what is often referred to as "life-settlement contracts." These contracts are often signed between someone who has a life insurance policy, but due to medical conditions is known to be dying, and an investor who seeks to make profits in the purchase of the life insurance policy. By selling a life settlement contract, the dying policyholder gives up the death benefits of the life insurance policy to the investor in return for a smaller lump sum payment while he or she is alive. The investor agrees to pay the policy's premiums and the lump sum amount and in return collects the death benefits after the policyholder has died. These exchanges are difficult to imagine, as the investor is in essence betting on (and looking forward to) the policyholder's death. In recent years however, such exchanges have become less frequent due to lower mortality rates, the introduction of new pharmaceutical products, and advancements made in the field of medicine. These advancements have made death a less predictable factor in life settlement contracts and have made these contracts less attractive to investors.[24]

Specialized Insurance Products

The insurance industry has recently been presented with a series of innovative products that tend to focus on very specific and unique needs of consumers. Typically, these specialized insurance products are not mass-market in nature and serve small, yet profitable, market segments. Unlike automobile insurance or homeowners insurance, these insurance products tend to cater to specific customer needs arising from the types of activities carried out by the individual, the individual's economic and demographic status, or an individual's unique consumption behavior. For example, highly active skiers who may engage in high-risk ski trips are able to purchase season pass insurance, which protects them against financial losses associated with injuries inflicted on the ski slopes. This type of policy, also referred to as "wipeout insurance," typically covers the cost of the season pass, which may no longer be of use due to the extent of the policyholder's physical injuries. The policy may also cover the medical expenses associated with evacuating the policyholder from the ski slopes.[25]

Another type of insurance product that has found great interest among high net worth (HNW) individuals is what is referred to as an *umbrella insurance policy*. Umbrella policies typically cover unexpected expenses that traditional insurance policies such as homeowners insurance or automobile insurance may not cover. They may, for example, cover costs arising from personal law suits against the policyholder. *Identity theft insurance* is another form of specialized insurance, which has grown in popularity over the years. Identity theft occurs when a criminal gains access to critical pieces of information such as the social security number or the driver's license number of the victim. This information is then used to obtain access to credit, and the activity will often subsequently contaminate the victim's credit records. There are typically three common forms of identity theft that might affect individual consumers. Financial identity theft occurs when the name or the social security number of the victim is stolen and then used to apply for, and potentially obtain, credit. Criminal identity theft happens when a criminal that has been stopped by law enforcement authorities does not present his or her true identity but proceeds to use someone else's name. This situation results in criminal records being issued for the named person rather than for the actual criminal. Identity cloning is the third form of identity theft, where the victim's name and personal information are utilized to establish a new life and identity for the criminal.[26]

The emergence of identity theft insurance as a popular consumer insurance policy is largely attributed to the explosive growth in incidents of identity theft in the U.S. It is estimated that the number of cases of identity theft doubles every year.[27] In order to protect themselves, consumers are able to purchase identity theft insurance through various financial services providers such as their homeowners insurance company, their credit card company, or as a separate stand-alone policy. These policies typically cover the costs associated with legal expenses and lost wages for the time needed to carry out the paper work and legal procedure necessary to recover from the damaging effects of identity theft.[28]

A specialized form of insurance that is most relevant to event organizers is what is referred to as *event cancellation insurance*. This type of insurance provides financial protection for organizers of entertainment, sports, or music events against the possible cancellation of their event due to unforeseen occurrences such as natural disasters or acts of terrorism. These policies witnessed a significant growth in sales after the tragic events of 9/11, and most major event organizers now regularly purchase such policies.[29] Another form of insurance policy, one which is most relevant to homeowners in areas that are vulnerable to flood, is *flood insurance*. Flood insurance is often required by mortgage companies to be included in the homeowners insurance policy for properties in specific flood zones where the risk of flooding is considered to be high.[30] In addition, homeowners may have the ability to purchase additional flood insurance coverage in case they themselves fear potential damage to their property resulting from floods. The increase in flood-related property damage in recent years, such as the devastation following Hurricane Katrina in 2005 have increased consumer appreciation for the need of having flood protection coverage.[31]

Product warranties are another popular and growing service category which in many ways resemble property and casualty insurance policies. Warranties are purchased by consumers to protect their purchases of electronics, appliances, automobiles, or other forms of consumer durable goods, against product failures. Typically, these warranty policies cover the cost of repairs and may even facilitate the replacement of failed products for a finite period following the purchase. Product warranties are frequently offered by electronics retailers, appliance stores and automobile dealerships as a standard part of the sales process. These warranties have certain limitations such as the length of time for which the purchased product is covered and the components that the warranty policy protects. These limitations have sometimes resulted in warranties that act more as a source of profits for the sellers than a means for protecting consumer purchases. For example, the profit margins for many home electronics extended warranties are estimated to be over 15 times the margins associated with the sale of the electronics products to which the warranties apply.[32]

Concerns in the Marketing of Insurance

One of the primary challenges in operating an insurance business is in having confidence in the truthfulness of statements made by a policyholder when filing a claim, or by an applicant when applying for an insurance policy. For example, a policyholder might claim that his vehicle has been damaged due to a hit-and-run accident, when in fact his own poor driving might have been the cause of the damage to the vehicle. Technology has begun to find its way into customers' service interactions with insurance companies. For example, some insurers use voice recognition software to detect cases in which customers may be making false statements in their conversations with a customer service representative on the phone. The customer service employee first asks the customer a series of simple, unthreatening questions. The customer's voice tones help calibrate the "truth detection" software. The customer is then asked specific questions related to the claim, and the truthfulness of the statements is then reported to the customer service employee. Studies show that through the use of this system, about one third of calls are given special attention, about half of which are eventually found to be fraudulent. The result of using this system has been a decrease in the settlement time for customers and a decrease in payout costs to the insurer.[33]

One form of technology currently being used by some automobile insurance carriers is designed to better predict the risk characteristics of their policyholders. This technology utilizes a "black box" device similar to those used on airplanes. The device can be activated for monitoring driving habits on a willing policyholder's vehicle and is able to characterize the driving style of the policyholder such as the tendency to speed and conduct high-risk maneuvering. This information would then be used as a predictor of risk, with subsequent adjustments being made to the policyholder's premiums. Due to its intrusive nature, this approach to the pricing of automobile insurance may not become a mass-market phenomenon. Many consumers may feel uncomfortable about the very notion of their every move as a driver being monitored and may choose not to purchase policies from insurers that use information collected from the black box device.[34] Nevertheless, this example representing an interesting demonstration of how new technologies can have direct impact on consumers' engagement with financial services.

One of the unique aspects of selling insurance is that, for the majority of consumers, the true quality of an insurance policy is largely unknown. The ultimate product of any insurance contract is the payment of claims in case the policyholder incurs losses. However, the willingness of an insurance company to make such payments is not known by the average consumer. This information may be obtained by examining complaint records filed at the state's Insurance Department. Nevertheless, most consumers do not know how to obtain this information, and rarely is this information publicly advertised by the insurance companies themselves. An additional factor that complicates the insurance purchasing process for consumers is the total lack of knowledge about the risk rates associated with accidents and unforeseen events that are being insured. For example, an individual who purchases a life insurance policy must have some estimate of his own mortality rate (probability of dying). However, most individuals do not have this information readily available when they assess the prices offered to them in a life insurance contract. Not knowing this information translates to uninformed decisions on price and features for an insurance policy. As discussed in Chapter 2, the great majority of consumers lack awareness of the risks associated with different aspects of their lives, for which they regularly purchase insurance products.[35]

TRANSACTION PROCESSING SERVICES

In this section we will discuss services that facilitate financial transactions for consumers. These services may facilitate the transfer of funds, provide consumers and service providers with critical financial information, and guide consumers in their financial decisions. The services that will be discussed are: checking accounts, debit cards, ATM services, and specialized services such as those provided by credit rating agencies and financial advisors. Exhibit 3.4 provides an overview of these products.

Checking Accounts

Checking accounts allow customers to deposit funds in a safe location for future retrieval. The concept of checking accounts dates back to Roman times, during which benches were placed by specialized merchants in commodity markets so that individuals might "check" or deposit their jewelry in return for access to currency. In fact, the term "check" originally referred to the premises where the deposits were made. The deposits placed in checking and savings accounts are secured by the physical infrastructure of the banking system. They are also used by the bank to issue loans to customers who need

Financial Product / Service	Typical Risk Determinants	Input	Output	Time frame
Checking Accounts	Not having access to deposited funds. Interest rate variability. FDIC insured up to $100,000	Deposits into the account, transaction fees.	Withdrawal of funds and earned interest, if applicable.	Withdrawal of deposited funds
Debit Cards	Fraudulent access to the account	Processing fees at non-participating ATMs, transaction fees, monthly fees (if applicable)	Access to cash, electronic payments for purchases	Immediate withdrawal of funds from the bank account
Credit Reporting	N/A	Fees for access to the credit report	Credit score and credit history	Information is typically disseminated online on an immediate basis

Exhibit 3.4 Transaction Processing Products and Services

funds for special needs. Certain regulatory requirements enforced by the Federal Reserve exist to determine how much money in loans can be issued by a bank. This quantity is a pre-specified multiple of the customers' deposits in the bank and is often referred to as the reserve ratio. Checking accounts are a mass-market product. Most individuals need to have access to the services of a checking account in order to deposit funds, pay bills, and maintain liquidity in their day-to-day finances. The four basic elements of financial services that relate to checking accounts are as follows:

- *Risk:* Deposits made into a checking account are insured by the Federal Deposit Insurance Corporation (FDIC). The FDIC guarantees the first $250,000 of balances in an account at one of its member banks. Therefore, unless higher amounts have been deposited, consumers can be confident that they will be able to retrieve their original deposits from the bank.
- *Input:* The amount deposited in a checking account, plus any monthly charges and transaction fees for activities such as the writing of checks or the use of ATM and teller services.
- *Output:* The ability to withdraw funds, write checks, and gain access to funds. Some banks also pay interest on deposits placed in a checking account.
- *Time Frame:* Deposits into a checking account might take several days in order to be cleared. Cash, on the other hand, is immediately available upon being deposited in the checking account. Checking accounts can be closed at any time, at the customer's request.

Similar to savings accounts, checking accounts are often provided by commercial banks, which are typically regionally clustered. In recent years, due to the deregulation of financial services, new players such as insurance brokers, financial advisers, and brokerage firms have begun to provide their clients with services that emulate checking accounts.

Traditionally, when an individual writes a check, the check is passed on from the recipient's (payee) bank to the bank of the individual writing the check (payer). For decades, this process involved the physical handover of the written check from the payee's bank to the payer's bank through a network of local and regional clearinghouses located in locations across the country and operated by the Federal Reserve. The process not only was expensive to carry out, but it also considerably slowed down the fund-transfer process. In 2004, the *Check Clearing Act for the 21st Century*, otherwise known as "Check 21" went into effect. According to Check 21, electronic images of checks have equal legal standing to their paper originals. As a result, the payee's banks can now scan a check once it has been deposited and pass on the electronic scan to the payer's bank in order to request a transfer of the appropriate amount of funds. This resulted in monumental gains in processing efficiency in the commercial banking business.[36] Despite the gained efficiency in the processing of checks, consumers' use of checks has witnessed a decline over the years, as the rate of use of credit cards, debit cards, and payment through mobile devices and electronic means have increased.[37]

Debit Cards

Similar to checks, debit cards tap into a customer's bank account deposits. The difference is that debit cards function through electronic means using established electronic fund exchange networks. Similar to bank checks, debit cards are a mass-market product, and most banks provide them as a standard or optional feature with their checking account services. The four basic elements of financial services that relate to debit cards are as follows:

- *Risk:* Debit cards do not represent any significant risks to the consumer as they facilitate immediate access to funds. The only risk that is present is attributed to the fraudulent use of the card. Many banks provide protection for their customers in case fraudulent use of the card is established.
- *Input:* Most banks do not charge fees for debit card use, but some do. However, the use of the card at nonparticipating ATM machines is often associated with transaction fees charged by the operator of the ATM device, which is debited from the accountholder's balance.
- *Output:* The output of the debit card transaction is the retrieval or transfer of funds from the customer's checking account. This retrieval might be in the form of cash or electronic debits applied to the account.
- *Time Frame:* Transactions involving debit cards are all immediate in nature. However, deposits that are made using a debit card can take several days before they are reflected in the account balance. New ATM technology, which will be discussed below, is in the process of being deployed by many banks in the near future to accelerate the processing of transactions using debit cards.

The use of debit cards in consumer purchases is expected to grow at a steady pace over the course of this decade, and some estimate that the associated rate of growth will be nearly three times the growth rate in the use of credit card transactions.38 There are numerous advantages and disadvantages to the use of debit cards and credit cards, which may be compared. In contrast to credit cards, which may result in considerable consumer borrowing, debit cards provide users with some degree of control. Because debit cards tap into existing balances in a bank account, the customers are limited in how much they can spend. The use of debit cards in retail outlets is also convenient since the option of obtaining cash directly from the cashier is often available. Although this option is also available with credit cards, many credit card companies charge interest for cash withdrawal transactions from the day the cash is issued to the customer rather than from the bill's due date. In addition, debit cards are better suited for small-ticket purchases, while credit cards are more appropriate for larger transactions that may require the borrowing of funds.

Variations of the debit card concept have emerged in recent years. For example, prepaid cards, which have a pre-determined amount of funds associated with them, are likely to significantly grow in consumer use over the next few years. Christmas gift cards are a prime example of this. It is estimated that half of the population purchases at least one gift card around Christmas time.[39] In addition, pre-paid cash cards are now being used to issue food stamps and child-support payments, and they are also used by the U.S. Navy to conduct payroll payments. A retailer's ability to process debit and credit card transactions usually results in higher transaction volumes and more spending by the customer. For example, a study conducted by McDonald's showed that the introduction of debit and credit card transaction-processing capabilities into a restaurant increases the average amount of consumer spending from $4.50 to $7.00.[40]

Nevertheless, it is important to note that credit cards present additional advantages to the consumer that debit cards typically do not. Many credit cards provide loyalty programs as well as special fraud protection features. In addition, consumers have been protected against fraudulent use of credit cards for decades by regulations such as the *Fair Credit Billing Act of 1974*. Furthermore, any billing errors that occur for credit cards are buffered from the customer through the billing cycle during which the customer may appeal the erroneous charges. In contrast, debit card errors do not have such a protection buffer, as the funds are immediately withdrawn from the cardholder's bank account. As a result, consumers' control over the outflow of funds is considerably reduced with debit cards compared to credit cards. Furthermore, the regulations that protect fraudulent use of a debit card are less protective of consumers. Debit cards are protected by *Regulation E* of the Federal Reserve, which is a 3-tiered system for fraudulent use of the card at $50, $500 and higher levels, while credit card fraud liabilities for consumers is limited by the *Fair Credit Billing Act* to a maximum of $50. Credit card transactions are further protected by the *Truth in Lending Act*, which requires full disclosure of financing and other charges to the consumer.[41]

Automated Teller Machines (ATMs)

Automated teller machines are devices that facilitate fund transfers, account information exchange, and the dispensing of cash. The first ATMs were installed in bank branches in metropolitan areas in the early 1970s. The first customers to find ATMs useful were those who were unable to visit their bank branch during regular bank hours, such as police officers and hospital employees who may often work odd shifts. Operators of ATM devices are able to realize profits through transaction fees, which they charge the users. ATM devices operated by a bank typically do not charge transaction fees to their own customers for most transactions.

The pattern of use of ATM devices is such that the per-machine volume of transactions using ATMs has historically been on a decline. This is largely due to the fact that we are increasingly becoming a cashless society, and there is less need to withdraw cash using an ATM device.[42] Nevertheless, new technologies are being deployed to improve the functionality and attractiveness of ATM devices for consumers. For example, ATM machines are outfitted with the ability to allow customers to link into the Internet and to obtain financial information relevant to their account transactions. In addition, ATMs are being deployed so that some are able to scan checks as well as cash deposits, and therefore allow account balances to be more quickly processed for such transactions.[43] New features are also being integrated by ATM manufacturers in order to improve account security, for example through biometric user authentication.[44]

Information Services

The final category of financial services that will be discussed relates to information-based financial services. We will first discuss credit rating agencies, which provide information to lending institutions as well as to consumers interested in obtaining credit. We will then discuss financial advisory services and brokerage services, which are often used to provide consumers with investment advice and to facilitate securities transactions.

There are three leading credit reporting agencies in the United States: Equifax, Trans Union, and Experian (formerly known as TRW). All three record credit-based information on any individual in the U.S. with credit activity. Credit activity would include events such as applying for a credit card, obtaining a loan at a bank, leasing a car, or making a late payment on a mortgage bill. The recorded information is then applied to credit scoring algorithms to produce a credit score. The resulting credit score can range from a low of 300 to a high of 850. The national credit score average is approximately 700.[45] Some of the factors that influence one's credit score include the amount of credit utilization, one's payment history for existing credit cards and loans, the number of times the individual has applied for credit, the income-to-debt ratio, the amount of revolving credit used, and other financially related factors. Individuals with credit scores below 600 are typically considered high risk and those with scores above 700 are considered qualified for competitive interest rates. Despite efforts to accurately record consumers' credit histories, numerous errors find their way into these records. By some estimates, as many as four out of every five credit records are erroneous, and one in four of these errors are sufficiently significant to cause one to be denied credit.[46] The high inaccuracy of consumer credit records and the critical impact of this information on consumer finances resulted in the introduction of regulations (Fair and Accurate Transaction Act of 2003) that require the credit reporting agencies to provide one free credit report per year for every individual in the United States upon the individual's request. The agencies are also required to inform consumers of any significant changes in their credit profile.

Another information-based financial service is financial advice. Financial advice can be provided through a variety of sources. Typically, financial advisers or stockbrokers provide customers with suggestions about which investment products to utilize. Financial advisers have been regulated by the *Investment Advisers Act of 1940* and the *Financial Advisory Act of 1941*. According to these regulations, individuals who are paid a fee by a client in return for financial advice must take their clients' best interests into account and not their own financial incentives. Brokers, on the other hand, are not bound by the exact same regulations and may find themselves in situations of conflict of interest because the investment advice they provide a client may not necessarily be in the best interest of the client. A broker, for example, may persuade a customer to purchase a mutual fund that has a high load (for example a large upfront fee for the customer) but an attractive commission for the broker. In addition, brokers might be tempted to encourage clients to conduct a large number of trades when in fact none or few might be required, a practice referred to as "churning." Many brokers earn commissions on trades made by their clients. Clearly, this practice may not be in the best interest of the client and may be challenged by regulators and customers.

CONCLUDING POINTS

One of the unique aspects of financial services marketing is the predictable shift in the types of products and services that individuals may need as they age. For example, in their 20s, most consumers' needs in financial services relate to transaction facilitation such as checking account services, debit cards, and credit card usage. Short-term collateralized loans or automobile leases may also be needed in order to purchase consumer durables in this stage of life. As one ages and advances professionally, an increase in disposable income often occurs. This facilitates the purchases of more expensive products and possible acquisition of a residential property. As a result, in the early 30s, a consumer may be interested in obtaining a mortgage and saving up for investments. The possibility for family life and birth of dependant children in the following years increases the need for financial products and services such as life insurance, college savings funds, financial advice, and pension planning. Beyond the midlife stage, consumers may need to tap into existing equity that they have built in their homes through home-equity loans and lines of credit. They may also find an increased need to deposit funds into their IRAs and pension plans in preparation for their retirement years. Those individuals and households who find themselves in financial distress by this time may also choose to take out reverse mortgages in their senior years, and some unfortunately accumulate considerable debt through credit card usage in this stage if life.

It is also important to note that since the deregulation of the financial services industry in 1999, the array of consumer choices available through any one financial services provider has significantly increased. The *Bank Modernization Act* allowed financial institutions to offer a much broader range of products and services to their customers. For example, it enabled banks to sell and underwrite insurance products, while insurance companies were allowed to offer deposit account services. The borderline between the various financial services therefore blurred at the turn of the century and has remained that way ever since. The blurring of the borders has made a large variety of financial services available to consumers, and has made it necessary for all financial services marketers to be well-educated about the array of financial products and services available in the marketplace.

CHAPTER QUESTIONS

1. What are the differences between home equity loans and home equity lines of credit?

2. What are the differences between loans and leases?

3. Define the following terms:
    a. Primary mortgage insurance
    b. Collateralized credit
    c. Time deposit
    d. Adjustable rate mortgage
    e. Demand deposit
    f. Check 21
    g. Umbrella insurance

4. What disadvantages do CDs present compared to savings accounts?

5. How has the practice of marketing credit cards evolved through the years?

6. What consumer concerns do you think might exist with credit card marketing practices?

7. What is the difference between term life insurance and universal life insurance?

8. How do credit and debit cards compare in terms of their consumer protection features?

9. What ethical mutual funds do you think would be attractive to today's investors?

ENDNOTES

1 C. Naser (2008), "Getting FDIC Insurance Shifts Right," *ABA Banking Journal*, Vol. 100, Iss. 12, pp. 38-40; S. Block (2008), "FDIC Limit Bumps Up to $250,000: Deposit Protection Included in Bailout Plan," *USA Today*, Oct 1, 2008, p. 1.

2 Nancy Michael (2009), "Branch and Deposit Trends: Facts and Fiction," *ABA Banking Journal*, Vol. 98, Iss. 2, pp. 14-15; Lauren Bielski (2004), "Is Free Checking Worth It?," *ABA Banking Journal*, Vol. 96, Iss. 3, pp. 31-35. See also, Bill Orr (2003), "Contrarian Forecast for 2010: Chilly for Branches, Sunny for E-Banks," *ABA Banking Journal*, Vol. 96, Iss. 3, pp. 56-57 and Michelle Pacelle, Carrick Mollenkamp, and Jathon Sapsford (2003), "Big Banks Signal They May be Gearing Up for Acquisitions," *Wall Street Journal*, June 12, page C1.

3 M. Bazerman and D. Moore (2008), *Judgment in Managerial Decision Making* New York: Wiley; S. Benartzi and R. Thaler (2001), "Naïve Diversification Strategies in Defined Contribution Savings Plans," *The American Economic Review*, Vol. 91, Iss. 1, pp. 79-98.

4 J. Kujala, A. Lamsa and K. Penttila (2011), "Managers' Moral Decision-Making Patterns Over Time: A Multidimensional Approach," *Journal of Business Ethics*, Vol. 100, Iss. 2, pp. 191-202; Allison Bell (2001), "Socially Conscious Funds Hold Their Own in the Face of the Slump," *National Underwriter*, Sept 24, Vol. 105, Iss. 39, pp. 11-12; See also: Toddi Gutner (2000), "Do the Right Thing - It Pays," *Business Week*, August 28, Iss. 3696, p. 266.

5 Jeff D. Opdyke (2004), "Selling Your Life Insurance to a Stranger," *Wall Street Journal*, Sep 21, p. D3.

6 *Country Forecast: United States (2011)*, Economist Intelligence Unit: London.

7 Ruth Simon (2004), "Your Unreliable Friend: Variable Rates," *Wall Street Journal*, Jul 4, 2004.

8 Stacey Buford (2004), "Mortgages Get More Exotic," *Wall Street Journal*, July 25, p. 3.

9 Timothy Mullaney (2004), "Real Estate's New Reality," *Business Week*, May 10, Iss. 3882, p. 88; James Hagerty (2004), "American Way: Some Take It, Some Leave It," *Wall Street Journal*, July 12, p. C1.

10 Peter Coy (2004), "When Home Buying by the Poor Backfires," *Business Week*, Nov 1, Iss. 3906, p. 68.

11 Timothy Mullaney (2004), "Real Estate's New Reality," *Business Week*, May 10, Iss. 3882, p. 88.

12 David Crook (2009), "If Your Credit Card Account is Closed, Your APR Jumps," *Wall Street Journal*, Oct 3, p. 4; Ruth Simon (2004), "Credit Card Fees Are Rising Faster – As Economies of Industry Change, Issuers Seek to Boost Income From Penalties," *Wall Street Journal*, March 31, p. D.1.

13 Mara Der Hovanesian (2009), "The Virtually Cashless Society," *Business Week*, November 17, Iss. 3858, p. 125.

14 Deborah Lagomarsino (2005), "Past Due Credit Card Bills Reach Record in the U.S." Wall Street Journal, Sept. 29, p. D2, citing figures from the American Bankers Association; see also: "Delinquencies Stable, But Still High," *Credit Card Management*, November 2003, Vol. 16, p. 9, citing figures reported by the American Bankers Association.

15 Linda Punch (2004), "Older Debtors, New Problems," Credit Card Management, Vol. 17, Iss. 5, pp 26-29; See also: Kelley K. Spors (2004), "Beware of Credit Cards at College," *Wall Street Journal*, Sept 5, p. 3.

16 L. Parrish and J. Frank (2011), "An Analysis of Bank Overdraft Fees: Pricing, Market Structure and Regulation," *Journal of Economic Issues*, Vol. 45, Iss. 2, pp. 353-36; Jim Barmlett, and Dave Kaytes (2004), "Credit Disconnect," *Credit Card Management*, Vol. 17, Iss. 1, pp. 54-57; Suein Hwang (2004), "Once Ignored Consumer Debts Are Focus of Booming Industry," *Wall Street Journal*, Oct 25, p. A.1; Kelley K. Spors (2004), "Credit Card Offers You Should Refuse," *Wall Street Journal*, Sep 26, p. 4.

17 For examples of such transactions consult: "A Rush to Bail out of Finance", Business Week, 8/18/2003-8/25/2003, Iss. 3846, p. 14. "MBNA Strikes and Agreement to Buy Credit Card Portfolio," *Wall Street Journal*, Nov 2, 2004, p. 1; Carrick Mollenkamp and Anne Davis (2004), "Computer Glitches Stall Wachovia Brokers," *Wall Street Journal*, Sep 14, p. C1.

18 Joseph Weber (2010), "Plastic that Looks Like Gold", *Business Week*, June 16, Iss. 3837, p. 70.

19 David Crook (2004), "If Your Credit Card Account is Closed, Your APR Jumps," *Wall Street Journal*, Oct 3, p. 4.

20 Ruth Simon and Jennifer Saranow (2004), "Credit Cards Start to Bump Up Rates," *Wall Street Journal*, Oct 6, citing a report by Bankrate.com; Jeanne Hogarth, Maureen English, and Manisha Sharma (2001), "Consumer Complaints and Third Parties: Determinants of Consumer Satisfaction With Complaint Resolution Efforts," *Journal of Consumer Satisfaction, Dissatisfaction and Complaining Behavior*, Vol. 14, pp. 74-87; Jeanne Hogarth, Marianne Hilbert, Jane Kolodinskly, and Jinkook Lee (2001), "Problems With Credit Cards: An Exploration of Consumer Complaining Behavior," *Journal of Consumer Satisfaction, Dissatisfaction, and Complaining Behavior*, Vol. 14, pp. 88-107.

21 Kate Fitzgerald (2010), "Mail Mania", *Credit Card Management*, Vol. 17, Iss. 10, p. 20.

22 Kaji Whitehouse (2009), "Auto Insurers Offer Discounts to Professionals," *Wall Street Journal*, April 7, p. D2.

23 Carol Marie Cropper (2004), "Premiums You can Retrieve", *Business Week*, May 10, Iss. 3882, p. 114; Christopher Oster (2004), "Life Insurers Charge Consumers More for Splitting Up Premiums," *Wall Street Journal*, September 15, p. D2; Christopher Oster (2004), "Life Insurers Raise Coverage Limits," *Wall Street Journal*, October 27, p. D3, citing a report by LIMRA International.

24 See: Jeff D. Opdyke (2011), "Life Insurance for Your Kids: Creepy, But ...," *Wall Street Journal*, August 22, p. 2, and, Jeff D. Opdyke (2004), "Selling Your Life Insurance to a Stranger," *Wall Street Journal*, September 21, p. D3, for additional details on these policies.

25 "Ski Pass Insurance Makes Debut," *Wall Street Journal*, January 7, 2004, page 1.

26 Jennifer Saranow (2008), "Insurers Add Benefits to Identity Theft Policies," *Wall Street Journal*, Oct 14, p. D2.

27 "Finding the True Extent of ID Theft," *Credit Card Management*, May 2004, Vol. 17, Iss. 2, p. 8, citing reports by the FTC and Gartner Inc.

28 B. Sheridan (2010), "What Your Identity is Worth Online," *Business Week*, October 18, p. 1.

29 Shaheen Pasha (2004), "Olympics Bring Heightened Risk, But Insurance Rates Are Stable," *Wall Street Journal*, August 4, page 1; Charles Fleming (2004), "Terrorism Insurance: Many Companies Are Going Without," *Wall Street Journal*, December 13, page C1.

30 Jeff D. Opdyke (2004), "Underwater With No Insurance," *Wall Street Journal*, Nov 16, page D2.

31 Theo Francis (2005), "In Katrina's Wake: Many in Areas Hit by Flood Lack Insurance," *Wall Street Journal*, Aug. 31, p. A5.

32 Consumer Reports (2005), *"Shopping Strategies to Get Best Values,"* Yonkers, NY: Consumers Union, pp. 13-22. Robert Berner (2005), "The Warranty Windfall," *Business Week*, Dec. 20, Iss. 3913, p. 84, citing figures reported by FTN Midwest Securities Corp.

33 Charles Fleming (2004), "Insurers Employ Voice-Analysis Software to Detect Fraud," *Wall Street Journal*, May 17, p. B1.

34 Kathy Chu (2004), "Auto Insurer Cuts Rates for 'Black Box' Testers," *Wall Street Journal*, August 12, page D2.

35 David Wessel (2011), "How Not to Outlive Your Savings," Wall Street Journal, Sep 30, p. D1; Daniel Kahneman and Amos Tversky (1973), "On the Psychology of Prediction," *Psychological Review*, Vol. 80, pp. 237-251; P. Slovic and B. Fischhoff (1977), "On the Psychology of Experimental Surprises," *Journal of Experimental Psychology: Human Perception and Performance*, Vol. 3, pp. 544-551.

36 Lauren Bielski (2004), "A New Era Begins: Making The Transition to a Revised Check Processing Scheme," *ABA Banking Journal*, Vol. 96, Iss. 6, p. 51.

37 Andrew Park, Ben Eglin, and Timothy Mullaney (2003), "Checks Check Out," *Business Week*, May 10, Iss. 3882, pp. 83-84, citing study conducted by Gartner; Jennifer Saranow (2004), "Electronic Ways Outpace Checks As Payment Means," *Wall Street Journal*, Dec 7, p. D2, citing a study conducted by the Federal Reserve; Reed Albergotti (2003), "Plastic Puts Fresh Crease in Cash," *Wall Street Journal*, Dec 16, p. D4, citing figures reported by the American Bankers Association and Dove Consulting.

38 Mara Der Hovanesian (2003), "The Virtually Cashless Society," *Business Week*, November 17, Iss. 3858, p. 125; Lauren Bielski (2004), "A New Era Begins: Making The Transition to a Revised Check Processing Scheme," *ABA Banking Journal*, Vol. 96, Iss. 6, p. 51.

39 Linda Punch (2004), "Beckoning the Unbanked", *Credit Card Management*, Vol. 17, Iss. 7, pp. 28-32; see also: Mara Der Hovanesian (2008) "The Virtually Cashless Society," *Business Week*, November 17, Iss. 3858, p. 125.

40 M. Polasik, J. Gorka, G. Wilczewski and J. Kunkowski (2010), "Time Efficiency of Point-of-Sale Payment Methods: Preliminary Results," *Journal of Internet Banking and Commerce*, Vol. 15, Iss. 3, pp. 1-11; See Jathon Sapsford (2004), "As Cash Fades, America Becomes a Plastic Nation," *Wall Street Journal*, July 23, page A1 for additional statistics and related figures.

41 Christopher Conkey (2004), "Holiday Shoppers Should Rethink How They Pay," *Wall Street Journal*, December 22, p. D3.

42 Jen Ryan (2010), "ATMs Try to Cash in with Extra Services," *Wall Street Journal*, August 11, p. D4.

43 David Gousnell (2004), "Hard-Core Enthusiasm for High-Tech ATMs," *Credit Card Management*, Vol. 16, Iss. 11, p. 16.

44 J. Ginovsky (2010), "Depositing Cash and Checks Simultaneously at ATMs," *ABA Banking Journal*, Vol. 102, Iss. 11, p. 24; David Gousnell (2004), "ATM Growth Rates Converge," *Credit Card Management*, Vol. 17, Iss. 8, p. 57.

45 C. Lourosa-Ricardo (2011), "How Does Your Credit Score Actually Work?" *Wall Street Journal*, March 6, 2011, p. 3.

46 M. Singletary (2010), "With Credit Scores it Should be Equal Access to All," *The Washington Post*, May 27, p. 12.

CHAPTER FOUR

Pricing

Pricing is one of the most important decisions in the marketing of financial services. Price serves multiple roles for the financial services organization as well as for the individuals who use those services. To the financial services organization, price represents the sole source of revenues. Most activities that an organization undertakes represent costs and an outflow of funds. When advertising, for example, one has to spend money purchasing advertising space in a newspaper or media time on radio or TV. When employing staff in a sales department salaries and benefits need to be paid. All of these activities represent an outflow of funds, and the only way to recover these expenditures is through revenues obtained by charging prices for the financial services provided. It is critical not only to appreciate the importance of price, but also to be certain that one's prices are at optimal levels. Pricing too low or too high can have detrimental effects on profitability of financial services organizations.

In addition, price is the most visible component of the marketing strategy of a financial services organization. Unlike advertising style, product strategy, or sales force incentives, which might be difficult to quantify precisely, price is always presented numerically, and can be observed and compared by consumers, regulators, and competitors. Therefore, a second function of price is to communicate to the marketplace the identity, market positioning, and intentions of a financial services organization. Lowering of prices or an upward movement of premiums might signal a shift in marketing strategy to competitors and may provoke reactions from them. This fact raises the strategic importance of price and highlights the great impact that price has been found to have in shifting the balance of power among competing financial services providers.

A third function of price is to serve as a signal of quality to customers. As mentioned in earlier chapters, the quality of a financial service may be highly elusive and vague. Determining whether one insurance policy is better than another, or if an investment advisor will provide recommendations that generate high returns on one's investment portfolio, is difficult if not impossible for many. It has been well established in consumer research that in such situations where quality is not clearly evident, consumers tend to rely on price as a proxy for quality.[1] They might therefore assume that higher-priced financial services are of better quality, and the lowering of prices may not necessarily be associated with more positive consumer impressions of the financial service. The potential for this unexpected relationship between price and consumer demand in specific markets further highlights the critical importance of setting prices correctly in financial services.

In this chapter, we will discuss methods for pricing financial services. The complexity of financial services prices and the cost structure of financial services organizations have a great impact on how financial services pricing is practiced. We will discuss the unique aspects of pricing in financial services and how it differs from the practice of pricing in other contexts. We will then discuss common approaches used for pricing specific types of financial services commonly used by consumers. This chapter will conclude with a discussion of strategic and tactical aspects of pricing financial services.

CHALLENGES IN PRICING FINANCIAL SERVICES

Financial services prices are unique in several ways. The unique aspects of price in financial services are important to recognize when developing marketing strategies and analyzing consumers' decision dynamics. Some of these unique aspects are listed below:

Financial Services Prices are Often Multi-Dimensional: One of the most notable characteristics of financial services prices is that they are complex and often consist of multiple numeric attributes. For example, an automobile lease is often communicated in terms of the combination of a monthly payment, number of payments, a down payment, the final balloon payment, wear-and-tear penalties, and mileage charges for driving over the allowed number of miles. Therefore, unlike the sticker price for the cash purchase of a car, which is a single number, the lease price consists of many different numbers. As a result, to evaluate an offered lease accurately, the consumer will have to conduct considerable amounts of arithmetic. To calculate the total dollar layout for an automobile lease, for example, the monthly payments and the number of payments have to be multiplied and added to the down payment. The complex numeric nature of financial services prices and the requirement of a minimal number of numeric computations make financial services prices among the most complex items that consumers have to evaluate in their purchase decisions. Research has established that conducting arithmetic tasks associated with the evaluation of a financial service price can be highly stressful, and consumers have a tendency to simplify such tasks by finding mental short-cut strategies that would allow them to avoid carrying out the demanding arithmetic.[2] These simplification strategies, some of which were discussed earlier in Chapter 2, may result in poor consumer decisions.

Elusive Measures of Quality: A second challenge in the pricing of financial services is the elusive and intangible nature of the quality of a financial service. In contrast to manufactured goods, which can be scientifically tested in laboratories and are often rated by well-established third party organizations such as Consumer Reports, J.D. Power and Associates, and the Insurance Institute for Highway Safety, the quality of financial services is far more difficult to determine. Objective levels of service quality as determined for example by the likelihood that a mutual fund will have good returns, the transaction processing accuracy and efficiency of a commercial bank, and the ability of a tax accountant to secure the highest possible tax returns, are difficult to assess. The fact that these measures of quality are difficult, if not impossible to quantify often forces consumers to examine other pieces of information, in particular price, as an indicator of service quality.[3] Therefore, while a high price may discourage some consumers from purchasing a financial service, it may also serve as a positive signal for others and may increase their desire to use the service.

Economic Forces: The pricing of financial services is further complicated by the fact that the attractiveness of a financial service may be affected by the general economic environment. For example, in order to appreciate the value of an investment option a consumer must compare the expected rate of return with the rates of return experienced in the financial markets. A change in the prime rate or U.S. Treasury rates might make an investment option look more or less attractive to the consumer. As a result, financial services providers need to take relevant economic indicators such as interest rates and stock market returns into account when setting prices for specific financial products and services.

Poor Consumer Price Knowledge: The pricing of financial services needs to take into account the fact that consumer memory for financial services prices is quite weak.[4] The unexciting and complicated nature of financial services often results in poor recall of the prices of financial services. For example, many consumers have a difficult time remembering the cost of their banking services, such as the monthly maintenance fees for checking account services and ATM transaction charges, or what yearly premiums they are paying for their automobile insurance. As a result, the general level of price knowledge with which consumers interact with financial services providers might be quite limited.

Difficulty in Determining Customer Profitability: An additional challenge presented in the pricing of financial services is that the profitability associated with a given customer may be difficult to assess. This is because a single customer may purchase multiple services from a financial services provider, some of which are highly profitable and others that represent losses. For example, a bank customer might use the bank's checking and savings account services, which may not be highly profitable to the bank. However, she may also conduct her investment and retirement planning, which are typically higher margin services, at the same bank. Therefore, while certain transactions with this customer may be perceived to be unprofitable, other transactions may compensate for this shortfall making the individual a highly valuable customer to the bank overall.

Indeterminable Costs: Determining the costs associated with a specific financial product or service might be a numerically challenging task given the fact that various elements of a financial services organization contribute to the service experience that is delivered to the customer. The limited ability to pinpoint costs accurately can therefore complicate the task of pricing a financial service.

Conflicts of Interest: The pricing of financial services is further complicated by the significant conflicts of interest that may exist in the selling process. For example, brokers may use different components of price, such as trading fees or commissions earned on the sale of specific financial products, as the means for their earnings. Therefore, the link between price and the incentive mechanism used to compensate the broker might influence the types of products that the broker would be inclined to recommend to the client. The expected broker behavior would be to recommend products with a price structure that provides her with higher commission earnings. This further complicates the pricing decision by introducing issues of trust and ethics to the already complex pricing process.

COMMON APPROACHES TO PRICING FINANCIAL SERVICES

The general approach to pricing can be visualized as a process of determining where on a continuous line one chooses to set the price charged to customers. The range of these possibilities is shown in Exhibit 4.1 as a spectrum of pricing possibilities. At the one extreme, one could choose to freely provide services to consumers by charging nothing (point A). While such an approach may result in a significant growth in one's customer base, it is typically financially unwise, as it will result in loss of significant amounts of profits. Such a pricing approach is only associated with short-term promotional objectives in which new customer acquisition is the primary objective. For example, an automobile road-side assistance policy might be freely offered to customers for a three-month time period in hopes that some of these customers will decide to continue the service by subscribing to it after the free trial period has ended. Alternatively, one could choose to price a financial

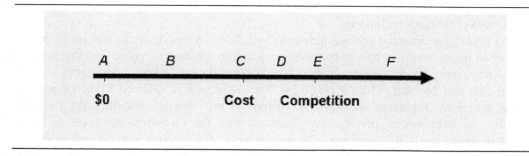

Exhibit 4.1 The Pricing Spectrum

service below cost (point B) or at cost (point C). These price points may also serve the general objective of new customer acquisition, but may be catastrophic in the long-term due to their harmful impact on profitability.

Furthermore, prices that are below cost often trigger competitors to engage in intensive price competition and may raise the attention of regulators who may consider the prices to be predatory and anti-competitive. This may result in legal actions against the company based on U.S. anti-trust laws, which are designed to promote healthy competition in all markets. Therefore, the benefit of remaining in the lower range of the price spectrum (points A, B, and C) would need to be very carefully examined in terms of its long-term strategic impact as well as short-term profit implications. Most financial services organizations seek to generate at least a minimal amount of profit. Therefore, a minimum constraint on their prices is the need to cover costs (areas beyond point C in Exhibit 4.1). This approach is often referred to as *cost-based pricing* and will be discussed shortly. The thought process behind cost-based pricing is to determine the costs of providing a given financial service and to apply a specific markup typical of one's line of business in order to ensure that appropriate levels of profitability are generated from offering the service.

Alternatively, a financial services organization may choose market share as its primary objective. Therefore, the relative position of one's prices versus those of key competitors might become the primary focus. To take away market share from a leading competitor, one may have to price below or at comparable levels to the competitor's price. This could represent areas between points C and E on the price spectrum and is often associated with what is referred to as *parity pricing*. Parity pricing involves choosing prices that are anchored around competing prices in the marketplace. Because higher prices may be interpreted by consumers as reflecting higher levels of quality in certain financial services, it is important to note that price points above E on the price spectrum may also be quite acceptable to consumers. The correct positioning of price in such a context would be an empirical issue only to be established through the application of formal market research techniques.

The price of a financial service may also be guided by the desire to maximize profits. In order to do so, one has to determine the maximum amount of value that the financial service represents to its customers and to translate the associated value into a dollar amount that can be charged as a premium. This approach is referred to as value-based pricing and may represent any of the various points discussed earlier on the price spectrum. In value-based pricing, one assumes that the customer perceives a unique benefit in using one's financial services or products. This unique benefit not only helps differentiate one from competitors, but also justifies charging prices that may possibly exceed those of the competition. The challenging task would then be to determine what unique features represent value to the customer and to quantify the dollar equivalent associated with the value of these features. This would be an empirical task as it requires thorough formal market research utilizing representative samples of consumers.

A final approach to pricing financial services is guided by regulatory constraints. In this approach, regulators would determine the specific prices or determine acceptable price ranges within which financial services providers would operate. According to this pricing approach – regulation-based pricing – all financial services providers have to respect regulators' price requirements. In the following section, we will discuss each of these four popular approaches to pricing financial services in detail. It is important to note that each of the approaches provide for a given price point on the price spectrum. However, rarely do financial services organizations choose a specific price based on a single approach to pricing. In order to set prices in an educated and well-informed manner, one would have to estimate the price based on all the approaches discussed here and then use managerial judgment and sound decision making to fine-tune the price. With each price point serving as an anchor, the final price is often determined by choosing a price point that best reflects a compromise among the various prices suggested by the different approaches.

1. Cost-Based Pricing

The cost-based approach to pricing is one of the oldest methods of pricing in both financial and non-financial services, as well as in manufactured goods.5 The motivation behind this approach is that one must cover at least the costs of running a business in order to survive financially. As a result, the cost of providing a financial service is used as the lower bound for prices. Prices are set in such a way that costs are covered and a particular level of profit is secured. This is done by applying a markup to the unit cost of the service. Price is set by this simple formula:

$$Price = Cost \times (1 + Markup)$$

The markup reflects the general objectives of the business and the financial risks of providing the service. Higher markups would be associated with higher levels of profits, while lower markups could enable the generation of a larger volume of customer transactions. In addition, the markups that are applied may reflect the company's norms and policies, the type of services it offers, and the risks that are associated with these service offerings. Services associated with higher levels of risk (for example, ensuring high-risk drivers, providing credit to applicants with poor credit histories) may justify higher markups, and depending on the type of financial service, the markups applied might vary.

To demonstrate how cost-based pricing is used, we will examine a hypothetical scenario where a commercial bank needs to determine how much each customer has to be charged, on a monthly basis, for banking services. The bank has 10,000 active accounts, and the bank's fixed costs, as reflected by the cost of the bank employees' salaries, the rent for the bank branch building, and other overhead expenses, is estimated at $40,000 a month. Considering the types of transactions that an average customer conducts and the costs of transaction processing (e.g., paperwork and other variable components of transaction handling), the variable cost to the bank is estimated to be $1 per account each month. This means that the total cost of operating the bank branch on a monthly basis is $50,000 ($40,000 + $1x10,000 accounts). Averaging this cost across all the 10,000 accounts would imply that the average cost per account is $50,000/10,000 or $5.00. Assuming that the bank uses a 50% markup for its services, the price that each accountholder should be charged is $5 x (1+0.5), or $7.50 per month.

Service	Cost Range
Debit from Checking	$0.10-$0.20
Cashing Checks	$0.20-$0.40
Deposit into Checking Account	$0.30-$0.35
Account Maintenance	$4.00-$5.00
Deposit into Savings Account	$0.60-$1.00
Withdrawal from Savings Account	$1.00-$2.00
Online Payment	$0.05-$0.15

Exhibit 4.2 Approximate Costs of Various Banking Services

Clearly, one of the challenges in this process is to determine what the average cost per account would be. For commercial banking operations, the Federal Reserve Board's *Functional Cost Analysis Table,* as well as estimates by other third-party organizations provides estimates for some of the common services utilized in commercial banking. Exhibit 4.2 provides the range of some of these cost estimates based on a variety of sources.[6] Precise figures can be obtained through formal surveys of financial institutions, and as one may see from the table, certain transactions are likely to be far more expensive for a bank to carry out than other transactions. For example, the cost of making deposits into a savings account is nearly five times the cost of conducting debits from a checking account. Similarly, depositing funds into a checking account can cost multiples of what online payments would cost. Knowledge of the frequency by which these different transactions or services are used by a typical customer helps provide an estimate of the overall cost of maintaining an account for a banking institution. Such estimates, which could also be obtained through analysis of one's customer base, could then be used to determine the prices that would be charged by the bank for its services by applying the appropriate markups.

There are several limitations associated with the use of cost-based pricing in financial services. Since different customers may utilize a financial service to different degrees, use of an average cost to determine the price charged to all customers may be somewhat unfair. Customers that rarely utilize a service would pay an equal price to those that heavily utilize it. As a result, the light users might subsidize the heavy users of the service. This may be remedied by charging customers on a per usage basis. For example, some commercial banks charge customers additional fees for use of bank teller services or for banking by phone. Customers who tend to use the more costly customer services, such as bank tellers excessively must therefore pay a proportionate fee for their high usage level of these methods of service delivery.

An additional limitation of cost-based pricing is the challenge of pinpointing fixed costs. The complexity of the cost structure of financial services organizations makes the allocation of fixed costs across the multitude of services provided by the organization a numerically challenging task. In addition, for certain types of financial services, the costs associated with running the business may be highly volatile and unpredictable. For example, a financial services organization's cost of credit is determined by the interest rates in the financial markets. When the prime rate increases, a credit card company's costs of securing funds also increases. Unless the rates charged to customers are accordingly adjusted, the credit card company may stand to lose considerable amount of profits. The volatility that this introduces into the relationship between costs and prices translates into price changes that may have to parallel cost volatilities. This is one reason why changes in the prime rate are typically followed within a few weeks by changes in credit card interest rates charged to customers.[7]

An additional limitation of cost-based pricing in financial services is the lack of consideration for the level of consumer demand that might exist at the computed price point. The prices that are arrived at through a cost-based pricing formula may or may not result in a sufficient number of customers in order for the business to break even. It is very important, therefore, to assess the receptiveness of the customer base to a price that is determined using a cost-based approach. Despite these limitations, cost-based pricing is often utilized in many financial services organizations as a primary approach for price determination. This is often the case for financial services that are highly commoditized and standardized in nature. Financial services such as commercial banking, transaction processing services, and insurance are services in which the underlying cost structure is often well established. Therefore, in these services, cost-based pricing may guide the final prices charged to the consumer more so than other approaches to pricing.

2. Parity Pricing

In the cost-based pricing approach, there is no assurance that the determined prices will appeal to consumers in the marketplace. The increasingly competitive nature of financial services, driven by the deregulation of the industry in recent years, has forced many financial services organizations to pay closer attention to prices offered by their competitors. The thought process behind parity pricing is to set prices in response to what the competition is charging. This does not necessarily imply that one's prices will be below that of the competitors. In fact, depending on the overall positioning of the company, one may choose to price below or above competing prices. To conduct parity pricing, one would have to establish the primary competitor. The primary competitor could be the market leader who has the highest market share, or the company that has the closest resemblance to one's own service offerings. It is critical to establish which of the competing financial services offers represents the most relevant and intense level of competition with one's own offering. This approach is appropriate for both price changes in a market in which one is currently active, as well as new financial services introductions into markets where one has never participated before. Once the key competitor has been identified, the price that is charged is then computed by applying a multiplier factor to the competitor's price:

Our price = Factor × Key Competitor's Price

The applied factor is determined by the overall marketing strategy of the company. A factor of less than 1.0 represents scenarios in which the key competitor is systematically being undercut. Care must be taken if such an approach is used because price wars might easily result. A factor of greater than 1.0 might be justified by perceived or actual service advantages over the competitor, and a strategy that capitalizes on customers' perceptions of quality associated with higher priced services. Such an approach would be less likely to trigger price wars, although it would most likely not generate the same volume of sales as the use of a factor below 1.0. To demonstrate the use of parity based pricing, Exhibit 4.3 shows prices charged by various competitors for a particular automobile insurance policy. The first step is to establish the key competitor.

In this case, our company (C) has determined that the key competitor is insurance company A, the current market leader. Parity-based pricing is used in this case to determine what price should be charged in the context of recent changes made by the competitor to its prices. The principle to follow is that the ratio of one's price to the key competitor's price must remain the same when the price is revised. The factor to be applied is therefore:

In our case, this would be computed as:

$$Factor = \frac{Our\ price\ last\ year}{Key\ competitor's\ price\ last\ year}$$

$$Factor = \frac{\$861}{\$938} = 0.918$$

Given that the leading competitor has adjusted its price to $887, our revised price is therefore computed as:

$$Our\ new\ price = 0.918 \times \$887 = \$814$$

	Market Share	Price Last Year	Revised Price
Company A	47%	$938	$887
Company B	21%	$852	$795
Company C (us)	7%	$861	**$814 ***
Company D	5%	$731	$731
Company E	3%	$1,019	$1,019

Exhibit 4.3 Yearly Premiums for Auto Insurance

This results in a revised price, which maintains the same relative difference with the key competitor's price. If the key competitor raises its price, one's prices should also be raised. There are several advantages to this approach. If all competitors follow price changes in a marketplace, this approach might result in market stability and prevent price wars since the relative differences in prices will not change dramatically. Use of parity pricing often requires that one competitor is used as the benchmark for others to consider as their key competitor. This benchmark company is referred to as the *price leader*, because its price changes lead others to change their prices. Often, the price leader is also the market share leader in a marketplace, and may in fact be the lowest priced competitor. However, a price leader may also operate at the higher end of the market and not be the lowest priced competitor in the marketplace. The challenge in such an entangled system of pricing is that, if one of the competitors violates the relative price differences with the market leader, the market attractiveness of the competing prices would be challenged. The brand that may have been priced closely to the price leader, for example, may shift its price down and become significantly more price competitive. This may trigger reactions from the price leader and others, followed by parallel shifts in prices by the remaining competitors in the market. The end result could be a drop in prices across all competitors in the market, which may further escalate into subsequent price cuts. The vicious cycle may continue until the competing companies have undercut one another to such an extent that profit margins have largely vanished. An additional limitation of parity-based pricing is that one's pricing strategy is driven by the key competitor's pricing strategy. Since a relative distance between one's price and the key competitor's price needs to be respected, one would have to adjust prices any time the competitor changes its price.

This eliminates the fundamental notion of independent strategic thinking in managing one's prices.

3. Value-Based Pricing

The use of cost-based pricing or parity pricing does not necessarily guarantee maximization of profits. This is because neither of these approaches takes into account the unique attributes and characteristics that consumers might value greatly in a financial service. In fact, both of these approaches may result in prices that are either above what consumers are willing to pay or below consumer price expectations. In the former case, this would result in a loss of market share, while in the latter case a loss in profits would result. The principle behind value-based pricing is to determine the price based on what customers perceive to be the value of the service. Often, financial services have specific attributes that make them valuable and attractive for customers. For example, an insurance company's name may appeal to those customers who would like to purchase their policies from established companies. Alternatively, the convenient location of a bank branch might represent added value to customers who live or work within the geographic vicinity of that specific branch. Similarly, the accessibility and friendliness of customer service staff at a mortgage company might increase the value that a customer places on interactions with the company.

The objective of value-based pricing is to quantify in monetary terms what each of these sources of value is worth to the customer, and to utilize this information in order to determine the price to be charged. The price that is charged for a service using the value-based approach would have to take into account the base price of the service, which may reflect the average market price or the prices of the most closely comparable services, supplemented by the monetary values associated with the additional features uniquely provided by the company's financial service offering:

Price = Base price + dollar value of our unique features

To demonstrate an example of value-based pricing, imagine how an insurance company may choose to price an automobile insurance policy. For example, the average premium charged a typical consumer by the various insurance companies in the marketplace may be $845 a year. However, our company provides a series of unique services to its customers, which may merit a higher price. For example, the company has recently been ranked as a top insurer by a third-party industry rating organization. In addition, the name of the company is well recognized and customer service is available through the phone 24 hours a day, 7 days a week—unlike some of its competitors. These unique features should be of value to the customers, and should be reflected in the price. Through consumer surveys, it is possible to quantify the dollar value of each of these unique features. For example, a consumer survey could ask consumers to assign dollar values to each of these unique features of the service, and the average dollar amount across all collected surveys could then be used to quantify the monetary value of each feature. Such a survey may reveal, for example, that the top ranking given to the company by a third-party organization is valued at $31, the well-recognized brand name is valued at $15, and having accessible customer service is valued at $25. These dollar figures could then be added to the base price (market average of $845 for competitors who do not possess these features) in order to determine the value-based price for this unique insurance policy:

$$Price = \$845 + \$31 + \$15 + \$25 = \$916$$

Value-based pricing encourages one to examine the sources of value in a service offering and to recognize the associated profits through the charged price. In the credit card business, for example, customers might find value in credit card offers that have fraud protection features or provide reward programs that are relevant to the types of purchases they usually make using the credit card. Similarly, an insurance company might find that customers value its well-recognized name to the extent that they are willing to pay extra for the peace of mind it presents to them. Customers of a commercial bank may find additional value in a bank that has a wide network of ATMs, weekend operating hours, and knowledgeable bank tellers. All of these features translate into opportunities to realize additional profits through higher prices, which customers might be willing to pay due to their own unique needs in the financial service.

What is especially helpful about this approach to pricing is that it encourages the financial services organization to examine and recognize sources of revenue (and value) which may not have been previously considered. This approach to pricing requires one to dissect the service into its subcomponents and to ensure that all possible valuable features of the service are accounted for in the price. An additional benefit to this approach to pricing is that it forces one to examine factors that either contribute to or diminish value in the consumer's mind. This would help facilitate the improvement of existing services and products. It may also pave the way for new product development and the introduction of added features in future financial services offerings. This not only helps one realize higher revenue potentials associated with innovation, but it may also encourage the organization to identify and eliminate service features that deplete value and result in customer dissatisfaction. For example, credit card customers may find depleted value in the services of a credit card company that has inaccessible customer service or stuffs its monthly statement envelopes with an avalanche of irrelevant promotional material. Recognizing this might help a financial services provider to eliminate value-destroying practices in the service delivery process. Because of the close link that the value-based pricing approach encourages between financial services marketers and customers, its use is growing in practice in both financial and non-financial pricing contexts.[8] Of the various approaches to pricing financial services, this approach is the most connected to customer feelings about the company's offerings, and often requires active gathering of customer feedback data in order to quantify the price.

4. Regulation-Based Pricing

The final approach to pricing is driven by the forces of legislation and regulation that may govern particular categories of financial services. In certain categories of financial services, regulators may play a significant role in determining prices. As will be discussed in the discussion of regulations in Chapter 10, the motivation behind many financial services regulations is to ensure that the prices charged to consumers are equitable and that all segments of the population would have access to financial products that are essential to their economic wellbeing. Given this, regulators might mandate price levels, and financial services providers may have very limited input in determining the prices that would be charged. Therefore, the computational effort related to cost-based, parity-based, or value-based pricing may be of limited application in this context because regulators would dictate prices or specify the allowable ranges for price.

An example would be the sale of flood insurance included in homeowners insurance policies and required by mortgage companies for properties located in flood zones. The rates charged for flood insurance coverage are managed through the National Flood Insurance Program of the Federal Emergency Management Administration (FEMA). Another example would be the premiums charged for the sale of reverse mortgages. In the case of reverse mortgages, customers are often required to pay an upfront fee to secure the transaction. The fee is often determined as a percentage of the total reverse mortgage amount. In the late 1990's, a notable proportion of senior citizens – the dominant customers for this product –who obtained reverse mortgages found themselves paying exceptionally high upfront fees, provoking the federal authorities to regulate these fees. The U.S. Department of Housing and Urban Development (HUD) has since established the maximum amount of premiums that can be charged for providing a reverse mortgage as a specific percentage of the value of the property.[9] Although the regulation does not spell out a lower bound, it constrains the upper bound of what a reverse mortgage contract could charge as upfront fees. When setting prices for any financial product or service, it is therefore essential to ensure regulatory compliance with any applicable price constraints that may be required by relevant regulatory bodies.

Determining Which Price to Use

The pricing approaches discussed above are often used in combination. For example, one may use cost-based pricing to arrive at a price. Parity-based pricing may be used to arrive at another price, and value-based pricing could be used to arrive at another price. The task of determining the final price may involve managerial judgment as to which of the estimated prices should weigh more heavily in determining the price charged for a financial service. For example, in a market that is highly competitive, a parity-based price might have more weight than the other pricing approaches. Alternatively, in a market where customers might value the unique features of a financial service, value-based pricing might be most relevant. As a result, the task of setting prices is a combination of the science involving the numeric derivation of the price points discussed earlier, and the art of judging what the ultimate price should be. The ultimate price might take one of these computed prices more into account than the others, or it may reflect an average of these prices.

CATEGORY-SPECIFIC PRICING PRACTICES

In this section, we will discuss unique aspects of pricing for several popular categories of financial services. In particular, tactics and approaches used in pricing credit products, savings products, investment and brokerage services, and insurance products will be discussed. These categories account for a significant proportion of consumer spending in financial services, and the unique aspects of each of these services require particular pricing approaches to be utilized. It is critical for financial services marketers to have a full understanding of the underlying process for pricing these particular types of services.

A. Pricing Credit Products

Credit products facilitate the lending of funds to a customer. As discussed in Chapter 3, these would include credit cards, home equity lines of credit, home equity loans, automobile loans, home mortgages, and other forms of financing within both consumer and business settings. Credit products have two fundamental characteristics. The first relates to whether the lending activity is collateralized or not. Collateralized lending (also called "secured" lending) occurs when an asset possessed by the borrower is used as collateral, such that it could be repossessed by the lender in case of default. Collateralized (secured) credit therefore presents the lender with relatively low risk in giving out credit. For example, the collateral used for a home mortgage is typically the property itself. Therefore, if the homeowner fails to make the regular mortgage payments, the mortgage company may have the right to gain possession of the collateral (the house) and to place the property on the market in order to recover its own investment. This lowers the risk for the lender because it not only motivates the customer to ensure timely payment of the mortgage bills (or risk losing the house), but the secured collateral also serves as a safety blanket for recovering the funds loaned to the customer. On the other hand, non-collateralized credit such as credit card debt is not associated with any specific asset that could be repossessed, and therefore represents a higher level of risk to the lender. If a customer decides not to pay his credit card balance, the credit card company typically has no assets to rely on as a means for recovering its funds and must rely on the functions of a collection agency. Therefore, when it comes to the pricing of credit, higher interest rates apply to non-collateralized credit where the lending risks are higher. This is one of the reasons why home equity lines of credit (which use the home as collateral), receive significantly lower interest rates than credit cards, which are non-collateralized, and can therefore be a cost effective way for consumers to conduct debt consolidation

A second dimension of credit pricing relates to the time frame, as discussed in Chapter 3. Credit can be extended to a customer in either revolving or non-revolving form. In the non-revolving form, there is a finite length of time in which the borrowed amount has to be repaid by the customer. Typically, non-revolving credit such as a home mortgage is long-term in nature. Revolving credit, on the other hand, has no specific time limit, but should be used by consumers as a short-term instrument for borrowing. An example of revolving credit is credit card debt or home equity lines of credit. Since revolving credit is of a short-term nature, associated rates of interest are often linked to short-term interest rates. Therefore, prime rate changes are often a leading indicator for interest rate changes for many revolving credit products. On the other hand, non-revolving credit is often associated with longer-term interest rates, such as the U.S. Treasury rates.

In addition to collateral and the revolving nature of credit, additional factors may determine the price that is charged for providing credit to a given customer. Two fundamental risk factors that influence the price of credit are *performance risk* and *interest rate risk*. Performance risk reflects the possibility that the customer is unable or unwilling to make the regular payments related to the loan. Customers with bad credit history represent higher levels of performance risk and are often charged higher interest rates. Performance risk is often assessed by examining a credit applicant's credit report. Interest rate risk, on the other hand, reflects speculations on interest rate trends in the near future. If the interest rates rise during the term of a loan, the lender suffers from a possible opportunity cost. The opportunity cost is presented by the fact that the lender could have realized higher interest earnings had it been able to lend out the funds using the higher rates. Interest rate risk, therefore, relates to the possibility that interest rates will increase during the term of a credit arrangement.

The interest rate for many credit products can take on two forms: fixed or variable. Fixed interest rates remain constant throughout the term of the loan. Variable interest rates however change during the life of the loan as a function of external variables such as the rates of interest in financial markets. Variable rates can therefore present borrowers with opportunities if general financial market rates decline, but also pose a financial risk to the borrower in times of rising market interest rates. Fixed rate loans are typically priced higher than variable rate loans to cover interest rate risk. It is also important to note that interest rates are not the only dimension of price in credit transactions that generate revenue for lenders. In fact, for many credit services, the price may materialize through additional credit components. For example, a credit card company could realize additional revenues by charging penalties for late payments on bills. Similarly, a mortgage company could earn additional revenues by charging customers for mortgage processing fees, origination fees, and for penalizing them for accelerating the repayment of the mortgage through prepayment penalties. In fact, research has shown that, in recent years, financial services providers have found such penalties to be a far more effective way of exercising higher prices than raising interest rates.[10] The transparent nature of interest rates and the highly competitive environment of the credit card business, which promotes low introductory APRs, has forced many credit card companies to utilize non-transparent aspects of price, such as penalties and fees, to improve their revenue base. This approach to pricing clearly raises ethical concerns related to the pricing of credit products because it exposes the possibility that consumers may not be aware of the total price that they are paying for commonly utilized financial services. Consumers typically do not pay sufficient attention to the non-interest dimensions of credit products. As a result, their estimates of the total cost associated with the price of a credit offering may be highly inaccurate.[11] This is further compounded by consumers' inability to conduct the necessary mental arithmetic. While the opportunities for exercising price increases through these non-interest dimensions of credit products exist, the potential for consumer deception and related ethical and regulatory concerns is equally problematic. This concern was a major force behind the *Credit Card Accountability, Responsibility and Disclosure Act of 2009* which was put in place in order to protect consumers against unfair price increases, unreasonable fees, and deceptive marketing practices, specifically in the context of credit cards.

B. Pricing Savings Products

Savings products involve consumers depositing their money with a financial organization such as a bank or a saving and loan institution. The financial organization ensures the safekeeping of the customer's funds and possibly facilitates additional transactions related to the deposited funds. By depositing funds into a savings account, the customer has in effect passed on the responsibility of keeping the money in a safe place onto the bank that now has to keep the funds in a secure location and possess the necessary infrastructure to facilitate the safekeeping and associated financial transactions. The safekeeping aspect of the bank's service allows it to justify charging prices for its service.

The first approach to pricing savings products is transaction-based: customers are charged fees for the transactions which they undertake. For example, the bank might charge each customer $10 a month for the maintenance of the accounts. This fee is justified based on the fact that the bank has to have a building, staff, a safe vault, and security measures to receive the customer's money and to keep the deposits in a safe place. In addition, fees might be charged based on the number and type of transactions, the number of ATM-based activities, and other forms of customer-driven banking transactions. The monthly maintenance amount and the additional charges associated with these transactions would then constitute the price that is charged to the customer.

It is important to note that the foundation of the modern system of banking relies on consumers depositing funds into financial instruments such as savings and checking accounts. This is because the deposited funds are subsequently used by the bank to issue loans. The bank is then able to realize interest earnings from these lending activities, which are in essence funded by the customers' own deposits. Therefore, an alternative approach to transaction-based pricing is to encourage customers to place large amounts of funds into their accounts in return for free banking services. This is the basis for the second approach to pricing savings products. For example, the bank might price its account services such that, as long as customers maintain a minimum balance, no fees would be charged for banking transactions and services. The minimum account balance provides the bank with the supply of funds that it needs in order to conduct its lending activities. The interest earned on these activities is what replaces the revenues that would have otherwise been earned though a transaction-based price.

To demonstrate how the two approaches to pricing savings products might work, imagine the following scenario: A commercial bank offers "free" banking services in which customers are required to maintain a minimum balance of $2,000 in their bank account. In return, the bank will provide all its account services for free to the customer. The bank is able to earn a 10% annual rate of return by lending the deposited funds to loan seekers. It has in essence earned 10% of the $2,000, or $200 a year, in the process. This amount is the minimum interest earnings, as some customers may choose to maintain balances in excess of the $2,000 minimum requirement. The $200 earnings would be the equivalent of charging customers a monthly fee of approximately $17 but not requiring them to maintain any minimum balances.

The minimum balance approach to pricing savings products has an intrinsic appeal among consumers. The term "free" associated with this pricing approach is considered to be one of the strongest terms in advertising and consumer communications. Commercial banks heavily utilize "free checking" offers as a mechanism to draw consumers into their branches.[12] However, a survey of bank administrators showed that in only 5% of cases in which free checking is offered, do banks make profits. In fact, the free checking approach is primarily used as part of a broader customer acquisition strategy by banks with the underlying philosophy that it will facilitate new customer acquisitions, and the eventual cross-selling of other financial services that the banks offer to these new customers. Therefore, by acquiring a new customer the bank may not necessarily profit from offering free banking services, but it may be able to sell much more profitable products such as insurance and investment services to the newly acquired customers. It is also important to note that the notion of free banking may be somewhat inaccurate. The terms and conditions that make a bank account free might be quite restrictive. For example, restrictions might exist on the number of checks written, access to customer service on the phone, and a requirement that direct payroll deposits into the accounts be made on a regular basis. Furthermore, customers may not recognize that they are indirectly paying for the service through the lost interest earnings on their balances.

From the bank's perspective, there are also risks associated with a minimum balance pricing approach because the interest earnings are a function of the interest rates. The interest revenues that the bank is able to earn through its lending activities on the deposited funds could deplete in a declining interest rate environment. Such a concern would not exist in a transaction-based pricing approach in which the customers' payment of fees based on their transaction volume is predictable and relatively risk-free.[13]

C. Pricing Brokerage and Investment Services

The pricing of services provided by brokers and investment houses for the sale of financial products and securities can be customized at the individual customer level or set as a fixed price applicable to all customers. Often, prices are assessed based on the unique needs of individual clients, the total amount of assets being managed, and even at times negotiated on an individual basis. Brokers, whose job is to facilitate the trading of securities for customers, have a multitude of approaches available to them for earning income. One approach is to charge trading fees for the purchase and sale of securities on behalf of a client. Trading fees might be flat regardless of the dollar amount of securities traded, or they may be based on a percentage of amounts traded. The brokerage business is divided into two general categories called full-commission brokers (FCBs) and discount brokers. FCBs generally charge higher prices for their services, but also provide financial advice and portfolio planning services to their clients. A full-commission broker may charge clients based on a percentage of total assets managed, charge a fixed yearly fee, or charge a fee which is a combination of the two. Discount brokers, on the other hand, typically do not provide advisory services, and pass on the task of determining an optimal portfolio of investments to the client. As a result, prices charged by discount brokers are often significantly lower than those charged by full-commission brokers, and discount brokers tend to rely more on securities trading fees.

Another commonly used investment product is the mutual fund, which is often managed by a professional fund management firm. Shares are sold to the public in a similar way to how shares of stocks are sold on the securities exchanges. Fund shares could be sold directly by the company itself or, as in most cases, sold through third parties. The price paid for a mutual fund share is the net asset value (NAV) as determined by the stock market value of the portfolio of stocks included in the fund at any given point in time. However, in addition to the NAV, mutual funds may have additional expenses associated with them. For example, a customer may be charged an upfront fee simply to purchase shares of the mutual fund (these are typically called "class A" shares). In addition, the customer may be required to hold those shares for a minimum length of time; selling the shares prior to that time may be associated with early withdrawal penalties ("class B" shares). The fund may also charge asset management fees, which are typically applied as a percentage of the NAV. If third parties are involved in facilitating the sale of mutual fund shares, they may also charge additional commissions and fees.

Conflicts of interest are often a concern in the pricing of brokerage and investment services. A significant proportion of a broker's earnings may be linked to the number of trades conducted by clients. Therefore, brokers may have an underlying incentive to encourage their clients to carry out a high number of securities trades. The technical term for this practice is *churning*. These trades may or may not be in the best interest of the client, but they can represent a significant source of revenue for the broker. Similarly, mutual funds may have commissions associated with them, and a broker may encourage a client to purchase shares of a particular mutual fund, not necessarily because of highly expected performance for the fund, but rather because of the high commissions associated with the sale of the mutual fund shares. In fact, some mutual fund companies that sell their funds through third parties may provide quotas and incentives for the sale of a minimal number of shares—a practice that is likely to bias the supposedly objective advice that clients should be receiving.[14]

D. Pricing Insurance Products

The pricing of insurance is one of the more elaborate forms of pricing in financial services. In order to determine the correct price of an insurance policy, one would have to have an accurate estimate of the probability of the event being insured. These probabilities are often captured in what is referred to as *actuarial tables*, which report the probability that an event will take place based on a series of predictors. For example, with the life insurance, mortality tables report the probability of an individual dying given the person's age, gender, smoking habits, and other factors that relate to the risk of death. An additional variable, that needs to be taken into account when pricing insurance, is the estimated cost of claims. For example, in term life insurance, the claim amount would be the total amount of life insurance coverage purchased, which is reflected in the face value of the insurance policy. In automobile insurance, one could utilize the average claim costs for the various types of events (e.g., collision, theft, vandalism) as a basis of analysis.

To demonstrate the procedure used for the pricing of an insurance policy, imagine a life insurance company that anticipates selling a $100,000 term life insurance product for 30-year-old males to 10,000 individuals. Based on the mortality tables for individuals in this age bracket[15], of these 10,000 policyholders 17 are estimated to die during the next year. Since the policies that are being sold have a $100,000 coverage, that means the beneficiaries of the 17 people, would receive 17 × $100,000 or $1.7 million. As a minimum, the premiums paid in that one-year time period by the 10,000 policyholders should cover this amount in order for the company to break even. That means that the average yearly premium should be $1.7 million divided by 10,000, which is $170 a year. This is the minimum price that the insurance company should charge simply to break even (assuming no marketing or administrative costs). When considering the additional risks that the company is undertaking and the profits that its shareholders might demand, a higher price could easily be justified. Cost-based, parity-based, or value-based pricing can then be used to determine what the end price should be.

The profits generated from the sale of insurance products, as reflected in the excess of premiums collected over losses paid out for claims is referred to as *underwriting profits*. However, insurance companies can realize additional profits beyond this simple activity-based source of profit. According to insurance regulations, insurance companies are required to hold portions of the premiums that are paid by policyholders in reserves. These reserves are in place in order to ensure that sufficient funds are available in case policyholders make a large number of claims. The interest earned on these reserves by the insurance company creates additional investment profits for the insurer. When determining prices and the resulting profits, investment profits must be also taken into account, as it may allow for a greater degree of flexibility in pricing, often in the form of lower more competitive prices. This helps explain some of the interest rate sensitivity experienced in insurance prices over the years. When interest rates are low, the interest earned on investments by an insurer are low, and insurance companies tend to compensate for the shortfall by raising premiums. The opposite tends to be true when interest rates are high.

In determining the final price of an insurance policy, several other factors play a significant role. The intrinsic risk associated with a policyholder is always a determinant of the policyholder's premiums. In the case of life insurance policies, it is known that the male death rate is higher than the female death rate; as a result, the premiums charged for males are typically slightly higher than that of females. Similarly, the health background of the individual, health history of the family, and unhealthy habits such as smoking and drinking represent risks to the insurance company. In addition, high risk activities such as skydiving, riding motorcycles, or scuba diving increase the risk of death and are often inquired about at the time of applying for life insurance. These risk factors may then be translated into higher premiums charged to policyholders.

The distinction between life insurance and property and casualty ("P&C") insurance is also important to recognize in pricing. Due to the availability of mortality tables, which predict a person's likelihood of death in a one-year time period, the outcomes of providing life insurance policies to a large group of individuals are predictable. Unless the life insurance applicants have not been truthful about their health background or risky behavior, or have suicidal tendencies, the expected amount of insurance policy payouts is relatively predictable. Background checks on applicants by insurance companies, investigators, and medical checkups are in place to ensure this. Property and casualty insurance claim probabilities, on the other hand, are less accurately predictable. The amount of damage in claims resulting from a car accident can be highly variable. An automobile accident might be associated with minor costs to fix a minor fender-bender, to catastrophic expenses related to the replacement of multiple vehicles, mounting medical bills, and related law suits. This is further compounded by the insurance company's liability for property and casualty coverage that it had sold a policyholder years after the accident. For example, if the policyholder or others involved in an accident had been injured in a car accident but the injury was recognized several years after the end of the policy, the policyholder's insurance company may still be liable for the related medical expenses. This is not the case for term life insurance policies, in which the end of the policy also typically represents the end of any legal obligations that the insurance company has towards a policyholder or the beneficiaries.

The higher level of uncertainty associated with property and casualty insurance not only makes it a more difficult task to price insurance products, but it also may justify charging higher rates since the company may have to bear additional levels of risk and uncertainty in its property and casualty insurance product offerings. What is also important to note is that prices for insurance products can be further adjusted based on perceptual factors that influence the consumer. For example, the well-recognized name of an established insurance company may justify for consumers additional premiums that could be charged. When pricing insurance products, the full line of the company's financial products and services may need to be taken into consideration, and opportunities for cross-selling may justify pricing products at attractive levels to help expand the appeal to the customer base. It is also important to note that the opposite end of the price spectrum, where excessively high insurance rates are charged, at times result in regulators interfering in the pricing process. For example, if it is established that insurance companies are realizing excessive profits in a particular state or are systematically over-charging policyholders, state insurance regulators may mandate rebate checks to be issued to policyholders and require the lowering of insurance rates for new policies and policy renewals.

STRATEGIC CONSIDERATIONS IN PRICING

In determining the price of a financial service, several strategic and tactical issues need to be taken into consideration. The long-term strategic framework of the service, as well as short-term profit and customer acquisition tactics that may be required can influence the final determination of price. Some of these considerations will be discussed below.

The Demand Function

Perhaps the most important consideration in setting prices in any market is the shape of the demand function. The demand function shows the relationship that might exist between price and sales volume. The techniques used to determine the shape of the demand function are beyond the scope of this book. However, as a minimum, a financial services marketer responsible for setting prices needs to have an approximate estimate of what the impact of a price change would be on sales volume. This estimate is often based on managerial judgment but may also be validated by formal market research techniques and test marketing, some of which will be discussed in Chapter 7.

For example, the marketing manager in charge of the sales of supplemental health insurance policies might recognize that a 10% reduction in premiums would result in a 35% jump in the number of new policies sold. It is therefore essential to estimate the net financial impact of such a price change on profits. In doing so, one would have to estimate the revised profit margins associated with new policies as well as the lost revenues from existing policyholders upon renewal at the lower premium levels. This numeric exercise is essential because profit maximization is only possible if an accurate assessment is made of the financial effects of such price changes. Readers are encouraged to consult a pricing textbook for the various methods used to determine consumer demand.

Price Complexity

An additional tactical pricing concern discussed earlier in this chapter is that financial services prices are intrinsically complex and multidimensional. As a result, consumers may have a difficult time determining what the exact price is that they are actually paying. For example, credit card companies charge customers interest for balances carried over from one month to the next. However, they can also realize revenues by charging transaction fees, late payment penalties, fees on ATM cash withdrawals, and other forms of non-interest charges. While the customer may pay attention primarily to the interest rate associated with the credit card, the remaining dimensions of the credit card might have a much greater financial impact on the customer as well as the credit card company's profits. Exercising price increases using the non-interest dimensions of the credit card has the tactical advantage of not attracting a high level of consumer attention because consumers may not be in tune with what the exact non-interest charge amounts are. This approach also allows a financial services provider to exercise price reductions without directly challenging competitors' prices by focusing away from the typical dimension of interest rates used by the industry to communicate and benchmark prices. While such an approach can help reduce the likelihood of price wars, it is important to note, however that in the context of price increases focused on non-interest components of price, the practice can be highly problematic from a consumer protection perspective. The fact that consumers may not be fully aware of the various pricing components through which they pay for a financial service not only raises ethical concerns, but has also become a focus of regulators in recent years.[16]

Promotional Pricing

Many financial services organizations provide promotions that in one way or another, find their way into the pricing of their services. For example, an investment company might offer customers who invest a minimum amount of funds a lump-sum dollar rebate. Alternatively, a bank might offer new customers small home appliances in return for opening new accounts with a minimum amount of deposits. Another promotional tactic practiced by life insurance companies is to provide customers with an introductory period of free coverage. Such a promotional offer may entice customers to sign for life insurance, and the insurance company would hope that some of these consumers would choose to continue their coverage by paying for the life insurance coverage following the free trial period.

Several advantages can be associated with promotional pricing. Promotional pricing generates a sense of connection and excitement about financial services which may otherwise be considered dry and boring by customers. In that sense, it is able to elevate consumer involvement and generate excitement for relatively uninteresting products. Promotional pricing also has the potential of being highly relevant to consumers with specific needs. This would require that the financial services organization conduct the necessary market research and segmentation studies in order to establish which promotional offers should be extended to which customers. A good match between a customer's needs and the promotional offer is likely to significantly increase the probability of sales. Therefore, data mining and segmentation techniques might prove to be highly effective tools in this context. The primary disadvantage of promotional pricing is that it may be difficult to determine and match each consumer to a relevant promotional program. In addition, from a strategic perspective, promotional pricing may attract customers who are price sensitive and deal-prone. These customers may not necessarily intend to develop a long-term relationship with the financial services provider and may not be highly profitable prospects for acquisition.

Environmental Forces Influencing Pricing

Several environmental considerations that are likely to influence the future of pricing in financial services also need to be taken into account. The first is the significant impact that the Internet has had on the price search behavior of consumers. The Internet has made the process of looking for the lowest priced financial services provider easier for consumers, and it has also made detailed product information readily available to the masses. For example, it is estimated that seven out of every ten homebuyers search the Internet for mortgage rates.[17] Similarly, the Internet is now beginning to facilitate price shopping in other categories of financial services such as property and casualty insurance, term life insurance, and commercial banking services. In addition, information available through the Internet is beginning to enable consumers to have a better assessment of the quality of financial services providers. For example, the Insurance Departments in most states often post the complaint rates that are associated with insurance companies operating in their state, on the Internet. Access to such information would allow consumers to have a more accurate assessment of the quality of an insurance company, and influence their reactions to the prices of the insurance policies offered in the marketplace.

In addition to the Internet, new technologies are reducing the costs associated with financial services transactions. Online banking and the use of ATMs for conducting transactions, that only a few years ago would be done by bank tellers, have resulted in monumental drops in the costs associated with commercial banking transactions. This has allowed commercial banks to realize much more attractive cost structures and has given them increased pricing flexibility so that transaction costs no longer create a restrictive lower-bound to prices. The increased flexibility has enabled banks to exercise higher levels of price competition within their local and regional markets. This trend is witnessed in the context of free online banking, which has been heavily promoted by the majority of commercial banks in recent years.

The lowered cost of transactions driven by new technologies may result in such drops in prices that price wars and margin depletion may become a real threat to the industry's financial future. Offshore outsourcing has also contributed to cost savings for many financial services organizations. Many labor-intensive low-technology operations, which were typically delegated to "back-office" operations in banks, have over the years been passed on to offshore facilities that conduct those operations in far more cost-effective ways. Offshore outsourced customer service call centers are an effective resource for many financial services organizations, some of which also conduct outbound telemarketing sales calls using these offshore facilities.[18] The improved cost structure associated with these practices has increased financial services providers' price flexibility greatly, and is likely to result in a higher level of price competition in the coming years.

An additional source of cost reductions has been large-scale consolidations and mergers that have taken place since industry deregulation in the late 1990s. In the past two decades, there has been a nearly 50% drop in the number of commercial banks and deposit-taking financial institutions operating in the United States. Consolidations and mergers have resulted in a smaller number of institutions, each managing a larger customer base. The result is that the larger consolidated financial services organizations are able to achieve economies of scale by serving a larger number of customers through existing infrastructures. This has resulted in cost savings by lowering the average per-customer transaction cost.

CHAPTER QUESTIONS

1. What are some of the differences that need to be considered in pricing life insurance as opposed to pricing property and casualty insurance?

2. Define the following terms:
   (a) Performance risk
   (b) Interest rate risk
   (c) Churning
   (d) Actuarial tables
   (e) Underwriting profits

3. What are some limitations that apply to the use of cost-based pricing in financial services?

4. What are the various roles of price in the marketing of financial services?

5. What differentiates the pricing of financial services from other pricing contexts?

6. What specific pricing practices in financial services markets would you consider unethical, and why?

7. What creative promotional programs in financial services can you identify that have a potentially strong consumer appeal?

ENDNOTES

1 A. Rao, (2005), "The Quality of Price as a Quality Cue," *Journal of Marketing Research*, Vol. 42, Iss. 4, pp. 401-405; W. Dodds, K. Monroe and D. Grewal (1991), "Effects of Price, Brand, and Store Information on Buyer's Product Evaluations," *Journal of Marketing Research*, 28 (August), pp. 307-319; A. Miyazaki, D. Grewal, and R. Goodstein (2005), "The Effect of Multiple Extrinsic Cues on Quality Perceptions: A Matter of Consistency," *Journal of Consumer Research*, Vol. 32, Iss. 1, pp. 146-153.

2 H. Estelami and P. DeMaeyer (2010), "An Exploratory Study of Divided Pricing Effects on Financial Services Quality Expectations," *Journal of Financial Services Marketing*, Vol. 15, Iss. 2, pp. 19-31; H. Estelami (1999), "The Computational Effect of Price Endings in Multi-Dimensional Price Advertising," *Journal of Product and Brand Management*, Vol. 8, Iss. 3, pp. 244-253; Hitch, G. (1978), "The Role of Short-term Memory in Mental Arithmetic," *Cognitive Psychology*, 10, 302-323; G. Wolters, M. Beishuizen, G. Broers, and W. Knoppert (1990), "Mental Arithmetic Effects on Calculation Procedure and Problem Difficulty on Solution Latency," *Journal of Experimental Child Psychology*, Vol. 49, No 1, pp. 20-30; S. Dehaene (1992), "Varieties of Numerical Abilities," *Psychonomic Science*, Vol. 6, No. 2, pp. 71-92; M.H. Aschcraft (1992), "Cognitive Arithmetic: A Review of Data and Theory," *Cognition*, Vol. 44, August, pp. 75-106.

3 Tser-Yieth Chen, Pao-Long Chang, and Hong-Sheng Chang (2010), "Price, Brand Cues, and Banking Customer Value," *The International Journal of Bank Marketing*, Vol. 23, Iss. 2/3, pp. 273-291; Viggo Host and Michael Andersen

(2004), "Modeling Customer Satisfaction in Mortgage Credit Companies," *The International Journal of Bank Marketing,* Vol. 22, Iss. 1, pp. 26-34.

4 Hooman Estelami (2005), "A Cross-Category Examination of Consumer Price Awareness in Financial and Non-Financial Services," *Journal of Financial Services Marketing,* Vol. 10, Iss. 1, pp. 125-139.

5 T. Nagle, J. Hogan, and J. Zale (2010), *The Strategy and Tactics of Pricing.* Upper Saddle River, NJ: Prentice Hall ; Kent B. Monroe (2002), *Pricing: Making Profitable Decisions.* 3rd Edition, McGraw-Hill: New York.

6 The reported figures are approximate ranges and interested readers are encouraged to consult the following sources: G. Michael Moebs (1986), *Pricing Financial Services.* Dow Jones-Irwin: Homewood, IL, p. 84; *Fed Letter* (1997), Federal Reserve Bank of Kansas: Kansas City, KS; *Board of Governors of the Federal Reserve System* (2002). The Federal Reserve System: Purposes and Functions.

7 David Crook (2004), "If Your Credit Card Account is Closed, Your APR Jumps," *Wall Street Journal,* Oct 3, p. 4; Ruth Simon and Jennifer Saranow (2004), "Credit Cards Start to Bump Up Rates," *Wall Street Journal,* Oct 6, citing a report by BankRate.com

8 T. Nagle, J. Hogan, and J. Zale (2010), *The Strategy and Tactics of Pricing.* Upper Saddle River, NJ: Prentice Hall; Michael Zack (2003), "Rethinking the Knowledge-Based Organization," *Sloan Management Review,* Vol. 44, Iss. 4, pp. 67-74.

9 Kathy Chu (2009), "Seniors Get Break on Mortgage Fees," *Wall Street Journal,* April 20, p. D2.

10 Ruth Simon (2004), "Credit Card Fees Are Rising Faster – As Economies of Industry Change, Issuers Seek to Boost Income from Penalties," *Wall Street Journal,* March 31, p. D.1.

11 Kelley K. Spors (2010), "Credit Card Offers You Should Refuse," *Wall Street Journal,* Sep 26, p. 4; Kelley K. Spors (2004), "Beware of Credit Cards at College," *Wall Street Journal,* Sept 5, p. 3.

12 Lauren Bielski (2004), "Is Free Checking Worth It?," *ABA Banking Journal,* Vol. 96, Iss. 3, pp. 31-35.

13 See G. Michael Moebs (1986), *Pricing Financial Services.* Dow Jones-Irwin: Homewood, IL, pp. 94-113, for additional comparisons between the two approaches.

14 Paula Dwyer (2003), "Mutual Funds: Is Your Broker Ripping You Off?" *Business Week,* June 9, Iss. 3836, p. 114; Daisy Maxey (2004), "Monthly Mutual Funds Review, The Year of Living Scandalously," *Wall Street Journal,* Sept 3, p. R.1.

15 Christopher Oster (2008), "Good News! Insurers Extend Your Lifespan," *Wall Street Journal,* June 24, p. D1; Stuart Klugman (1991), *Bayesian Statistics in Actuarial Science.* Springer; G. Michael Moebs (1986), *Pricing Financial Services.* Dow Jones-Irwin: Homewood, IL, pp.

16 Ruth Simon (2004), "Fee Accounts Face Scrutiny By Regulators," *Wall Street Journal,* Oct 5, p. D.1; Christopher Oster (2004), "Life Insurers Charge Consumers More for Splitting Up Premiums," *Wall Street Journal,* Sep 15, p. D2; Kortney Stringer (2003), "The Weird Science of Getting a Car Rental Deal," *Wall Street Journal,* Dec 30, p. D1.

17 J. Ginovsky (2010),"Online Will be Customers' Chief Criterion," *ABA Banking Journal,* Vol 102, Iss. 10, p. 28; T.Mullaney (2004), "Real Estate's New Reality," *Business Week,* May 10, Iss. 3882, p. 88.

18 V. Yanamandram (2010), "Are Inertia and Calculative Commitment Distinct Constructs? An Empirical Study in the Financial Services Sector", *International Journal of Bank Marketing,* Vol. 28, Iss. 7, pp. 569-584; Manjit Kirpalani (2003), "The Rise of India," *Business Week* (2004), Dec. 8, Iss. 3861, p. 66-74; P. Davies (2004), *Offshore Outsourcing and the Global Services Solution.* Chicago: Nicholas Brealy International.

CHAPTER FIVE

Advertising

Advertising is a fundamental part of most successful marketing strategies in both financial and non-financial services. It is the primary mechanism by which marketers create awareness among consumers about their products and services. However, it has a special role in the marketing of financial services since financial services are generally intangible. The intangible nature of financial services stems from the fact that they cannot be touched, tasted, felt, or visualized. As a result, consumers' perceptions of quality are often based on the image associated with the company. This places the burden of informing consumers about the beneficial aspects of a financial service on the shoulders of the advertiser. While the quality of manufactured goods might be easily visible to the consumer through the observation of the product's physical features, the quality of financial services is a largely unobservable construct. The training and knowledge of a financial advisor, the transaction accuracy of a credit card company, or the financial strength of an insurance company are largely unknown measures to the masses. As a result, the financial services advertisers have to educate consumers on the unique and beneficial features of their services. Financial services advertising facilitates the differentiation of a company from its leading competitors. This is an especially important task when consumers may not possess the required background knowledge and product information to appreciate the merits and weaknesses of competing financial services. Advertising is one of the few ways to achieve differentiation in financial services.[1]

Advertising in financial services can be formally defined as marketing communications carried out through the mass media or direct marketing means, with the intention of motivating the purchase of specific financial products or encouraging particular forms of financial behavior. Various forms of media can be used to execute advertising campaigns. Broadcast media such as television and radio, as well as print media such as newspapers and magazines, are often used to execute advertising campaigns for financial services. In addition, a growing trend in financial services marketing involves using direct advertising methods such as direct mail and direct e-mail to elicit consumer responses. These methods create a sense of personalization and help generate leads for subsequent sales. In addition, advertising may not only have the objective of selling specific products, but it may also be used simply to encourage specific forms of financial behavior in consumers. For example, advertising may be used to increase public awareness of the needs for retirement planning and savings, or to encourage the purchase of insurance products to protect oneself against catastrophic financial losses.

In this chapter, we will first discuss the unique aspects of advertising in financial services, including the differences that exist between financial and non-financial services advertising. We will then examine several frameworks that help explain the function and effectiveness of advertising in financial services. The dynamics of executing advertising campaigns will then be discussed. The chapter will conclude with a discussion of the strategic and financial aspects of effective advertising in financial services markets.

UNIQUE ASPECTS OF ADVERTISING IN FINANCIAL SERVICES

Several factors differentiate the advertising process in financial services from advertising in other contexts or markets. Appreciating these distinctions is important in order to capitalize on the unique role that advertising can play in the successful marketing of financial services.[2]

(A) Vague Product/Service Attributes: One of the challenges in advertising financial services is that consumers may not be fully aware of the various dimensions that constitute a financial service. For example, while shopping for automobile insurance, consumers may be focused on the premiums and the brand names of the insurance companies. However, they may not fully understand the exclusion terms of the contract, which identify the circumstances under which the insurance company can choose *not* to provide insurance protection. Similarly, consumers faced with a choice between mortgages may focus on the interest rate and closing costs, but fail to consider the escrow account requirements of the mortgage contract, origination fees, and late and prepayment penalties associated with the mortgage. Consumers' limited knowledge and education about the choices facing them in the marketplace can result in inefficient and uncompetitive market conditions – a phenomenon often referred to as *market failure* by economists. As discussed in Chapter 2, consumers can only process about seven pieces of information at any one point in time. This limits their ability to fully understand the financial services presented to them in advertisements. Furthermore, research has shown that consumers' education on financial services is generally very poor. The academic curricula of most primary and secondary education systems fail to inform and educate the young on the fundamentals of financial decision making adequately, resulting in uninformed and often suboptimal decisions in consumers' purchases of financial

services.[3] The difficulty in understanding financial services offers is further compounded by the fact that financial services are generally uninteresting and unexciting. This makes the task of appreciating the differences among financial services more challenging for the average person. Advertising is one of the few ways to overcome this challenge because it may facilitate consumer education, and can help consumers understand the unique benefits of a financial service.

(B) Quality is Intangible: One of the other challenges facing financial services advertisers is the fact that the quality of financial services is rarely quantifiable. This may also be true for consumers who have already used a financial service as it is for those who are considering using it for the first time. For example, the claims payout behavior of an automobile insurance company is generally unknown to the majority of the company's customers. This is because, insurance companies operate through the sharing of risks across a large number of customers, and as a result most policyholders do not experience losses. It is the rare few that do who may have an accurate assessment of the payout behavior of the insurance company. Similarly, the long-term future returns of a mutual fund would be unknown for many years after the purchase of shares of the fund. It is the task of the financial services advertiser to create an understanding and appreciation for the underlying qualities of an advertised financial offer. In the context of an insurance company, statements about the efficiency of the claims processing procedures of the company or overall customer satisfaction, may accomplish this. In the case of a mutual fund, revealing the qualifications of the fund manager or the past performance of the fund may help convey the sense of quality that consumers may expect. Without advertising, these aspects of quality would be largely unknown to the masses.

(C) Unexciting Products: Financial services transactions typically are not carried out on a frequent basis, and generally do not create a great deal of excitement and interest for most individuals. For example, consumer involvement with the benefits of an insurance policy, the rates of return on an investment product, or the checking account services provided at a commercial bank rarely cause a great deal of excitement and enthusiasm. In addition, the quantitative and contractual nature of financial services requires considerable cognitive effort and mathematical processing before consumers can fully appreciate the merits of an advertised offer. This makes the process of advertising financial services more difficult since the audience will generally be uninvolved in absorbing and appreciating the presented information. Financial services are usually not associated with high levels of consumer involvement, excitement, symbolism, or emotions; in addition, they are more complex than consumer goods. The high level of complexity associated with financial services makes evoking positive emotional responses more challenging than it would be for consumer goods such as automobiles, clothing, or electronics.

(D) Limited Ability to Visually Communicate Financial Products: One of the unique

challenges in advertising financial products is the fact that they may not always be communicated to consumers in ways similar to how consumer goods are advertised. For example, an automobile manufacturer may feature pictures of a car in a magazine ad or footage of the car's handling abilities in a television advertisement. Similarly, fashion clothing, consumer electronics, home hardware, and even food products can be featured in advertisements using images and photographs. Visualization of these products increases the sensory input of the consumer and creates a sensation similar to the consumption of the product. This increases the cognitive and emotional impact that advertising generates in the consumer. Contrast this with a situation in which one attempts to advertise an insurance policy or an investment product. The challenge to the advertiser is to determine how to present and communicate visually such abstract and intangible products. The challenge is further compounded by the fact that, as discussed earlier, the quality of financial services is a largely elusive measure. The challenges in visual communication of financial services often require experienced, attentive, and creative development of ad content in order to excite the viewer about the useful aspects of the financial service.

(E) Regulations: The practice of financial services advertising is further complicated by the large number of regulations that restrict the contents of financial services advertisements, and the number of regulatory agencies that closely monitor and influence ad content. One of the primary objectives of regulations in financial services markets is to ensure that marketers do not present consumers with misleading information. From an advertiser's perspective, this objective translates into elaborate and complex sets of criteria that need to be met in order to attain regulatory compliance. Therefore, the advertiser's creative process may become restricted due to these regulations, and often requires the involvement of compliance specialists to oversee the content of a financial services advertisement. Regulatory bodies such as the Securities and Exchange Commission, the Federal Reserve, the Federal Trade Commission, as well individual states' regulators have a profound influence on the content of financial services ads, and possess considerable punitive powers to punish those who violate their regulatory requirements. Such restrictions and regulations are far less present in advertising other forms of services and goods, making the task of financial services advertising a highly unique specialization.

(F) Variable Prices: Another challenge in the advertising of financial services is the fact that price is often not a constant and varies as a function of each individual's unique circumstances. For example, the premiums for an automobile insurance policy would vary from one consumer to the next depending on age, driving history, and vehicle type. Similarly, the interest rates charged in credit arrangements such as consumer loans may vary as a function of the applicant's credit history and credit score. This complicates the process of featuring prices in financial services advertising far more than in other contexts. For example, while the sticker price of an automobile could be

easily advertised, the lease price may require the disclosure of specific consumer credit characteristics that need to be satisfied in order for the lease rate to be secured. The limitations in featuring price in financial services advertising reduce the diagnostic impact of financial services ads on consumer decisions, and constrain consumers' commitment in decision making.

FRAMEWORKS FOR FINANCIAL SERVICES ADVERTISING

There are various frameworks that can be used to describe successful advertising in financial services. In this chapter, four specific frameworks will be discussed. The first framework relates to the consumer's decision making process. Using this framework, one would examine how a consumer goes about recognizing the need for a specific financial service and the subsequent steps that the consumer would need to follow in order to identify and obtain access to the service. This framework allows one to identify the specific steps in the consumer's decision making process that require additional advertising effort in order to result in incremental sales. The second framework that will be presented relates to the communications process by which advertisers connect to the masses. Using this framework, one would dissect the steps that are taken by advertisers in order to attract consumers' attention and to create memorable advertisements. This framework can also be used to quantify the logistics of consumer communications and to identify steps in the advertising process that can help improve consumers' awareness of a financial service.

The third framework that will be discussed relates to the classification of consumers' motivations and needs when purchasing financial services. In this framework, the relationship between ad content and consumers' underlying motivations to seek financial services will be examined. The logic behind this framework is that the contents of an advertisement must relate to psychological and emotional forces that trigger purchases of specific financial services and products. The final framework that will be discussed relates to the execution style of the ad, which may include the use of humor, emotions, and other approaches to the delivery of ad content. The effectiveness of various ad execution styles and their relevance to particular types of financial services will be discussed using this framework.

It is important to note that there is no general consensus on which framework is the most valid to describe successful financial services advertising. The applicability of a given framework depends upon the specific financial service being marketed, market characteristics and the overall strategy of the company. In addition, practitioners in advertising view the characteristics of successful advertising differently, and generally do not converge on best practices. Therefore, it is critical to present a comprehensive perspective of the various frameworks that are commonly used to identify successful advertising practice in financial services.

Framework 1: The Consumer Decision Process

The consumer decision process, as discussed in Chapter 2 consists of several distinct steps. The first step in the process is *need recognition*, in which the consumer recognizes that there is a discrepancy between what is ideal and what is experienced.[4] Financial services advertisements that focus on the need recognition step attempt to create a sense of discrepancy between ideals and the consumer's actual experienced state. This can be accomplished by raising perceptions of what is considered ideal. For example, the ideal level of insurance coverage can be raised by informing consumers in an ad of the amount of financial protection needed in order to recover from economic losses resulting from an accident or mishap.

Reminding consumers of the unfavorable state of their existing insurance coverage can also highlight discrepancies between ideal and actual states. For example, a company selling term life insurance policies might present an advertisement that portrays the head of a household who has the responsibility of a mortgage and must also overlook the future of two dependant children but has no life insurance coverage to financially protect them. By doing so, the advertiser has created a sense of insecurity in the viewer by highlighting "what is" as opposed to "what should be," causing the viewer to recognize the necessity of having life insurance coverage. Similarly, a company selling supplemental health insurance might focus the advertisement on informing viewers of the financial needs that arise in case they are unable to work due to medical conditions or accidents. Supplemental health insurance policies often cover portions of expenses such as lost wages, health care bills not covered by insurers, and other related expenses that traditional insurance policies do not cover. However, consumers' lack of knowledge of this fact and the unique benefits of supplemental policies may be used as a primary focus of an advertisement in order to help them recognize their need for such coverage.

The second phase in the consumer decision process, which was discussed in detail in Chapter 2, is *information search*. In this phase, consumers who have recognized their need for a particular financial service begin to gather relevant information about various competitors in the marketplace. A financial services advertisement targeted to consumers in this phase would need to focus on creating memorable messages that consumers would be able to recall in subsequent phases of the decision process. Brand names that are memorable, advertising content that is unique, and ad messages that have a long-lasting impact on the consumer's mind would characterize successful advertising in this phase of the decision process.

Pre-purchase evaluation is the next phase in the consumer decision process. It consists of an elaborate process in which consumers evaluate the various alternatives available to them in the marketplace and, based on the attributes that the alternatives possess, form a judgment as to which one represents the best option. Financial services advertising that focuses on this phase of the decision process would attempt to create uniquely beneficial perceptions of the product or service being advertised. Attributes that market research would have established to be the most relevant in the consumer's mind would typically be used as a basis for differentiation. For example, an investment firm might highlight the individualized nature of the advice and support that it provides to its clients because it has empirically established this to be of primary importance to many of its investors.

The final steps in the consumer decision process are *purchase, consumption, and post-purchase evaluation.* To tap into the purchase and consumption phases of the decision process, advertising content could focus on creating trials for financial services such as insurance and warranty products. For example, a direct mail campaign could promote a three-month trial of an automobile roadside assistance insurance policy that would facilitate consumer consumption of the service. Following this trial period, a certain percentage of consumers who have found the peace of mind associated with having the service available to them would subsequently subscribe to the policy. In addition, the content of an advertisement might highlight the post-purchase impact of consumer decisions in a financial services context. The content may for example, include testimonials from customers who have had a good experience with the claims service of an insurance company, report customer satisfaction ratings, or highlight the many benefits available to clients of a particular financial services provider.

It is important to recognize that each of the steps in the decision process would be most relevant to specific types of financial services. If the average consumer generally does not recognize that he may need a particular type of financial service, advertising focused on the need recognition phase of the decision process would be required. On the other hand, if consumers are generally aware of their needs but do not know which competitors offer particular benefits, an advertising focus on information search and pre-purchase evaluations is needed. In such cases, advertising content should help differentiate one's offerings from those of competitors. It is also important to recognize that most financial services advertisements focus on the first three steps of the consumer decision process, during which initial preferences are formed.

Framework 2: The Communication Process

A second approach to characterizing financial services advertising is to dissect the process by which advertisers communicate to their target consumers. One may do this by identifying the stages that an advertiser must complete in order to attract the consumer's attention and to create positive memorable messages.[5] There are three general stages that need to be completed in order for this to take place:

1. Exposure: This stage consists of the presentation of an advertisement in the environment in which the consumer is present. Examples include billboard advertising displayed in a public area where the consumer is walking, a print ad that is included in a newspaper that the consumer is reading, or a commercial that is featured on a cable channel that the consumer might be watching. It is generally established that the average consumer is exposed to hundreds and by some estimates, thousands of commercial messages every day.[6] It is important, therefore, to recognize the difference between *environmental exposure*, and *cognitive exposure*. Environmental exposure occurs when an ad is present in the consumer's environment. While such a presence is a positive event for the advertiser, it does not guarantee that the consumer notices the advertisement. For example, despite being present on a street where the consumer is walking (environmental exposure) the consumer may fail to see the billboard. However, if the consumer's senses come into contact with the ad, *cognitive exposure* would result. Cognitive exposure represents the consumer's sensory processing of advertisements. Cognitive exposure is therefore a more difficult objective to achieve than environmental exposure, simply because of the massive number of ads consumers are exposed to regularly.

2. Attention: Formally, attention can be defined as the allocation of mental effort by the consumer to the advertised material.[7] In this phase, the consumer further processes information that has been presented in the advertisement. The consumer may decide to ignore some of the presented information or to dedicate additional mental effort to the contents. Therefore, a filtering process takes place during which ads that are considered irrelevant or uninteresting are quickly screened out. Success in this phase depends upon being able to direct the ads toward the appropriate target audience and developing ad content that is sufficiently interesting to motivate consumers to pay attention to the details of the advertised information.

3. Information Processing: Information processing is a complex phase in which the consumer allocates significant elaborative effort into conducting cognitive and diagnostic assessment of the information presented in the advertisement. The resulting elaboration often results in an assessment of the message being conveyed in the ad and an agreement or disagreement with the stated message. For example, the consumer may need to evaluate the statements made in an ad by a brokerage firm about its outstanding personalized attention to the client, or an insurance company's claims about its competitive rates. The consumer's analysis of these statements would then result in a general conclusion of agreement or disagreement with the claims being made. It is therefore important, especially in the context of financial services, that the claims made in an advertisement be convincing to the target audience and not considered exaggerated or superficial. The elaboration involved in this phase, as well as the repeated execution of the advertisement in the media, would help reinforce memorable messages that will subsequently influence consumer perceptions and decisions.

The framework of the communications process for advertising financial services provides a powerful diagnostic tool. It helps a financial services advertiser determine the bottlenecks that may limit consumers' ability to remember the advertised message. Each of the phases of the communications process is associated with specific probabilities that reflect the likelihood that a consumer will complete that particular phase of the process. As stated earlier, consumers are exposed to hundreds, if not thousands, of commercial messages on a daily basis. As a result, the likelihood of any one message receiving notable levels of cognitive exposure is very low. Similarly, consumers may be exposed to a large number of advertisements, but choose to ignore most of them. Even when an ad is not ignored, the chances of the consumer processing the presented information, agreeing with the statements being made, and remembering the ad, such that it would affect subsequent decisions, are less than certain.

Understanding where in this process the probabilities drop helps a financial services advertiser recognize areas where additional advertising effort is needed. For example, if exposure is the primary bottleneck in the process, additional advertising effort such as increased print ad placements or more frequent radio or cable TV spots might be needed. On the other hand, if consumers fail to pay significant attention to the ad, the advertising style and method of execution might need to be changed in order to create catchier ads. If consumers do not remember the advertisement, creating more memorable ads, perhaps by using humor or emotions, might be helpful. Understanding which of these steps needs to be fine-tuned is an empirical task that would require conducting formal market research such as focus groups and consumer surveys.

Framework 3: Hierarchy of Consumer Needs

Understanding the underlying motivations to consumers' purchases is a focus of psychological research and is the basis for the third framework for identifying successful financial services advertising strategies. Underlying human needs have been classified by psychologists into several distinct hierarchical categories that often motivate consumer action, including the purchase of goods and services. The hierarchy is often referred to as *Maslow's hierarchy of needs*, named after the psychologist who first conceived this approach to dissecting human motivation.[8] The first category of consumer needs relates to survival, as reflected by the human desire to protect oneself from dangers that threaten one's physical existence. In the classical definition of Maslow's hierarchy, this category of human needs relates to a desire to seek protection from *physical* danger posed by environmental forces. In the context of financial services, however, it relates to the basic notions of financial security and the ability to obtain access to financial resources needed to secure a minimal level of material existence. This motivation can be seen in consumers' desires to have the ability to obtain access to deposits made in a bank account when needed and to conduct daily transactions to purchase goods and services that are necessities for human existence. Advertisements that focus on this level of Maslow's hierarchy might for example feature insurance products that demonstrate how the product can protect the policyholder against catastrophic losses. Typically, these types of ads would portray consumers in a state of distress, reflecting the fundamental human desire for survival.

The next general level in Maslow's hierarchy relates to consumers' desires to gain acceptance and status within their social group. Advertisements that relate to this phase of consumer needs attempt to convey a sense of belonging. They give the impression that a product, or a financial service such as a lease that may facilitate the purchase of an automobile, would help the consumer become part of a social group or obtain an elevated status relative to others in the group. Financial services that relate most to this stage in Maslow's hierarchy are those that provide access to credit to facilitate the purchase of high-priced manufactured goods (for example, loans, leases, credit cards) or services related to asset growth and wealth accumulation (for example, brokerage and investment services).

The highest stage in Maslow's hierarchy relates to consumers' recognition of their own roles and responsibilities in life. This is reflected in an individual's beliefs surrounding life values, family, religion, and the possible preservation of these values for future generations. In this phase, consumers' consumption decisions reflect the development of their self-identity. Financial services that best relate to this phase are those that facilitate asset growth, financial planning, and even specific categories of mutual funds that are guided by social responsibility themes. Ads in this category may highlight the long-term benefits of an investment service not only to the client, but also to the client's offspring and future generations.

Framework 4: Ad Execution Style

Successful advertising can capitalize on a variety of execution styles. We will examine three execution styles commonly used in financial services advertising: Humor, rational arguments, and emotional advertising.

1. Humor: This is the style most fitting to mass-marketed financial services such as automobile insurance, mortgages, commercial banking, and credit cards. Humor has the advantage of attracting consumer attention while conveying the unique benefits of the product in an exciting and attracting form. This is especially important in view of the fact that financial services are generally unexciting and uninteresting for most consumers. For example, the automobile insurer GEICO has consistently over the years utilized humor as its primary ad execution style. GEICO's approach to advertising through humor has not only had a positive impact on sales, but has also helped differentiate the company from competitors. Some of GEICO's ads have also resulted in numerous advertising awards being given to the ad campaigns.[9]

While humorous advertising works well with commoditized categories of financial services such as property and casualty insurance and mortgages, it is not as effective with the more involved and complex categories of financial services such as investment planning, financial advisory services, and life insurance. The major drawback of the use of humor in financial services advertising is that the humor itself might become the primary focus of the consumer's attention. Unless the advertiser carries out considerable repetitions of the ad, consumers may fail to pay sufficient attention to the name or identity of the financial services provider that is being advertised. Therefore, while they may remember the ad and the humorous situation that was communicated, they may fail to remember the company name or the specific financial product that was advertised.[10]

2. Logical Arguments: Logic can be an effective way to promote specific financial services that may require elaborate consumer evaluations.[11] Ads that utilize this approach are especially effective in the pre-purchase evaluation phase of the consumer decision process. Two examples of this form of advertising are a financial services provider that communicates the tax benefits of its investment products and an insurance company that conveys the many supplemental benefits that it provides its customers to surpass those offered by the competitors. The logical and rational nature of financial services makes this an attractive approach to advertising specific types of products and services. This approach is especially well-suited for products that require calculated consumer thought such as investment and brokerage services, home mortgages, and property and casualty insurance.

3. Affective Impact: Certain categories of financial services may be attributed to specific affective or emotional states in consumers' minds and relate to driving psychological motivations in purchase decisions.[12] For example, life insurance, which is intended to protect a policyholder's dependants in case of the policyholder's death, is often associated with powerful emotions and a sense of concern about the future of the beneficiaries. Similarly, a college savings plan, which provides for the education of one's children, is an emotionally relevant financial product as it may help determine the future of the next generation. Emotions can therefore serve as a potentially strong force for advertising such financial products. Financial services that may utilize emotions in their advertising include insurance, retirement planning, and college funds.

ADVERTISING BASICS

In this section, we will review the fundamentals of the advertising process. The dynamics by which advertising influences sales will be examined, and the methods used for measuring the impact of advertising on sales, will also be discussed.

Advertising Execution

Three measures are used to describe how advertising campaigns are carried out. The first characteristic is *reach,* and it reflects the number or proportion of target consumers who will be exposed to the ad campaign at least once. The higher the reach, the larger the group of consumers exposed. The second measure used to characterize an ad campaign is referred to as *frequency*, which reflects the number of times that the average person is exposed to the ad campaign. The higher the frequency, the more often the audience is exposed to the same ad content. Finally, the *Gross Rating Point* (GRP) is the product of reach and frequency. The higher the GRP, the more impact the advertising campaign is likely to have. Advertising campaigns are typically planned based on gross rating points.

One of the measures that is used to quantify and price the reach component of an ad campaign is "cost per thousand" also referred to as CPM. This figure estimates the dollar amount of advertising expenditure that is needed in order to reach a thousand consumers using a particular medium. Typically, print media such as newspapers have lower CPM costs than broadcast media such as cable TV. This is largely due to the relative impact that the medium might have on the consumers' sensory inputs and the resulting sales effects of exposure to the advertisement.

When determining the optimal advertising strategy, it is important to establish the nature of the relationship between advertising and sales. This is usually reflected in what is referred to as the *advertising response function*, which plots the relationship between ad frequency and resulting sales. Exhibit 5.1 shows several possible examples of what an advertising response function could look like. An advertising response function such as the one shown in curve A reflects a scenario in which small amounts of advertising will influence the consumer greatly; however, the effect will plateau and have no significant incremental impact beyond a certain point. In contrast, curve B shows a scenario in which advertising may not have much impact until a minimum threshold is reached; beyond that point, the impact of advertising will grow, and every additional dollar spent on advertising is associated with a significant rise in sales. Similarly, curve

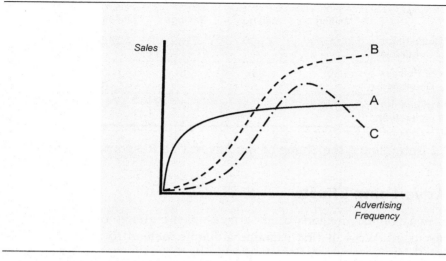

Exhibit 5.1: The Advertising Response Function

C not only demonstrates a lower-bound threshold effect, but it also shows a diminishing effect at frequency levels beyond an upper threshold. This effect might reflect consumers' disinterest and possible repulsion resulting from excessive exposure to a particular advertising message, and suggests that high levels of advertising must be avoided.

The strategic importance of the advertising response function is that it helps identify the optimal level of advertising expenditure. In scenario A, it is clear that advertising beyond a certain frequency level will not generate significant incremental sales. Therefore, incremental advertising expenditures should not be undertaken beyond the threshold point. In scenarios B and C, however, a minimum threshold amount of advertising must be reached before any notable effects on sales are observed. In scenario C, the diminishing effects of advertising at the higher frequency levels highlights the importance of cutting back on excessive advertising effort, not only to save on costs, but also to preserve consumer sentiment towards the advertised product or service. Advertising beyond the upper threshold in scenario C is not only wasteful, but also potentially damaging to the product or company being advertised.

It is also important to recognize that the shape of the advertising response function might significantly vary from one competitor to another. Furthermore, advertisers need to be able to contrast various ad execution strategies and identify ads that are most effective in the marketplace. Formal market research is often needed to achieve both these objectives, and an overview of some of the techniques used will be discussed below.

	One Mailing	Two Mailings	Three Mailings	Four Mailings	Five Mailings
Number of Households Contacted	3,000	2,500	3,250	2,800	3,200
Number of Policies Generated	30	28	78	112	118
Response Rate (# of policies divided by # contacted)	1.0%	1.1%	2.4%	4.0%	3.8%

Exhibit 5.2 Determining the Shape of the Advertising Response Function

Measuring Advertising Effects

In this section, two popular methods used to measure the effects of advertising on sales will be discussed. We will first examine a simple method for determining the shape of the advertising response function. As discussed above, knowing the shape of the advertising response function is critical in order to optimize advertising expenditures. We will then examine a method to determine the relative performance of different executions of an advertisement. Both approaches are commonly used in financial services advertising. However, their proper execution requires a basic understanding of statistics and market research techniques, which is beyond the scope of this book. Interested readers are therefore encouraged to consult an advertising or marketing research textbook for additional technical details related to these methods.[13]

(A) Determining the Shape of the Advertising Response Function: Research techniques using test markets and controlled experiments are often applied in order to determine the shape of the advertising response function. Exhibit 5.2 shows an example of how such a test market may be conducted. The table reports the results of a test market that has examined consumer responses to different levels of direct mail frequencies. A list of over 10,000 households was randomly split into five different groups, as can be seen in Exhibit 5.5. Each group received mailings at a different level of frequency. Subsequently, the number of newly generated policies was calculated for each of the five groups. The results are reflected in the response rate associated with each level of mailings. The response rates provide a picture of the advertising response function, which in this case relates new policy generation (sales) to advertising effort (frequency of mailings).

As can be seen from the table, there is no notable increase in sales response when moving from a single exposure to two exposures. The doubling of the costs associated with this move cannot be justified by a sales increase. However, moving to three exposures causes a significant increase in sales. This increase seems to continue until four exposures have been reached, but plateaus beyond that point. Knowledge of this pattern of response is extremely helpful for determining when to spend more or less money on advertising. As shown in the table, it seems that spending on advertising in order to achieve an exposure level of two is sub-optimal because a single exposure could achieve similar results. Similarly, five exposures have less of an effect than four exposures, suggesting diminishing effects of advertising.

(B) Comparing the Efficacy of Different Advertisements: One of the challenges in developing an effective advertising strategy is to establish which of the various executions of an advertising campaign will have the greatest impact on consumers. This task is largely an empirical undertaking carried out using formal market testing. For example, different groups of consumers can be presented with different versions of an ad. Their responses can then be recorded for statistical analysis, which would then establish the most effective version. This can be achieved by utilizing focus groups in which different groups of consumers are exposed to different ads or by using test markets in which different test cities are used to run different versions of the ad.

For example, using two focus groups, each exposed to a different ad, consumer responses in each group can be captured by administering a questionnaire and obtaining preference ratings for the ads on a 1-to-5 scale (with for example, 1 being "dislike the ad very much" and 5 being "like the ad very much"). The average rating for each group can then be produced, and statistical tests for establishing differences in averages between the two groups could be applied to establish which of the two ads is most favored by consumers. In the context of two test cities that run two different versions of an advertisement, the number of new policies that are generated could be tracked, or the dollar volume of policy sales following the ad campaign could be recorded for subsequent analysis. Statistical tests should also be carried out to establish if the differences observed between the two test cities are simply a result of noise or if they reflect underlying differences resulting from the execution of two different ads. Readers are encouraged to consult a text on statistics for the related technical details on the necessary statistical tests.

SUCCESS FACTORS IN FINANCIAL SERVICES ADVERTISING

Several factors influence successful advertising in financial services. In this section, we will discuss some of these factors. In assessing the quality of an advertising campaign, one may use the factors outlined below as a checklist to diagnose potential areas for improvement.

1. Having a Unique Selling Proposition: A fundamental requirement for advertising financial services is to possess a *unique selling proposition*. A unique selling proposition reflects the one attribute that a financial services provider must possess that makes it uniquely superior to its competitors. Not possessing a unique selling proposition implies that there is no basis for differentiation between one's offering and other choices that the consumer might have. In financial services advertising, identifying the unique selling proposition is even more critical than in other contexts because the amount of time that a consumer will commit to paying attention to an advertisement is generally limited to a few seconds, and the products being advertised are often quite complex. As a result, the advertiser must make the unique selling proposition a fundamental feature of the ad's execution objectives.

For example, GEICO features cost savings as a consistent unique selling proposition throughout most of its advertising campaigns. The typical GEICO ad would feature the unique selling proposition of GEICO by stating that a simple call to GEICO could result in significant savings on car insurance premiums. Metropolitan Life on the other hand, for many years focused on the payout behavior of the company's insurance product as its unique selling proposition as reflected by the *"Get Met, it pays"* slogan. Similarly, Allstate Insurance's unique selling proposition is the integrity and accessibility of its agents, as reflected by the *"You are in good hands"* message often included in its ads. Not having a unique selling proposition makes the task of producing convincing advertising campaigns a challenging and often expensive one. It is therefore essential that financial services advertisers expend sufficient effort in understanding the underlying attributes and unique benefits of the financial products and services for which they're advertising.

2. Target Marketing: Successful financial services advertising requires that the financial services being promoted are relevant to the targeted groups of consumers. While this is true of all advertising, it is especially true in financial services marketing since consumer needs in financial services significantly vary from one consumer to the next. Furthermore, the abundant availability of data on consumers and access to segmentation tools make accurate target marketing possible. However, a mismatch between the financial service being advertised and the target audience could result in a complete loss of advertising effectiveness. For example, selling homeowners insurance policies to college students, most of whom may not yet own homes, promoting high-end investment products to low-income families, and advertising a home warranty product to renters would be highly ineffective uses of advertising dollars driven by a total lack of appreciation for the needs of the ad's target audience. In contrast, advertisements selling term life insurance policies to new parents and automobile insurance to drivers whose policies are about to expire are wise target-based applications of advertising in financial services.

3. Creating Memorable Ads: Successful advertising often requires the completion of all phases of the communication process – exposure, attention, processing – as discussed earlier in this chapter. However, the creation of a memorable advertising message is critical to generating a long-term impact. Memorable ads might be recalled years after the consumer has been exposed to them, with subsequent effects on sales. This can be achieved through creative execution of advertising, use of humor or emotions, and a carefully planned schedule of media exposures. It has been established that, when purchasing advertising time and frequency, a minimum frequency level of three exposures is necessary for creating memorable messages.[14] In addition, use of memorable brand names, celebrities, and creative jingles can help improve consumers' recall of the ad. Maintaining a consistent ad execution style and focusing on a single unique selling proposition throughout the ad campaign further enhance consumer memory and the long-term effects of an ad campaign.

4. Facilitating Consumer Action: The fact that financial services are often individually customized to specific consumer needs, and typically require one-on-one contact in order to be sold means that advertisers should facilitate the process for consumers to contact the financial services provider.[15] This may require the inclusion of toll free telephone numbers, web site addresses, instructions on how to obtain additional information, and the address of the nearest agent or retail location where the product or service could be obtained. Advertisements that do not provide this information may not be very effective, especially for financial services providers that have a low market share and lack a well-recognized brand name or large scale presence in the retail environment.

5. Coordinated Use of Media: A successful advertising strategy used in a variety of markets is referred to as *coordinated media campaigns*. This involves the simultaneous use of various media to display ads with similar messages. For example, a TV ad featuring a celebrity might be combined with mobile device advertising embedded in mobile apps. Targeting consumers through various forms of media with the same message significantly improves the impact of the advertising campaign. For example, a $300,000 television advertising campaign for an insurance policy may result in 200 new policies. In contrast, a coordinated media campaign might be achieved by reducing the TV advertising budget to $200,000 and utilizing the remaining $100,000 in mobile advertising, resulting in 250 new policies. The incremental policies generated (50) are attributed to the reinforcing impact of the combined media, both of which contain the same underlying message. Clearly, such an effort would require careful targeting and coordination between the different types of media options used.

6. Use of Direct Marketing: Financial services advertising has recently become more reliant on the use of direct marketing techniques, reflected in an array of activities such as advertising on mobile devices, Internet banner advertising, direct mail, direct e-mail, direct response advertising and telemarketing. These forms of advertising are uniquely capable of initiating personal communications between the financial services provider and potential or existing customers. Direct marketing serves multiple objectives: it helps facilitate contacts with consumers and may motivate them to take further action by requesting additional information related to the service being advertised. This may help to create a direct line of communications with the financial services provider. By doing so, direct marketing allows one to separate serious leads from the less likely prospects and to prioritize selling efforts. For certain types of financial services, in which customization and personalization of products are typical (for example, insurance, investment services, home mortgages), it is critical for direct marketing to be integrated with follow-up sales procedures in order to ensure maximum results.

Direct marketing presents several strategic advantages to financial services organizations. It enables one to communicate the details of certain financial services offers, which in some cases may be elaborate and complex. Furthermore, it is a form of advertising that is easily measurable. Direct marketing campaigns and associated promotional material often have tracking information that consumers communicate in their contacts with the company, providing objective measures of which advertisements have been most effective. This helps one gauge the response rate associated with various direct advertising materials that may have been sent out to consumers. It also helps quantify the financial benefits of different direct advertising approaches using the estimated response rates. Return on investment computations can then be carried out in order to determine the financial feasibility of a direct marketing campaign.

Direct marketing has been shown to be most effective with existing customers of financial institutions.[16] For example, consumers have a tendency to open direct mail envelopes received from financial services providers with whom they currently transact. Therefore, consumers with established relationships with a company typically exhibit response rates that are higher than those consumers with whom no prior relationships exist. From a strategic perspective, use of direct marketing is therefore most effective on current customers. Direct marketing techniques also enable the use of segmentation tools which will be discussed in Chapter 8, resulting in higher levels of precision and target marketing ability. This has proven to be especially true at times of industry consolidation. Mergers and acquisitions in the financial services sector facilitated by the Bank Modernization Act have over the years resulted in the formation of mega-databases, which consist of massive amounts of information on a large number of customers, increasing the efficiency of advertising efforts using direct marketing techniques.

One of the more popular forms of direct marketing has been direct mail.[17] The typical response rate for direct mail solicitations is quite small - often well below 0.5%.[18] This means that only 5 of every 1,000 households who are mailed an offer will respond. It is important to note that direct marketing response rates have fallen over the years. For example, prior to the turn of the century response rates exceeding 1% were common in the credit card direct solicitation business. The decline in response rates is associated with the fact that consumers increasingly consider direct marketing material as junk mail, and the mass of direct mail material received by consumers has become excessive. Nevertheless, the low response rate has not discouraged mailings of financial services solicitations, which now account for a significant proportion of mail solicitations received by consumers.

Electronic means of direct marketing are also heavily utilized by financial services organizations. These include advertising on mobile devices through mobile sites or embedded advertising in mobile apps. Another form of direct marketing is direct e-mail. Direct e-mail has witnessed trends similar to direct mail. In the early 1990s, the response rate to direct e-mail solicitations was around 10%, while typical response rate to such solicitations have dropped to as low at 5 per 100,000 and even lower figures in some cases.[19]

Several factors account for the decline in response rates for direct e-mail. These include the use of spam blockers to protect Internet users, and anti-spam legislation, which has limited the distribution of e-mailed direct marketing material. Furthermore, the constant threat of computer viruses has resulted in consumer reluctance to open direct email solicitations. Research also indicates that consumers are reluctant to provide their e-mail addresses to marketers. Almost seven in every ten individuals refuse to provide their e-mail address in business transactions because they recognize that promotional direct e-mails and spam are likely to follow.[20]

It is no surprise that loyalty-marketing programs utilizing email which could theoretically be a highly cost-effective mechanism for marketing to existing customers rarely succeed.[21] This is especially true in the context of financial services in which an underlying sense of trust and security is essential for establishing a transactional relationship. Similar difficulties have also been experienced in the context of telemarketing. The Telemarketing Act of 2003, which will be discussed in Chapter 10, prohibits financial services marketers from making outbound telemarketing calls to individuals who have chosen to be on the national "do not call" list. The use of telemarketing call screening features provided by some telecommunications companies have further complicated the task of telemarketing financial services.

With the increasing amount of restrictions in consumer communications, driven by regulations and technological forces, the greatest challenge in advertising financial services is in finding the means for reaching and connecting with the target audience effectively. To do so, a methodical approach needs to be taken to determine the appropriate advertising objectives, identify the intended ad message, and establish effective advertising media. The steps in this process will be discussed in the next section.

Step 1: Determining the objectives of the advertisement

Step 2: Determining the available budget

Step 3: Estimating the return on investment

Step 4: Establishing the ad content

Step 5: Selecting among media choices

Step 6: Campaign execution

Step 7: Quantifying the effects of the ad campaign

Exhibit 5.3 Steps in Advertising Financial Services

STEPS IN ADVERTISING FINANCIAL SERVICES

Several steps are essential for successful execution of advertising campaigns in financial services. These steps are outlined in Exhibit 5.3 and will be discussed below. We will also discuss and highlight the unique aspects of these steps as they relate to specific financial services.

(1) Identification of Advertising Objectives: The first step is to determine the objectives of the advertising campaign, reflecting the overall marketing strategy of the company. For example, the objective of an advertising campaign might be to generate new policies for an insurance product or to increase the level of consumer awareness of the brand or the company. Recognizing and identifying the exact objective of an ad campaign is critical to accurate assessment of its merits and potential. Examples of popular advertising objectives in financial services are target levels for customer inquiries, new policies signed, and advertising recall.

(2) Budget Determination: The next step in the advertising process is to determine the budget required to carry out the ad campaign. Often, the required budget is significantly different from what is available, and may be dictated by organizational budgetary constraints. For example, the budget available for advertising a particular financial service might be determined based on a percentage of the total premium revenues generated in the prior year. Clearly, an increase in the intensity of an advertising campaign would require higher budget allocations and may call for the abandoning of traditional budget-setting approaches for advertising. The total budget that is required to execute an advertising campaign is a function of the reach and frequency (and hence the gross rating points) necessary to create consumer response and the cost of media used to secure this level of exposure. The associated dollar figure, therefore, needs to have been estimated prior to negotiations with higher levels of management, in order to ensure the availability of sufficient funds for executing an effective advertising campaign.

(3) Computing the Return on Investment (ROI): The next step in the advertising process

is to determine the return on investments associated with the advertising campaign. Four items of information are needed in order to conduct this estimation, one of which is an estimate of the lifetime value of an acquired customer. The lifetime value of the customer is the total profit that an acquired customer represents to the company. It is quantified as the sum of the profits associated with the stream of transactions that the customer will undertake with the company over the years. In addition, an estimate of the total number of consumers who will be exposed to the advertising campaign is required. An estimate of the percentage of reached consumers who will eventually purchase the advertised financial product or service is also required. This conversion estimate may range from a low of 0 to a high of 1. Advertisements that are more memorable, are run more frequently, or are more relevant to their target audiences are likely to have a greater impact on consumers, resulting in higher conversion levels. Finally, the total dollar expenditure identified in Step 2 is needed in order to compute the return on investment for the ad campaign. With this information at hand, the return on investment can be computed by applying the following formula:

$$ROI = \frac{\text{lifetime value of customer} \times \text{conversion rate} \times \text{reach}}{\text{total advertising campaign expenditure}} - 1$$

To demonstrate the computation of the return on investment for an advertising campaign, consider the following example. A direct-mail campaign focusing on 40-year-old heads of household in order to sell a $250,000 term life insurance policy is being developed. The ad campaign is reaching 200,000 households at a cost of $325,000 (reach=200,000; ad campaign expenditure=$325,000). To determine the lifetime value of the customer, the management estimates that a new customer will renew her policy for about four years and that a customer will generate profits of approximately $600 (net of all costs and benefit payouts) each year. As a result, the lifetime value of an acquired customer over the four-year time period is estimated at 4x$600 or $2,400. Based on past experiences with such advertising campaigns, the management estimates that 1 in every 1,000 individuals mailed will become a policyholder (conversion rate=0.001). Applying these estimates to the above formula would result in an ROI estimate of 48%. The estimated ROI can then be examined against benchmarks used by the company in the past in order to determine whether the ad campaign should be executed. The ROI computation shown here is a rather simplified approach encompassing many assumptions and more complex mathematical models may be needed to accurately reflect the underlying dynamics of advertising effectiveness within a given business. Clearly, negative return on investment estimates would make the advertising campaign an unlikely prospect for further action.

	Newspaper	Magazine	Radio	TV	Direct Mail	Tele-Marketing	Mobile Apps
Checking & Savings Accounts			✓	✓		✓	✓
Automobile Insurance			✓	✓	✓	✓	✓
Homeowners Insurance	✓	✓		✓	✓	✓	✓
Life Insurance	✓			✓	✓		
Investment Services	✓	✓		✓			✓
Retirement Planning	✓	✓		✓			

Exhibit 5.4 Media Preferences for Various Types of Financial Services

(4) Developing the Contents of the Ad: Once the return on investment computation has shown favorable results, the next step in the advertising process is to develop the contents of the ad, as reflected in its execution style and informational content. In this step, the services of advertising agencies that specialize in producing financial services ads are required. These specialized agencies often also engage the support of legal experts who can determine the compliance of advertising content with existing regulations. Often, testing of ad content using small-scale samples, focus groups, or test markets may be needed.

(5) Media Selection, Scheduling and Campaign Execution: The next step in the advertising process is to determine the media that will be used. Exhibit 5.4 shows a simplified table of some of the more common forms of media that can be used for different types of financial services. In general, financial services that are more complex and require the communication of detailed information tend to rely on print forms of advertising. Television advertising, which capitalizes on multiple sensory inputs, tends to be the most effective although often the most expensive. Once the media for an ad campaign has been determined by the ad agency, a media schedule needs

to be developed in order to achieve the original objectives of the ad campaign which had been identified in step 1. This task is often carried out by the advertising agency that has been hired to carry out the campaign. There are specific media scheduling and campaign execution strategies that are most effective in certain forms of financial services. For example, an effective ad-scheduling tactic is to advertise in pulses, with heavy advertising in one month, reduced advertising the following month, and a return to high advertising levels in the third month. This tactic tends to result in more sales and higher levels of consumer response than a constant and steady level of ad spending. Interested readers are encouraged to consult an advertising textbook for the details of various advertising campaign execution styles.[22]

(6) Measurement: The final step in the advertising process is to assess the impact of the ad campaign through formal market research or examination of company records. It is critical to measure and record sales levels and other advertising responses following an ad campaign in order to determine the financial effects of the invested advertising dollars. Such measures may help fine-tune the advertising strategy of the company and provide estimates for optimizing future advertising campaigns. For direct advertising campaigns, such measures are obtained through the tracking of consumer inquiries following the ad campaign and the use of tracking numbers, which can pinpoint the exact promotional material to which the consumers are reacting. For ads delivered through mass media such as television, radio, and newspapers, the tracking of consumer responses may be considerably more difficult and might require examining aggregate changes in sales for the months following the ad campaign, or the purchase of market research data from specialized research firms.

REGULATIONS AND FINANCIAL SERVICES ADVERTISING

As pointed out earlier in this chapter, the large numbers of regulations that limit the contents of financial services ads result in creative challenges for advertisers. Regulatory bodies such as the Securities and Exchange Commission (SEC), the Federal Reserve, the Financial Industry Regulatory Authority (FINRA), and the insurance departments of the individual states closely monitor the contents of financial services advertisements. Regulations, restrictions, and rules of conduct enforced by these regulatory authorities impose specific limitations on what can or cannot be included in the ads.

The primary objective of regulating financial services advertisements is to protect consumers against misleading advertisements. In addition, regulations are in place to ensure that consumers have the necessary information available to them prior to making decisions on financial services. The types of regulations that are in place vary depending on the financial service category. For credit products, the cost of credit is a critical decision-making variable, and the Truth in Lending Act dictates some of the restrictions that apply to ad content. Conversely, for savings products, the Truth in Savings Act needs to be closely examined. For investment and brokerage services, the rules and guidelines set by the Securities and Exchange Commission and the Financial Industry Regulatory Authority regulate much of the ad content. Similarly, the Department of Insurance of the state in which an insurance company is operating typically regulates advertisements for insurance products. Readers are encouraged to examine additional resources on regulations governing financial services advertising in order to ensure regulatory compliance.[23] Furthermore, the legal advice of attorneys specialized in financial services advertising regulations may be necessary to ensure regulatory compliance. Below, we will examine some of the regulations that have a direct influence on advertising specific financial services.

Advertising Commercial Banking Services: Advertising of commercial banking services is monitored through the various regulations enforced by the Federal Reserve as well as the Office of the Comptroller of the Currency. For example, the *Truth in Savings Act* specifies items of information that depository institutions should disclose about deposit accounts featured in their advertisements. Terms such as the rate of interest, applicable fees, and terms of the deposit such as the minimum length of time that is required prior to withdrawal of the funds need to be clearly communicated to consumers. For credit products, the *Truth in Lending Act* (regulation Z of the Federal Reserve) dictates that the true cost of credit must be communicated in written form to consumers. Regulation Z also establishes the method to be used to determine the cost of credit and requires that lenders communicate this information in the form of the annual percentage rate (APR). Regulators may also monitor advertisements to ensure that banks do not exaggerate the extent to which they claim to make credit available to customers as a means for generating leads. In addition, commercial banks, which are ensured by the Federal Deposit Insurance Corporation (FDIC), need to mention their coverage status with the FDIC in their ads and other consumer communications.

Advertising Insurance: Each state's department of insurance regulates insurance advertising. The objectives of insurance advertising regulations are two-fold. The first objective is to prevent the creation of biases in consumer assessment of the probability of catastrophic events. This objective relates to the established fact that consumers typically are unaware of the risks and probabilities for events for which they purchase insurance products, as discussed in Chapter 2. For example, insurance advertising that bolsters the fear of catastrophic events through dramatic imagery is not allowed. Negative outcomes of disasters should also not be overstated in insurance advertisements. The second objective of insurance advertising regulations is to prevent the creation of inferences that suggest that an insurance company is unusually generous in its payout behavior. As a result, insurance advertisers have to take great care not to exaggerate either the severity of harmful events or their own willingness to pay out customer claims. In addition, images of currency and checks should not be included in advertisements for insurance products as they may make consumers infer unconsciously that the insurance company has a high propensity to payout claims and is usually generous.

An additional objective in insurance advertising is to prevent misleading information from being communicated to consumers. Formally, an ad can be considered misleading when it causes individuals with average levels of intelligence to arrive at inferences that conflict with reality. In order to establish if such inferences are a result of the advertisement, formal market research utilizing third-party companies and random samples of consumers would be used. Insurance advertising is further restricted by the terminology that may be used.[24] Terms such as "liberal" and "generous," for example, cannot be used as they boost impressions of the payout behavior of the insurance company. Similarly, references to words such as "financial disaster" and "catastrophic" are not allowed because they may exaggerate the extent of the harm consumers might face if they do not have insurance coverage. The fact that insurance prices vary from one consumer to the next due to varying risk levels also limits the pricing terminology that can be used in insurance advertising. Therefore, terms such as "low," "budget," and "low-cost" cannot be used.

Advertising, Investment and Brokerage Services: The advertising of investment and brokerage services is regulated by the SEC as well as FINRA. These regulators require that advertisers ensure that consumers understand that past returns of an investment may or may not be realized in the future. As a result, statements to this effect need to be mentioned in consumer communications, including advertisements in mass media and direct mail. Advertisements for mutual funds must also encourage potential investors to seek the detailed technical information on the fund by requesting the fund's prospectus. The ads should facilitate such action by providing consumers the necessary contact information. Additional Securities and Exchange Commission rules should be consulted for the details of information that must be included in mutual fund advertisements. Readers are encouraged to further examine sources specializing in financial services advertising regulations for additional details.[25]

CHAPTER QUESTIONS

1. What unique benefits and drawbacks do you think mobile advertising might have in the context of advertising the following types of financial services:
    (a) Discount brokerage services
    (b) Automobile insurance
    (c) Retail banking
    (d) Home mortgages

2. Define the following terms:
   (a) Environmental exposure
   (b) Cognitive exposure
   (c) Reach
   (d) Frequency
   (e) GRP
   (f) CPM
   (g) Advertising response function
   (h) Unique selling proposition

3. What are some limitations of using humor in financial services advertising?

4. When considering some of the leading providers of property and casualty insurance, what unique selling propositions could you associate with each of them? Provide three examples.

5. What are the stages in Maslow's hierarchy and how do they relate to the advertising of financial services?

6. Develop the layout of a print ad for each of the following financial products:
   (a) A credit card for which, 1% of your spending will be donated to the charity of your choice.
   (b) An investment advisory service, that provides financial advice to investors of all size, at a cost of $45/hour.

7. Considering your ad design in question 6:
   (a) What considerations do you need to give to specific advertising regulations that restrict the contents of your ad?
   (b) Given the success factors outlined in this chapter for good advertising practice in financial services, how do your ads stack up?

8. What other industries can you think of that exhibit advertising strategies similar to what is observed in financial services markets? What specific consumer decision characteristics may contribute to such similarities?

9. What conditions create deceptive advertising in financial services? Can you identify examples based on your exposure to financial services ads in mass media?

ENDNOTES

1 A. Pergelova, D. Prior and J. Rialp (2010), "Assessing Advertising Efficiency," *Journal of Advertising Research*, Vol. 39, Iss. 3, pp. 39-54; W. Boulding, E. Lee, and R. Staelin (1994), "Mastering the Mix: Do Advertising, Promotion, and Sales Force Activities Lead to Differentiation?" *Journal of Marketing Research*, 31 (May), pp. 159-172; A. Chakravarti and C. Janiszewski (2004), "The Influence of Generic Advertising on Brand Preferences," *Journal of Consumer Research*, Vol. 30, No. 4, pp. 487-502.

2 For more detailed discussions of these differences, readers are encouraged to consult the following sources: Christine Ennew, Mike Wright, and Trevor Watkins (1989), "Personal Financial Services: Marketing Strategy Determination," *International Journal of Bank Marketing*, Vol. 7, Iss. 6, pp. 3-8; Alec Benn (1986), *Advertising Financial Products and Services*. Quorum Books: New York, pp. 1-13; Tina Harrison (2000), *Financial Services Marketing*. Pearson Education Ltd: Essex, pp. 214-216.

3 H. Estelami (2009), "Cognitive Drivers of Suboptimal Financial Decisions: Implications for Financial Literacy Campaigns," *Journal of Financial Services Marketing*, Vol. 13, Iss. 4, pp. 273-283;P. Lunt (2005), "Consumer Choice and Financial Services," *Consumer Policy Review*, Vol. 15, Iss. 3, pp. 104- 112; Anthony Santomero (2003), "Knowledge is Power: The Importance of Economic Education," *Business Review*, The Federal Reserve Bank of Philadelphia, Fourth Quarter 2003, p. 1; Sandra Braunstein and Carolyn Welch (2002), "Financial Literacy: An Overview of Practice, Research, and Policy," *Federal Reserve Bulletin*, Vol. 88, Iss. 11, pp. 445- 457.

4 Roger Blackwell, Paul Minard, and James Engel (2005), *Consumer Behavior*. South-Western College Publishing; J. Hammond, R. Keeney, and H. Raffia (1999), *Smart Choices*. Harvard Business School Press: Boston, MA; Newell, A. and H.A. Simon (1972), *Human Problem Solving*. Englewood Cliffs, NJ: Prentice Hall.

5 W. McGuire (1978), "An Information Processing Model of Advertising Effectiveness," in H.L. Davis and A.J. Silk (eds.), *Behavioral and Management Science in Marketing*. New York: Ronald, pp. 156-180; W. McGuire (1973), "Source Variables in Persuasion," in I. de Sola Pool et al (eds.), *Handbook of Communication*. Chicago: Rand McNally, pp. 229- 232.

6 Mark Ritson (2012), "Advertising's Death Rattle May Soon Drown Out the Optimists," *Marketing*, Sep. 12, 2002, p. 18; Theo Poiesz and Henry Robben (1994), "Individual Reactions to Advertising: Theoretical and Methodological Developments," *International Journal of Advertising*, Vol. 13, Iss. 1, pp. 25-53;; Jack Trout (2000), *Differentiate or Die: Survival in Our Era of Killer Competition*. John Wiley and Sons: New York.

7 Roger Blackwell, Paul Minard, and James Engel (2005), *Consumer Behavior*. South-Western College Publishing.

8 Tina Harrison (2000), *Financial Services Marketing*. Pearson Education Ltd: Essex, pp. 55-57; A. Maslow (1970), *Motivation and Personality*. Second Edition, Harper & Row, New York; A. Maslow (1970), *Motivation and Personality*. Second Edition, Harper & Row, New York.

9 "Echo Awards: GEICO Direct Auto Insurance," *Direct Marketing*, Nov. 1999, Vol. 62, Iss. 7, p. 52.

10 Thomas Cline, Moses Altsech, and James Kellaris (2003), "When Does Humor Enhance or Inhibit Ad Response?" *Journal of Advertising*, Vol. 32, Iss. 3, pp.31-45; Amitava Chattopadhyay and Kunal Basu (1990), "Humor in Advertising: The Moderating Role of Prior Brand Evaluation," *Journal of Marketing Research*, Vol. 27, Iss. 4, pp. 466-476.

11 Alec Benn (1986), *Advertising Financial Products and Services*. Quorum Books: New York, pp. 69-76.

12 For a more detailed discussion of emotions in financial services advertising, interested readers are encouraged to examine the following sources: Tina Harrison (2000), Financial Services Marketing, Pearson Education Ltd: Essex, p.p. 207-208; A. Maslow (1970), *Motivation and Personality*. Second Edition, Harper & Row, New York; Alec Benn (1986), *Advertising Financial Products and Services*. Quorum Books: New York, pp. 69-76.

13 David Aaker, George Day and V. Kumar (2010), *Essentials of Marketing Research.* New York: Wiley; Donald Lehmann, Sunil Gupta and Joel Steckel (1997), *Marketing Research.* Upper Saddle River, NJ: Prentice Hall; Alec Benn (1986), *Advertising Financial Products and Services.* Quorum Books: New York.

14 Herbert Krugman (1972), "Why Three Exposures May be Enough," *Journal of Advertising Research,* Vol. 12, Iss. 4, pp. 11-14; Larry Percy and Richard Elliott (2002), *Strategic Advertising Management.* New York: Oxford University Press; R. Batra, J. Myers, and D. Aaker (1995), *Advertising Management.* New York: Prentice Hall.

15 M. Barrett (2008), Financial Services Advertising: Law and Regulation. Clarus Press: Dublin ; A. Benn (1986), *Advertising Financial Products and Services.* Quorum Books: New York.

16 Kin-nam Lau, Haily Chow, Connie Liu (2010), "A Database Approach to Cross-Selling in the Banking Industry: Practices, Strategies, and Challenges," *Journal of Database Marketing & Customer Strategy Management,* Vol. 11, Iss. 3, pp. 216-234; Justin Hibbard (2004), "Banks Go beyond Toasters," *Business Week,* Dec 20, citing research by the TowerGroup.

17 Edward McKinley (2005), "Opt Out? Mail Offers Reach Record Highs," *Credit Card Management,* Vol. 18, Iss. 1, p. 50; Kate Fitzgerald (2004), "Mail Mania", *Credit Card Management,* Vol. 17, Issue 10, p. 20.

18 J. Turner (2007), "Improving Direct Response Rates When Loan Rates Are High," *ABA Banking Journal,* Vol. 39, Iss. 3, p. 52;"Behind 2003's Direct-Mail Numbers," *Credit Card Management,* April 2004, Vol. 17, Issue 1, p. 20, citing figures produced by Synovate Mail Monitor of Chicago.

19 C. Rose (2011), "Applying Spam-Control Techniques to Negate High Frequency Trading Advantage," *International Journal of Management and Information Systems,* Vol. 15, Iss. 2, pp. 105-110; ;Stephen Baker (2003), "The Taming of the Internet," *Business Week,* December 15, Issue 3862, pp. 78-81.

20. "How Spam Undermine Loyalty Efforts", *Credit Card Management,* Jan 2004, Vol. 16, Issue 11, p. 8, citing figures reported by the Federal Trade Commission.

21 Stephen Baker (2003), "The Taming of the Internet," *Business Week,* December 15, Issue 3862, pp. 78-81; "How Spam Undermine Loyalty Efforts", *Credit Card Management,* Jan 2004, Vol. 16, Issue 11, p. 8

22 Alec Benn (1986), *Advertising Financial Products and Services.* Quorum Books: New York, pp. 85-102; W. Wells, J. Burnett, and S. Moriarty (2002), *Advertising Principles and Practice.* Upper Saddle River, NJ: Prentice Hall.

23 Readers are encouraged to consult the following sources for more thorough discussions of these regulations: Alec Benn (1986), *Advertising Financial Products and Services.* Quorum Books: New York;
Gene A. Marsh (1999), *Consumer Protection Law in a Nutshell.* St. Paul, MN: West Group.

24 Alec Benn (1986), *Advertising Financial Products and Services.* Quorum Books: New York, provides a detailed overview of restrictions on the terminology that can be used in insurance advertising, on pages 175-177. Benn also discusses the regulatory motivations behind some of these restrictions. Interested readers are also encouraged to consult the NAIC web site at www.naic.org

25 A. Poddar, J. Mosteller, E. Scholder (2009), "Consumers' Rules of Engagement in Online Information Exchanges," *Journal of Consumer Affairs,* Vol. 43, Iss. 3, pp. 419-448; Gene A. Marsh (1999), *Consumer Protection Law in a Nutshell.* St. Paul, MN: West Group; "Banks Warned About Marketing," *Wall Street Journal,* Sept 15, 2004, p. 1; Alec Benn (1986), *Advertising Financial Products and Services.* Quorum Books: New York, pp. 168-171.

CHAPTER SIX

Distribution

In this chapter, we will discuss the logistics of how financial products and services are made available to the marketplace. The distribution of financial services is a critical part of the marketing process that not only involves the logistics of making the relevant products available to customers, but also involves legal and ethical concerns that may significantly constrain a financial services organization's activities. This is primarily due to the fiduciary responsibility that is placed upon many companies and individuals selling financial services which may require them to be accountable for the financial well being of their customers. Financial services can be made available to customers through a variety of channels. Services such as checking and savings accounts are often available at retail branches of commercial banks, and transaction-processing services such as money transfers may be provided in a variety of outlets including bank branches, retail stores and supermarkets. The sale of property and casualty insurance is predominantly conducted by agents and brokers, and the buying and selling of securities is for the most part done by brokerage firms or through their online websites.

The choice of distribution systems for financial services is driven not only by the norms of the specific financial service category, but also by the changing trends in the marketplace and customers' shifting preferences. Shifts in customer preferences can, for example, be witnessed in the growing use of hand-held mobile devices for the trading of stocks, the steady growth of online banking services, and a move towards commoditized distribution of insurance products.[1] In this chapter, we will discuss the distribution systems used in financial services marketing. As will be seen, the proper design and implementation of distribution strategies and a flexible distribution infrastructure are critical components of running a successful financial services organization.

STRATEGIC ROLE OF DISTRIBUTION IN FIANANCIAL SERVICES MARKETING

Distribution is a vital part of the marketing process in both goods and services marketing. Without proper distribution, products and services would have no way to reach the consumer. This is especially true in financial services since the distribution networks in many financial services have a significant influence on the company's ability to reach its target customers. For example, mutual fund companies have found over the years that third party distributors such as brokers, advisors, and banks have great influence on consumers' decisions regarding mutual funds. As a result, nearly 90% of the sale of funds today is done through third parties rather than the direct sales of the funds' shares by the fund company itself.[2] Similarly, insurance companies sell their policies mostly through agents and brokers in the retail environment because they recognize the economic and logistic efficiencies gained by using such a process.

It is important to recognize some of the differences that exist between distribution and other marketing activities such as pricing, advertising, and product development. In most financial services organizations, distribution is the least flexible of all marketing activities. To appreciate this, consider the amount of effort that is required to make changes in the marketing program of a financial institution. For example, changes in the price of a financial product might require several days or weeks to implement. Changing the advertising content or media schedule for a financial service might be a matter of several weeks. However, making changes to the distribution strategy of a financial services organization requires considerably greater effort and a significantly longer time horizon. Expanding distribution might require setting up new branch offices, hiring new sales people, and developing an agent network. Limiting the distribution of a financial service may require the reverse of the above processes. These changes would not only require considerable investment and organizational effort, but they may also take months, if not years, to implement successfully, and may also have significant legal implications.

One of the other unique aspects of the distribution process, especially in financial services, is that the actions of the participants in the distribution network such as agents, salespeople, and brokers can be controlled through reward and compensation systems. These parties can be directed to more aggressively promote specific products, based on what is communicated to them in the form of incentives, commissions, and other forms of monetary and non-monetary rewards. The underlying psychology of these participants has a great impact on the way optimal incentive programs are designed. For example, the incentives for a broker might be based on the number of securities trades that the broker's clients carry out during the year. Such an incentive system would motivate the broker to recommend high numbers of trades to clients. However, the resulting effects on the clients' portfolio performance may be questioned on the grounds that the trades may have been partially motivated by the broker's self interest and therefore not necessarily have been in the best interest of the clients. Alternatively, disconnecting broker compensation from clients' trade volume, providing a higher base salary, and linking compensation to portfolio returns is likely to result in better management of the clients' portfolios. By implementing such a change in the incentive system, the broker may shift focus from trade facilitation to the objective management of clients' investment portfolios.

In fact, one of the biggest challenges in the distribution process and the design of appropriate sales incentive systems in financial services is the intrinsic conflicts of interest that exist in many financial services transactions. Conflicts of interest arise from the fact that the incentives that motivate members of the distribution network such as agents and brokers may not necessarily be designed to force these parties to focus on the best interests of their clients. In fact, such incentive systems have sometimes resulted in the introduction of new regulations and penalties imposed by regulators.[3] This is a distinctly different picture from what one would see in most other marketing contexts. For example, an individual purchasing an automobile at a car dealership cannot fault the salesperson for recommending a vehicle that may not match the car buyer's exact needs or not disclosing to the buyer how he will be compensated for the sale of the vehicle. However, if a broker recommends the purchase of a financial product to a client and fails to disclose the incentive structure that determines his own compensation structure, legal questions and possible repercussions may result. Such conflicts of interest have in recent years, been the focus of considerable attention for several powerful regulatory bodies.[4]

It is important to recognize that the choice of the distribution system used in a financial services organization impacts all elements of the marketing program. For example, the choice of where the product is sold may influence its pricing. Financial services that are made available through automated channels such as the technology-based means of the Internet and ATM devices are typically associated with lower prices. For example, the commissions paid by customers for stock trades conducted online are often considerably lower that the commissions charged for trades made using a broker in a brokerage office or by phone. Similarly, the choice of where and how a financial service is made available to consumers has a significant impact on the perceptions that consumers form of the financial services organization. The sale of financial products through low cost networks may be associated with a low-quality image. In contrast, financial services that are made available through more costly channels such as branch office locations or personal sales visits may imply a higher degree of customer care and individualized attention, resulting in positive perceptions of service quality. The choice of the distribution system used for a financial product or service can therefore have a profound impact on the image associated with the company, and customer perceptions of price and quality.

DISTRIBUTION SYSTEMS USED IN FINANCIAL SERVICES MARKETING

As in most other markets, there are two general approaches for making products and services available to customers. The first approach is *direct distribution*, which requires the company's own employees to be in direct contact with customers to sell its products and services. For example, a commercial bank that operates several retail branches comes into contact with its customers through its own bank tellers and retail staff. Similarly, an insurance company that sells direct to customers would come into contact with its customers through its own sales staff and the company's customer service operations. Other examples of direct selling include scenarios in which a financial services provider utilizes its website to sell financial services such as insurance and mortgage products, or deploys its own sales force to call customers to pitch its products.[5]

As shown in Exhibit 6.1, the second approach to distributing financial services is *indirect distribution*, which involves the use of third parties to mediate sales transactions. These third parties take on the forms of agents and brokers. For example, an insurance company could utilize a national network of *captive agents* to sell its insurance products to the marketplace. These agents, while not employees of the insurance company, have the ability to represent the insurance company and its products to consumers. Similarly, a mortgage company could utilize mortgage brokers to sell its mortgage products to homebuyers. The brokers, who are also typically not employees of the mortgage company, have the primary task of facilitating transactions between customers and the company. However, in contrast to agents, brokers may carry mortgage products from various companies, and their motivation to sell products from any given financial services provider may be influenced by the sales incentives provided by the company.

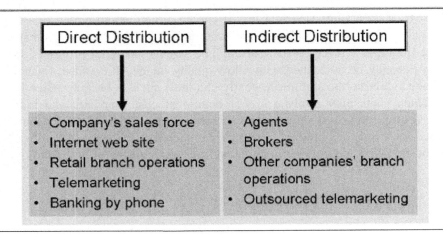

Exhibit 6.1: Distribution Strategies in Financial Services Markets

In the indirect approach to the distribution of financial services, the extent of control exercised by a financial services provider on the selling activities of the participants (for example, agents and brokers) might be limited when compared to the amount of control available in the direct approach. With a direct distribution system on the other hand, the company's own employees are in direct communication with the customer, and the ability of the company to control the nature of their communications and sales processes is greatly enhanced. In the direct approach, since the company's own paid employees carry out the customer contact activities, the ability to manage customer relationships tends to be significantly greater than in the indirect approach.[6]

Industry trends indicate that the selling of financial services is shifting away from traditional methods that involve human interactions. As will be discussed in this chapter and as shown in Exhibit 6.2, technology is having a profound impact on the distribution of financial services. Customers may come into contact with their financial service provider through the Internet, ATM devices, or by phone. Customers may also come into contact with a financial services provider through the traditional methods of distribution which involve human contacts. For example, instead of utilizing an ATM device to withdraw cash from a checking account, the customer could withdraw cash from her account by visiting a teller at her local bank branch. Similarly, instead of purchasing insurance policies on the Internet, a customer could approach an agent's office. However, the shift away from these human contacts is evident in several trends observed in recent years. In financial services, significant cost savings are often associated with the use of technology rather than humans in the distribution, selling, and customer service processes. In fact, some financial services organizations penalize customers for the use of human contact

Technology-Based Channels:	Commercial Banking	Property and Casualty Insurance	Mutual Funds	Residential Mortgages
Own ATM	✔			
Competitor's ATM	✔			
Internet	✔	✔	✔	✔
Phone	✔	✔		
Traditional Channels:				
Branch/ office	✔		✔	✔
Agent		✔		
Broker		✔	✔	✔

Exhibit 6.2: Popular Distribution Channels for Various Financial Services

points in their choice of transaction methods. For example, certain banks may charge customers additional fees for visiting a bank teller at a branch or for calling the customer service line on the phone, rather than conducting their transactions using an ATM device or online.[7]

Depending on the financial service category, various distribution methods are used for making services available to the customer. For example, in the U.S., many of the major insurers use agents to sell most of their policies. Agents are typically not employees of the insurance company, but are tasked with presenting the company's products and services in a retail environment that is physically accessible to the public. Insurance sales also take place through insurance brokers. The distinction between agents and brokers is that agents are typically required to represent only a single company's products, while brokers may be able to represent competing companies. Insurance products are also made available to the public through online mechanisms and by phone. The growing use of the Internet by the masses, increased sophistication of the consumer base, and the commoditization of many financial products has made technology-based approaches to distribution a cost-effective approach for the sale of insurance as well as other forms of financial products and services.[8] Retail branches of commercial banks have also begun to account for a significant share of insurance sales in the U.S.

The wide geographic presence of bank branches and their immediate access to a large population base makes these branches an attractive choice for the sale of many types of financial services. Since the deregulation of the financial services sector in 1999, commercial banks have become active participants in the selling of financial products other than the traditional banking products and services which they had been associated with for decades. Retail banking services can be provided to customers in a variety of ways. A bank customer could conduct her banking transactions through a teller at a bank's branch location, for example. The same customer could choose to utilize the bank's ATM device, or even a competing bank's ATM device, to conduct basic transactions such as depositing and withdrawing funds or obtaining account balances. The consumer could also utilize the Internet web site of the bank to conduct simple tasks such as obtaining account balances or more complex tasks such as paying bills online. Trends indicate that Internet banking is experiencing notable growth and is likely to make consumers' bill payments using checks relatively obsolete in the near future.[9]

The distribution of mortgages can also be achieved through various channels. A mortgage company may come into contact with customers directly through its branch locations, which accept and process applications and disburse funds to homebuyers. The company could also utilize brokers who would represent it in contacts with homebuyers. The broker may for example, take on the responsibility of prescreening applicants and conducting basic administrative tasks that the company would otherwise need to carry out by itself.

Multiple layers of brokers could also be utilized to make funds available to end customers. A mortgage company could also come into contact with homebuyers through its Internet web site. The use of the Internet for the promotion of mortgage products has witnessed a growing trend in recent years. The mortgage business is unique in the sense that, after mortgages have been issued to homebuyers, they may be sold from one mortgage company to another and exchanged on the mortgage-backed securities markets.[10] The existence of mortgage-backed securities markets has increased the array of choices available to investors, with a special benefit to institutional investors who seek the unique risk characteristics of mortgages in managing their investment portfolios.

In the context of mutual funds, a variety of mechanisms for distributing and selling of funds exist. A fund company could operate its own offices, which customers could visit in order to obtain information and advice on the funds, and to purchase fund shares and conduct other related transactions. Alternatively, a fund company could utilize its web site as a means for making its products available to the public. In addition to these direct approaches, fund companies typically utilize third parties for the sale of their funds. These third parties could include entities such as commercial banks and brokerage houses that promote the company's funds and make the funds available to their own clients. Third parties may also include other fund companies who choose to make the company's funds available to their client base as a means for increasing the variety of investment choices that they offer.

THE AGENCY SYSTEM

Efficiency Gains and Agent/Broker Intermediation

As highlighted above, third parties may have a crucial role in the sale and distribution of financial services. This is because the direct selling of financial services may require a large amount of investment in infrastructure, the setting up of retail locations and branch offices, and the hiring and training of a specialized sales force. In many cases, these costly requirements make the direct selling of financial services economically infeasible. As a result, financial organizations may choose to utilize agents or brokers for selling their products to the market at large. The logistical efficiencies gained by this approach may have a monumental impact on the marketability and cost effectiveness of a financial product.

As highlighted earlier and shown in Exhibit 6.3, the distinction between agents and brokers is that agents typically only represent a single financial services provider or a small set, while brokers can represent multiple providers and may also have an intrinsic responsibility to help their clients identify the best option among the choices

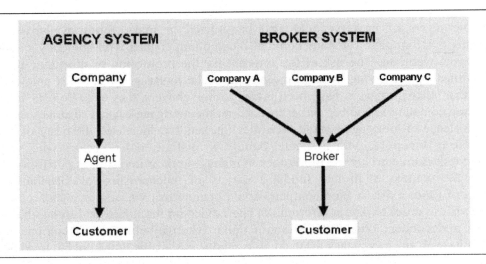

Exhibit 6.3 Distribution through Agents and Brokers

presented to them. An agent that represents only a single financial services provider is referred to as a captive agent, whereas one that represents multiple companies is referred to as an independent agent. There are several advantages to the use of agents and brokers in distributing financial services. In addition to the logistical efficiencies mentioned above, for the financial services organization the costs of engaging agents and brokers in the sale and distribution of its products are far more favorable than what it costs to set up its own retail presence. This is because the agent/broker is the primary party who undertakes the investments needed to create the retail infrastructure and often accepts the financial burden of setting up an office and hiring the necessary staff. In most agent/broker arrangements, the agent or broker is not an employee of the company, and therefore represents little or no payroll and benefit expenses to the company. This results in little or minimal upfront investments needed from the company in order to build its network of retail locations. In addition, the use of agents and brokers may enable a quicker response to poor performance by an agent or a broker through the termination of their contracts.[11] The flexibility and cost effectiveness of this system is one of the primary reasons why a significant share of sales is attributed to agents and brokers, across a variety of financial services.

One of the disadvantages associated with the use of agents and brokers in the sale and distribution of financial services is the difficulty in achieving coordination in marketing activities, and maintaining consistency in service quality across agents' or brokers' offices. This is largely due to the fact that the agent or broker is not an employee of the company and may have limited motivation to comply with company objectives. In addition, conflicts of interest may at times influence the nature of the relationship between the agent or broker, and the customer. As will be discussed below, the agent or broker may choose to take on business from unattractive market segments. An agent or broker may for example, sell insurance policies to individuals who are in high-risk categories and charge inappropriately low premiums in order to make a sale. Since agents and brokers are not direct employees of the company, they may also proceed to conduct marketing activities in ways that are not consistent with the financial services organization's business objectives and in some cases, they may place the company at considerable risk by undertaking activities that violate not only company norms, but also existing regulations.

Challenges in Managing an Agency/Brokerage Distribution System

A financial services provider using intermediaries such as agents and brokers is vulnerable to what economists refer to as *moral hazard*. Moral hazard occurs when an agent or a broker is placed in the unique position of negotiating the terms of a sales transaction, such as price or policy limits, on behalf of the financial services provider.[12] Since the agent or broker is only serving as an intermediary, he is insulated from any direct risks in making decisions on behalf of the company and may proceed to pass on high risks to the company by selling financial solutions to risky customers. For example, moral hazard could occur because the agent has chosen to charge a price that is too low, or has sold policies to individuals whose risk levels are beyond acceptable norms by the company. In the context of brokers who may have no pre-determined commitments towards a single financial services provider and can sell products of competing companies, moral hazard may transpire in the form of switching a customer to a competing financial services provider because of more attractive commissions. In addition, moral hazard could occur when an agent or broker sells customers inappropriate and uncompetitive products, which may eventually result in customer dissatisfaction or legal repercussions. In all these cases, the decisions made by the agent or broker present no immediate risk to her and could therefore be guided by self-interest, placing the interests of the financial services provider or the customer at significant risk.

Moral hazard could be controlled through various mechanisms such as the use of explicit contractual agreements between the company and its agents or brokers. These contractual agreements would spell out the specific requirements of how sales transactions should take place. Surveillance technologies for ensuring the execution of these requirements can be deployed by monitoring the interactions between an agent/broker and customers. Technologies such as call monitoring, which enable the company to understand the relationship between an agent/broker and the clients, and random audits of customer contracts are essential and widely used practices of ensuring contractual compliance by agents and brokers, in a variety of financial services. Alternatively, the direct selling of financial services to customers and the complete bypassing of agents and brokers could eliminate moral hazard altogether. Clearly, such an approach may also compromise a sense of trust that might have developed between the company and its agent/broker network over the years, with potentially harmful long-term effects on sales and agent/broker morale. The use of self-contained technologies such as the Internet and ATM devices could however eliminate human contacts, and the associated negotiations that often result in cases of moral hazard, altogether.

Several problematic agent/broker behaviors can occur in the distribution of financial services through an agency/brokerage system or even through the actions of the company's own employees, who in their own way may act as agents by responding to the company's sales incentive structure designed to increase sales. For example, *churning* is a term used to describe a practice by stockbrokers in which a broker advises clients to conduct an excessive number of trades. The underlying motivation by the broker is to maximize his own commission revenues. *Contingent commissions* are another problematic practice. These are additional lump sum commissions that a company such as an insurance provider or a mortgage company provides its brokers for exceeding a certain volume of sales. This practice has in recent years, been the target of legal challenges because it conflicts with the objective of seeking the best results for the clients. In the context of securities trades, "suitability" guidelines set by the Financial Industry Regulatory Authority (FINRA) mandate that broker-dealers that recommend to their clients the sale or exchange of a security should have reasonable ground for making such recommendations, taking into account the customer's financial position and background.[13]

Another controversial practice in the brokerage business is what is often referred to as *revenue sharing*. Revenue sharing occurs when the distributor of a financial product such as a broker charges a financial services provider a fee for listing its services on its preferred list, which is then distributed to its clients. This practice may represent a challenge to the brokers' responsibility to provide clients with recommendations based on the clients' best interests, rather than the broker's own compensation incentives. For example, a mutual fund that is listed on a preferred list and promoted to clients may not necessarily be a superior fund, but has found its way on the list simply because of the fees that are paid to the brokerage firm by the fund company. A similarly problematic practice in the brokerage business is referred to as *directed brokerage*. This practice has been outlawed by the Securities and Exchange Commission.[14] It occurs when a brokerage firm requires a mutual fund company to conduct its securities trades using the services of the brokerage firm in return for featuring the mutual fund on the preferred list distributed to clients. Similar to revenue sharing, this practice questions the basic responsibility of a broker to keep the clients' best interests in mind. Despite the ban, cases of directed brokerage continue to be prosecuted by regulators.[15]

Incentive Systems

Various incentive mechanisms exist to encourage and motivate sales by agents and brokers. A fundamental requirement in managing a sales force is to define sales territories for agents and brokers in a fair and equitable way. This can be achieved through geographic partitioning of territories or other means that would ensure a minimum volume of sales in any given territory. Sales compensation bonuses that are based on performance and are consistent with the financial services organization's objectives would ensure that the agent or broker keeps those objectives in mind in daily transactions and interactions with customers. For example, if a financial services provider is concerned with customer satisfaction, bonuses can be given to agents, based on customer satisfaction survey results inquiring about customers' experiences with the sales process in a financial transaction. A more formal approach to managing agents and brokers utilizing contracts that clearly communicate shared objectives may further enhance the synergy that is often needed in a sales and distribution system. Agents and brokers may also find non-monetary incentives attractive and relevant. For example, advertising support in which a financial services organization advertises its brand using mass media either regionally or nationally is likely to be welcomed by agents and brokers. Such advertising campaigns would result in the strengthening of the brand name and translate into higher volumes of traffic in agent/broker offices. In addition, support in the form of employee training for the development of agent/broker marketing plans may help motivate and organize the marketing activities undertaken, in a manner consistent with the company's overall mission and objectives.

DETERMINING DISTRIBUTION SYSTEM CHARACTERISTICS

In determining an optimal distribution approach for a financial services organization, two fundamental characteristics of the distribution system need to be carefully considered. The first relates to the size of the distribution system as reflected by the number of individuals involved in the selling and servicing of a financial service. The second characteristic that needs to be established relates to the scope of distribution outlets in which the financial service is made available.

1. Determining the Size of the Distribution System

In order to determine the staffing and resource needs for the distribution of a financial service, both inbound and outbound customer contacts must be considered. Outbound contacts include scenarios in which the sales staff needs to proactively contact existing customers or prospects in order to initiate sales. Examples would be an insurance agent who calls customers to sell supplemental insurance products, or a stock broker who contacts potential investors to promote specific investment services.

Three factors need to be taken into account when determining the size of an outbound distribution system. The first is the total number of customers that need to be contacted during the course of a year (N). In addition, estimates are needed for the number of customers that each staff member could contact on a yearly basis (C). Finally, an estimate of the number of times an individual customer/prospect needs to be contacted by a salesperson during the course of a year, whether for the creation of new sales or the maintenance of existing relationships, is needed (T). The appropriate size of the outbound distribution system based on these inputs can then be computed using the following formula:

$$\text{Number of outbound staff needed} = \frac{N \times T}{C}$$

For example, an insurance agent's office may want to reach 10,000 individuals (N) in a given year in order to retain their business and to sell additional products. The agency estimates that a typical staff member could contact as many as 20 customers in a day. This translates to approximately 5,000 customer contacts (20 contacts per day x 250 working days a year) on a yearly basis (C) per staff member. In addition, the management may have a goal of attempting to reach each of the 10,000 targeted individuals 3 times a year (T). Therefore, the number of outbound staff needed is estimated to be:

$$\text{Number of outbound staff needed} = \frac{10,000 \times 3}{5,000} = 6$$

A similar approach can be taken in order to estimate the size of the inbound operations. These operations are often attributed to the servicing of sold financial products and services. Examples of inbound distribution operations would include a bank branch that customers visit in order to conduct their commercial banking transactions, a mutual fund company that operates a branch office and is visited by investors who may seek financial advice, or the customer service phone line of an insurance company that receives calls related to claims, policy renewals, and other policy-related activities. In order to estimate the number of inbound staff, three specific inputs are needed. These are the number of customers who are to be served in a given year (N), the average number of yearly visits/calls expected for each customer (V), and the average number of customers that an individual staff member is able to serve on a yearly basis (C). The number of inbound staff can then be computed as follows:

$$\text{Number of inbound staff needed} = \frac{N \times V}{C}$$

For example, consider a new bank branch that is being set up in a location where about 5,000 customers are expected to be served yearly (N). It is estimated that the average customer will visit the bank branch once a month (V=12 times a year) and that a bank teller is able to process approximately 50 customer transactions every day (C=50/day x 250 working days a year = 12,500). Based on these inputs, the estimated number of staff needed to serve in-bound operations of the branch would be:

$$\text{Number of inbound staff needed} = \frac{5,000 \times 12}{12,500} = 4.8$$

Typically the number of staff computed would be rounded up in order to make sure sufficient human resources exist to serve the customers. Therefore, in this case, 4.8 would be rounded up to 5. The total number of staff needed to operate the distribution functions of a financial services organization is the sum of the inbound and outbound staff, plus any administrative and managerial employees. In the example provided above, assuming that the entire distribution process can be administered by a single manager, a total head count of 12 employees (6 outbound + 5 inbound + 1 manager) would be called for.

2. Determining the Scope of Distribution

The scope of distribution relates to the variety of locations in which consumers could obtain access to a particular financial product or service. For example, a financial transaction such as the withdrawal of cash from one's bank account can be conducted at the bank's retail branch, the bank's own ATM device, or the wider network of competing ATM devices available at other banks. In addition, the customer may be able to withdraw funds at a competing bank's branch located across the country. This is an example in which a financial service has a wide scope of distribution. On the other hand, certain financial services may be very selectively distributed. For example, the availability of investment advice, brokerage services, and life insurance products is intentionally limited due to the highly customized nature of these products. In these categories, customers are encouraged to visit specific locations devoted to providing the specialized services needed to address customer needs effectively. For example, the amount of individual attention and the level of professional skills needed to advise a client on investment decisions may only be available on a limited scale. At the same time, some of these services are becoming accessible through mobile hand-held devices, making them into mass-customized services.

It is important to note that the scope of distribution of financial services has consistently widened over the past two decades. This is largely due to the deregulation of financial services which occurred at the turn of the century. This allowed competitors from various backgrounds to provide a variety of financial services to the marketplace. As a result, the types of locations where customers can obtain access to financial services have become much more diverse. In contrast to a decade ago, it is now possible to obtain not only checking account services, but also to seek investment advice, gain access to insurance products, and conduct complex transaction processing services from a single commercial bank branch. Most of these services would have traditionally been delivered at different locations, often by different companies. The notion of "one-stop shop" bank branches serving the numerous financial needs of customers was further facilitated by the Bank Modernization Act, which eliminated many of the legal barriers that limited cross-category competition in financial services.

The expansion of distribution outlets to a large extent can be attributed to merger and acquisition activity among financial services providers. Often, one financial institution may decide to acquire another institution, or a subset of its customer portfolio, in order to gain access to that institution's customer base.[16] For example, many credit card companies purchase each other's portfolios of customer accounts in order to gain economies of scale and to obtain specialized access to specific customer segments.[17] The buying and selling of these customer accounts is partially driven by the fact that larger credit card companies operate at more efficient levels. In addition, these types of acquisitions may be attractive to the acquiring companies since they provide immediate access to well-defined customers with established histories of transactions and great potential for the cross-selling of supplemental services.[18] Geographic expansion has also been linked to the growing trend of mergers and acquisitions in financial services, where one financial institution may seek to expand into a new region of the country by purchasing some or all of the distribution branches of an existing financial services provider.[19]

The scope of distribution may have a significant impact on customer perceptions of the financial services organization. When distribution is limited and only certain outlets provide the financial service, customers may associate a high level of exclusivity with the service experience. At the same time, selective distribution may become an inconvenient aspect of the customer experience and a wider range of access may be needed, perhaps through the application of information technology. The hand-held mobile devices and the Internet have played a major role in widening the scope of distribution for financial services. Financial services organizations of all sizes make their services available not only through personal customer contacts with their employees, but also through their mobile and Internet sites. The move towards electronic distribution of financial services has further been accelerated by market pressure and the need to keep up with distribution capabilities of competing financial services providers as well as the communications technologies widely adopted by consumers.

Research suggests that, despite the growing trend of mergers in the financial services, the net results on the attractiveness of the merged organizations can be mixed. For example it has been found that mergers may result in loss of share value in bank-to-bank mergers.[20] In three out of every ten cases, such mergers result in a drop in share values. However, mergers between banks and insurance companies are typically far more successful. In almost seven out of every ten bank-to-insurer mergers share values tend to increase. This result suggests that consolidation and mergers among financial services providers must take into account the unique strengths that one organization brings to the other to benefit the combined distribution and sales processes. Bank-to-bank mergers may result in efficiency gains in transaction processing and shared infrastructure but do not create new selling and distribution opportunities for the combined organization. On the other hand, mergers between banks and insurance companies not only result in infra-structural efficiency gains, but they also provide greater efficiencies through opportunities for the cross-selling of additional services offered by the combined organization.

THE IMPACT OF TECHNOLOGY ON FINANCIAL SERVICE DISTRIBUTION

As discussed earlier in this chapter, technology is having a revolutionary impact on the distribution of financial services. Explosive growth in certain channels of distribution for financial services has already been witnessed. Consumer use of mobile devices capable of providing them with detailed financial data has made this medium a growth opportunity not only for connecting with customers but also for transacting with them. Other evidence on the replacement of traditional distribution systems with technologically enabled means has been mounting for years. For example, the number of consumers paying bills online has steadily grown over the years, and the use of the Internet by consumers for identifying providers of credit and mortgage products has continuously grown. In addition, the sophistication by which ATM devices function and the technological ability to utilize biometric user authentication has opened new possibilities for how ATM-based transactions can replace the physical branch infrastructure of retail banks.

Technology manifests itself in various forms. While the Internet has been the most revolutionary influence the past decade, mobile phone and ATM technologies are also having a profound impact. ATM devices are being designed to serve not only as a tool for processing financial transactions, but also as a means for information acquisition, customized and individualized advertising of financial solutions customized to individual customers.[21] From the customer's perspective, many advantages can be attributed to the use of technology in the distribution of financial services. The widespread availability and accessibility of the Internet and ATM devices create convenient means for transacting with financial institutions. From a financial services provider's perspective, the use of technology also helps remove the expensive human interface from the transaction process. The presence of bank tellers, brokers and agents in the exchange process not only introduces the potential for human error, but also may at times result in incidents of moral hazard discussed earlier in this chapter. The use of technologies that eliminate the human bargaining process and standardize the distribution and sale of financial services may be most appropriate for financial services categories that are commoditized in nature, such as commercial banking services and property and casualty insurance.[22]

The cost efficiencies obtained through the use of technology are difficult to ignore when designing and implementing sale and distribution strategies for financial services. For example, it is estimated that the average transaction completed in a bank branch costs approximately one dollar. Banking online would bring down the average transaction cost to less than a dime.[23] As one can see, the cost efficiencies gained by serving customers online are monumental, and it is no surprise that many commercial banks heavily promote this means of interaction to their customers.

FINANCIAL SERVICES DISTRIBUTION STRATEGY

When considering the appropriate design for the distribution system used in a financial services organization, it is essential to determine carefully the size and scope of the organization's distribution needs. The distribution mechanisms used by a financial services organization should be reflective of its company image, target market, and internal capabilities. Deviations from this principle may in fact inhibit growth in particular distribution outlets. For example, a brokerage firm that has a strong presence in the discount brokerage business but does not provide full commission brokerage services (which typically cater to high-net-worth clients), may have a difficult time moving up-market using the same company name. It is important to recognize that the same principle holds true in consumer markets for durables and packaged goods. Moving up-market or down-market often requires the establishment of separate brand identities. Examples would be Honda's move to the semi-luxury category of automobiles through the introduction of Acura and a similar move by Toyota though the creation of the Lexus brand name.

The way in which the U.S. population clusters around particular income and wealth brackets also affects the distribution choices of financial services organizations. For example, it is estimated that there are approximately 10 million American households who do not have bank accounts. This particular population group, while not attracted to traditional commercial banking services, has in fact benefited from the use of technologies such as pre-paid cash cards and ATMs and financial services such as check-cashing services as a means for maintaining liquid assets without the need to open a bank account.[24] Another interesting trend in the distribution of financial services in the U.S. has been a drop in the number of financial institutions due to mergers and acquisitions over the past decade. The number of deposit taking financial institutions such as commercial banks and savings and loans institutions has dropped by nearly 40% during the past two decades.[25] The result is that a smaller number of organizations have become responsible for a much wider scope of operations.

One of the other challenges facing financial services organizations that use technology to replace human-based transactions is the evolving nature of the customer relationship experience. Ever since the first ATM replaced a bank teller, a fundamental issue in financial services marketing has been to determine how a financial services organization could maintain a human touch without the presence of human interactions. This is an especially important question for the older and more affluent segments of the population, who are adapted to the personalized human interface in their daily transactions. On the other hand, the younger generation's heavy reliance on technology has limited their desire for human contacts in financial transactions. Nevertheless, meeting the preferences of these two different population segments is a challenge that must be addressed by almost every financial services organization today.

What is also important to recognize is that consumer awareness and education about financial products and services is improving. The increasing use and accessibility of information on financial services and the more advanced levels of consumer education on financial matters may reduce the power of distribution personnel such as sales staff, agents, and brokers, in influencing customer decisions. As a result, traditional face-to-face selling would be expected to decline in popularity for a great majority of financial services.[26] It is important to note, however, that distribution systems based on the human interface would still be a necessary component of the sales process for many financial services, especially those that are non-commoditized and need to be customized to the individual needs of customers, such as life insurance, financial advisory services, and tax accounting.

One of the other fascinating aspects of the distribution of financial services is the growing reliance on offshore outsourcing for serving customer needs. Offshore outsourcing takes place when a service organization utilizes a customer service center that is located abroad to serve local customers' needs. This is a growing practice, which has been implemented not only in financial services organizations, but also by software developers, airlines, and consulting firms. Reliance on offshore outsourcing is itself a result of the technology-driven cost efficiencies of the Internet. The low cost of voice over IP operations has made it possible for organizations to financially benefit from the lower wage rates in offshore customer service operations.[27] Despite the financial benefits of offshore outsourcing, the impact of the practice on customers' service experiences remains a matter of debate, especially as it relates to the ability of offshore operations in meeting the unique needs of American customers within specific categories of financial services.[28]

Legal concerns must also be taken into account when developing a distribution strategy for a financial services organization. Incentive systems and sales instructions provided to members of the distribution system can have a great impact on their actions and behaviors. Legal cases in which agents or brokers in securities and insurance markets have undertaken tasks that have subsequently resulted in punitive measures or legal actions by regulators are frequently cited in the business press. Additional legal constraints must also be respected when hiring new employees into the sales and distribution system of a financial services organization. For example, financial advisers are guided by the *Financial Advisory Act of 1940* and need to complete specific licensing requirements. Similarly, insurance sales people are regulated by the insurance department of their individual states and are required to complete specific licensing requirements specified by the state. Similar licensing requirements apply to mortgage brokers, tax accountants, and stockbrokers. The costs for training these individuals, therefore, must be computed into the strategic plans of a financial services organization.

The increased use of technology, consumers' growing comfort with the use of new technologies, rising levels of consumer education on financial decision making, and the cost efficiencies gained by using new technologies as the means for transaction processing are revolutionizing the distribution methods used by financial services marketers. The inefficiencies associated with traditional face-to-face methods of providing financial services can no longer be ignored, and the competitive pressure for cost reduction will help create new interfaces for providing financial products and services to customers. This trend is further compounded by the reduced use of cash in consumer transactions and a marketplace that is becoming more information-based rather than currency-based. Marketing managers developing both short-term and long-term plans for their organizations must therefore work closely with information technology professionals to ensure proper integration of technology in their marketing and distribution strategies.

CHAPTER QUESTIONS

1. What specific financial services do you think are best suited for distribution through the following channels:

    (a) Mobile apps
    (b) Automated Teller Machines
    (c) Captive agents
    (d) Retail banks

2. What are some factors that make the distribution of financial services different from distribution in other marketing contexts?

3. What are the different approaches used in order to distribute financial services?

4. A mortgage broker is considering expanding operations by opening a new branch location. It is estimated that, in order to be fully functional, the new branch would have to serve approximately 10,000 outbound customers and 20,000 inbound customers a year. In addition, it is estimated that each staff member is able to make 10 outbound customers or alternatively serve 25 inbound customers on a daily basis. It is expected that three outbound calls and two inbound calls per year would occur for each customer or prospect. How many staff members does the new branch require?

5. What emerging channels of distribution do you think will have a great impact on the future of financial services?

6. What are some advantages and disadvantages to using an agent or broker

system for distributing financial services?

7. Define the following terms:
   (a) Moral hazard
   (b) Churning
   (c) Captive agent
   (d) Contingent commissions
   (e) Broker
   (f) Revenue sharing

ENDNOTES

1 R. Kwong (2011), "Outside Help May be Vital to Satisfy Demand: Corporate Apps," *Financial Times*, Feb, 14, p. 3; "Note to Banking Industry: Whopping Operational Cost Savings are Up for Grabs," *Business Wire*, Oct 18, 2010.

2 R. Pozen, T. Hamacher and D. Phillips (2011), *The Fund Industry: How Your Money is Managed.* New York: Wiley.

3 For related examples, consult the following sources: David Bogoslaw (2009), "How Banks Should Manage Risk," *Business Week (Online)*, September 15; Christopher Oster (2004), "Insurance Probe Targets Policies for Consumers," *Wall Street Journal*, Oct 19, p. D1; Theo Francis and Vanessa Fuhrmans (2004), "Insurance Probe Expands its Focus on Improper Payments to Brokers," *Wall Street Journal*, Oct 21, p. C.1; Paul Davies (2004), "Intel Employee Sues Insurer Over Commissions," *Wall Street Journal*, Oct 22, p. C.3.

4 R. Pozen, T. Hamacher and D. Phillips (2011), *The Fund Industry: How Your Money is Managed.* New York: Wiley; Tom Luricella (2004), "Brokerage Firms Begin to Reveal Details of Sales Pacts," *Wall Street Journal*, Oct 1, p. C.1; Christopher Oster (2004), "Insurance Probe Targets Policies for Consumers," *Wall Street Journal*, Oct 19, p. D1; Theo Francis and Vanessa Fuhrmans (2004), "Insurance Probe Expands its Focus on Improper Payments to Brokers," *Wall Street Journal*, Oct 21, p. C.1

5 Philip Kotler (2011), *Marketing Management.* Prentice Hall: Upper Saddle River, NJ, pp. 489-495; Douglas Dalrymple, William Cron, and Thomas DeCarlo (2003), *Sales Management.* Wiley: New York; Thomas Ingram, Raymond LaForge, Ramon Avila, Charles Schwepker, and Michael Williams (2003), *Sales Management: Analysis and Decision Making.* Southwestern College Pulishing;.Robert Peterson and Thomas Wotruba (1996), "What is Direct Selling? Definition, Perspectives, and Research Agenda," *Journal of Personal Selling and Sales Management*, Vol. 16, Iss. 4, pp. 1-15; Dominique Xardel (1993), *The Direct Selling Revolution.* Cambridge, MA: Blackwell Publishers; Filipe Coelho and Chris Easingwood (2003), "Multiple Channel Structures in Financial Services: A Framework," *Journal of Financial Services Marketing*, Vol. 8, Iss. 1, pp.22-34.

6 Rosann Spiro, William Stanton and Greg Rich (2007), *Management of a Sales Force.* New York: McGraw-Hill; C. Easingwood and C. Storey (1996), "The Value of Multi-Channel Distribution Systems in the Financial Services Sector," *The Service Industries Journal*, Vol. 16, Iss. 2, pp. 223-241. G. Frazier (1999), "Organizing and Managing Channels of Distribution," *Journal of the Academy of Marketing Science*, Vol. 27, Iss. 2, pp. 226-240. Filipe Coelho and Chris Easingwood (2003), "Multiple Channel Structures in Financial Services: A Framework," *Journal of Financial Services Marketing*, Vol. 8, Iss. 1, pp. 22-34.

7 Lauren Bielski (2004), "Is Free Checking Worth it?," *ABA Banking Journal*, Vol. 96, Iss. 3, pp. 31-35.

8 Jennifer Saranow (2004), "Incentives to Pay Bills Online – Financial Institutions Give Cash to Induce Customers to Use Web-Based Services," *Wall Street Journal*, December 8, p. D2; "Contrarian Forecast for 2010: Chilly for Branches, Sunny for E-Banks," *ABA Banking Journal*, Vol. 96, Iss. 3, pp. 56-57.

9 Ben Eglin, and Timothy Mullaney (2003), "Checks Check Out," *Business Week*, May 10, Iss. 3882, pp. 83-84,

citing a study done by Gartner; Filipe Coelho and Chris Easingwood (2003), "Multiple Channel Structures in Financial Services: A Framework," *Journal of Financial Services Marketing*, Vol. 8, Iss. 1, pp. 22-34.

10 "A Safer Fannie and Freddie," *Business Week*, 5/10/2004, Iss. 3882, p. 136; Joseph Hu (2001), *Basics of Mortgage-Backed Securities*. New York: Wiley.

11 William Cron, and Thomas DeCarlo (2010), *Sales Management: Concepts and Cases*. Wiley: New York; Thomas Ingram, Raymond LaForge, Ramon Avila, Charles Schwepker, and Michael Williams (2003), *Sales Management: Analysis and Decision Making*. Southwestern College Publishing.

12 J. Kimball Dietrich (1996), *Financial Services and Financial Institutions*. Upper Saddle River, NJ: Prentice Hall, pp. 188-189.

13 Christopher Oster (2004), "Insurance Probe Targets Policies for Consumers," *Wall Street Journal*, Oct 19, p. D1; Theo Francis and Vanessa Fuhrmans (2004), "Insurance Probe Expands Its Focus on Improper Payments to Brokers," *Wall Street Journal*, Oct 21, p. C.1; Amy Borrus (2004), "Brokers Aren't Advisors," *Business Week*, Aug 30, Iss. 3897, p. 55.

14 Judith Burns (2005), "NASD Charges Firms on Fund Sales," *Wall Street Journal*, June 9, 2005, p. C15; Kaja Whitehouse (2003), "Wealthy Clients Dismiss Brokers; In Survey, Rich Register Their Concern That Advice is Incomplete or Biased," *Wall Street Journal*, Nov. 11, p. D2, citing study conducted by the Spectrem Group.

15 D. Johnsen (2010), in J. Boatright (ed), *Finance Ethics: Critical Issues in Theory and Practice*. New York: John Wiley & Sons.

16 Ben Wright (2001), "Acquire or be Damned," *Global Investor*, Feb. 2001, Iss. 139, p. 36.

17 Monica Roman (2003), "Oh-So Popular Sears Card", *Business Week*, April 14, Iss. 3828, p. 43; "A Rush to Bail out of Finance", *Business Week*, 8/18/2003-8/25/2003, Iss. 3846, p. 14; Burney Simpson (2004), "A Turning Point for Retailers" *Credit Card Management*, Vol. 17, Iss. 2, p. 43.

18 Joseph Weber (2003), "Plastic that Looks Like Gold", *Business Week*, June 16, Iss. 3837, p. 70.

19 Lauren Bielski and Orla O'Sullivan (2003), "Branch Mania," *ABA Banking Journal*, Vol. 95, Iss. 8, p. 30.

20 Ken Smith and Eliza O'Neil (2003), "Bank-to-Bank Deals Seldom Add Value," *ABA Banking Journal*, Vol. 95, Iss. 12, pp.7-9, citing figures reported by SECOR Consulting.

21 David Gousnell (2004), "Hard-Core Enthusiasm for High-Tech ATMs," *Credit Card Management*, Vol. 16, Iss. 11, p. 16; Jen Ryan (2004), "ATMs Try to Cash In With Extra Services," *Wall Street Journal*, August 11, p. D4.

22 Kathryn Waite and Tina Harrison (2002), "Consumer Expectations of Online Information Provided by Bank Websites," *Journal of Financial Services Marketing*, Vol. 6, Iss. 4, pp. 309-322.

23 G. Michael Moebs (1986), *Pricing Financial Services*. Dow Jones-Irwin: Homewood, IL, p. 84; *Fed Letter* (1997), Federal Reserve Bank of Kansas: Kansas City, KS; *Board of Governors of the Federal Reserve System* (2002). The Federal Reserve System: Purposes and Functions. Books for Business.

24 S. Rhine, W. Greene, and M. Toussaint-Comeau (2006), "The Importance of Check-Cashing Businesses to the Unbanked: Racial/Ethnic Differences," *The Review of Economics and Statistics*, Vol. 88, Iss. 1, pp.146-159; Sally Law (2006), "Attracting the Non-Customer," *US Banker*, Vol. 116, Iss. 2, p. 36; Linda Punch (2004), "Beckoning the Unbanked", *Credit Card Management*, Vol. 17, Iss. 7, pp. 28-32; Mara Der Hovanesian (2003) "The Virtually Cashless Society," *Business Week*, November 17, Iss. 3858, p. 125.

25 F. Mishkin (2007), *The Economics of Money, Banking, and Financial Markets*. New York: Pearson; Michelle Pacelle, Carrick Mollenkamp, and Jathon Sapsford (2003), "Big Banks Signal They May be Gearing Up for Acquisitions," *Wall Street Journal*, June 12, p. C1.

26 "Note to Banking Industry: Whopping Operational Cost Savings are Up for Grabs," *Business Wire*, Oct 18, 2010; Jennifer Saranow (2004), "Electronic Ways Outpace Checks as Payment Means," *Wall Street Journal*, Dec 7, p. D2, citing a study conducted by the Federal Reserve; Bill Orr (2004), "Contrarian Forecast for 2010: Chilly for Branches, Sunny for E-Banks," *ABA Banking Journal*, Vol. 96, Iss. 3, pp. 56-57

27 R. McIvor (2010), *Global Services Outsourcing*. New York: Cambridge University Press.

28 R. Hira and A. Hira (2008), *Outsourcing America: The True Cost of Shipping Jobs Overseas*. New York: American Management Association.

CHAPTER SEVEN

New Product Introduction in Financial Services Markets

The new product introduction process is a fascinating aspect of financial services marketing. A new product can be introduced at a considerably quicker pace in financial services markets than in most other markets. This is largely attributed to the fact that the introduction of new financial products and services does not necessarily require the development of entirely new physical objects or the deployment of elaborate and technologically sophisticated product development procedures.[1] Rather, the introduction of a new product in most financial services may require expanding or limiting contractual obligations to the customer, or changes in the form in which a financial transaction or process is presented to the marketplace.

Reliance on long product development cycles that are typical of the manufacturing sector or consumer packaged goods markets is often not the case in financial services. For example, when new electronics products or home appliances are introduced to the marketplace, a significant amount of time and money is expended conducting research in order to conceive a potentially profitable new product and to test its technical and financial feasibility. This extensive level of research may not necessarily be needed for financial services due to the comparatively lower costs of product introductions and the limited technological nature of financial services. As a result, the speed at which new financial services can be introduced to the marketplace is typically higher than in most other services or goods markets, and the road to innovation and creativity can be an exciting and rewarding one. The rate of innovation in financial services has accelerated in the past two decades as a result of deregulatory forces that have enabled financial services organizations to introduce new financial solutions to the marketplace.

An example of a new financial product is a limited form of travel insurance called season pass insurance, designed for the unique needs of highly active skiers. A season pass insurance (also referred to as "wipe out" insurance), provides skiers with specific policy benefits often not covered by existing travel insurance policies on the market. The policy provides a skier who gets injured on the ski slopes, the ability to redeem the monetary value of the season ski pass if the injuries sustained prevent her from engaging in physical activity during the skiing season. In addition, the policy may cover the medical expenses for emergency evacuation of the policyholder from the ski slopes. Despite the fact that this policy may not be relevant to the masses, a particular segment of the market, namely highly active skiers, find such policies very attractive, and sufficient numbers of them purchase these policies every year to make this new category of insurance products economically attractive for the insurance industry.[2] The existence of ski pass insurance has not only helped individual skiers enjoy more security while engaging in a high-risk sport, but it also has helped the industry experience growth in the seemingly stagnant category of travel insurance.

In the home mortgage business, new breeds of mortgage products such as "flex mortgages" and 40-year mortgages helped fuel much of the real estate boom of the past decade. Flex mortgages provided homebuyers with the added flexibility of skipping a mortgage payment or two: a situation that some households may confront at times due to the unpredictability of household finances and fluctuating cash flows. Variations of these mortgages allowed the homeowner to switch from a 20-year to a 30-year (or longer term) mortgage, or to change payment preferences during the term of the mortgage. Clearly, this type of mortgage was of special interest to particular segments of the population who desired the level of payment flexibility provided. The introduction of flex mortgages changed the traditional notion of what a mortgage is, and enabled a large number of individuals who may not have otherwise been able to purchase homes to become homeowners.[3] It is important to acknowledge that while such innovations improved the lives of many, they have also been widely blamed for much to the financial crisis of the past decade, as such mortgage products in some cases encouraged irresponsible spending by financially constrained homebuyers.

Another example of a financial service that came to life due to concerns over information security and consumer privacy is identity theft insurance. This product protects the policyholder with the financial coverage needed to recover from cases of identity theft. The typical policy covers the legal filing costs, attorney fees, and other relevant expenses associated with recovering from a case of identity theft. The introduction of this type of financial service was a direct response to the explosive growth in cases of identity theft that had been experienced in the early part of the previous decade.[4] Its creation helped consumers gain peace of mind in online transactions and other contexts where the buyer-seller relationship may be challenged by geographic distance, and by doing so, supported the growth of online commerce.

As may be evident from the above discussion, many interesting new products are regularly introduced to the financial services marketplace. These products can be introduced in a variety of ways, including the expansion as well as the constraining of a traditional financial product's performance features. In this chapter, we will discuss methods that financial services marketers often utilize for identifying new product opportunities. We will also discuss the science behind consumer decision processes and the cognitive strategies that consumers may use in order to evaluate these new products and services. We will also gain exposure to two popular techniques that are used to test new concepts and to establish the potential profitability and market acceptability associated with new financial services.

NEW PRODUCT OPPORTUNITIES IN THE PRODUCT ATTRIBUTE SPACE

As discussed earlier in Chapter 2, financial services often possess several standard input attributes: (a) the monetary input, (b) the time frame in which a financial service is in effect, and (c) the risk associated with the financial transaction. As also discussed in detail in Chapter 2, the output of a financial service is typically some form of financial or nonfinancial attribute, such as the total mortgage amount provided for the purchase of a house or the insurance protection offered by an insurance policy. These fundamental attributes (risk, time frame, monetary input and output) are present in the majority of financial services and are referred to as the *core attributes* of a financial product or service. The rational consumer would need to rely on the values of the core attributes to form an objective assessment of a financial offer. However, in addition to the core attributes, other non-core attributes may also play a significant role in consumer decisions regarding financial products and services. For example, while the interest rate (monetary input), the length of the mortgage (time frame), and the credit profile of the mortgage applicant (risk) may be the primary determinants of the total mortgage amount that a mortgage applicant may be able to obtain (monetary output), other attributes may also contribute to the applicant's overall impression of a mortgage offer. The applicant may for example be concerned with factors such as the reputation of the mortgage company, the friendliness and accessibility of the customer service staff, and the physical location and cleanliness of the branch offices.

The difference between core and non-core attributes is the extent by which they impact the objective value of a financial offer. Core attributes (for example, the interest rate on a mortgage) typically have significantly greater impact on consumers than non-core attributes (for example, the cleanliness of a branch office). However, the very existence of non-core attributes provides opportunities for financial services marketers to not only differentiate themselves from their competitors, but also to identify new product opportunities that may be highly relevant to unique groups of consumers. Flex mortgages, which were discussed earlier, reflect the introduction of a new attribute—namely payment flexibility—to the traditional mortgage product. While the addition of this attribute may be considered unimportant to many homebuyers, individuals who seek payment flexibility may find this attribute of immense importance. Exhibit 7.1 provides additional examples of how the introduction of new non-core attributes or variations on existing attributes in financial services may influence consumer decision processes and help create new categories of financial services.

Another example is the evolution of the mutual fund business. Investors purchasing shares of mutual funds typically focus on the core attributes of fund performance (output), upfront and back-end loads (input), and the reputation of the fund (risk). However a new breed of mutual funds focused on a non-core attribute of investing – ethical investment philosophy – helped create a new category of mutual funds. Ethical funds may steer away from investing in companies that are known to conduct activities that are ethically considered incorrect. For example they may choose not to invest in companies that have manufacturing operations that use child labor or those that are polluting the environment. While the ethical philosophy of a fund may not have a direct positive impact on the objective output of the fund (its investment returns), it may be very relevant to an investor who is concerned about the greater question of how the fund returns

Product / Service	Core Attributes	Non-Core Attributes	New Product
Mutual Fund	Fund's load (input), performance (output), company name (risk), time restrictions (time frame)	Socially responsible investment focus	Socially Responsible Mutual Funds
Mortgage	Interest rate and monthly payments (input), mortgage amount (output), applicant's credit score (risk), length of mortgage (time frame)	Payment flexibility	Flex Mortgages
Auto Insurance	Premiums (input), total coverage (output), company name and driver's record (risk), length of coverage (time frame)	Ability to receive customer service online and by phone	Direct Insurance
Travel Insurance	Premiums (input), total coverage (output), company name (risk), length of coverage (time frame)	Coverage for skiing accidents	Season Pass Insurance for Skiers

Exhibit 7.1: Core and Non-Core Attributes Used for New Product Introduction

are secured. Non-core attributes can therefore help introduce new dimensions to the consumer experience, and can be used as a basis for serving new customer needs in an otherwise cluttered marketplace.

HOW NEW PRODUCTS AND SERVICES ARE CREATED

Financial services and other types of services and goods share a common process for new product development. New products are introduced to the market because they can significantly improve the consumer's experience or help serve unique consumer needs that are not satisfied by existing products and services on the market. This is often achieved in one of two different ways. The first is the introduction or modification of existing product attributes. For example, until the middle of the 20th century, the majority of motorcycles sold were large, heavy, and difficult to ride. In the 1960s and 1970s, manufacturers such as Honda, Suzuki, and Kawasaki recognized that there might be a much larger consumer base potentially interested in riding motorcycles but unable to do so due to the prohibitively large physical size of motorcycles and their high sticker price at the time. This led these manufacturers to focus on the size of the motorcycle as the key product attribute for creating a new consumer experience, which resulted in the introduction of smaller motorcycles such as mopeds and scooters.[5] By introducing ease of handling as a new attribute to the motorcycle riding experience, the category of scooters and mopeds was created, changing the picture of the industry. The same process can be observed with financial services such as flex mortgages, which are fundamentally traditional mortgage contracts with the added dimension of payment flexibility, or wipe-out insurance, which is fundamentally a travel insurance policy for which the attribute characterizing the conditions in which the policy is activated is specifically designed to cover only the unique needs of highly active skiers. All of these products were developed through the *modification* of existing product attributes.

A second approach to new product development is the *merger* of the existing categories in the marketplace. For example, when Chrysler introduced the first minivan in 1985, it fundamentally merged two different categories of vehicles: the van and the station wagon. The introduction of the minivan resulted in the automotive industry's creation of a totally new class of vehicles that were specifically designed to meet the unique needs of families. A similar process can be associated with many new product introductions in financial services. For example, the debit card is a result of the merger of the credit card and the personal checking account. Similar to using checks, using a debit card results in the withdrawal of funds from one's bank account. On the other hand, debit cards, like credit cards, provide the convenience of mass-market acceptance, ease of use, and the use of electronic networks for fund transfers and information exchange. Similarly, the merger of gift certificates and credit cards resulted in the creation of the gift card category. These new products add a notable level of convenience to the consumer experience, and have therefore received mass consumer acceptance.[6]

METHODS FOR IDENTIFYING NEW PRODUCT NEEDS

A variety of techniques are used to identify new financial product opportunities. In this section, we will review four common approaches and discuss their advantages and disadvantages. The first approach capitalizes on organizational learning and what the existing management perceives consumers' needs to be. The second and third approaches capitalize on informal and qualitative data that are collected from the consumer. The final approach represents a more structured and quantitative approach to consumer data collection through the use of formal surveys with large consumer samples.

1. Observational Methods

A common approach to identifying new product opportunities in financial services it to utilize what the existing employees may already feel to be the needs of the customers. For example, managers of a commercial bank branch may have noticed long customer lines forming in the bank teller area inside the bank branch. Further discussion with the bank tellers and a study of the transactions that take place may reveal that a significant proportion of the customers who come to the branch do so with the sole purpose of depositing funds. This may help the management conclude that the flow of traffic in the customer service area may be improved by introducing an "instant deposit" machine. These are ATM-like devices that only facilitate the depositing of funds and unlike ATMs do not dispense cash. Through this product introduction customers can directly deposit their cash or checks and do not have to wait in long lines to see a teller. Their ability to improve the flow of customer traffic in bank branches and to reduce the load on bank tellers and ATM machines has made them an attractive choice for some commercial banking operations.

Similarly, the management of a mortgage company may recognize that a significant number of their applicants and subsequent mortgage holders are purchasing homes that are over 50 years old. The purchase of these older homes presents the homeowner with additional risks resulting from malfunctioning components such as electrical and plumbing systems, and the potential failure of the heating system. This unique characteristic associated with older home purchases may help the management recognize that a notable proportion of their customers may ultimately find a need for some form of a home warranty product. Home warranties provide homeowners with financial protection to cover repair costs in case of malfunctioning systems in the home. The result might be the introduction of specific home warranty products by the mortgage company to its existing customer base.

It is important to note that human intuition may not necessarily be the only method for identifying new product opportunities. In fact, new product opportunities may be identified through observation of other modes in which a financial services organization interacts with its customers. For example, surveillance video of a bank branch may be able to reveal that long lines are accumulating at either the bank teller area or the ATM area of the bank. This may prompt the management to examine the cause for the accumulation of the long lines, thereby identifying the transactions that may be accelerated either through the introduction of new services or the modification of existing ones. Similarly, while the managerial intuition of a mortgage company may provide insights into the potential need of homebuyers for home warranty products, a close examination of existing mortgages and the ages of homes purchased with these mortgages may provide the same potential for identifying new product opportunities.

While the observation method for identifying new financial services is frequently utilized, there are several drawbacks to this approach. One obvious drawback is that this approach may be highly biased by what data becomes available at the time or location where the observations are being made. For example, the location of a bank branch may result in a series of observations that are most relevant and specific to customers who live or work in the vicinity of that specific branch. As a result, the views and opinions of customers in other geographic locations may not necessarily be represented in the observations that are made, and the wider spectrum of consumer opinions and the full range of potential new product opportunities may not be captured through this approach. Nevertheless, the minimal costs associated with this technique make it a very attractive approach for many organizations in pursuit of new concepts, both from within and from outside of the financial services sector.[7]

2. Open-Ended Questioning

A second approach that is frequently used in identifying new product opportunities is what is often referred to as qualitative or open-ended questioning. This approach advances the observation method discussed above by facilitating direct communication with customers of a financial services organization. Often, this requires conversing with a representative sample of customers through means such as intercept interviews in a bank branch, where customers are stopped and asked to respond to a series of general questions, or reached through telephone interviews, or via email. This technique requires one to utilize an open format of questioning to probe the specific needs that customers might have and to identify new services of potential interest to them. The primary consideration in this method is not to restrict the scope of customer responses, but rather to allow customers to express their opinions and thoughts freely. In an interview, the customer might be asked an open-ended question such as: "What factors prevent you from using the instant deposit machine in this bank branch?" Responses obtained from a sample of customers on the above question can then be studied, categorized into various types of answers, and then tabulated in order to identify what the majority of customers believe is restricting them from using this service.

For example, Exhibit 7.2 provides some of the categories of answers that customers of a retail bank provided in response to this question, and the associated percentages. Certain categories of customer responses seem to dominate. The majority of customers expressed that they do not feel comfortable depositing their funds in a machine and would instead prefer to interact with a bank teller. In order to market an instant deposit machine to this customer segment successfully, individualized training of customers and image advertising aimed at making customers more comfortable with the process of using the device may be needed. From examining the numbers provided in Exhibit 7.2, it is also obvious that a significant percentage of customers are under the assumption that the device does not provide them with a receipt. This reduces the sense of assurance that they seek when depositing their funds with a banking institution. Marketing activity can therefore focus on communicating to customers that the deposit machines do in fact produce receipts, thereby directly confronting these customers' uninformed concerns related to the service.

The open-ended questioning approach is a relatively quick method for obtaining objective evidence on the nature of consumer response to a new financial service as well as to an existing service that may be experiencing difficulty gaining acceptance in the marketplace. Typically, the required sample size associated with this method is anywhere between 50 to 300 respondents. However, sample size estimation using market research methods may be needed to determine the minimum required number of customers that needs to be interviewed.[8] Since respondents are allowed to provide a range of responses in an open-ended fashion, the method requires thorough study of the open-ended comments that consumers have provided. In this examination, a team of two or three trained market researchers reads the customers' responses and classifies them into the various response categories using a technique called *content analysis*.[9] Content analysis is a means for quantifying what is otherwise qualitative verbal or written data. Once the customers' statements have been grouped into categories of response, the number of customers that provided different forms of response can then be tabulated and subjected to further numeric analysis. This is a very powerful feature of the technique because it translates what would otherwise seem like simple human expressions into quantifiable figures such as the percentages reported in Exhibit 7.2.

Don't like to drop money in a machine ... need to deal with a human	62%
Don't think the machine produces a receipt	44%
Need to see a teller about other services	19%
Location of the box is too public	2%
Other	5%

Exhibit 7.2 Tabulation of Customers' Responses

3. Focus Groups

Focus groups further advance one's ability to conduct open-ended questioning by engaging groups of customers rather than an individual customer. The fundamental idea behind a focus group is very similar to that of open-ended questioning, with the distinct difference of the use of a group of customers gathered in a common location rather than individual interviews with one customer at a time. In a focus group, a small sample of potential or existing customers—typically about 10—are invited to a focus group facility. The facility often consists of a room with a conference table around which everyone sits. Focus groups also utilize a trained market researcher as a moderator who presents the participants in the focus group session with a series of general questions aimed at soliciting their opinions. The flow of the discussion is then managed by the moderator. The moderator has the unique and sometimes challenging responsibility of ensuring that all participants are heard and that all issues that may have been of concern to the client (e.g., the financial services company concerned with the launch of a new product) are addressed. In addition, the focus group participants' thoughts may be recorded through both video and audio recording of the session, for subsequent analysis. Often, focus group results are provided in written format to the client, and these results may then help identify new product opportunities or provide the necessary insights into how to improve the marketing of a newly introduced financial service.

What is unique about the focus group approach is that the setting of a focus group often provides the ability for the client (the management of the financial services organization) to observe the conversations taking place between the focus group moderator and the participants (existing or potential customers). This enables the management not only to gain first-hand experience of what the customers are thinking but to also provide feedback to the moderator on different lines of questions that may be introduced to the group discussion. Focus group facilities that enable this are equipped with a one-way mirror separating the observation room from the group meeting area, which allows the client to freely observe the participants' responses without interfering in the group dynamics in the adjacent room. Communication between the client and the focus group moderator is typically achieved through a computer monitor located near where the moderator sits or the hand delivery of a note from the observation room to the moderator.

The use of focus groups is a widely accepted approach for identifying new product opportunities in financial services, consumer packaged goods, durables and industrial products. Typically, focus groups last about one to two hours. However, due to the expenses associated with the unique setup requirements of focus group facilities, the cost of recruiting participants, and the consulting fees of moderators and other professionals involved, the total cost of a single focus group session can run in the $5,000 to $15,000 range, and may even exceed these figures in certain cases. Despite the costs, the insights gained in a focus group session may be of great value as they may facilitate critical corrections to the marketing program of a financial services organization, and can help identify new product opportunities that could not have been identifiable through other means.

4. Attribute Ratings

A more technical approach for identifying new product and service opportunities is achieved by asking customers to rate the importance of various attributes for an existing financial service on numeric rating scales. The customer may be asked for example to rate the various aspects of a commercial bank on a scale of 1 to 5 (with 5 being "very important" and 1 being "not important at all"). The customers' ratings of the attributes may then provide insights into what weaknesses a particular financial service might have or what potential opportunities might exist for the introduction of new services.

In analyzing attribute-rating data, two approaches are often used. One approach is to examine the service attributes by computing the average rating associated with that particular attribute. While this approach is relatively simple, it presents the numeric challenge of establishing whether differences in averages across the various attributes truly exist. This problem stems from the fact that the average attribute ratings for various service attributes are often in close proximity to one another, and identifying significant differences across the averages can become a difficult statistical task requiring large sample sizes.[10] An alternative approach that often remedies this problem is to use what is referred to as *top box analysis*. In top box analysis, one simply determines the percentage of consumers who checked the top box (for example checked off the number 5 on a 1-to-5 attribute rating scale), for a given attribute. This approach can identify variations in consumer

Attribute	Percent of Customers Rating the Attribute as 'Very Important'
Location of the bank branch	83%
Account maintenance fees	42%
Minimum balance requirements	19%
Availability of loans	51%
Online banking capabilities	72%
Availability of insurance products	7%

Exhibit 7.3 Top Box Figures for Importance of Various Bank Attributes

responses much more clearly than using the average ratings. It also often requires smaller sample sizes to detect differences in ratings across the various attributes.

As can be seen in Exhibit 7.3, various attributes of a commercial bank are profiled by reporting the percentage of customers who rate each attribute as a 5 (top box). The higher the number, the greater the importance of the corresponding attributes. This method can therefore identify attributes that have the most impact on the customer. From the numbers reported in Exhibit 7.3, it can be inferred that bank location is the most important attribute. This if followed by the availability of online banking and accessibility to bank loans. The least important attribute seems to be the availability of insurance products at the bank.

The obtained attribute rating information can also be used in order to profile the importance of the attributes in combination with how well a given financial institution and its competitors perform on that attribute. Exhibit 7.4 demonstrates a typical example of this process. The first column reflects the top box percentages obtained through a consumer survey of the attributes relevant to commercial bank branches. The remaining columns communicate the performance of a given bank as well as its competitors on those attributes. The data for these latter columns may be obtained either through subjective assessment conducted by independent consultants or the formal collection of additional market research data using consumer surveys designed to estimate the performance of the various competitors on these fundamental attributes. The goal of this approach is to identify specific attributes that have two characteristics. First, the attribute has to be of great importance to the customer and second, existing competitors should not be providing the attribute to the customers (or doing a poor job of doing so). In the example provided in Exhibit 7.4, this combination can be found for "weekend

Attribute	Percent of Customers Rating Attribute as "Very Important"	Our Bank	Competitor 1	Competitor 2
Number of Branches	80%	Good	Excellent	Excellent
Branch Appearance	58%	Excellent	Excellent	Good
Advertising and Company Image	81%	Good	Excellent	Poor
Online Banking	56%	No	No	Yes
Weekend Operation	75%	No	No	No
Size of the ATM Network	20%	Moderate	Large	Small

Exhibit 7.4 Analysis of Competitors' Service Offerings

operations," which is rated as important by 75% of consumers. Since none of the banks provide such a service, this particular attribute clearly represents a new service opportunity for the bank. While this relatively minor modification to the service attributes may not be considered a totally new service, as we had pointed out at the beginning of this chapter the modification of an existing service attribute (for example, hours of operation), may change the spectrum of the banking experience for both existing and future customers and provide the added potential of attracting new segments of the market who may, in this case, need banking services on weekends.

5. Conjoint Analysis

Conjoint analysis is a technique that is used to determine how consumers form their overall impressions of a new service or product based on its attributes.[11] Through the use of this technique, one is able to explain how consumers value each individual service attribute and predict how these attribute values are combined to form an overall judgment of an existing service, as well as new services not yet introduced to the marketplace. This process can then help identify promising new services for market introduction. For example, consider credit card offers, which vary in terms of their interest rates, their annual fees, as well as their refund and benefits programs. In designing a new credit card offer, a credit card company would need to determine how each of these different attributes are evaluated by the consumer and the extent to which each helps improve or deplete consumer opinions. For example, one might be interested in knowing the extent to which changing the annual percentage rate (APR) for a credit card from 3% to 6% might impact consumer impressions. Alternatively, one might be concerned with the effects of charging an annual fee for the card or providing a reward program that gives customers a refund as a percentage of charges made to the card.

Conjoint analysis enables one to address these questions in a numeric and scientific manner. In conjoint analysis, one provides a consumer with an array of hypothetical service offerings and asks for the consumer's general perceptions of each offer using a rating scale, such as a like-dislike numeric response scale. The service characteristics are varied through changes in the attributes described to the consumer, and the resulting changes in consumer ratings are then measured. By doing this, one is able to quantify the effects that a given attribute has on consumer preferences for the service. One would also be able to estimate the extent to which variations in any attribute influence consumer perceptions of the service. This enables the identification of service characteristics that are likely to result in the most favorable consumer responses.

In order to conduct conjoint analysis, all hypothetical combinations of the various attributes under consideration need to be presented to the consumer. Exhibit 7.5 provides an example of the eight possible hypothetical credit card offers associated with different levels of introductory APRs (3% and 6%), the charging of annual fee ($0, $25), and the availability of a loyalty program (yes, no). The presented offers in Exhibit 7.5 reflect all possible combinations that could be created by varying each of the attributes at their two corresponding levels. Each of the eight hypothetical credit card offers is then presented to the consumers. Exhibit 7.6 provides an example of what one of the eight credit card descriptions presented to the consumer would look like, and the response scale that would be used by the consumer to rate the described offer. As can be seen in Exhibit 7.6, the consumer, having looked at the description, is asked to make an evaluation of how

Offer	Introductory APR	Annual Fee	Loyalty Program
1	3%	$0	Yes
2	3%	$0	No
3	3%	$25	Yes
4	3%	$25	No
5	6%	$0	Yes
6	6%	$0	No
7	6%	$25	Yes
8	6%	$25	No

Exhibit 7.5: Credit Card Offers for Use in Conjoint Analysis

```
                 Introductory APR:      6%
                 Annual Fee:            $0
                 Loyalty Program:       None




        How much do you like or dislike this offer?


            Dislike it                         Like it
            Very Much                          Very Much

                 1... 2... 3... 4... 5... 6... 7... 8... 9... 10
```

Exhibit 7.6 Sample Offer Description and Response Scale for Conjoint Analysis

attractive or unattractive the described offer is using a rating scale provided at the bottom of the page. In this case, a 1-to-10 (dislike-like) scale is used. Each consumer will examine all 8 offers. However, it is critical that the order of presentation of the individual offers be randomized for each individual consumer so that the collected data are not biased by any pre-specified order in which the services are presented to the consumers.

The consumer's ratings are then captured for all eight offers. Exhibit 7.7 shows the pattern of responses for a consumer who has completed the rating task. To determine the extent to which each attribute contributes to this consumer's ratings, the variations in the ratings across the various offers will be used. For example, when presented with an offer in which the credit card has a 3% introductory APR, no annual fee, and a loyalty program, this consumer's response was very positive, rating it a 10 on the 1-to-10 response scale. In contrast, when the credit card offer has a 6% introductory rate, an annual fee of $25, and no loyalty programs, only a rating of 2 points on the 1-to-10 scale was observed.

From the pattern of ratings provided by this consumer, one is able to make several observations. First, it seems obvious that the loyalty program has a positive impact on the evaluations. This is evident by the fact that, when most offers in which a refund program is present are compared to similar offers in which the refund program is not present, significant increases in ratings can be observed. Similarly, a comparison of offers in which the introductory APR levels are high versus those in which the introductory APR level is low demonstrates that a high APR will influence the consumer evaluations negatively. A similar approach can be used to establish that the presence of an annual fee would in fact negatively influence this consumer's assessments.

Offer	Introductory APR	Annual Fee	Loyalty Program	Consumer Rating
1	3%	$0	Yes	10
2	3%	$0	No	7
3	3%	$25	Yes	5
4	3%	$25	No	3
5	6%	$0	Yes	8
6	6%	$0	No	5
7	6%	$25	Yes	4
8	6%	$25	No	2

Exhibit 7.7 Ratings Provided by an Individual Consumer

Loyalty Program:

Yes	6.75
No	4.25

Annual Fee:

$0	7.50
$25	3.50

Introductory APR:

3%	6.25
6%	4.75

Exhibit 7.8 Average Attribute Ratings

In order to more systematically evaluate shifts in consumer ratings, Exhibit 7.8 shows the computed average ratings for the various levels of each of the attributes. For example, by estimating the average ratings for all the offers that have a loyalty program (offers 1,3,5,7) versus those that do not (offers 2, 4, 6, 8), one can quantify the overall effect that the loyalty program has on the consumer ratings. For offers in which the loyalty program is available, the average rating is 6.75. For offers in which there is no loyalty program available, the average rating is 4.25. Similarly, it is established that, when an annual fee is charged, the average rating for those offers (3, 4, 7, and 8) is 3.5, whereas when no annual fee is charged, an average rating of 7.5 results. The corresponding shift in consumer ratings from a low introductory APR level to a high level reveals a change in average scale points from 6.25 to 4.75.

These shifts reflect the degree to which changes in financial service attributes influence the consumer. The offering of the loyalty program improves the consumer's evaluations by 2.5 points (from 4.25 to 6.75). In contrast, charging an annual fee results in a reduction in consumer evaluations by 4 points (shift in ratings from 7.5 to 3.5). Similarly, a high introductory APR level of 6% results in a 1.5 point drop in the consumer's evaluations, versus an APR level of 3% percent (drop from 6.25 to 4.75). The magnitude of these shifts represents the extent to which the consumer's overall evaluations are influenced by each attribute. From these results, it appears that, for this consumer, the annual fee seems to be a very important factor. As a product feature, this consumer would not like to see an annual fee required by the credit card company. The second most important feature for this consumer seems to be the presence of a loyalty program, and the least important attribute seems to be the introductory APR.

The conjoint analysis technique is not only used in financial services marketing but also in many other consumer and industrial contexts in which the underlying decision process and the contribution of each attribute to the overall evaluation of the offered services needs to be estimated. By some estimates, conjoint analysis is the most popular market research technique for new product development.[12] There are many advantages to this technique. One particularly attractive feature of conjoint analysis is that it allows the financial services marketer to work with small sample sizes— typically in the range of 50 to 100 consumers—thereby reducing the overall cost of data collection.[13] Another attractive feature of the methodology is the ability for one to dissect the service evaluation process for each individual consumer, as was done above. Replicating the above process for another consumer may reveal a slightly or perhaps drastically different thought process. One is therefore able to understand and estimate the decision process that each individual consumer (or segments of consumers) follows when evaluating financial service offers. This is an especially useful benefit of the technique because it allows one to detect the potential existence of market segments using conjoint analysis data. If different groups of consumers who have completed a conjoint task exhibit very different ways of evaluating the various attributes, a segment-based approach to marketing of the service may be called for. These segmentation possibilities will be further discussed in Chapter 8.

The major limitation of conjoint analysis is that the number of offer descriptions that a consumer is able to see is typically limited to about 20 since higher numbers may quickly result in consumer fatigue and lack of interest.[14] The fatigue and disinterest associated with very large conjoint tasks may possibly result in inaccurate responses, thereby providing unreliable data for further analysis. In addition, since the consumer is presented with hypothetical descriptions of offers, the context in which the consumer is exposed to these offers is artificial in nature. The consumer recruitment process for conducting a conjoint study may also affect the results. Consumers might be drawn into a research facility in return for monetary compensation and asked to examine the various profiles presented to them. The resulting reactions to these profiles in the controlled laboratory setting and the artificial environment that it represents may not necessarily reflect what consumers will actually do in the marketplace when faced with similar financial services. The result is that the external validity of conjoint studies needs to be validated through replication or through the test marketing approaches discussed below when designing new financial services.

TESTING MARKET ACCEPTANCE OF NEW FINANCIAL SERVICES

Once a new financial service has been identified through the techniques discussed above, it is critical for a financial services organization to establish and validate the attractiveness of the service to the marketplace by field-testing. The idea behind a field test is to examine closely how a new financial service is received by a test group of consumers often referred to as a "test market." The test market could be a city chosen because of its representative demographics or a series of bank branches or brokerage offices where customers are presented with the new service. The reactions exhibited by these customers are then used as an indicator of how attractive the service might be to the market in general.

There are two popular forms of test market studies conducted in financial services. One approach focuses on percentage response rates related to new services pitched to consumers, while the other approach focuses on the average dollar volume associated with the use of a new financial service. The first approach therefore requires one to estimate the rate of consumer response to a new financial service offer by focusing on the percentage of consumers who express interest by for example inquiring about it or subscribing to it. The objective of this type of test market is to establish if one form of service offering will result in significantly higher levels of response than an alternative offering. The method capitalizes on one's ability to establish statistically any significant differences in percentage response that might exist between consumers who received one service pitch versus another. The second form of test market is used to establish whether one financial service results in significantly higher levels of monetary transactions such as the level of customer account balances held in a bank or the dollar amount of stocks purchased through a broker. The objective in this approach is to establish if the monetary volume (for transactions or account balances) is different for accountholders who have subscribed to one service offering instead of another. For example, one might be interested to know if offering a no minimum balance requirement (versus requiring a minimum balance) on checking account services creates significant drops in customer's account balances. Each of the two approaches mentioned will be discussed in more detail below.

Test Markets for Determining the Consumer Response Rate

Consider the case of a bank that has recently developed a new mortgage program for homebuyers with a special interest rate protection component. The essence of the protection plan is that prospective homebuyers who have completed their mortgage application could lock in at lower rates following their initial mortgage agreement with the bank, should the rates drop prior to the closing (purchase of the property). Clearly, such a policy might be considered quite attractive by homebuyers because it provides them with an added level of assurance about getting the lowest possible rates, especially at times when interest rates fluctuate greatly. If the rates drop in the marketplace following their initial agreement with the mortgage company, they will no longer be tied to the higher rate used at the time of signing the mortgage agreement and can benefit from the lower rates that have followed. However, from a financial services marketing perspective, it may be unclear whether this particular service offering might have any significant degree of attraction to homebuyers.

In order to establish whether or not this particular offering might be attractive to the marketplace, a test market experiment could easily be carried out. The idea is to choose two comparable consumer groups (perhaps located in different cities or contacted at different branches of the bank) with similar demographics and to present each group with a different mortgage offer. One group (perhaps applicants in one city) would be exposed to the new mortgage offering with the mortgage protection feature, and the other group (applicants in the other comparable city) would be presented with the traditional mortgage product that the bank offers. In the example that will be discussed below, two comparable mid-western cities were used to test the new mortgage offering.

Consumers in one city (city 1) were used as the test group. Consumers in another comparable city (city 2) were used as the control group to whom the new mortgage offer was not introduced. The existence of the control group is critical to such tests because it provides a baseline for analysis and comparison. If the overall mortgage market is experiencing fluctuations due to seasonality or economic conditions, the effects should be more or less equally experienced in the two cities. This helps identify changes in baseline sales that are occurring due to external reasons not related to any specific marketing activities.

$$P_1 = 300 / 10,000 = 0.03 \qquad P_2 = 540 / 9,000 = 0.06$$
$$n_1 = 10,000 \qquad n_2 = 9,000$$

$$Z = \sqrt{\dfrac{P_1 - P_2}{\dfrac{P_1(1-P_1)}{n_1} + \dfrac{P_2(1-P_2)}{n_2}}} = 2.11$$

Exhibit 7.9 Testing for Response Rate Differences

As a result, any significant differences that are observed between the two cities could be primarily attributed to differences in the marketing activities of the company. It is critical, therefore, that both cities possess similar characteristics in terms of size, demographics, geography, and economic conditions.

The test market was carried out over a 6 month time period. The following figures emerged: Of the 10,000 people contacted in city 1 (control city) by direct mail to promote the bank's mortgages, 300 applied for mortgages; of the 9,000 people contacted in city 2 (test group), 540 applied. Therefore, the corresponding success rate for the two groups, as reflected by the percentage response rate exhibited were 3% (P_1=300/10,000=0.03) and 6% (P_2=540/9,000=0.06). As a financial services marketer, one is therefore faced with a seemingly simple question of how effective the new mortgage offering is in attracting new customers. To establish whether the response rates are different at statistically significant levels, one would have to conduct a statistical test for differences in proportions, as shown in Exhibit 7.9. Conducting this statistical test is essential since anytime one examines two different groups of consumers, different results are very likely to emerge and the chances of obtaining the exact same results are slim. It is important, therefore, to establish that the observed difference is a result of differences in the offers being made and not external factors or a small sample size.

The formula shown in Exhibit 7.9 is designed to help establish the answer to this very important question. The formula takes into account the response rate in the two groups (P_1 and P_2) as well as the sample sizes in each of the two groups (n_1 and n_2), in order to compute a "z-score". If the computed z-score is greater than 1.96, we would conclude that the two groups have not responded at equal rates, and that there is a significant difference between the two groups in terms of their response rate. This represents a test of difference in proportions at what statisticians refer to as the "95% confidence level", which is quite typical of the norms used in marketing research.[15] Interested readers are encouraged to examine texts on marketing research and basic statistics for possible variations on the simplified approach presented here. In our case, since the z-score of 2.11 exceeds the threshold level of 1.96, we can conclude that the new mortgage offer has resulted in a significant improvement in response rates and provides a level of consumer response that exceeds the base levels established in the control group.

While the example above focused on two different cities as the basis of testing, one does not always need to utilize such a geographically large scale of testing to conduct test markets. It is also possible to select a handful of bank branches randomly and to use their customers as the control group (whereby the pitch is unchanged), and use a different randomly selected set of branch locations in which to present the new mortgage offer (and thereby conduct a test of its effectiveness). The key to this approach is to ensure that the branches chosen to recruit the control group are similar to those chosen to recruit the test group, in terms of basic characteristics such as customer demographics, account type, and other factors that might influence customers' responses.

Testing Changes in Transaction Volume or Account Balances

The second approach to testing the market acceptance of a new financial offering focuses on volume changes in customer transactions or changes in account balances, resulting from the introduction of the new offering. When a new service is introduced by a financial services organization, a critical question is how it impacts the volume of transactions that an average customer might undertake. For example, if a credit card company introduces a new credit card with unique reward program features, would one expect the dollar volume of customer transactions using that card to change? Alternatively, a bank may be considering the launch of a no minimum balance free checking service, whereby customers would receive free checking account services regardless of the amount of funds deposited in their account. The bank might like to know if the no minimum balance component of the new service would result in a decrease in the account balances. To establish this, a similar testing approach to what was described in the previous section would have to be taken. Two different groups of customers would be presented with different service packages. The first group would receive the service offer in its original form (control group), whereas the second group would experience the modified service (test group). Differences in average transaction volume for the two groups would then be computed. A statistical test, which will be described below, would then be conducted in order to establish if the new service resulted in any changes in transaction volume or account balances.

Consider the example of a commercial bank that is interested in testing the effects of a no minimum balance free checking service on customers' checking account balances. Traditionally, most commercial banks offer free checking services only if the customer maintains a minimum balance in her checking account. With the proposed new checking account, there are no minimum balance requirements in order for the customer to receive free checking services. While this may represent a highly attractive marketing pitch, the management of the bank is concerned about potential drops in account balances and a reduction in interest earnings from these potentially lower account balances. To carry out the test, bank branches were randomly split into two comparable groups. In one group of branches, new customers were offered the bank's traditional checking service (control group), whereas in the second group of branches, the new checking service was offered to customers (test group). Over a 6-month period, it was found that, for the 900 individuals who opened a standard checking account (control group), the average monthly balance was $3,215 (and the standard deviation in monthly balances was $550). Of the 700 people who opened the new no minimum balance free checking account (test group), the average monthly balance was $3,150 (and the standard deviation in monthly balances was $470).

The question facing the bank's management is whether or not the no minimum balance offering has resulted in the lowering of account balances. While there is an obvious difference in the averages for the two groups, this is always expected because the averages for two different groups of individuals would rarely match exactly. As a result, it is unclear if this difference is simply due to randomness or if it represents a deeper underlying difference that would replicate if we used a different pair of consumer groups or if we had conducted the test on a much larger scale. To establish whether the difference in average account balances can be attributed to the introduction of the new checking account service, one would have to conduct the statistical test for differences in averages, shown in Exhibit 7.10.

In the formula presented in Exhibit 7.10, X-bar, s, and n correspond to the sample average, standard deviation, and sample size, respectively, for each of the two groups under study. This formula also produces a z-score which can then be used to assess if the observed differences are statistically significant. If the z-score is larger than 1.96, we would conclude that the two services have resulted in differences in average account balances. Similar to the approach discussed earlier, the number 1.96 is used to represent a statistical test of differences in averages at the "95% confidence level." In our case, since the computed figure of 2.56 exceeds the threshold of 1.96, we can conclude that the new checking account service has indeed resulted in a drop (although small) in average account balances at statistically significant levels. Clearly, this may have implications on the bank's overall marketing strategy and profit projections associated with the new checking service. Financial computations would be needed to determine if the drop in interest earnings associated with the lower account balances would be offset by the profits gained by expected increases in the number of new customers. Interested readers should consult a text on statistics for additional details on the techniques discussed in Figures 7.9 and 7.10, sample size requirements, and possible variations to the simplified version of the approaches presented.[16]

$$X_1 = \$3{,}215 \qquad\qquad X_2 = \$3{,}150$$
$$S_1 = \$550 \qquad\qquad S_2 = \$470$$
$$n_1 = 900 \qquad\qquad n_2 = 700$$

$$Z = \left| \frac{X_1 - X_2}{\sqrt{\dfrac{S_1^2}{n_1} + \dfrac{S_2^2}{n_2}}} \right| = 2.56$$

Exhibit 7.10: Testing for Differences in Account Balances

THE PRODUCT LIFE CYCLE

It is important to recognize that the new product development process discussed in this chapter is part of a larger process under the generic title of the *product life cycle*, which is used to describe the new product introduction and market acceptance process in all markets, financial or otherwise. The notion of the product life cycle is that, similar to living organisms, products go through multiple stages in their own existence, from birth to death. Similar to a living organism, a new product is first conceived and created. This stage is referred to as the *incubation phase* and is characterized by intensive research, development, and scientific testing, similar to test market approaches discussed above. The length of time that companies spend in this phase varies by industry; for new market introductions that are not technologically sophisticated, the length of this stage tends to be short. On the other hand, for products and services that are technology based, the length of time associated with this stage could span years and even decades.[17]

Once a product has cleared the incubation period, the next stage in the product life cycle is the *introduction* phase. In this phase, the marketing of the product to the marketplace commences. Financial services that are in their introduction phase today are specialized insurance services and new technologies for transaction and payment processing.[18] The eventual market acceptance of these products will only be determined in time. The introduction phase is characterized by a relatively slow growth rate in sales and a strong need by the company introducing the new service to invest in building the market and educating consumers on the benefits of its innovation. In financial services, this may require investing in high levels of advertising to educate the masses on the unique benefits of a new financial service and building a well-trained sales force to promote the product to consumers, brokers, agents, and other retail channel members.

Once the market has demonstrated its acceptance of a new product or service concept, a growth in sales volume is expected to result. This helps to start the *growth* phase of the product life cycle. In this phase, significant growth in sales volume is observed. For example, in financial services, identity theft insurance would represent a service in its growth phase, with growth rates trailing the alarming rates at which cases of identity theft are observed nationally.[19] The result of such growth is that, in this phase of the product life cycle, new competitors begin to enter the market. However, the high rate of growth in sales and consumers' strong interest in the product reduces competitors' incentives to undertake cutthroat competition. The ability to realize lucrative profits is most prominent in this stage of the product life cycle. From a strategic perspective, a financial services marketer that was a pioneer in conceiving the service during the incubation and introduction stages needs to hold on to its first-mover advantage. The pioneer product typically has the strategic advantage of being the most preferred by consumers because it has an established and proven track record.

Once the market has been saturated and the rate of growth in sales has declined, the *maturity* phase of the product life cycle begins. The maturity phase may also result from shifting demographics in which the mass of consumers in the market who were originally interested in the service may have aged and no longer need the service or product. In the maturity phase, due to the shrinking number of customers in the marketplace, profit margins tend to decline, and in some cases competitors who find these margins to be unattractive choose to leave the market and pursue more attractive options in other markets. This typically results in a lower number of competitors, which is a healthy effect as far as industry margins are concerned. Examples of financial services that are in the maturity phase today would be savings accounts services.[20] Savings accounts are likely to remain in the maturity phase for a long time due to the basic transaction processing and cash-flow management capabilities that they present to customers, while providing interest on the deposits.

Products and services that begin to lose consumer interest eventually move into the decline phase of the product life cycle. In this phase, overall market sales decline on a year-to-year basis. Eventually the financial product or service might be abandoned not only by consumers but also by companies that offer it. This is because the service providers may recognize the bleak future ahead and the declines in margins associated with staying in that business. An example of a financial service that is in a decline phase is the travelers' check, which, due to the use of credit and debit cards, and pre-paid cash cards has become irrelevant to the majority of the traveling public.[21]

It is important to recognize that the product life cycle concept is one that does not apply to an individual financial services provider, but rather to the entire market. It describes shifts in overall market growth as a function of time rather than as changes in individual companies' sales. However, from the perspective of strategic market planning, as shown in Exhibit 7.11, it has had a great deal to offer financial services marketers in identifying which elements of their marketing program they need to focus on at each stage of the product life cycle. Exhibit 7.11 demonstrates marketers' organizational priorities at each stage of the product life cycle as well as tools and approaches available to focus on these priorities. It also highlights the critical role that innovative financial services can play in the creation of new categories of services and the corresponding benefits that they present not only to consumers, but also to the companies introducing them.

During the incubation phase the financial services organization should be focused on extensive market research, customer interviews, and the scanning of new technologies to identify emerging opportunities. Once these opportunities are identified, transformed into new products and services, and introduced to the market, the focus shifts towards market development. Studies of the product life cycle in general have established that market pioneers typically experience much higher margins than their competitors and experience better consumer brand recognition, than competitors that follow in the later stages of the product life cycle. They are also often perceived as the established brand by consumers, and are therefore favored not only in the short run, but also for most of the life cycle of the product or service. This phenomenon is often referred to as the "pioneering advantage," and highlights the long-term rewards for innovation and risk taking.[22]

In the introduction phase, the pioneer needs to develop the market's interest in the product by educating consumers on the unique benefits and features of the new product. In this phase, consumers need to be convinced that the new product is capable of improving their experience beyond what existing products, technologies, or services are delivering. Once the market interest has picked up and growth is witnessed in the marketplace, the focus of the organization needs to shift to managing growth. This often requires significant expansions in resources, branch outlets, and infrastructure. Therefore, in the growth phase most financial services organizations are focused on training and mobilizing the organization in a coherent and well-organized fashion. In addition, the attracting of new customers through advertising and promotional activities forms an additional dimension of focus in this stage. Once the market growth rate subsides and the maturity phase of the product life cycle has been reached, the focus of the organization tends to be on maintaining profitable operations. This can be achieved by finding pockets of customer segments which have not yet been effectively served and by developing variations of the basic product or service to create new needs in the marketplace. Once the market has begun its decline phase, a financial services organization may have several options, the most dominant of which is to divest from the product altogether. However, remaining in the business may also provide a viable option if other competitors are exiting, as it will result in increased market share, be it in a shrinking marketplace.

Stage of the Product Life Cycle	Company Focus	Marketing Tools and Approaches Used
Incubation	Identify unserved customer needs and keep the competition in the dark	Focus groups, test markets, observation, research and development
Introduction	Educate the masses	Advertising, sales force management, customer education
Growth	Educate the organization	Training the organization, growth management, competitive assessment, advertising, promotions
Maturity	Profit maintenance	Segment the market and target the more attractive segments, developing new markets, direct marketing
Decline	Exit, de-marketing, and competitive acquisition	Drop uncompetitive services, divest from the business, acquire competitors to gain market share

Exhibit 7.11 The Impact of the Product Life Cycle on the Marketing of Financial Services

Several points are important to recognize in the context of new product introductions in financial services. The first point is that, in many financial services organizations, new concepts are often developed by internal insight rather than external market research.[23] The management of a financial services organization might have developed an understanding of what new services consumers might potentially be interested in and not seek confirmation using market research approaches such as formal consumer surveys or focus groups. The managers' insights and intuitions on possible new service features can, however, guide further testing of new concepts using the techniques discussed in this chapter, and other similar market research approaches. The importance of empirically based market testing is increasing due to the increased intensity of competition, higher levels of consumer awareness about financial decision making, and the introduction of innovative technologies in financial services.

It has also been suggested that product testing in financial services often evolves into full-scale product launches if the product is found to have acceptable consumer response during the initial testing phase.[24] This is largely attributed to the fact that the cost of launching new financial services is typically considerably lower than what the new product launch costs would be for durable, industrial, and consumer packaged goods. Small-scale market testing may therefore suffice as a signaling mechanism for determining market interest in a new financial service. However more accurate assessments would have to rely on large-scale market tests and formal market research. One of the drawbacks of conducing large-scale market research is that it may provide the competition with insights on one's marketing strategy and eliminate the strategic advantages that could potentially be gained by surprising competitors and catching them off guard with the introduction of a new financial service. What is also interesting regarding the new product development process is that in general, larger organizations are often more resourceful in their use of test markets than smaller organizations.[25] The availability of a large network of bank branches, broker locations, and customers is a luxury available only to the larger financial organizations. This enables these organizations to conduct large-scale tests, whereas the smaller organizations may not have the number and diversity of branch locations or customers needed to secure the sample sizes needed to conduct scientific statistical testing.

SECONDARY SOURCES OF INFORMATION

While most new financial services are conceived either through management intuition, exploration of internal data sets, or more formal approaches to market research, there is also an abundance of secondary data available to financial services marketers. The opportunity to gain general knowledge of trends in the marketplace through existing secondary data sources needs to be taken into account in the initial phases of developing new concepts. These sources include data on the demographics of the target population, which is often a good purchase predictor for many financial services. In addition, a variety of standard data sources exist on the changing trends in the financial services sector. The following is a list of some of the popular information sources and publications which may be consulted. It is important to note that the list provided below is not necessarily comprehensive and there may be other publications and resources which may fit individual applications best. Furthermore, the evolving nature of the organizations that produce these reports and the changing information needs of their subscribers may result in content variations from the details provided below.

Consumer Demographics:

US Census Bureau (cenus.gov): Provides detailed demographic information, population estimates, and demographic forecasts. These forecasts may be helpful to understanding market potential for financial products and services that are age-specific (for example pension plan, life insurance, mortgages, etc.)

Statistical Abstract of the United States: Summary of demographic profile of the United States and future projections.

Industry Trends:

Standard and Poor's Industry Surveys: Provides detailed analysis of the major industries in the US, general forces affecting markets, and expected trends in the near future. Several sections of the Surveys focus on various categories of financial services.

Hoovers (hoovers.com and related publications): Provides company information, industry analysis and related market intelligence. Financial services providers that may seek to promote credit and savings products to specific organizations may find this information useful.

Trade Journals, Magazines, and Association Reports: Specialized trade and industry publications focusing on specific categories of financial services.

Datamonitor Industry Market Research Reports: Database of industry reports. Reports are produced for major industry sectors of the U.S. as well as other regions of the world. Reports include market forecasts, market sizing, competitive share analysis and other related topics.

Thomas Register of American Manufacturers: Directory of manufacturers in the U.S. and Canada. Manufacturers categorized based on product offerings, brand names offered, and other business indicators. Financial services providers that may seek to promote credit and savings products to specific organizations may find this information useful.

Research Publications: Research and academic publications focusing on trends and behavioral patterns of consumers in financial markets. Examples of relevant sources include *Credit Card Management, ABA Banking Journal, International Journal of Bank Marketing,* and *Journal of Financial Services Marketing,* and *Journal of Financial Services Research.*

Advertising Exposure:

Television Audience Measurement: Information on the ratings of television programs obtained though consumer diaries or electronic cable-box devices from participating samples of households. Nielsen, Information Resources Inc. (IRI) and Arbitron are examples of companies that supply such information.

Leading National Advertisers: Provides a list of the top advertisers in the United States, based on annual levels of media spending.

Simmons Market Research: Detailed information on buyer behavior, purchase propensity, and related media exposure, across a wide range of product markets, including an array of financial products and services.

Information on Competitors:

Published Information by Competitors: For publicly traded financial services companies, annual reports may provide insights on competitors' strategies and capabilities. Furthermore, press releases by competitors or information disseminated through their web sites to their customers and investors may be helpful in assessing the competition.

Published Information by Third Parties: Press reports, trade publications, and industry analyses may be used to gauge the capabilities, resources, and intentions of competitors. Some of these sources of information may be identified through electronic databases of published articles and reports, such as ABI/Proquest (American Bibliographic Index) and Lexis-Nexis, as well as Internet search engines.

CHAPTER QUESTIONS

1. What is the purpose of the control group in testing new financial services?

2. What potential limitations do you see in the use of content analysis in new product development for financial services?

3. Considering the emerging consumer trends, what new financial services do you think must be introduced into the marketplace?

4. For each stage of the product life cycle, identify several relevant financial services.

5. Two groups of similar consumers were sent the identical credit card offer, which provides a 2% discount on the credit card balance for each month. The difference is that for one group (group A), the offer was also mentioned on the outside of the envelope with large fonts and bright colors (new offer); for the other group (group B), the pertinent information was included only in the promotional material inside the envelope (old offer). The following is the results of this test:

   Group A: Of the 2,590 people mailed, 27 responded.
   Group B: Of the 1,890 people mailed, 12 responded.

   Based on these results, do you believe there to be a significant difference in the response rates for the two groups?

6. GranPrixAuto Bank is a national provider of automobile loans, insurance, and credit services focusing on the driving public and automobile owners. The company currently offers a credit card with no specific benefits to its customers. It has tested on a small scale a new credit card that, upon the payment of a yearly $30 membership fee, will provide a 2% discount on gasoline purchases and hotel stays at participating hotels and gas stations. This new offer has been promoted to a select group of new account applicants and also promoted to existing credit card customers. Since its introduction early in the year, 839 customer accounts for this new offer have been created. The average monthly balance on these cards is $1,229 (standard deviation of $394).

Checking Account Interest Rate	Savings Account Interest Rate	Teller Service Fees	Average Rating
1%	2%	None	2.68
1%	2%	$1	2.29
1%	3%	None	3.65
1%	3%	$1	2.94
2%	2%	None	4.35
2%	2%	$1	3.83
2%	3%	None	5.15
2%	3%	$1	4.42

Exhibit 7.12 Conjoint Analysis Results for a New Banking Service

The management believes that this credit card can result in an increase in credit card spending; it cites the fact that, for a randomly selected sample of 1,000 of its traditional customer accounts, the average monthly balance is only $1,121 (standard deviation of $291). In your opinion, is their observation correct or not? What reservations might you have on making such an assessment?

7. The following is a result of a conjoint analysis study conducted in order to determine the attractiveness of a possible new service to be offered by a commercial bank. Three (3) dimensions of the bank were systematically varied, each at two levels. These were: Interest rate earned on the checking account (1% versus 2%), interest rate earned on the savings account (2% versus 3%), and charging customers for use of bank teller services (no charge versus $1 per visit). A research company contacted 64 consumers recruited from a research panel and administered the corresponding conjoint analysis task. Offers were rated on a 1-to-7 scale by the participants, with 1 being "very bad" and 7 being "very good." Average ratings across all respondents for each of the eight offers were produced and are shown in Exhibit 7.12. Based on these results, what tradeoffs do you think exist between the various service attributes?

8. In your opinion, what indications can be used to determine where a particular financial service is in the product life cycle?

9.   What potential drawbacks do you see in the use of top box analysis?

10. Does the product life cycle concept apply to a single brand/company or to the entire market?

11. What is meant by the pioneering advantage? Can you identify financial services companies that enjoy a pioneering advantage today?

ENDNOTES

1 N. Umashankar, R. Srinivasan and D. Hindman (2011), "Developing Customer Service Innovations for Service Employees," *Journal of Service Research*, Vol. 14, Iss. 2, pp. 164-172; A. Oradanini and A. Parasuraman (2011), "Service Innovation Views Through a Service-Dominant Logic Lens: A Conceptual Framework and Empirical Analysis," *Journal of Service Research*.

2 V. Senner and S. Lehner (2009), "Skiing Equipment: What is Done Towards More Safety, Performance and Ergonomics," in S. Ujihashi (ed) *The Impact of Technology on Sport*. Taylor & Francis Group: London;"Ski Pass Insurance Makes Debut," *Wall Street Journal*, Jan 7, 2004, p. 1.

3 P. Gopal and J. Shenn (2011), "Forecast: A Milder Mortgage Meltdown," *Business Week*, Feb 21, p. 1; R. Simon (2004), "Creative Mortgages Fuel Home Sales," *Wall Street Journal*, March 16, p. D1; Stacey Buford (2004), "Mortgages Get More Exotic," *Wall Street Journal*, July 25.

4 B. Sheridan (2010), "What Your Identity is Worth Online," *Business Week*, Oct. 18, p. 1; "Finding the True Extent of ID Theft," *Credit Card Management*, May 2004, Vol. 17, Iss. 2, p. 8, citing reports by the FTC and Gartner Inc.

5 T. Brown (2009), *Change by Design: How Design Thinking Transforms Organizations and Inspires Innovation*. New York: Harber Business. D. Frenken, P. Saviotti, and M. Trommetter (1999),"Variety and Niche Creation in Aircraft, Helicopters, Motorcycles and Microcomputers," *Research Policy*, Vol. 28, Iss. 5, pp. 469-488.

6 Burney Simpson (2004), "A Turning Point for Retailers" *Credit Card Management*, Vol. 17, Iss. 2, p. 43, citing a report by Value Link.

7 M. Maddock, L. Uriatre and P. Brown (2011), *Brand New: Solving the Innovation Paradox*. New York: Wiley.

8 Donald Lehmann, Sunil Gupta and Joel Steckel (1997), *Marketing Research*. Upper Saddle River, NJ: Prentice Hall, pp. 286-293.

9 N. Malhotra (2009), *Marketing Research: An Applied Orientation*. New York: Prentice Hall; Robert Weber (1990), *Basic Content Analysis*. Sage Publications.

10 R. Peterson and W. Wilson (1992), "Measuring Customer Satisfaction: Fact and Artifact," *Journal of the Academy of Marketing Science*, Vol. 20, Iss. 1, pp. 61-71.

11 Donald Lehmann, Sunil Gupta and Joel Steckel (1997), *Marketing Research*. Upper Saddle River, NJ: Prentice Hall; Paul Green and Vithala Rao (1971), "Conjoint Analysis for Quantifying Judgmental Data," *Journal of Marketing Research*, Vol. 8, Iss. 3, pp. 106-110; Jordan L. Louviere, David A. Hensher, Joffre D. Swait, and Wiktor Adamowicz (2000), *Stated Choice Methods: Analysis and Application*. Cambrdige: Cambridge University Press

12 Paul Green, Abba Krieger, and Yoram Wind (2001), "Thirty Years of Conjoint Analysis: Reflections and Prospects," Interfaces, Vol. 31, Iss. 3, p. S56; Dick Wittink and Philippe Cattin (1989), "Commercial Use of Conjoint Analysis: An Update," *Journal of Marketing*, Vol. 53, Iss. 3, pp. 91-96.

13 Paul Green and Vithala Rao (1971), "Conjoint Analysis for Quantifying Judgmental Data," *Journal of Marketing Research*, Vol. 8, Iss. 3, pp. 106-110; Donald Lehmann, Sunil Gupta and Joel Steckel (1997), *Marketing Research*. Upper

Saddle River, NJ: Prentice Hall; Norman Anderson (1981), *Foundations of Information Integration Theory.* New York: Academic Press.

14 Dick Wittink and Philippe Cattin (1989), "Commercial Use of Conjoint Analysis: An Update," *Journal of Marketing,* July 1989, Vol. 53, Iss. 3, pp. 91-96; Donald Lehmann, Sunil Gupta and Joel Steckel (1997), *Marketing Research.* Upper Saddle River, NJ: Prentice Hall, pp. 555-556.

15 David Aaker, George Day and V. Kumar (2001), *Essentials of Marketing Research.* New York: Wiley; Graham Hooley (1999), *Quantitative Methods in Marketing.* International Thomson Business; Gary Lilien (1992), *Marketing Models.* Upper Saddle River, NJ: Prentice Hall.

16 N. Weiss (2011), *Elementary Statistics.* Reading, MA: Addison Wesley.

17 N. Harmancioglu, D. Cornelia and R. Calantone (2009), "Theoretical Lenses and Domain Definitions in Innovation Research," *European Journal of Marketing*, Vol. 43, Iss. 1/2, pp. 229-263.

18 K. Bamberger, D. Mulligan (2011), "Privacy and the Books and on the Ground," Stanford Law Review, Vol. 63, Iss. 2, pp. 247-315; M. Kasavana (2010), "Emergent Service Delivery Technologies," *Journal of International Management Studies*, Vol. 5, Iss. 2, pp. 159-167.

19 Jennifer Saranow (2009), "Insurers Add Benefits to Identity Theft Policies," *Wall Street Journal,* Oct 14, p. D2.; Jane Black (2002), "Your New Weapon vs. ID Theft," *Business Week Online,* 12/11/2003.

20 Lauren Bielski (2004), "A New Era Begins: Making The Transition to a Revised Check Processing Scheme," *ABA Banking Journal,* Vol. 96, Iss. 6, p. 51; Ihlwan Moon (2004), "I'll pick up the Check – with my Cell Phone", *Business Week,* June 21, Iss. 3888, p. 80; Andrew Park, Ben Eglin, and Timothy Mullaney (2003), "Checks Check Out," *Business Week,* May 10, Iss. 3882, pp. 83-84, citing study done by Gartner.

21 L. Courtney (2008), "Regulating the Cross-border Movement of Prepaid Cards," *Journal of Money Laundering Control*, Vol. 11, Iss. 2, pp. 146-171; T. Gutner (2003), "Cash Card for Travelers," *Business Week,* October 20, Iss. 3854, p162.

22 H. van Heerde, S. Srinivasan and M. Dekimpe (2010), "Estimating Cannibalization Rates for Pioneering Innovations," *Marketing Science*, Vol. 29, Iss. 6, pp. 1024-1039; G. Carpenter and K. Nakamoto (1989), "Consumer Preference Formation and Pioneering Advantage," *Journal of Marketing Research,* Vol. 26, Iss. 3, pp. 285-298.

23 J. Mollick (2009), "Determinants of Perceived Customer-Centrism in Managing Information About Customers," *Journal of the Academy of Marketing Science*, Vol. 15, Iss. 1, pp. 9-15; Jonas Matthing, Bodil Sanden, and Bo Edvardsson (2004), "New Service Development: Learning From and With Customers," *International Journal of Service Industry Management,* Vol. 15, Iss. 5, pp. 479-485Eric Stevens and Sergios Dimitriadis (2005), "Learning During Developing and Implementing New Bank Offerings," *The International Journal of Bank Marketing*, Vol. 23, Iss. 1, pp. 54-72.

24 C. Ennew and N. Waite (2006), *Financial Services Marketing: An International Guide to Principles and Practice.* London: Butterworth-Heinemann; Tina Harrision (2000), *Financial Services Marketing.* Pearson Education Ltd: Essex, p. 109.

25 J. Jiwani and J. Husain (2011), "Strategic Impact of Incentive Programs for Loan Officers of Micro-Finance Institutions," *Journal of American Academy of Business*, Vol. 17, Iss. 1, pp. 33-42.

CHAPTER EIGHT

Segmenting Financial Services Markets

Market segmentation is a fundamental requirement for successful implementation of marketing strategies in most financial services. However, market segmentation is a commonly utilized approach to marketing not only in financial services, but also in markets for consumer packaged goods, durables, and industrial products. Segmentation is the breaking down of a market into smaller groupings of consumers, referred to as "segments," based on the commonality of individual consumers' needs. In the automotive industry, for example, manufacturers typically target each consumer segment with products that match the unique needs of the segment. While some manufacturers may target the high end of the market, others might focus on consumers who seek value and are less concerned about the luxury aspects of a vehicle. In addition, each manufacturer may produce vehicles that meet the varying needs of different sub-segments, such as sports vehicles, minivans, sedans, and trucks. By doing so, the manufacturers present the market with an array of differentiated products that capitalize on the common needs of specific groups of consumers.

In financial services, the concept of market segmentation is also widely practiced. For example, different automobile insurance providers focus on different customer segments based on each segment's specific needs for insurance coverage. Some insurance companies focus on price-sensitive consumers who may care little about the personalized service provided by agents and are primarily concerned about low premiums. Another set of insurance companies focus on the upper tier of the market by insuring high-end luxury vehicles whose owners may care more about service than price. An array of other insurers exists between these two extremes, each serving the unique needs of specific segments of consumers. Similarly, the banking industry is segmented such that different commercial banks focus on the needs of different market segments. While certain banks provide highly personalized service at their retail branches, others reduce access to customer service and instead focus on competitive fees, for example, by providing free checking account services. Other banks may focus on reaching younger customers by providing versatile online banking services, or cater to the special needs of busy professionals by keeping some of their bank branches open during weekends and evening hours.

A unique aspect of segmentation in financial services is that the resources needed to conduct accurate market segmentation are abundant, when compared to most other marketing contexts. There is a wealth of customer data and segmentation tools available to financial services marketers that can be used to classify individuals into specific market segments and to predict their current financial needs and future purchase behavior. Financial services marketers are fortunate since they have access to rich internal databases on their existing customers, accumulated through years of repeated transactions. Furthermore, the ability to purchase a wealth of external information on individual consumers, such as their credit histories and past purchase behavior, through specialized data providers, greatly enhances the segmentation possibilities available to financial services marketers. The objective of this chapter is therefore to provide a fundamental understanding of the market segmentation process in financial services. We will also examine popular segmentation techniques that are used by financial services marketers. Finally, we will discuss how market segmentation is transformed into marketing action by examining segment-based marketing strategies used by financial services organizations.

AN EXAMPLE OF SEGMENTATION AT WORK

To appreciate how the market segmentation process works, we will first examine how segmentation is carried out in the market for credit cards. As shown in Exhibit 8.1, the credit card market can itself be broken down into different segments based on individuals' specific needs. The wide variety of credit cards available reflects the variations in consumer needs, across market segments. At the lower end of the market credit cards with no specific benefits can be identified. These cards fundamentally provide transaction processing capabilities so that the customer could purchase a product of interest by using the card at a retail location. The next tier of credit cards provides additional benefits to the cardholder, through rewards programs such as airline miles. These cards link the rewards given to the cardholder to the amount of usage of the card. By doing so, they provide a direct incentive for increased use of the card. Another category of credit cards is the benefit-oriented cards, which are those that provide pre-defined benefits to the cardholder. The benefits may for example, include refunds applied to the monthly account balance and additional discounts for purchases made at specific retail outlets. The objective of these cards is to target specific market segments that appreciate the unique

Card Type	Key Benefits Sought by Target Segment
Basic	Transaction processing
Loyalty	Rewards such as airline miles or discounts
Premium	Access to specific benefits secured by the card
Small-Business	Rewards, transaction processing, detailed account information
Super-elite	Unique benefits, personal concierge, high spending limit

Exhibit 8.1 Credit Card Types and Their Target Segments

benefits associated with using the card, and are willing to function within the rules of the reward mechanisms for the card, such as shopping at specific retail outlets where the benefits apply.

Premium-oriented credit cards serve a higher tier of the market. This category includes some of the cards issued by American Express, Diners Club, and others who charge an annual membership fee. In return for the annual fee, certain privileges and membership benefits are granted to the cardholder. These benefits might for example, include free automotive insurance for car rentals using the card, access to entertainment events such as concerts for which tickets are difficult to obtain, and other benefits programs that are relevant to the specific needs of the cardholder. Another segment in the credit card market that has significantly grown in recent years is credit cards for small businesses. Customers in this particular segment are attracted to the unique credit card features needed to run a small business. For example, these credit cards often provide expense reporting services for business planning and tax purposes, and provide the accountholder with special discounts on common business expenses such as shipping and travel.[1]

Another segment of credit card users consists of cardholders demanding a super-elite card. These cards, such as the American Express *Black* card or Visa's *Stratus* card, often have annual membership fees in the thousands of dollars, making them out of reach for most individuals. In some cases, membership is only possible by an invitation extended from the credit card company and in order to qualify for such an invitation, the individual must have the potential to spend tens of thousands of dollars on the card yearly. In return, the card may provide cardholders with benefits such as a personal concierge, privileged access to exclusive restaurants, and personalized customer-care benefits that the typical credit card does not provide. These cards also serve as symbols of wealth and status due to their exclusive nature and therefore have social image benefits beyond their functional features.[2]

As may be evident from the above description, the variety of credit cards available on the market, allow credit card companies to target consumers with distinctly different needs and tastes. The variations in consumer needs reflect the underlying segments to which each individual cardholder belongs. The segment-based approach to marketing credit cards therefore enables credit card issuers to approach each consumer with a credit card offer that is most relevant to his needs and by doing so, the card issuers gain significant efficiencies in their marketing activities. These efficiencies are also witnessed in other financial services markets where segmentation can be applied, as will be discussed in more detail below.

THE SEGMENTATION PROCESS

What is Market Segmentation?

Market segmentation is the process by which the overall mass of consumers is broken down into distinct groups of consumers, called segments, such that consumers within each segment are very similar to one another, while consumers in different segments are very different from one another. By breaking up the market into market segments, the financial services marketer would be able to present relevant products and services that appeal to the specific needs of each segment. Therefore, consumers in each market segment will be more likely to receive pitches for financial services that best match their unique needs. Furthermore, each segment could be reached though modes of communications and choices of media that best match their viewing or reading patterns. Therefore, for example, if a given market segment is known to consist of sports enthusiasts, targeting it would require more concentrated advertising effort in such outlets as ESPN and Sports Illustrated. The increased marketing efficiencies gained by this approach typically result in significant cost savings and higher profit levels for financial services providers.

As pointed out earlier, market segmentation is especially important in financial services marketing due to the ability to profile and target each individual consumer. For example, the availability of individual consumers' credit records through credit reporting agencies enables financial services marketers to understand better the credit usage behavior of each individual and to predict the types of financial products and services he needs. In addition, financial services marketers are better able to manage the relationship that they develop with prospects, some of whom will eventually become clients through the use of effective segmentation tools. The abundance of individual-level data, availability of segmentation tools, and the precision of current targeting methods further enable one to differentiate between profitable prospects and less profitable ones and to enhance the long-term profitability of the business.

Strategic Benefits of Market Segmentation

There are several competitive advantages that may be gained by adopting a segment-based approach in marketing financial services. The financial services industry is dominated by a small group of very powerful players. In credit cards, commercial banking, and online brokerage services, the top ten competitors account for a substantial portion of the business. Smaller financial services companies might therefore benefit from not challenging the larger, well-established competitors directly. A direct challenge would occur if for example, a smaller player attempts to attract existing customers of the larger competitors. This situation may be avoided through market segmentation, by focusing on market segments that have not effectively been served by the larger players. This segment-based approach to competition not only minimizes the likelihood of marketing confrontations and hostile reactions by the larger well-established companies, but it also ensures that a greater number of consumers in the market are served with products and services that are most relevant to their unique needs.

The market segmentation process is highly scientific and is driven by data collected from a representative sample of consumers with the aim of identifying their unique needs and characteristics. The scientific and objective nature of segmentation removes ambiguity and confusion from the marketing process and helps align and mobilize the workforce in financial services organizations. In the absence of the objective and scientific techniques used for market segmentation, important marketing decisions would be vulnerable to the errors of subjective assessments regarding the identity and size of the various market segments. With formal segmentation techniques being integrated into the marketing process, marketing efforts would not suffer from confusion regarding the exact characteristics and identity of the various market segments. The scientific approach to segmentation would ensure that the segments that are identified are distinct from one another, and that they vary in terms of their financial needs.

Exhibit 8.2 The Market Segmentation and Targeting Process

Steps in Market Segmentation

As shown in Exhibit 8.2, the process of market segmentation typically starts with data collected from a sample of consumers. The data could be obtained through consumer surveys, internal databases, or from market research providers and credit reporting agencies that provide individual-level information on consumers. The types of data that could be used for market segmentation include demographics such as gender and age, income, wealth levels, credit scores, and other related measures that can help identify the unique financial needs of individual consumers or households. It is essential that the measures used to conduct market segmentation have managerial appeal and are accurate and reliable.

Once these measures have been obtained, the next step in conducting market segmentation is to utilize specialized market segmentation software, which would scientifically break up the market into its corresponding segments. Formal computer-driven techniques are used to achieve this. While the details of the methodology used to conduct computer-based segmentation are beyond the scope of this book, we will review the basic components of Cluster Analysis, which is one of the more popular approaches used for conducting market segmentation. The final step in market segmentation is to utilize the identified segment characteristics for developing a marketing plan to target particular segments. This topic will be discussed in Chapter 11, which details strategic planning and organizational alignment in financial services organizations.

Data Sources Used for Conducting Market Segmentation

Two sources of data are frequently used for market segmentation. The first source constitutes of internally collected data that an organization might systematically and naturally accumulate as it conducts its business. For example, data on customer age, gender, transaction volume, and account balances provide a basic picture of the various customers that an organization currently serves. In addition, many financial services organizations regularly administer customer surveys through which they measure customer satisfaction ratings as well as other measures related to consumer perceptions of the products and services that they provide. The accumulation of these measures can help provide the necessary inputs for conducting market segmentation.

Financial services marketers are at an advantage over other marketing professionals due to the abundance of customer information that is available to them. For example, a credit card company has a significant amount of information on the types of products a customer purchases, as well as the basic demographics and credit histories of each customer. A commercial bank may know a customer's income due to direct deposit fund-transfers made into the customer's account by her employer. Moreover, the bank may have an understanding of the customer's purchase patterns, mortgage payments, and other financially diagnostic information. These items of information may provide insights into underlying market segments and customer needs.[3]

A second source of data used for segmentation is obtained through external suppliers. This approach is often used when a financial services provider is seeking prospects rather than using its own customers as a focus of its marketing activities. Externally purchased data could for example, include credit scores obtained from credit reporting agencies or segment identifiers obtained from segmentation data specialists. We will review these sources of segmentation data in more detail below.

1. Internally Collected Data

Internally collected data are sourced from the existing information technology infrastructures of a financial institution. Four different types of data can be associated with internal resources that a financial institution might maintain:

(A) Customer Demographics: Most financial institutions possess data warehouses, which contain some basic customer demographic records such as the date of birth and the address where an individual customer lives. Other types of information that may also be automatically collected include household size, gender of the accountholder and, in certain financial institutions where wealth management is the focus, the total assets held by the client.

(B) Life Stage: Demographic information can be combined and transformed into a commonly utilized measure referred to as *life stage*. A customer's life stage reflects the person's advancement through what is considered to be a typical set of phases through which individuals pass during the course of their lives. These stages are often mapped against specific age ranges. For example, in their 20s, many individuals may have begun working, are completing college, and are in the initial phases of professional and career development. In their 30s and 40s, many individuals are occupied with the process

of building assets, forming families, owning homes, and raising young children. In their 50s and 60s the focus of many individuals is to support children who may be leaving for college. During this phase, people also begin to prepare for their retirement. The powerful potential that life stage segmentation presents to financial services marketers is in its ability to predict the types of financial services that an individual will need as a function of the individual's age.[4] For example, at a younger age, one might primarily use services that facilitate transaction processing abilities such as checking accounts and credit cards. In the mid stages of life, mortgages, investment products, college funds, and insurance services become more relevant. Knowledge of an individual's life stage can therefore be tremendously helpful in facilitating effective marketing of specific types of financial services which the individual is most likely to need.

(C) Psychographics: Psychographics reflect an individual's state of mind. For example, an individual's interests might be reflected by one's hobbies and recreational activities, which may be an indicator of the psychological state of the individual. In addition, psychological measures could be obtained to assess a consumer's general attitudes towards a specific financial services provider or financial behavior in general. For example, there are distinct differences in consumers who primarily invest in mutual funds and those who primarily invest in stocks. Mutual fund investors are typically more risk averse and conservative than those maintaining a portfolio heavy in stocks. Furthermore, psychological variations across consumers might be reflected in their level of financial knowledge, their attitudes towards saving and borrowing, and the motivations underlying the purchase of specific financial products. A good example of this is the purchase of life insurance from well-established insurers. Those consumers who purchase life insurance policies from established companies have a psychological need for the reassurance gained by feeling that a well-established company will financially protect their dependants in case they pass away. For these individuals, the peace of mind of obtaining their policy from an established company outweighs any cost savings that may result from obtaining policies from lower-priced but less known competitors.

A challenge of using psychographic measures for market segmentation is that these measures are often not readily available. As a result, financial services marketers would have to obtain this information through market surveys. Often, these surveys could be conducted on existing customers who may be willing to take the time to fill them out. However, for prospects and individuals with whom the company may have had no previous interactions, collecting such data might be significantly more difficult and expensive. Because of this, the use of psychographic measures for market segmentation is much more popular in consumer durables and consumer packaged goods marketing and may be relatively less applicable to certain types of financial services.

(D) Transaction Records: Financial services providers often have detailed records

of their customers' transactions. This information can help provide the data necessary to identify such important measures as a customer's loyalty towards the company and purchase patterns exhibited in the past for the various products and services offered by the company. In certain financial services categories, such as automobile and homeowners insurance, in which service contracts have to be renewed on a regular basis, the frequency of renewals and the tendency for an individual customer to switch back and forth between competitors may provide valuable information in order to distinguish between different customer segments and to prioritize marketing effort towards the more loyal and valuable customers.

2. Externally Purchased Data

In addition to internal data available to many financial services organizations, secondary data could be obtained from third-party organizations. In the United States, several companies specialize in providing data to marketers interested in conducting market segmentation. The data provided by these organizations may enable the financial services marketer to assign each individual, whether a prospect or an existing customer, to a specific pre-defined market segment. This can help the marketer quantify the value that an individual presents to the company and to define specific marketing actions that need to be taken. Two types of data are generally obtained through external suppliers: credit-based information and geo-demographics.

Credit Based Information: A powerful tool that is commonly used by financial services marketers for identifying prospects and classifying existing customers is the individual credit scores obtained through credit reporting agencies. Agencies such as *Equifax*, *TransUnion*, and *Experian* provide these scores for each individual in the United States that has an established credit history. Individuals' credit histories are recorded by these agencies as an individual engages in credit-related activities such as opening a credit card account, obtaining a bank loan, or taking out a mortgage. Each individual's collected records and an associated credit score are then made available for sale by these agencies. The credit scores range from a low of about 300 to a high of 850. The score helps quantify the credit worthiness of an individual (the higher, the better). The credit scores are computed based on a series of factors, such as the amount of an individual's credit utilization (percentage of the total available credit used), the individual's payment history on existing accounts (for example, late payments on credit card bills), the number of times an individual has applied for credit, and the individual's income-to-debt ratio. The national credit score average is 678, and where an individual consumer stands on the credit score scale helps to determine the types of financial products and services the person might be most receptive to.[5] For example, individuals with credit scores below 550 might need financial services such as debt consolidation or home equity loans to cope with their credit needs. On the other hand, an individual with a credit score of 750 might be associated with very low credit risk behavior and a disciplined financial style receptive to products and services such as mutual funds and financial advisory services.

Geo-demographics: The term geo-demographics implies a combination of geographic information related to a person's place of residence and demographic information identifying the structure of the individual's household. Based on a household's address, geo-demographic segmentation specialists assign the household to a specific segment with pre-defined sets of demographic characteristics. Through this method, each household's likelihood of obtaining various types of financial services can also be predicted and quantified. A financial services marketer interested in selling a specific type of product could then quickly identify which households and neighborhoods would represent the most attractive prospects. Claritas is one of the major suppliers of geo-demographic data in the United States. Given a prospect's mailing address, Claritas would be able to assign that particular household to a pre-specified market segment. The market segment association would then help predict the basic demographics of the household such as the annual income, the age of the head of the household, and ownership status of the property. In addition, the expected patterns of financial needs can be predicted for each household. These patterns would include measures such as the particular financial services that the household is likely to be interested in obtaining, as well as channels of distribution for financial services (for example, online instead of retail agents) that the household is likely to prefer. Furthermore, each household could be described in terms of their media preferences, as well as basic lifestyle measures such as hobbies and sports activities most likely pursued by members of the household. This information can be used for advertising and target marketing. Geo-demographic segmentation data would therefore be tremendously useful for financial services marketers, especially in the context of new customer acquisitions.

CLUSTER ANALYSIS

Cluster analysis is one of the most popular approaches used for conducting market segmentation.[6] It is a technique that is widely applied not only for segmenting financial services markets but also heavily used by marketers of consumer packaged goods and industrial products. Cluster analysis computer algorithms are widely available through standard statistical packages such as *SAS* (Statistical Analysis System) and *SPSS* (Statistical Package for the Social Sciences). The cluster analysis technique has been used for several decades by consultants, brand managers, and marketing practitioners worldwide. The objective of this section of the chapter is to provide a general overview

Individual's Name	Age	Credit Score	Average Credit Card Balance	Household Income
J. Powers	29	650	$845	$78,000
D. Steenkamp	38	680	$1,290	$154,000
R. Fader	42	710	$1,126	$229,500
N. Davidson	24	590	$980	$110,000
.	.	.	.	.
.	.	.	.	.
.	.	.	.	.
.	.	.	.	.

Exhibit 8.3 Sample Data Input Needed for Cluster Analysis

of what cluster analysis does and to develop an understanding of its overall capabilities. Readers interested in obtaining a more detailed foundation for the technique are encouraged to consult a multivariate statistics textbook.[7]

The popular use of cluster analysis for market segmentation is largely due to its scientific foundation. Cluster analysis utilizes a computer algorithm that is able to objectively identify the segments that exist in a given marketplace as well as the corresponding characteristics associated with consumers in each of the identified segments. Cluster analysis is a data driven technique and therefore always starts with data collected from a sample of consumers. The data could be obtained from consumer surveys or the typical sources of information such as internal data warehouses, which were discussed earlier in this chapter. Sample data could include measures such as the customer's age, income, wealth, and credit score. A sample data set containing these data elements could then be submitted to the cluster analysis procedure. Exhibit 8.3 provides the first four observations from a sample data set that could be provided as inputs to cluster analysis.

The objective of cluster analysis is to form segments of consumers so that consumers in the same segment are very similar to one another in terms of the input data provided, but consumers in different segments are distinct from one another. In order to appreciate how the cluster analysis process works visually, Exhibit 8.4a provides data on six individual consumers. Each person is plotted on the two-dimensional space of age and credit score. Exhibit 8.4b shows one possible segmentation scheme *not* produced by cluster analysis, which fails to reveal a convincing segment structure. This is because the individuals that have been grouped in the same segment seem to vary significantly in terms of age and credit score. In segment 2, for example, two older individuals with high credit scores are grouped with an individual who is young and has a low credit score. In addition, the two segments seem to be visually close to one another and not distinct.

The goal of cluster analysis is to group these individuals so that those placed in the same segment exhibit very similar levels of the age and credit score. Furthermore, once these segments have been formed, they need to be distinctly apart from one another. Exhibit 8.4c shows a different way of grouping the customers, obtained through cluster analysis. Customers have been grouped into two different market segments, this time using cluster analysis.

As can be seen, the market segments seem to be more clearly defined. For example, the age and credit scores of individuals who are classified into the same segment are roughly in the same range. Moreover, a significant distance between the two market segments exists, and the two segments seem to represent two distinct groups of people. The ability to group individual consumers into the various clusters is the primary accomplishment of cluster analysis. By doing so, this methodology is able to create a better understanding of the typical individual that belongs to each of the various market segments that constitute a marketplace. The wealth of this information becomes evident in the generated output which not only includes the variables originally fed into cluster analysis, but can also include detailed information on other measures that might be available on individuals whose data were included in the cluster analysis data set.

The output of cluster analysis consists of a series of tables. Exhibit 8.5 shows the output of cluster analysis applied to the data set that was partially exhibited in Exhibit 8.3. As one may see from Exhibit 8.5, there are three distinct segments that are identified using cluster analysis. The three segments seem to differ significantly in terms of basic demographics such as age and income as well as behavioral measures such as credit scores and customer perceptions of the bank. Segment A seems to be the youngest segment while segment B seems to be the oldest. Segment B also possesses the highest credit scores and income levels. Segment C, on the other hand exhibits the lowest credit scores and income levels. By examining the variations across the segments on these key measures, the financial services marketer could then determine which segment represents the more attractive opportunities.

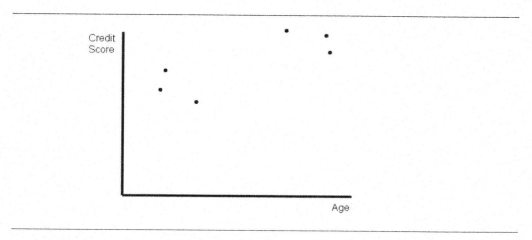

Exhibit 8.4a Plotting Consumers on the Two Dimensions of Age
and Credit Score

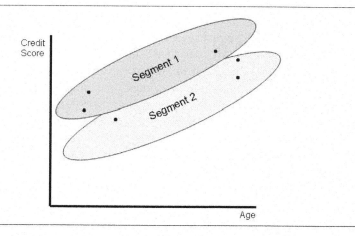

Exhibit 8.4b Grouping Consumers into Segments
(not produced by cluster analysis)

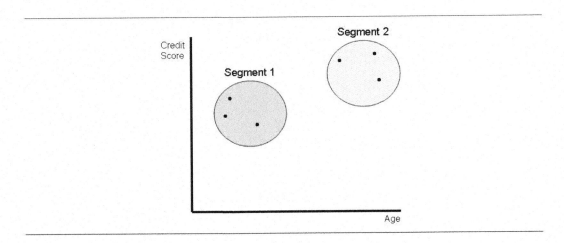

Exhibit 8.4c Segments Developed by Using Cluster Analysis

Exhibit 8.5 also provides additional diagnostic information on the identified market segments, such as the size of the segment. This is done by computing the percentage of consumers in the input data set that are classified into the various segments. For example, segment B is found to be the largest segment, whereas segment C is found to be the smallest. Furthermore, cluster analysis allows one to assign each individual customer to one of the three identified market segments. This is an important capability that may be critical in subsequent market targeting efforts. For example, individual consumers could then be reached through marketing communications in order to measure their response rates to the company's marketing pitches, and to establish variations in consumer response across market segments. Depending on the amount of internally collected date available on the customers of a financial services organization, additional diagnostic information can also be obtained by linking the data to customers' segment assignments obtained from cluster analysis. For example, the last row in Exhibit 8.5 reports the average number of direct mail pieces that have been sent out to customers in each of the three segments, based on company records. The segment that has received the highest number of direct mail solicitations (segment C) also represents the least attractive of the three segments, as reflected by its low credit scores and income levels. Segment B, which is the most attractive segment (highest credit scores, highest incomes, most favorable evaluation of the bank), has only received less than one quarter the amount of promotional material received by segment C. Such observations are critical to financial services marketing realignment efforts in which inefficiencies may become easily detected through the application of market segmentation tools.

	Segment A	Segment B	Segment C
Average age	28	46	37
Average credit score	590	505	750
Average income	$105,200	$167,900	$42,350
Average rating of the bank by consumers in this segment (on a 1-10 scale, 10 being "excellent")	5.5	8.9	8.3
Percentage of Respondents	45%	47%	8%
Names of individuals belonging to each segment	J. Powers N. Davidson L. Kemp .	D. Hansen R. Johnson P. Meyer .	E. Little J. Packer N. Danto .
Average number of direct mail pieces sent out per quarter to each individual	1.2	0.4	1.7

Exhibit 8.5: Example of Cluster Analysis Output

Several limitations need to be acknowledged with respect to cluster analysis. The first is that the input variables provided to cluster analysis may largely determine the segments that eventually emerge. It is possible, therefore, that the set of identified market segments and associated descriptions would vary as a function of the input variables provided to cluster analysis. The choice of one set of input variables instead of another may result in a different picture of the market segments. This may lead to inconsistent segment descriptions arising from different choices of input data. It is therefore critical to ensure that a sensible and coherent set of variables is used consistently across market segmentation studies and over the years.

It is also important to appreciate some of the other limitations of cluster analysis.[8] It is critical to limit the number of input variables provided to cluster analysis to about ten. Using a larger number of variables may result in confused descriptions of the market segments and also introduce statistical constraints when the input variables are correlated with one another. Correlated variables used to run cluster analysis can result in unreliable segment definitions and compromise the reliability of the results. Furthermore, cluster analysis typically requires relatively large sample sizes. This may not be a major concern for segmenting existing customers of financial services organizations because large amounts of data may have already accumulated in exiting databases. However, segmenting prospects for which little or no data might be available through internal data sources might prove to be considerably more difficult and expensive.

TARGETING CUSTOMER SEGMENTS

Market segmentation strategies have the potential to facilitate effective and efficient marketing of financial services. For example, it is well-established that life stage and age can predict financial services needs relatively accurately.[9] This is an encouraging fact since these measures are far more easily obtained than measures related to lifestyle and psychographics. The ability to use demographics and life stage data as a means for conducting market segmentation is one of the differentiating factors that distinguish marketing in financial services from marketing in other contexts. In the marketing of automobiles or consumer durables for example, demographics often do a poor job of predicting segment assignments and purchase behavior.[10] To conduct market segmentation, marketers in these categories must often rely on psychographic and perceptual measures, which may have to be obtained through large-scale consumer surveys. This is often not the case in segmenting financial services markets because basic demographics may help predict consumers' financial needs well.

Social class is another measure that can be used for market segmentation, especially in predicting consumer activity in savings and investment products.[11] Age and gender also relate to financial services in interesting ways. For example, men and women may vary in their knowledge of specific financial services, and older consumers have distinctly different preferences in their interactions with financial institutions than younger consumers.[12] Some of these preferences are driven by cultural differences between the generations while others are related to the physiological changes related to aging. Older consumers demand more personal attention and require clear disclosures associated with financial services that they use. Natural limitations associated with the process of aging also lead older consumers to require modes of communications which compensate for the aging human body. For example, research has shown that older consumers require financial statements printed using larger fonts, which is a direct result of the deterioration of vision associated with aging.

The approaches taken by a financial services organization to attract specific market segments are largely a function of who their target customers are and what competing financial services are currently being offered in the marketplace. In most cases, financial services organizations would have to undertake market segmentation studies in order to determine the unique needs of the various customer segments prior to designing and implementing a marketing plan. For example, technology could be implemented to target younger market segments. Use of mobile banking services, the Internet, and ATM devices can help attract the newer generations of consumers who are more receptive to technologically-based interfaces and those consumers who do not demand face-to-face interactions in their service encounters. The more traditional interfaces of a financial institution provided by bank tellers, brokers, and agents can be deployed to serve more traditional and mature market segments who demand personalized attention and face-to-face service interactions.

Similarly, market segmentation can be used in association with pricing strategies adopted by a financial institution. Depending on the price sensitivity of a given market segment, different price points and product types can be pitched. Financial services marketers can also choose to widen the breadth of products available to their customers in order to implement multi-segment marketing strategies. A wide range of financial services would allow a financial services marketer to serve multiple market segments simultaneously. The multi-segment approach to marketing financial services has become much more prevalent since the deregulation of the financial services sector, which has allowed financial institutions to deliver a much wider range of products and services to their existing customers.

Many competitors in the financial services sector have chosen to focus their marketing efforts on specific market segments through well-defined services. GEICO (Government Employees Insurance Company), as the name suggests, was for many years a provider of insurance products to employees of federal and state governments as well as members of the armed forces. Over the years, the company has expanded its reach beyond government-based customers by providing low-cost insurance products to the masses. The low-cost positioning of the brand is facilitated by the company's strategy to remove insurance agents from the distribution process and to sell its products directly to consumers. The cost savings associated with not having to run expensive agent operations at the retail level are passed on to customers in the form of lower premiums. By doing so, the company has attracted a unique segment of consumers who may not find a need for an agent as their contact point with the company, but would rather pay lower insurance premiums. Similarly, Haggerty is an automotive insurance company that is focused on providing insurance coverage for antique and collector cars. Haggerty's clients who purchase these types of vehicles may value the specialization of the company in serving this unique market. Both GEICO and Haggerty carry out effective segment-based approaches to marketing through which the specific needs, preferences, and requirements of well-defined market segments are translated into relevant financial services.

Segment Targeting Through Predictive Models

In this section, we will provide a short overview of the predictive models used to target customer segments in financial services. The objective in predictive modeling is to examine data on existing customers in order to establish the characteristics that constitute an attractive customer for the business. For example, by examining data on existing customers, a credit card company could assess which credit card applicants eventually proved to be profitable accountholders and which turned out to be risky customers. The characteristics of these applicants can then be used to identify attractive prospects from prospect lists obtained through third-party firms or other data sources to which the credit card company may have access. Predictive methods are used primarily as the means for assigning potential customers to general categories such as good or bad prospects. These category assignments can then be used to prioritize, develop and execute specific marketing programs aimed at attracting new customers.

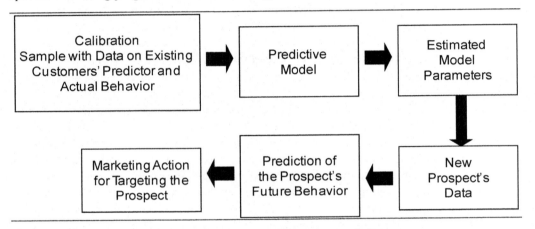

Exhibit 8.6 Use of Predictive Modeling

Customer Name	Age	Credit Score	Average Credit Card Balance	Household Income	Timely Payment of Bills
R. Watkins	24	520	$739	$38,200	No
T. Hall	48	480	$280	$64,500	Yes
D. Woodson	22	670	$589	$129,500	Yes
J. Randall	34	640	$1,390	$312,000	No

Exhibit 8.7 Sample Data Needed for Predictive Modeling

Prospect Name	Age	Credit Score	Predictive Function Value	Prediction of Timely Payment of Bills	Marketing Action
K. Saunders	35	540	296	Yes	Direct Mail
R. Wilson	28	390	188	No	Ignore
D. Wiseman	32	410	204	No	Ignore
J. Patterson	48	610	305	Yes	Telemarketing
N. Potter	26	750	252	Yes	Email promotion
.	.	.	.	.	.
.	.	.	.	.	.
.	.	.	.	.	.

Exhibit 8.8 Marketing Actions Determined by Predictive Modeling

Two predictive techniques are commonly used by financial services marketers. One is called Discriminant Analysis, and the other is Logistic Regression. Both techniques are widely used to classify potential customers and are also well established in the direct marketing practice.[13] Both techniques are designed to enable one to predict an individual consumer's future behavior (for example, customer profitability) based on a set of predictor data on the consumers (for example, income, age, and occupation). The fundamental difference between the two techniques is the statistical methodology used to form the link between the predictor variables and the predicted behavior. Since the focus of this book is not to engage in detailed technical discussions of statistical methods, readers are encouraged to consult a multivariate statistics book for the details of each of these techniques.[14] We will, therefore, provide an overall perspective of what predictive techniques are capable of achieving without providing detailed technical information.

As shown in Exhibit 8.6, the objective of predictive modeling is to use the information from a database of existing customers (referred to as the "calibration data set") to learn and predict what the behavior of other individuals not included in the original data set, might be. A sample of consumers would be needed, as in cluster analysis. Also similar to cluster analysis, some of the elements of the data used for predictive modeling such as income, age, and credit score could aid in prediction and classification. The key difference, however, is that, in addition to the predictor variables, the data should also provide measures of the individual's behavior—for example, whether the customer has been paying his bills on time.

Exhibit 8.7 provides an example of a calibration data set. Similar to the data used for cluster analysis (Exhibit 8.3), the input data for predictive models constitutes basic measures on the customer such as demographics and credit-related data. Note that an additional piece of information on customers' actual behavior, namely, the timely payment of bills, is shown on the column on the right. This measure would have been established through analysis of the customer's account history or through other means that have historically helped the financial institution classify its customers based on their debt management behavior.

The task of predictive methods is to find the mathematical link between the predictors and the subsequent consumer behavior. Once this mathematical framework is established, it would then be possible to apply the mathematics to the predictor data obtained from new prospects in order to predict (and hence the term "predictive modeling") what a new prospect's future behavior might emerge to be. For example, using age, income, and credit score information on a credit card applicant, one would then be able to predict if the individual is likely to pay his bills on time. This allows one to classify and target individual consumers and to prioritize marketing activities.

Exhibit 8.8 provides a demonstration of how the predictive approach could be applied to a new data set in order to classify new prospects and to determine specific marketing actions that need to be taken with each individual consumer. Based on a prospect's classification as determined by the predictive model (column titled "prediction of timely payment"), the financial services organization could then choose to deploy different levels of promotional activity (column titled "marketing action") to attract those prospects who are of most interest.

Once each prospect has been classified, specific marketing actions can be prescribed to optimize the efficacy of marketing efforts. Predictive models, therefore, enable one to segment customers for whom no specific company-related history may exist. This may help increase the attractiveness of the services that are pitched to new prospects and possibly increase the response rate associated with the individual marketing campaigns.

SEGMENTING CUSTOMERS BASED ON EXISTING RELATIONSHIPS

The focus of this chapter has so far been on developing a fundamental understanding of the segmentation process in financial services markets. The combined use of segmentation techniques with predictive models enables one to target individual consumers with relevant financial products and services, resulting in the eventual creation of new customer accounts. While this is a highly appealing approach for acquiring new customers, financial services organizations also often segment their existing customer accounts, based on the extent of the customer's relationship with the company. Customers who have had a longer stream of transactions, or have been more profitable for the company are often provided with special treatment and care. As a result, loyal customers are viewed as a separate market segment from non-customers, or those with whom little business with the company has taken place.

A focus on these loyal customers is what is generally referred to as *Customer Relationship Management* (CRM). This focus is especially important in light of the cost efficiencies that CRM presents to most organizations. The cost of attracting a new customer is often significantly higher, and in some cases exponentially greater, than the cost of retaining an existing customer. Some practitioners estimate this cost difference to be on average a ratio of 5 to 1, and even greater for certain categories of goods and services.[15] The magnitude of this cost difference highlights the importance of keeping existing customers satisfied using customer relationship management practices which will be briefly discussed here, and detailed further in Chapter 9.

One of the fundamental aspects of customer relationship management is to recognize that the total profit that an organization is able to realize is a function of two generally independent variables. The first variable is the number of customers that the organization is able to attract. This is largely driven by market share, which is often determined by the use of traditional practices of marketing related to brand building, advertising, and competitive pricing. The second variable that drives profitability is the dollar amount of profits generated from a single customer. The profit generated from a single customer can fluctuate greatly from one organization to another and from one customer to the next.

Efforts that an organization could undertake in order to boost profits from each individual customer, could significantly outweigh efforts made to acquire new customers. For example, it might be easier to increase average profits from a single customer by 25%, by selling more profitable products or bundling and cross-selling additional financial services than it is to increase market share by 25%. An increase in market share would require aggressive advertising of the brand, possibly cutting prices, and may eventually lead to retaliation by existing competitors in the form of price and advertising wars. On the other hand, existing customers who have established a relationship with the financial services provider are often open to transacting further with the company. Efforts to increase the volume and profitability of business conducted with existing customers might, therefore, prove to be far more profitable than new customer acquisition efforts.

Formally, CRM is defined as the marketing activities, processes, and procedures that an organization has in place in order to establish and strengthen its communications and repeated transactions with existing customers.[16] These activities, therefore, are focused on developing procedures that improve individual customers' experiences with the financial services organization. Ideally, this results in customer satisfaction and generates repeat purchases, as research has shown that CRM practices can have a positive, enduring, and predictable effect on company profitability.[17] In fact, studies in a variety of service contexts suggest that the increase in customer loyalty resulting from CRM activities is a critical determinant of company profitability. It is therefore critical to understand what factors create loyalty and enduring customer relationships, especially in the context of financial services.

Patterns of Loyalty in Financial Services

Loyalty rates, as measured by individuals' likelihood to remain customers of a company are generally higher in financial services than in most other markets. The majority of customers of most financial services providers tend to stay with the same service provider year after year, and switching between competitors is less common than in other marketing contexts. However, it is important to recognize that the high customer retention levels in financial services may not necessarily represent loyalty resulting from customer satisfaction with the service provider. In financial services, customer retention is often driven by customers' lack of initiative to seek alternative financial services providers.[18]

An example of this is a customer who has a checking account at a local bank branch and recognizes that she may be paying banking fees that are higher than what many of the competing banks offer their customers. She may also not be very happy with the quality of service she receives at the bank. Despite this, she may choose to forgo the idea of switching to another bank. Switching banks would require having new checks issued, linking payroll direct deposits to a new bank account, as well as other adjustments and inconveniences associated with the switching process. The customer may, therefore choose to stay with the same bank since the effort required to switch banks can be considerable. The resulting outcome for the bank has been the retention of this customer, although it is not reflective of the customer's true satisfaction with the bank. In financial services, customer retention is therefore not necessarily indicative of customers' true loyalty and satisfaction levels.

Research suggests that the defection rates in financial services are lower than corresponding figures in most other markets. Depending on the industry, non-financial companies may lose about one fifth of their customer base every year. Financial institutions, on the other hand, typically lose less than 10% of their customers on a yearly basis, and in some financial services categories, the average figures are below 5%.[19] These figures may be deceptively encouraging for financial institutions, however, as they seem to suggest high customer retention levels and no urgent need to attend to customer defection issues. It is important to note that customer defection is a costly event. Even a small customer defection rate implies the costly acquisition of new customers to replace lost ones. It can therefore pose a significant threat to the long-term stability of any organization. For example, with a defection rate as low as 10%, half of the customer base of a company would be lost within 5 years. It is therefore essential to identify and eliminate factors which may contribute to customer defection.

One of the disturbing facts about customer defections is that many customers leaving a financial services provider do not complain or provide any early warnings prior to their departure. What is also disturbing is that only about one in ten of those customers who have chosen to leave, are ever asked by their financial services provider about the reason for their departure.[20] Nevertheless, the pattern of customer defections in financial services has steadily grown over the years, and certain categories of financial services have been more affected by defections than other categories. Credit cards, home mortgages, and automobile insurance are for example, categories in which higher than average rates of defection have been evident. In addition, these categories have exhibited drops in customer loyalty levels due to increased price competition and changing consumer attitudes regarding switching financial services providers.

It is not surprising, therefore, that efforts to retain existing customers have become more important to financial services organizations and that organizational efforts aimed at holding on to existing customers are becoming increasingly necessary. The way in which credit card companies manage their relationships with their existing customers demonstrates this well. Credit card companies are often aware of their own customer's value and may use this information in their dealings with the customer. Based on a customer's transaction profile and history, the customer is assigned a profit score. The higher the score, the more important is the customer to the credit card company. Therefore, when a customer makes a phone call to the credit card company's customer service line, the profit score might determine the speed of the response to the call.[21] A customer with a high profit score might be placed at the front of the call queue and have a very short wait time, while a customer with a low profit score might have to wait a longer time period before talking to a customer service representative.

Customer relationship management in the credit card business is facilitated also by the promotion and selling of additional products to the customer through promotional inserts placed in the envelopes with the monthly bills mailed out to customers. Credit card companies that practice customer relationship management are often very sensitive towards customer defection and may undertake considerable effort to encourage a customer who is considering closing an account not to do so. Customer service employees may also be trained to handle customer complaints and instructed to provide special incentives such as reduced rates or improved rewards programs, which might be needed to convince dissatisfied customers to continue using their credit card.

A critical component of customer relationship management is the existence of procedures for satisfactory resolution of customer complaints. Studies in both non-financial and financial services suggest that customer complaints not only serve as a source of

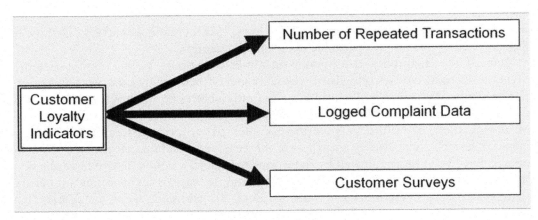

Exhibit 8.9 Customer Loyalty Indicators

information on how to improve the organization, but they also serve as a means to rebuild customer loyalty levels beyond levels achieved by most other means. In a classic study of retail banking services for example, the loyalty rate as reflected by the percentage of surveyed customers who stated that they would "most definitely" continue using the bank varied significantly by the complaint experience of the customer.[22] Customers who never experienced any problems and never had a reason to complain exhibited a 46% loyalty figure (46% stated they would most definitely continue using the bank). Customers who did experience problems and were dissatisfied with the resolution they received in response to their complaint only exhibited a 9% loyalty figure. What is intriguing is that customers who experience problems with the bank and were satisfied with the resolution to their complaint exhibited a loyalty figure of 62%. This figure is almost 1.5 times the level reported by customers who never had any problems with the bank (46%). By effectively resolving a customer's complaint, the customer loyalty indicator was in effect boosted by approximately 50%. It is therefore not surprising that customer service professionals and researchers have suggested that customer complaints can be a "gift" from the customer to the service organization.[23] Complaints provide a unique opportunity not only to regain the customer's business, but also to identify areas that need to be improved in running a business.

Measuring Customer Loyalty

Several approaches are used for measuring customer loyalty, as shown in Exhibit 8.9. The first approach capitalizes on what is known about the customer's history of transactions with the financial institution. For example the number of transaction cycles in which a customer has remained with the service provider enables one to assess the level of loyalty exhibited by that customer. A customer who has renewed an automobile insurance policy with a company for 10 years is therefore likely to be more loyal than one who has just recently signed up. The fact that most financial services organizations have records of their customers' past transactions often provides them with an easy-to-measure indicator of customer loyalty.

A second approach to quantifying customer loyalty is through the analysis of customer complaint reports. High numbers of customer complaints are usually early warning signs for customer defection. Therefore, high complaint rates may be indicators of possible defection and lack of loyalty. Furthermore, the management can use the information captured through a customer complaint report in order to improve the service. The captured information can also be used to fine-tune the types of sales pitches offered to the customer in the future so that the products and services marketed to the customer match the specific needs of the customer more closely. This may help improve customer loyalty levels in the future.

Despite the marketing intelligence potential that customer complaint reports present, the majority of customers rarely complain prior to defecting to a competitor, especially in the context of financial services. In fact, it is estimated that in most services, less than 5% of dissatisfied customers ever express a complaint to the service provider.[24] The low complaint rates are partially a result of the distressful elements that typify the complaining process and customers' lack of knowledge as to whom to complain to. A third approach to measuring customer loyalty is to obtain attitudinal measures through customer surveys. Many financial services organizations regularly survey their customer base to determine their likes and dislikes as well as general perceptions of the service. This information can provide opportunities to pinpoint areas in which service quality is lacking or to identify customer segments that may be unhappy with the service and may potentially defect in the near future. Loyalty measures such as customers' intentions to continue using the financial services provider can be included in such surveys as a means for quantifying and tracking customer loyalty.

What is interesting about customer loyalty measures in financial services is that, of the three measures mentioned above, the first—customer purchase history—is the only readily available measure. Obtaining customer loyalty measures through attitudinal surveys or through the analysis of customer complaints is a much more challenging task. Customer surveys are not only expensive to administer, but also fail to secure a 100% response rate. Similarly, the diagnostic ability of customer complaint data to serve as an indicator of customer loyalty is also limited by the fact that most customers who are unhappy with a service do not express their dissatisfaction in the form of a formal complaint, and may eventually defect without any record of their reason for switching. As a result, reliance on internally collected data on existing customers' behaviors and loyalty

	Segment 1	Segment 2	Segment 3
Average Age	32	23	57
Average Credit Score	590	505	750
Average Household Income	$77,592	$32,900	$142,490
Average Monthly Balance	$937	$1,182	$1,592
Percent of Accounts	36%	12%	52%
Percent of accounts fully paid	45%	12%	71%

Exhibit 8.10 Cluster Analysis Output for Credit Card Data set

levels is critical in understanding customer defection drivers and in improving customer retention rates.

The abundant availability of customer data and the accessibility of credit-related information on individual customers make market segmentation a readily available tool in financial services marketing. Segmentation-based strategies are a wise approach to the marketing of financial services due to the diversity of customer needs and the strategic advantages gained by adopting segment-focused approaches to prevent direct confrontations with the larger financial services companies, which may be more efficient and effective in serving the masses. For many financial services organizations, niche-oriented marketing strategies, which include offering specialized products to smaller market segments rather than to the masses, may prove to be highly profitable strategies that can only be facilitated through the effective use of market segmentation.

CHAPTER QUESTIONS

1. In your opinion, what are the various market segments that may exist in the following categories of financial services? Please describe each segment in terms of demographics, consumer psychology and product needs.
    (a) Commercial banking
    (b) Residential mortgages
    (c) Automobile loans

2. Exhibit 8.10 shows the summary of the results of cluster analysis conducted on a credit card customer data set. How would you describe the various segments in this market? Which segment do you think is the most valuable, and what marketing strategy would you propose to target it?

3. List the limitations associated with the use of cluster analysis.

4. Which financial services providers can you identify who have successfully used a segment-based approach in their marketing campaigns?

5. What consumer characteristics can be used to segment consumers in the student loan business?

ENDNOTES

[1] M. Somer (2011), "The Impact of Credit Card Policies on Small Businesses," *Communities & Banking*, Vol. 22, Iss. 3, pp. 8-9.

[2] J. Goldwasser (2010), "Air-Miles Cards for International Travel," Kiplinger's Personal Finance, Vol. 64, Iss. 3, p. 61.

[3] Depending on the type of financial service, certain elements of customers' personal information may not be allowed for use in target marketing and segmentation. Compliance specialists must be consulted to ensure that the utilized data are consistent with regulatory requirements.

[4] C. Chang, R.Ho and C. Lee (2010), "Pricing Credit Card Loans With Default Risks: A Discrete Time Approach," Review of Quantitative Finance and Accounting, Vol. 34, Iss. 4, pp. 413-438.

[5] J. Terrance, J. Stewart and D. Martin (2010), "The Value of Credit Card Benefits," *Financial Services Review*, Vol. 19, Iss. 3, pp. 227-244.

[6] Donald Lehmann, Sunil Gupta and Joel Steckel (1997), *Marketing Research.* Upper Saddle River, NJ: Prentice Hall; Art Weinstein (1993), *Market Segmentation.* Probus Publishing Company: Chicago.

[7] J. Hair, W. Black, B. Babin and R. Anderson (2009), *Multivariate Data Analysis.* Upper Saddle River, NJ: Prentice Hall, pp. 469-518; Richard A. Johnson and Dean W. Wichern, Applied *Multivariate Statistical Analysis.* Upper Saddle River, NJ: Prentice Hall, pp. 726-799.

[8] Interested readers should consult multivariate statistical analysis books such as: J. Hair, W. Black, B. Babin and R. Anderson (2009), *Multivariate Data Analysis.* Upper Saddle River, NJ: Prentice Hall; Art Weinstein (1993), *Market Segmentation.* Probus Publishing Company; David Aaker, George Day and V. Kumar (2001), *Essentials of Marketing Research.* New York: Wiley; Donald Lehmann, Sunil Gupta and Joel Steckel (1997), *Marketing Research.* Upper Saddle River, NJ: Prentice Hall.

[9] K. Tsiptsis and A. Chorianopoulos (2010), *Data Mining Techniques in CRM: Inside Customer Segmentation.* New York: Wiley.

[10] Thomas Yaegal (1987), "Using Life Cycle Segmentation to Build and Effective Sales System," *Journal of Retail Banking*, Vol. 9 (Fall), pp. 53-62; Philip Kotler and Paul Bloom (1984), *Marketing Professional Services.* Englewood Cliffs, NJ: Prentice Hall; Hooman Estelami and Donald Lehmann (2001), The Impact of Research Design on Consumer Price Recall Accuracy: An Integrative Review, , 29(1), pp. 36-48; Hooman Estelami (1998), "The Price is Right ... or is it? Demographic and Category Effects on Consumer Price Knowledge," *Journal of Product and Brand Management*, Vol. 7, No. 3, 254-266.

11 B. Ambrose, S. Agarwal and J. Campbell (2007), *Household Credit Usage: Personal Debt and Mortgages.* New York: Palgrave; William O'Hare and Joseph Schwartz (1997), "One Step Forward, Two Steps Back," *American Demographics,* September 1997, pp. 53-56. Diane Crispell (1994), "The Real Middle Americans," *American Demographics,* October 1994, pp. 28-35; "The Solvency Trap," *Wall Street Journal,* May 2, 2005, p. A18.

12 Sandra Timmermann (2005), "What Working Women Want: Crossing the Gender Gap to a Secure Retirement," *Journal of Financial Services Professionals,* Vol. 59, Iss. 3, pp. 29-32; Nancy Dailey (2003), "Why the Typical Sales Techniques Don't Work With Women," *National Underwriter,* Vol. 107, Iss. 2, p. 8; George Moschis, Danny Bellenger and Carolyn Folkman Curasi (2003), "Financial Service Preferences and Patronage Motives of Older Consumers," *Journal of Financial Services Marketing,* Vol. 7, Iss. 4, pp. 331-340.

13 Alan Tapp (2009), *Principles of Direct and Database Marketing.* Upper Saddle River: Prentice Hall. James Rosenfield (1991), *Financial Services Direct Marketing: Tactics, Techniques, and Strategies.* Financial Sourcebooks; Alec Benn (1986), *Advertising Financial Products and Services.* Quorum Books: New York.

14 J. Hair, R. Anderson, R. Tatham, and W. Black (1998), *Multivariate Data Analysis.* Upper Saddle River, NJ: Prentice Hall; Richard A. Johnson and Dean W. Wichern, Applied *Multivariate Statistical Analysis.* Upper Saddle River: Prentice Hall.

15 Roland Rust, Timothy Keiningham, Stephen Clemens, and Anthonly Zahorik (1999), "Return on Quality at Chase Manhattan Bank," *Interfaces,* Vol. 29, Iss. 2, pp. 62-72; Thomas Petro (1990), "Profitability: The Fifth 'P' of Marketing," *Bank Marketing,* September 1990, pp. 48-52; R.D. Buzzell and B.T. Gale (1987), *The PIMS Principles.* New York: The Free Press; C. Fornell and B. Wernerfelt (1987), "Defensive Marketing Strategy By Customer Complaint Management: A Theoretical Analysis," *Journal of Marketing Research,* Vol. 24, pp. 337-46.

16 Philip Kotler (2011), Marketing Management. Prentice Hall: Upper Saddle River, NJ, p. 50.

17 V. Zeithaml (2009), *Delivering Quality Service.* New York: Free Press; Roland Rust and Anthonly Zahorik (1994), *Return On Quality: Measuring the Financial Impact of Your Company's Quest for Quality.* Burr Ridge, IL: Irwin; G. Easton and S. Jarrell (1998), "The Effects of Total Quality Management on Corporate Performance: An Empirical Investigation," *Journal of Business,* Vol. 71, Iss. 2, pp.253-307; James Heskett, Thomas Jones, Gary Loveman, W. Sasser Jr., and L. Schlesinger (1994), "Putting the Service Profit Chain to Work," *Harvard Business Review,* 73 (November-December), 88-99; James Heskett and W.E. Sasser, and L. Schlesinger (1997), *The Service Profit Chain.* New York: The Free Press.

18 Ron Garland (2002), "Estimating Customer Defection in Personal Retail Banking," *The International Journal of Bank Marketing,* Vol. 20, Iss. 7, pp. 317-324; Bill Orr (2003), "Are NSF Fees on the Way Out?" *ABA Banking Journal,* Vol. 95, Iss. 5, p. 55; Justin Hibbard (2004), "Banks Go Beyond Toasters," *Business Week,* Dec 20, citing research by TowerGroup.

19 Frederick Reichheld and Thomas Teal (2010), *The Loyalty Effect: The Hidden Force Behind Growth, Profits, and Lasting Value.* Cambridge, MA: Harvard Business School Press; Bill Orr (2003), "Are NSF Fees on the Way Out?," *ABA Banking Journal,* Vol. 95, Iss. 5, p. 55.

20 K. Stewart (1998), "An Exploration of Customer Exit in Retail Banking," *International Journal of Bank Marketing,* Vol. 16, Iss. 1, pp. 6-14; F. Reichheld (1996), "Learning From Customer Defections," *Harvard Business Review,* March-April, pp.56-69; C. Fornell and B. Wernerfelt (1987), "Defensive Marketing Strategy By Customer Complaint Management: A Theoretical Analysis," *Journal of Marketing Research,* Vol. 24, pp. 337-46. S.M. Keaveney (1995), "Customer Switching Behavior in Service Industries: An Exploratory Study," *Journal of Marketing,* Vol. 59, No. 2, pp. 71-82; M. Colgate and R. Hedge (2001), "An Investigation Into the Switching Process in Retail Banking Services," *The International Journal of Bank Marketing,* Vol. 19, Iss. 4/5, pp. 201-212.

21 V. Zeithaml (2009), *Delivering Quality Service.* New York: Free Press; Diane Brady (2000), "Why Service Stinks," *Business Week,* October 23, Iss. 3704, p. 118

22 Tina Harrison and Jake Ansell (2002), "Customer Retention in the Insurance Industry: Using Survival Analysis to Predict Cross-Selling Opportunities," *Journal of Financial Services Marketing,* Vol. 6, Iss. 3, pp. 229-239.

23 J. Barlow, C. Moller and T. Hsieh (2008), *A Complaint is a Gift: Loyalty When Things Go Wrong.* Berrett-Koehler Publishers.

24 T. Keiningham, L. Aksoy and L. Williams (2010), *Why Loyalty Matters.* Dallas: BenBella Books; Hooman Estelami (2000), "Competitive and Procedural Determinants of Delight and Disappointment in Consumer Complaint

Outcomes," *Journal of Service Research*, Vol. 2, Iss. 3, pp. 285-300; Jeanne Hogarth, Marianne Hilgert, Jane Kolodinsky, and Jinkook Lee (2001), "Problems with Credit Cards: An Exploration of Consumer Complaining Behaviors," *Journal of Consumer Satisfaction, Dissatisfaction, and Complaining Behavior*, Vol. 14, pp.88-107; Frederick Reichheld and Thomas Teal (2001), *The Loyalty Effect: The Hidden Force Behind Growth, Profits, and Lasting Value.* Cambridge, MA: Harvard Business School Press.

CHAPTER NINE

Customer Satisfaction with Financial Services

C ustomer satisfaction is an essential component of a successful long-term exchange between a financial services provider and its customers. This is because financial services are typically long-term in nature and involve both the customer and the company in a series of transactions that may span years, if not decades. For example, a life insurance policy, a mortgage contract, or investment advisory services involve exchanges that may commit both the customer and the financial services provider to long-term obligations and interactions. As a result, ensuring that customers are satisfied with the services they receive is critical to the long-term success of all financial services organizations. This view is further reinforced by the abundance of opportunities that exist for monitoring and improving the quality of services provided by financial institutions. In most financial services organizations, the natural accumulation of data on customer transactions enables one to assess service quality using existing organizational data warehouses. Furthermore, the high level of contact between the customer and the service provider, which is typical of some financial services, facilitates the collection of additional customer survey data in order to help quantify customer satisfaction levels and to provide the diagnostics needed to improve customers' experiences with the company.

To appreciate the importance of adequate service quality, one only needs to consider the catastrophic effects that poor quality service could have on customer satisfaction. In brokerage and financial advisory services, for example, the effects of uneducated and miscalculated advice on the life savings of a client can be potentially devastating. In the commercial banking business, the delayed transfer of funds between accounts or inaccurate monthly statements can create significant amounts of customer distress. In the health insurance business, failure to make timely payments to health care providers may create unnecessary inconveniences for customers who, due to their medical condition, may already be in a highly vulnerable state. In financial services, the effects of service quality on the well being of customers can therefore be profound.

The strategic significance of proper customer care has become more evident over the years as the number of choices of financial services providers available to customers has grown. This has resulted in lower loyalty rates and a higher propensity for customers to switch between financial services providers. Often customer dissatisfaction is the trigger for this switching behavior. In light of research that suggests that customers of financial institutions often provide no lead information on their intent to leave, the importance of ensuring adequate levels of customer satisfaction is further heightened.[1] In this chapter, we will discuss the effects of customer satisfaction and examine commonly used techniques for measuring the level of customer satisfaction with a financial service. We will also discuss procedures that are used to improve the quality of services provided by financial services organizations.

Benefits of Customer Satisfaction with Financial Services

There are numerous strategic advantages that are gained by having satisfied customers, especially in financial services settings. In general, customers tend to be more receptive to additional financial services offered by a service provider with whom they are satisfied. As a result, opportunities for increased profit margins by cross-selling additional products and services are much greater for customers who are satisfied than for those customers who are dissatisfied. For example, a commercial bank that has a large customer base of checking accountholders who are satisfied with its retail operations is much more able to convince these customers to obtain additional financial products such as insurance, mortgages, and credit cards than a bank whose customers are generally unhappy with its service.[2]

In fact, research indicates that satisfied customers tend to be less price sensitive than dissatisfied customers.[3] Satisfaction with a financial services provider reduces a customer's *post purchase dissonance* behavior. Post-purchase dissonance is a retrospective mental process that customers often use to justify a purchase decision that they have already made. For example, a customer that has obtained a mortgage from a specific bank may revisit the decision several weeks after signing the mortgage papers in order to feel a sense of reassurance that the decision made was in fact the correct one. The tendency to engage in post-purchase dissonance behavior is much greater when a customer is unhappy with the service.[4] In such a context, customers may revisit components of the decision process, such as the service attributes or price, in considerable detail. This may trigger a heightened level of alertness to price and increases the customers' price sensitivity. In contrast, satisfied customers tend to appreciate the value offered by the financial services institution and as a result tend to be less price-sensitive. They also tend to shop competitors less frequently since they have a better appreciation for the benefits of their current financial services provider.

One of the unique aspects of financial services is the profound impact that word-of-mouth has on customer decisions. Getting advice from a friend, family member, or a colleague on which insurance company to use or where to obtain a home mortgage often has a much greater impact than any form of mass media advertising might have. Individuals typically place a great deal of weight on recommendations made by their immediate social group when determining their choice of financial services providers.[5] The net effect of this is that customer satisfaction can serve as a powerful tool for promoting a financial product or company. Satisfied customers may in fact play a pivotal role in recommending the company to others and championing the company's products.

Ensuring a high level of service quality may result in customers who then help further expand the company's market base without the need for investing in the typically high expenditures associated with advertising campaigns. As shown in Exhibit 9.1, the quality of a financial service can be broken down into three separate components: (1) objective performance, (2) the quality of human contacts with the customer, and (3) company image.

Objective Performance: For example, the objective performance of an investment product such as a mutual fund might be reflected in the returns generated at the end of each year. Similarly, the objective performance of an insurance product might be reflected in the willingness of the insurance company to pay claims filed by policyholders. What is interesting about the objective performance of financial services is that, in most cases, customers may have difficulty in assessing it. For example, the returns of a mutual fund may not be known for many years after the investment decision has been made. Similarly, the willingness of an insurance company to pay claims may not be known to many customers who have never filed a claim. Nevertheless, better performing products – for example funds generating higher returns, or insurance companies with higher levels of customer benefits – are perceived more positively by the market than those for which performance is lacking.

Human Interactions: In addition to the objective performance of a financial service, the nature of the interactions that take place between employees of the financial services institution and its customers have a great influence on customer perceptions of the company and its service quality. In fact, the perceptions of these interactions may, under specific circumstances, have an impact that far exceeds that of objective performance criteria. The manner in which a customer service representative talks to the customer, the friendliness of the bank teller, or the responsiveness of an insurance agent may greatly impact customer impressions of the service. As will be discussed in this chapter, understanding the human aspects of interactions between a financial services company and its customers is critical to successful development of strategies aimed at improving customer satisfaction levels.

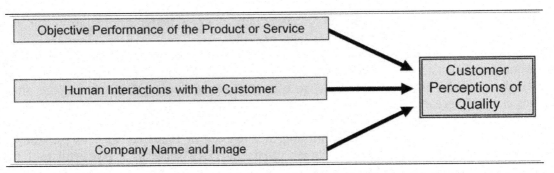

Exhibit 9.1: Drivers of Quality Perceptions in Financial Services

Company Image: Perceptions of service quality in financial services is also influenced by the image of the company, as reinforced through advertising and general communications in the mass media. Image building strategies that capitalize on developing a well-recognized company name help strengthen customer views of a financial services provider and enhance customers' confidence and feelings of security associated with its products and services. For example, an insurance company may spend considerable effort in establishing its name in consumers' minds through advertising on television and radio. The contents of the advertisements may focus on the financial backing and long-established history of the company, improving consumer confidence in the ability of the insurance company to respond to customer claims in times of need.[6] As a result, customer perceptions of the quality of services provided by a financial services company may be a direct function of the image developed through carefully designed advertising campaigns – a topic extensively discussed in Chapter 5. It is important to point out that consumers' reliance on company image, built through advertising must not lead to deceptive or misleading ad campaigns which may boost perceptions of the company beyond its capabilities and true performance levels. Such actions would not only be questioned on ethical grounds, but could also be challenged by regulators and can be harmful to company's image in the long-run.

A customer's overall satisfaction with a financial services provider may therefore be a highly subjective phenomenon. While the true objective performance of a financial product or service may influence customer satisfaction in certain categories of financial services, the qualitative and subjective dimensions of image and the personal human touch may significantly influence customer perceptions and their overall satisfaction with the service.

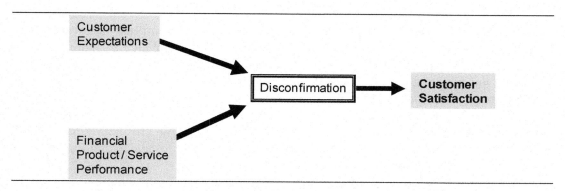

Exhibit 9.2 General Model of Customer Satisfaction Formation

DETERMINANTS OF CUSTOMER SATISFACTION

Customer satisfaction is a function of two underlying components. As shown in Exhibit 9.2, the first component is the customer's expectations of what the quality of the service should be. For example, the customer at a commercial bank might have some expectations as to how long one should wait before one is served by a bank teller. Similarly, the customer of an insurance company might have general expectations of the manners and behavior that should be exhibited by a customer service employee responding to a phone inquiry. These expectations form the baseline used by customers to judge their actual experiences with the financial services provider.

The second component which determines customer satisfaction with a financial services provider is the actual performance exhibited by the company and its employees. This might, for example, be reflected in the length of time the customer has to wait before talking to a teller at a bank branch, or the politeness and courtesy shown by an insurance company's call center employee responding to the customer's phone call. The discrepancy between customer expectations and service provider performance forms the basis for customer satisfaction assessments and is often referred to as *disconfirmation* in the customer satisfaction literature.[7] The larger the disconfirmation, the greater the impact is on customer satisfaction. Performance that significantly falls short of customer expectations is likely to create customer dissatisfaction and, in extreme cases, distress and departure. In contrast, performance that exceeds customer expectations is likely to result in customer satisfaction and, in extreme cases, a state of customer delight.

It is important to acknowledge, as done earlier in this chapter, that in financial services the notion of performance might be difficult to precisely quantify. The ultimate measure of performance for an insurance company or a mutual fund may not necessarily be evident to many customers. Furthermore, performance in many financial services is only meaningful in light of other factors that influence the financial markets. For example, the performance of a mutual fund can only be judged when compared to the returns observed on the securities markets. As will be seen in this chapter, certain aspects of a financial service's performance may dominate consumer perceptions of the exchange. As a result, an accurate understanding of how customers form their performance perceptions of a financial service is critical to understanding how to improve customer satisfaction with the service.

While the disconfirmation of expectations framework is a highly intuitive concept, it provides the financial services marketer with the tools not only to understand the underlying dynamics of customer satisfaction, but also to identify factors that result in customer dissatisfaction. Exhibit 9.3 provides several examples of the extent of impact that disconfirmation may have on a bank customer. Customer expectations of the length of waiting time for a teller at a bank branch as well as the actual performance of the bank as reflected by the customer's actual waiting time are reported. As can be seen in scenario 1, when the performance matches customer expectations, no detrimental effects on customer satisfaction result. In scenario 2, however, the waiting time exceeds the customer's expectations, resulting in customer dissatisfaction. In contrast, scenario 3, in which the waiting time was shorter than the customer's original expectation, results in customer satisfaction. Scenarios 4-6 exhibit how the scale of a customer's original expectations may impact satisfaction judgments. For example, the magnitude of disconfirmation in scenario 4 is identical to that of scenario 2. However, since the original expectation of waiting time in scenario 4 was significantly greater than the expectation level in scenario 2, the effects on customer satisfaction are less prominent. This is because human perceptions are formed on a relative basis. For example, a four minute delay on a 10-minute expected wait time (actual waiting time of 14 minutes) is considered to be less problematic than the exact same delay on a 1-minute expected wait time.[8]

What is appealing about the framework discussed above is that both expectations and performance are measurable constructs in most financial services settings, and their possible effects on customer satisfaction can be predicted. In a financial services organization, various measures of performance are naturally collected in the regular operations of the business through customer transaction logs and traces of data available in the company's internal data warehouses. For example, a bank teller's customer log or the security cameras located at the bank provide measures of the actual waiting time that customers experience while conducting their banking activities at the bank branch. Customer expectations can then be measured utilizing customer surveys and the research

Scenario	Expectation	Performance	Dis-confirmation	Impact on Satisfaction
1	1 minute	1 minute	0	No effect
2	1 minute	5 minutes	- 4 minutes	Dissatisfaction
3	1 minute	½ minute	+½ minute	Satisfaction
4	10 minutes	14 minutes	- 4 minutes	Mild dissatisfaction
5	10 minutes	10 ½ minutes	+1/2 min	No Effect
6	10 minutes	1 minute	+9 minutes	Delight

Exhibit 9.3 Examples of the Effects of Disconfirmation on Customer Satisfaction

techniques which will be discussed in this chapter. Additional data on performance and customer expectations can be collected through customer surveys and the monitoring of customers' banking activities, to quantify the magnitude and direction of disconfirmation experienced by customers.

MEASURING CUSTOMER SATISFACTION

In financial services, customer satisfaction can be measured through a variety of methods. Some of the more common approaches are listed below:

a. *Customer Retention Cycle:* A financial services provider could examine the number of years that a customer has been using its services. The assumption in the use of this measure is that customers that have been using the company's services for a long time are likely to be satisfied with its services. Despite the intuitive appeal of this measure as an indicator of customer satisfaction and its use in a variety of contexts, it may be limited in providing an accurate representation of the underlying level of customer satisfaction, especially in certain categories of financial services. This is because in many financial services, customers may choose to stay with the same service provider for a long time despite a lack of full satisfaction with the services received.[9] The inconvenience and effort needed to switch financial services providers often prevent customers from switching. As a result, a customer who may not be satisfied with a financial services provider may remain a customer due to lack of desire to expend the effort needed to switch.

b. *Number of Cross-Sold Services:* A more accurate measure that may help to quantify the satisfaction level of a customer is reflected in the number of different financial products and services that the customer has decided to obtain from the company. For example, a bank customer who not only obtains his checking account services, but also his auto insurance policy and home mortgage through the same bank is likely to be more satisfied with the bank's services than a customer who chooses to obtain these additional products elsewhere. Therefore, the propensity for a customer to obtain additional products and services form a financial services provider may be used as an indicator of the customer's satisfaction level.

c. *Customer Complaint Records:* Records of customer complaints obtained through customer service interactions may provide insights into the number of dissatisfactory customer service incidents, the types of financial products that are generating customer dissatisfaction, and the possible causes of customer dissatisfaction. It is important to note, however, that the diagnostic value of customer complaint frequencies as an indicator of customer satisfaction levels may be somewhat limited. Research demonstrates that the majority of customers typically choose not to complain to their service provider due to the distress associated with the complaining process and a lack of knowledge of how to proceed with a complaint, and whom to approach when reporting a complaint. In financial services, self-attribution – the association of a dissatisfactory transaction to one's own poor decisions – is also often cited as a reason for consumers' failure to express their complaints directly to the financial services provider.[10] As a result the diagnostic and predictive ability of this measure in determining customer satisfaction levels may be limited.

d. *Customer Satisfaction Surveys:* One of the more commonly utilized approaches for measuring customer satisfaction is to conduct formal customer satisfaction surveys.[11] Survey measures obtained through direct communications with customers regarding the quality of their experience with the services provided tend to be more accurate, more diagnostic, and more representative of the customer's true feelings than the previous three approaches listed. In a typical customer satisfaction survey, customers are contacted through telephone, mail, or e-mail and are asked specific questions about the quality of their service experience. They may be asked to rate specific attributes of the service such as the cleanliness of a bank branch, the politeness of the bank employees, and the accuracy of their monthly bank statements in order to quantify satisfaction with the various attributes of a bank's services. A rating scale, such as a 1-to-5 scale with 5 representing "very satisfied" and 1 representing "very dissatisfied," can be used to capture customer opinions. The result is a series of ratings that can be quantified using simple statistical techniques, such as computing average ratings, to provide a measure of customer satisfaction levels with the various attributes of a financial service. A similar questioning approach can be used in the survey to ask consumers to rate the importance of each of the service attributes. The value of this latter measure is to identify those service attributes that may have a great impact on customer satisfaction levels. The combination of the satisfaction and importance ratings of the attributes can help identify those service attributes which are important to customers, but for which quality is lacking. These identified attributes can then be used to prioritize areas of improvement for the financial services provider, with the eventual goal of increasing customer satisfaction levels.

Dimensions of Customer Satisfaction with Financial Services

Research in services marketing has established that customer satisfaction is driven by a set of well-defined dimensions that characterize the service experience. Five specific dimensions of the service experience help determine a customer's level of satisfaction with the service provider. These dimensions are based on seminal works done by Parasuraman, Zeithaml, and Berry which have helped uncover the underlying drivers of customer per-

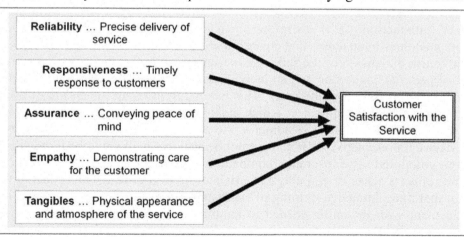

Exhibit 9.4: Determinants of Customer Satisfaction with a Service Experience

ceptions in service encounter shown in Exhibit 9.4.[12] The first dimension is referred to as *reliability*. This reflects the degree to which the financial services provider delivers what it has promised to its customers. For example, a commercial bank is expected to provide accurate monthly statements and to clear funds in a timely manner in fund transfer transactions. An insurance company is expected to process customer claims in a timely manner and have accessible customer service staff. An investment advisor is expected to be knowledgeable about investment products and to be aware of current trends in the financial markets.

The second dimension of the service experience is referred to as *responsiveness*. It reflects a service provider's propensity to attend to customer needs. This might be reflected in a mortgage company's speed of processing mortgage applications or a bank teller's willingness to undertake complex transactions requested by a customer. For a credit card company, it may be reflected in the speed at which a customer's application for an increased credit limit is processed. Responsiveness is therefore often reflected in the promptness and willingness exhibited by a financial services organization in dealing with customer requests.

The third dimension of the service experience is *assurance*. It reflects a sense of confidence conveyed by a financial services provider to its customers regarding its ability to take care of their needs. Assurance can, for example, be reflected in a customer's feelings of trust that an insurance company is willing and able to protect its policyholders financially. In the brokerage business, assurance may be reflected in a client's confidence that the advice provided by a broker regarding an investment decision is well-informed. It is important to note that in financial services such as insurance and investment services, in which considerable risk may exist, assurance may be a significant driver of customer satisfaction. It is therefore critical for financial services providers to facilitate customer interactions that create a feeling of trust and confidence.

The fourth dimension of the service experience is referred to as *empathy*. It reflects a sense of personal connection and an individualized focus on the customer's needs, especially during distressing circumstances. This is a highly relevant dimension of a financial service, especially in categories in which customers may be experiencing considerable losses or risks. For example, a customer's interaction with an insurance company's customer service representative after an automobile accident is likely to be highly distressed and even emotional. The insurance company's interactions with this customer should therefore reflect a sense of empathy towards the difficult circumstances facing the customer at that time. Intensive training of customer service employees is needed in order to equip them with the skills needed to handle customers who may be experiencing such unique difficulties. A customer service employee needs to convey a sense of empathy and cooperation in order to be positively perceived within this critical context of the service exchange.

The final dimension that characterizes the customer's service experience is referred to as *tangibles*. Tangibles represent the physical characteristics of the setting in which a service is delivered to the customer. For example, in the context of a commercial bank, it can be represented by the cleanliness of the bank's branch location and the availability of parking space. For an insurance company, tangibles may be reflected in the ease-of-use of its web site, and the clarity of the claims statements sent out to customers. In the brokerage business, tangibles may be reflected in the general appearance of the broker and the organization of the brokerage office.

The combination of these five dimensions helps determine the level of customer satisfaction with a financial services provider. It is important to note that the extent to which each of these service dimensions contributes to customer satisfaction might vary from one financial service to another. In the retail banking business, for example, the dimensions of tangibles and reliability dominate, and other measures such as empathy and assurance tend to be less relevant.[13] This is because retail banking is a highly standardized process with customer exchanges that tend to be programmatic and predictable. In addition, due to the fact that commercial banks are fundamentally retail outlets with a physical presence, tangibles tend to influence customer perceptions. In the insurance category, dimensions such as empathy, assurance, and responsiveness tend to be more relevant. This is especially true for those customers who have actually needed to utilize the claims services of an insurance company due to an accident or mishap. As outlined earlier, the willingness of an insurance company to attend promptly to the needs of a customer in distress is critical to a satisfactory customer experience.

It is therefore important for financial services organizations to establish empirically which aspects of the service experience most affect their customers. The empirical determination of the relative importance of the various dimensions of service in any given financial service is achieved through formal market research conducted using customer surveys. A commonly utilized questionnaire called SERVQUAL has been used by financial services organizations for nearly two decades.[14] SERVQUAL consists of a list of over 30 specific questions that relate to each of the dimensions of service discussed above, as well as additional aspects of the service. Customer research utilizing these questionnaires can then be done in order to assess how well a financial services organization operates with respect to each of these dimensions and if it meets customer expectations. The diagnostic information collected can then be used to improve service quality.[15]

IMPROVING CUSTOMER SATISFACTION USING GAP ANALYSIS

An important aspect of managing a financial services organization is to improve the products and services provided to customers. A popular technique for guiding such improvements is *gap analysis*. The objective of gap analysis is to dissect the service process into a series of distinct constructs. For example, the process of serving customers includes consideration of the delivered service, as well as the customer's original expectations. Gaps between these two constructs may result in poor customer service. Similarly, in running a financial services organization, the management may have preconceived assumptions regarding what customer expectations of the various aspects of the service are. However, gaps between these assumptions and customers' actual expectations are likely to result in dissatisfactory service encounters for customers. The objective of gap analysis is therefore to identify specific steps in the service production process where important gaps may exist and to help improve the quality of the service by minimizing these gaps.[16]

According to this technique, several important gaps need to be monitored closely in order to improve service quality. As discussed earlier in this chapter, one critical gap is between customer expectations and the actual service received. Efforts to minimize this gap either by improving the delivered service or by lowering customer expectations to reasonable levels would help reduce the chances of dissatisfactory customer experiences. Another important gap relates to the internal operations of the service organization. The gap between what the customer actually experiences and what the financial services organization instructs its people to deliver may suggest that the organization is not fully informed of its own mandate. For example, if the bank specifies that its customers should not wait longer than three minutes to talk to a bank teller, and the actual delivered service is reflected by an average waiting time of seven minutes, a clear shortfall in the bank's service delivery is evident. This gap represents a potential disconnect between what is delivered and what the management is demanding to be delivered. Similar to the first gap discussed in this chapter, reduction of such a gap would likely result in an increase in the quality of service experienced by customers.

An interesting aspect of gap analysis is that many of the gaps can be measured objectively using formal market research techniques. For example, in a commercial banking operation, customer expectations can be measured by surveying customers on what they would consider to be a reasonable waiting time for a bank teller. Average figures for this measure represent a quantification of customer expectations. To quantify customers' actual experiences, teller log data obtained from branch teller operations can be used. The average actual waiting time can then be computed and the difference between this measure and the average produced by surveying the customers' expectations would represent the gap in the service process. Not only is the magnitude of this gap informative of where disconnects in the service process may exist, but continuous monitoring of it may also help determine the degree of improvement or depletion in service quality over time.

Exhibit 9.5 provides an example of how some of the gaps in the service process can

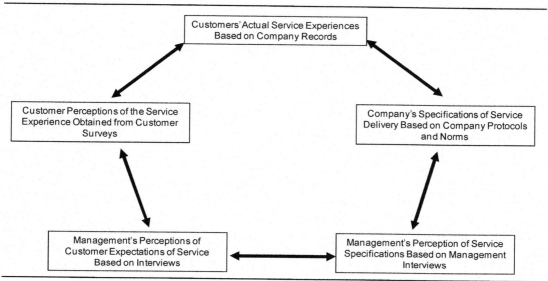

Exhibit 9.5 Sample Measures Used to Identify Service Gaps

be quantified. For example, to quantify gaps between the actual service delivered to customers and the management specifications of what the delivered service should be, service specification instructions to the service personnel need to be examined. If the bank management has instructed the employees a target waiting time of two minutes, the gap between this and the actual customer experience, which for example may be an average of eight minutes of waiting, represents an area in which improvements can be implemented. As shown in Exhibit 9.5, other gaps can also be quantified to establish where in the service production process disconnects may exist.

By using gap analysis, one could utilize additional layers of gaps to characterize the service process. For example, the gap between expected service and perceived service can be quantified. In addition, the gap between perceived service and delivered service can be quantified. Gap analysis can also be used to dissect the internal aspects of the service production process by quantifying the discrepancy that might exist between the delivered service and the service delivery specifications identified by the management. By doing so, significant disconnects would reflect a lack of discipline in the organization to deliver a pre-specified execution of the service to its customers. Furthermore, attempts can be made to quantify any gaps that might exist between what the management assumes to be the customers' expectations and the customers' actual expectations. This is an extremely important aspect of gap analysis that may help identify misperceptions of market demands on a financial services organization.

The diagnostic nature of gap analysis suggests that one could identify the step in the service production process in which improvements can be made. In financial services, the gaps between customer expectations, perceived experiences, and actual experiences tend to dominate a customer's overall impressions of the service. For example, one may find that a customer service employee responding to a call was not as responsive (actual service) as the company claims its employees to be (expected service). Therefore, communicating an image of the company that emphasizes responsiveness may have elevated customer expectations beyond a point where the delivered service exists. Similarly, an investor who uses a broker may believe that her investment returns are below what her colleagues experience with their brokers, despite not knowing their exact investment returns. A gap between actual (the investor's actual return) and perceived performance (based on perceptions of other's investment returns) may dominate her impressions of the broker's performance. It is important to appreciate that the relative importance of the various gaps in the service process may vary from one financial service to another. It is therefore critical for financial services organizations to develop a clear understanding of which gaps are the primary drivers of dissatisfaction for their customers. This would help guide the steps needed to eliminate such gaps, with the eventual goal of elevating customer satisfaction levels.

Certain prescriptive guidelines can be arrived at using gap analysis. For example, in order to eliminate any significant gaps between customer expectations and their actual experience, it is important for financial services institutions not to over-promise. For example, a brokerage firm must take care not to elevate customers' expectations of the amount of personal attention they might receive, especially if the number of brokers available to meet with customers is limited. Similarly, a commercial bank must take care not to exaggerate the speed of customer service at its branches, which would inflate customer expectations of the speed of service beyond what the bank is actually capable of delivering. Such raised expectations are likely to result in customer dissatisfaction and may set up the financial services provider for failure. To ensure that no significant gaps exist between what the customers experience and what the management specifies to be the customers' experiences, regular monitoring of customer service interactions is critical. For this very reason, many customer service operations in financial services organizations randomly monitor the communications that take place between their staff and customers. For example, they may randomly evaluate the conversations that a customer service representative has with customers on the company's customer service telephone lines and reward those representatives who exhibit outstanding levels of customer care.[17]

To ensure that management teams in a financial services organization have an accurate understanding of customer needs, they may need to regularly monitor market research results. This may require the administration of customer surveys or conducting focus groups with existing and prospective customers, with the aim of quantifying customer expectations of specific aspects of a financial service. A similar research approach can be applied on the management of the company in order to quantify their perceptions of what customer expectations are. The gap between the managers' perceptions of customer expectations and the customers' actual expectations can then be quantified to inform and educate the management on the emerging needs of the market and possibly guide organizational realignment to meet the identified needs.

BENEFICIAL EFFECTS OF CUSTOMER SATISFACTION

From the above discussion, it may be clear that the actions taken by a financial services organization aimed at improving customer satisfaction may have a profound impact on the strength of the relationships developed with its customers. The specific actions that are needed to ensure an enduring relationship vary depending on the type of financial service as well as the market position of the financial services provider with respect to its competitors. For example, in order to improve the human interface and to personalize customer interactions in the commercial banking business, bank tellers may need to be trained to recognize frequent customers. This may be especially helpful in an era where technologies such as ATM devices and the Internet have reduced the degree of human contact in the customer service experience.

Marketing practices aimed at improving customer satisfaction can also focus on developing better management techniques for dealing with customer complaints. In many financial services, complaining customers are typically in a state of distress and extreme dissatisfaction. As a result, it is critical for the customer service staff responsible for handling customer complaints to possess a level of specialized training often needed to help distressed customers resolve their concerns. In operational settings where the timely processing of customers is critical, such as bank teller lines or customer service phone queues, increased capacity will speed up customer service and reduce the likelihood of dissatisfactory experiences. In commercial banking, the physical atmosphere of the bank, the availability of parking space, and a wide ATM network may be factors that ensure positive customer perceptions of their service experience. Identifying which specific service attributes most influence customer perceptions of quality can therefore greatly improve a financial services organization's ability to satisfy and even exceed customer expectations.

Emerging research indicates that a positive correlation between employee satisfaction and customer satisfaction may exist in many organizations. This has been found to be true not only among financial services organization, but also in other service contexts.[18] As a result, for example, it has been observed that employees who are satisfied with their jobs tend to be more positive in their interactions with customers and are willing to expend more effort to deliver quality service, compared to employees who are unhappy with their jobs. As a result, the customer exchanges exhibited by satisfied employees tend to be more satisfactory not only for the customers, but also for the employees themselves. Research also indicates that satisfied employees not only result in a higher level of satisfaction among customers, but also may generate work efficiencies that result in higher levels of profitability for the company.[19]

One of the unique aspects of managing financial services organizations is the ability to monitor the quality of customer service interactions systematically. The systematic collection of personal and transactional data on customers provides objective measures that can be used to identify approaches for improving customer experiences. For example, in most financial services organizations, customer service calls are randomly recorded. The objective of this practice is to monitor the quality of exchanges that take place between an employee and the customers. The recorded data can be used to train individual customer service employees on how to improve their customer interactions and can also be used to determine their monetary compensation levels. The latter measure helps provide additional incentives for the customer service employees to ensure that quality service is provided to customers. Such close monitoring of the customers' service experiences also allows the management to continuously assess shifts in service quality and to implement corrective actions when necessary.

CUSTOMER RELATIONSHIP MANAGEMENT

In addition to the beneficial impact of service quality management on customer satisfaction, such efforts are often found to have positive effects on profitability and the ability of the company to retain customers for longer periods of time. This is a critical aspect of the profit generation process because the profits that are generated by

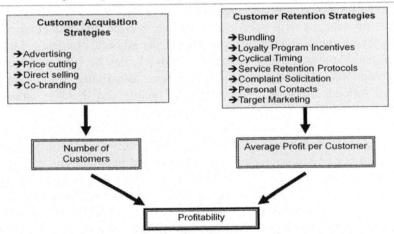

Exhibit 9.6 Drivers of Profitability in Financial Services

a service organization are typically dissected into two independent components. As shown in Exhibit 9.6, the first component is the average profit that is generated from a single customer and the second component is the total number of customers. While improving either of these two factors will result in profit increases, increasing the number of customers is often a more challenging task in the saturated and competitive markets that characterize most financial services. Increasing the number of customers would require one to engage in customer acquisition strategies typically involving high levels of advertising expenditures, costly sales force expansions, and price cutting. As a result, the focus of many financial services organizations today is on customer relationship management, as also discussed in the previous chapter. A fundamental principle behind customer relationship management practices is to increase the profits generated from a single customer. This increase could be achieved by ensuring that customers remain loyal to the company for a long time period, or that they purchase additional services that present supplemental sources of profits to the company.

Cross-selling of financial services is one of the most effective ways of to build stronger relationships with customers. For example, the customer of a commercial bank who has a checking account may also decide to purchase his life insurance policy as well as his automobile insurance policy from the bank. These additional transactions not only present increased profits obtained from the same customer, but also create a stronger bond between the customer and the bank, reducing the customer's propensity to defect to competitors. In addition, existing customers tend to be much more receptive to the marketing pitches of the company, and the return on investment in marketing activities to these customers tends to be significantly higher than corresponding figures associated with new customers.[20] Existing customers who are happy with a financial services provider may also serve as advocates and promote its various financial services to friends, family, and colleagues. This, as highlighted earlier, is critical because personal recommendations

Type of Account	18-24 years old	25-34 years old	35-49 years old	50 and higher
Checking Account Only	60%	40%	45%	65%
Checking Account and Credit Card	30%	15%	10%	5%
Checking Account and Auto Insurance	5%	35%	29%	10%
Checking Account and Mortgage	5	10%	35%	25%

Exhibit 9.7: Product Crossover Matrix (percentage of customers in each age bracket who obtain different combinations of banking services)

and word of mouth have profound effects on consumers' financial decisions.

One of the tools that can be used to identify potential cross-selling opportunities is the *product crossover matrix*. In a product crossover matrix, tabulations are made of the various product combinations that existing customers purchase from the company. Exhibit 9.7 provides an example of how a bank's customers are grouped into various categories depending on the combination of services that they obtain through the bank. For example, in the 18-24 year old age bracket, 60% of customers only have checking accounts. On the other hand, 30% of the bank's customers in this age bracket obtain both their checking account services and their credit cards through the bank. Therefore, for this age bracket, credit cards might be a suitable product to cross-market through the bank.

Similar figures are reported for customers in other age brackets. This type of analysis enables a financial services provider to determine how the propensity to supplement its core services (for example checking accounts) with additional products and services (for example credit cards) may vary by customer segments (for example by age). The percentage distributions provided in Exhibit 9.7 suggest that for the 25-35 years old age bracket, promoting automobile insurance policies might be a fruitful cross-selling endeavor, whereas for the 35-49 year olds, mortgages might represent the best opportunities for cross-selling. Such an analysis would be able to identify cross-selling opportunities which are likely to increase the strength of the relationship with an existing customer, resulting in a longer stream of profitable transactions.

METHODS FOR STRENGTHENING CUSTOMER RELATIONSHIPS

In an effort to retain existing customers, financial services providers must examine all possible activities that may foster a stronger relationship between them and the customer. Below, we will examine some common approaches used to enhance customer loyalty in financial services.

Bundling

A practice that has found increasing application in financial services marketing is bundling. The basic idea behind bundling is to provide customers with a multiple array of financial services under a single brand umbrella and, in some cases, using a single price rather than pricing the different services separately. For example, one may open a checking account, purchase auto insurance, and obtain a mortgage from the same commercial bank. The bundling of multiple financial services under a single financial services provider reduces the customer's incentives to switch to competitors. Two different forces drive the increased loyalty associated with this practice. The first relates to the convenience of having multiple services provided by a single company. The customer would no longer have to shop around for different services at different locations and would be able to obtain all the needed services from a single provider in one location. The convenience gained in this process represents additional value in transacting with a financial services provider and may therefore increase the customer's desire to continue doing business with it.

The second force that accounts for the loyalty effects of bundling relates to its influence on reducing customer defection rates. The fact that multiple services and contracts are bundled under the same service organization makes the task of switching to competing financial services providers more difficult for the customer. As a result, the customer may find the effort required to switch financial services providers to be prohibitive and inconvenient. For example, it has been established that customers who pay bills online are less likely to defect to competitors than other customers.[21] The bundling of online banking services with existing services offered by a bank could therefore not only improve the experience of the customer by providing the conveniences associated with online banking, but it may also discourage customers from switching to other banks due to the more involved role the bank plays in serving the customer's multiple banking needs. In certain categories of financial services, bundling may also be associated with discounts. For example, automobile insurance companies often provide "multi-policy" discounts to those customers who obtain multiple auto insurance policies from them, or obtain their homeowners insurance from the company. This monetary incentive reduces the customer's desire to switch insurers. The net effect of bundling strategies is to not only retain a larger number of customers, but also to retain them for longer periods of time. Care must be taken to comply with regulations in carrying out bundling strategies. For example, in commercial banking the bundling of certain services (for example offering loans) with other services (for example offering deposit accounts) may be restricted by existing regulations. Such a practice may be interpreted as a "tying" engagement whereby the issuance of a loan would be subject to the use of the bank's other services - a practice often challenged by regulators.

Individually Catered Incentives

Another approach that may be used to strengthen customer relationships and to enhance loyalty, is to market products and services that are catered towards the unique needs of individual customers. These needs could be identified based on a customer's transaction history or additional background information which may be available to the company. For example, a credit card company could examine customer transaction histories to identify the kinds of products and services a customer would best relate to. This information can be used to promote products and services targeted to the customer's individual needs.

Cyclical Timing

Another practice that helps customer retention relates to the timing of financial services providers' contacts with customers. Many financial services are cyclical in nature. For example, insurance policies for automobiles and homes are often renewed on an annual or semi-annual basis. The cyclicality of policy renewals provides a window of opportunity for competitors to penetrate one's customer base. It is during this critical time period that a financial services provider may need to undertake additional marketing and selling efforts to ensure the retention of those customers whose contracts are up for renewal.

Employee Protocols

As highlighted earlier, the role of customer contact employees in securing loyalty levels is critical to all service organizations. Customer service employees therefore need to be trained in the procedures for interacting with complaining customers. Special attention may also have to be given to the more severe cases of customer defection and flight. Customer service employees need to have a clear understanding of policies and methods for dealing with the retention of valuable customers who, due to an unsatisfactory experience, may be at great risk of being lost.

Complaint Solicitation

Most successful marketing organizations, whether financial or non-financial, benefit from proactive and resourceful complaint solicitation practices. Complaint solicitation mechanisms such as the availability of 1-800 customer complaint phone lines and customer feedback forms, which enable customers to express their concerns about general as well as specific shortcomings of the service, can provide diagnostic information on how to improve service quality. In addition, the information captured in consumer complaint reports could facilitate improvements, which may subsequently result in higher retention levels for future customers and reduce cases of customer defection.

Facilitating Personal Contact

Personal human contact between the employees of a financial services organization and the customer is critical for specific market segments that demand a human interface in their financial services interactions. This is especially true for older customers who may prefer personal communications and tend to require more individualized attention.[22] Therefore, depending on the market segments that are the focus of a financial services organization's marketing plan, accessibility of human contacts through bank tellers, brokers, or agents might be a critical requirement for building customer loyalty. In some financial services, the personal relationship between the financial services provider and the customer may at times override many of the objective performance aspects of the company. For example, a customer might choose to purchase an insurance policy from an agent whom he has known for many years without paying much attention to the competitiveness of the price of the policy or its underlying benefits. The personal connection between the customer and the agent would therefore play a greater role in customer retention than the more objective and arguably important aspects of the company's offerings.

Customer Prioritization

A good practice in most financial services organizations is to be aware of the customer's profit potential while interacting with them. Knowledge of this measure may influence the nature of the interactions with the customer, and in some cases in which highly profitable customers are involved, may motivate additional degrees of flexibility to provide the level of customer care needed to ensure customer retention. Customer complaints from highly profitable customers should therefore be treated generously and with great attention.

In general, most financial services organizations adopt some form of prioritization mechanism for their customer base. The prioritization mechanism could be captured through measures of profitability assigned to individual customers, as mentioned above, or through general classification of a customer's potential profitability. In financial services organizations ranging from commercial banks and insurance companies to investment brokers and financial advisors, customers with higher income and higher asset levels typically represent higher levels of profitability and are generally preferentially treated. For example, households with dual career professionals are typically high income and tend to accumulate large sums of assets, both financial and non-financial. The financial resources of these households makes them attractive to their commercial bank, which may benefit from the interest gained on the large balances held in their checking and savings accounts, as well as the investment brokers who may find the asset management fees to be lucrative due to the high dollar value of the assets being managed. On the other hand, retired individuals may have lower transaction volume and limited asset holdings for investments and may therefore be perceived by a financial services provider as less profitable. The lower level of profitability associated with some customers may therefore make them less attractive to a financial services provider. These differences in customer profitability may sometimes be manifested in how customers are treated. While these cross-customer differences in service quality may reflect a financial services organization's preferences for serving more profitable customers, the differences also represent concerns about social equity and fairness that may negatively influence a large proportion of the population that may not be perceived as profitable by financial service providers.

Target Marketing

The customer relationship management aspect of financial services often goes beyond complaint management practices and the resolution of customer concerns. Effective customer relationship management in many financial services may also require a better understanding of the underlying financial needs of individual customers. This understanding can often be gained through a study of the transaction history of the customer. Such an understanding would enable the financial services provider to market more meaningful and relevant services to the customer not only in order to generate incremental sales and profits, but also to help customers achieve their personal financial goals.

The ability to identify customer needs and to pitch relevant products is a unique aspect of marketing financial services such as credit cards, insurance, and commercial banking. The intimate knowledge that companies providing these types of services have of the financial dealings of their customers provides them with additional insights that can be used to identify relevant customer segments and associated product needs. Using segmentation techniques, financial services marketers are able to develop programs catered towards the unique needs of specific segments within their existing customer base. For example, if the credit card history of a segment of customers indicates a high level of purchase activity in toy stores, the credit card reward programs promoted to these customers may need to relate to children and products they might need: school supplies, clothing, toys, etc. A relevant offer to target this market segment might be a credit card that offers discounts or rewards points at select toy stores or a card that donates a percentage of its monthly balance to an education fund for the cardholder's children. Similarly, if the credit card activity for a different segment of customers exhibits a great deal of traveling (hotel bills, purchases of airline tickets, shopping in diverse geographic locations), the promotions presented to this specific segment must reflect travel benefits such as airline miles, hotel discounts and the banking needs of frequent travelers such as travelers' checks. By examining relevant customer information, a financial services provider can not only develop a product offering that matches the customer's needs, but also strengthen ties and relationships with the customer, thus increasing long-term retention rates.

RETURN ON INVESTMENT FOR CUSTOMER RELATIONSHIP BUILDING ACTIVITIES

The efforts undertaken by a financial services provider to improve customer satisfaction must in one way or another result in financial returns in order to be economically justifiable. It is therefore critical to be able to quantify the financial effects of investments made to improve service quality. Similar to other forms of investments that a company may undertake, customer satisfaction efforts represent an outlay of funds that must be recovered in order to be considered financially feasible. Four specific parameters are needed to approximate the associated return on investment (ROI) for service quality improvements:

- *The average life-time profits from a single customer (P):* This is a measure that depends on the types of services that the typical customer obtains from the financial services provider and also the number of different services obtained. Typically, this measure would be estimated based on historical analysis of revenues and costs of the service offerings.

- *The percentage profit impact of the service quality improvement (Δ):* This is a managerial estimate of the extent to which average customer profits (P) would change as a result of the increased business generated service quality improvements. This figure is usually determined by managerial judgment but may also be quantified more objectively based on the effects of prior service improvement efforts that may have been undertaken by the company.

- *The total number of customers affected by the service improvements (N):* This is an estimate of the customer base that would find the service improvements sufficiently attractive to engage in additional business with the company.

- *Service program improvement investment (I):* An estimate of the costs associated with the service improvements to achieve the results listed above.

Most of the above measures are judged estimates provided by the management or external consultants who may be informed of the expected results of specific service quality improvements. Prior experience in a particular category of services may also help provide reliable estimates of the above measures. The result is that a return on investment computation can be conducted in order to assess the financial feasibility of customer satisfaction improvement efforts:

$$ROI = \frac{N \times \Delta \times P}{I} - 1$$

To demonstrate the application of the above framework, consider a commercial bank branch that contemplates improving the layout of the branch and making it more user-friendly for customers. The management of the branch estimates that the profit from a single customer (P) is currently $3,200. The management also estimates that about 1,500 of the branch customers (N) would find the improved service highly attractive. Furthermore, the estimated incremental percentage impact on profits generated from each of these customers is 20% (Δ), and the investment for this improvement is estimated to be $650,000 (I). The resulting return on investment using the formula above is 48%.

This approach to quantifying the financial impact of service quality improvements in financial services has a high degree of managerial appeal. For example, the bank could assess whether an ROI of 48% matches the company norms. Furthermore, it allows the bank to compare the ROI of this particular quality improvement program with ROI figures for other types of activities that may also help improve service quality. This would facilitate the optimization of company efforts not only in improving service quality, but also in improving profits. It is important to acknowledge that the ROI computation presented here is somewhat simplistic and has relied on many convenient assumptions. Service improvement efforts that entail an outlay of investments over extended periods of time, or more elaborate assumptions on customer response, would require more sophisticated computations of ROI, by for example accounting for the in-flow and out-flow of funds and the time-value of money.

CONCLUDING POINTS ON CUSTOMER SATISFACTION

Several concluding points need to be addressed in the discussion of customer satisfaction. The first is that a small proportion of customers typically account for the majority of profits generated by financial services organizations. In the credit card business, for example, customers that pay off their balances at the end of every month tend to be the least profitable. On the other hand, those who use the card frequently and carry over significant balances from month to month tend to generate the highest amounts of profits. As a result, customer service improvement efforts may need to prioritize which customers are to be the first recipients of the benefits of these efforts. An additional factor that is important to recognize is the availability of segmentation tools and techniques that can be applied to internal data warehouses to help identify customers that exhibit the highest levels of loyalty. The abundance of personal and transactional information in financial services organizations enables the cross-selling of products that are not only profitable, but also relevant and beneficial to the customer. As a result, systematic and scientific application of segmentation tools in order to better target customers with relevant services is critical to building a satisfying long-term relationship with customers.

Finally, it is important to recognize that the defection rates in financial services are typically considerably lower than corresponding rates in other goods or services markets. As highlighted earlier in this chapter, this pattern of behavior is largely a function of customers' unwillingness to undertake the considerable effort needed to switch financial services providers. Nevertheless, even a small rate of customer defection can translate into significant loss of customers in the long-run. Since dissatisfied customers may eventually leave, the incremental value of customer satisfaction programs and effective complaint management procedures is in helping retain them. Studies on complaint resolution statistics indicate that customer complaints may provide the company with the unique opportunity to boost customer loyalty levels through satisfactory resolutions. Therefore, a disciplined and well-organized approach to service quality management is essential to the long-term health of most financial services organizations.[23]

CHAPTER QUESTOINS

1. Define the following terms:
   (a) Post-purchase dissonance
   (b) Disconfirmation
   (c) Gap analysis

2. What are some justifications for placing a high priority on customer satisfaction in financial services organizations?

3. Design a short questionnaire that you would use to measure customer satisfaction with a credit card company.

4. Of the five dimensions of customer satisfaction with a financial service which one do you think is the most influential in the following financial services:
   (a) Transaction processing services
   (b) Homeowners insurance
   (c) Credit cards
   (d) Reverse mortgages
   (e) Financial advisory services

5. Which gaps do you think most effect customer satisfaction with the following financial services:
   (a) Credit cards
   (b) ATM machines
   (c) Travel insurance
   (d) Brokerage services
   (e) Life insurance
   (f) Financial advisory services

ENDNOTES

1 C. Varela-Neira, R.. Vazquez-Casielles and V. Iglesia (2010), "Explaining Customer Satisfaction with Complaint Handling," *International Journal of Bank Marketing,* Vol. 28, Iss. 2, pp. 88-112; J. Dawes, K. Mundt and B. Sharp (2009), "Consideration Sets for Financial Services Brands," *Journal of Financial Services Marketing,* Vol. 14, Iss. 3, pp. 190-202; M. Durkin, A. O'Donnell and J. Crowe (2008), "Relationship Disconnect in Retail Banking," *Journal of Financial Services Marketing,* Vol. 12, Iss. 4, pp. 260-271.

2 B. Murthi, E. Steffes and A. Rasheed (2011), "What Price Loyalty? A Fresh Look at Loyalty Programs in the Credit Card Industry," *Journal of Financial Services Marketing,* Vol. 16, Iss. 1, pp. 5-13; Justin Hibbard (2004), "Banks Go Beyond Toasters," *Business Week,* Dec 20, citing research by TowerGroup; A. Rucci, S.P. Kim, and R. Quinn (1998), "The Employee-Customer-Profit Chain at Sears," *Harvard Business Review,* Vol. 76, Iss. 1, pp. 82-98; L. Schlesinger and J. Heskett (1991), "Breaking the Cycle of Failure in Services," *Sloan Management Review,* Vol. 32, Iss. 1, pp. 17-28; T. Frischmann and S. Gensler (2011), "Influence of Perceptual Metrics on Customer Profitability: The Mediating Effect of Behavioral Metrics," *Journal of Financial Services Marketing,* Vol. 16, Iss. 1, pp. 14-26.

3 T. Keiningham, L. Aksoy and L. Williams (2010), *Why Loyalty Matters.* Dallas: BenBella Books; Roland Rust and Anthonly Zahorik (1994), *Return On Quality: Measuring the Financial Impact of Your Company's Quest for Quality.* Burr Ridge, IL: Irwin; G. Easton and S. Jarrell (1998), "The Effects of Total Quality Management on Corporate Performance: An Empirical Investigation," *Journal of Business,* Vol. 71, Iss. 2, pp.253-307; James Heskett, Thomas Jones, Gary Loveman, W. Sasser Jr., and L. Schlesinger (1994), "Putting the Service Profit Chain to Work," *Harvard Business Review,* 73 (November-December), 88-99; James Heskett and W.E. Sasser, and L. Schlesinger (1997), *The Service Profit Chain.* New York: The Free Press; *The Loyalty Effect: The Hidden Force Behind Growth, Profits, and Lasting Value.* Cambridge, MA: Harvard Business School Press.

4 G. Raab, G. Goddard, R. Ajami and A. Unger (2010), *The Psychology of Marketing,* London: Gower; T. Keiningham, L. Aksoy and L. Williams (2010), *Why Loyalty Matters.* Dallas: BenBella Books

5 C. Lymperpoulous and I. Chaniotakis (2008), "Price Satisfaction and Personnel Efficiency as Antecedents of Overall Satisfaction from Consumer Credit Card Products and Positive Word of Mouth," *Journal of Financial Services*

Marketing, Vol. 13, Iss. 1, pp. 63-71; K. File and R. Prince(1992), "Positive Word-of-Mouth: Customer Satisfaction and Buyer Behavior", *International Journal of Bank Marketing*, Vol. 10 No. 1, pp. 25-9; R. Bruce Money (2000), "Word-of-Mouth Referral Sources for Buyers of International Corporate Financial Services," *Journal of World Business*, Vol. 35, Iss. 3, pp. 314-321.

6 Tina Harrison (2000), *Financial Services Marketing*. Pearson Education Ltd: Essex, pp.200-226; Alec Benn (1986), *Advertising Financial Products and Services*. Quorum Books: New York, pp. 5-24; G. Michael Moebs (1986), *Pricing Financial Services*. Dow Jones-Irwin: Homewood, IL, pp. 94-113.

7 V. Zeithaml (2009), *Delivering Quality Service*. New York: Free Press; Richard Oliver (1980), "A Cognitive Model of the Antecedents and Consequences of Satisfaction Decisions," *Journal of Marketing Research*, Vol. 17, Iss. 4, pp. 460-469; A. Parasuraman, Valerie A. Zeithaml, and Leonard L. Berry (1988), "SERVQUAL: A Multiple Item Scale for Measuring Consumer Perceptions of Service Quality," *Journal of Retailing*, Vol. 64, No. 1, pp. 12-40.

8 Terence Oliva, Richard Oliver, and Ian MacMillan (1992), "A Catastrophe Model for Developing Service Satisfaction Strategies," *Journal of Marketing*, Vol. 56, Iss. 2, pp. 83-95; Steven Taylor (1997), "Assessing Regression-Based Importance Weights for Quality Perceptions and Satisfaction Judgments in the Presence of Higher Order and/or Interaction Effects," *Journal of Retailing*, Vol. 73, Iss. 1, pp. 135-159.

9 T. Frischmann and S. Gensler (2011), "Influence of Perceptual Metrics on Customer Profitability: The Mediating Effect of Behavioral Metrics," *Journal of Financial Services Marketing*, Vol. 16, Iss. 1, pp. 14-26; Ron Garland (2002), "Estimating Customer Defection in Personal Retail Banking," *The International Journal of Bank Marketing*, Vol. 20, Iss. 7, pp. 317-324; Bill Orr (2003), "Are NSF Fees on the Way Out?," *ABA Banking Journal*, Vol. 95, Iss. 5, p. 55; Diane Brady (2000), "Why Service Stinks," *Business Week*, October 23, Iss. 3704, p. 118. *The Loyalty Effect: The Hidden Force Behind Growth, Profits, and Lasting Value*. Cambridge, MA: Harvard Business School Press; Alan Tapp (2005), *Principles of Direct and Database Marketing*. Upper Saddle River: Prentice Hall. James Rosenfield (1991), *Financial Services Direct Marketing: Tactics, Techniques, and Strategies*. Financial Sourcebooks.

10 J. Dawes, K. Mundt and B. Sharp (2009), "Consideration Sets for Financial Services Brands," *Journal of Financial Services Marketing*, Vol. 14, Iss. 3, pp. 190-202; Jeanne Hogarth, Marianne Hilgert, Jane Kolodinsky, and Jinkook Lee (2001), "Problems with Credit Cards: An Exploration of Consumer Complaining Behaviors," *Journal of Consumer Satisfaction, Dissatisfaction, and Complaining Behavior*, Vol. 14, pp.88-107; Frederick Reichheld and Thomas Teal (2001), *The Loyalty Effect: The Hidden Force Behind Growth, Profits, and Lasting Value*. Cambridge, MA: Harvard Business School Press; Jeanne Hogarth, Marianne Hilgert, Jane Kolodinsky, and Jinkook Lee (2004), "Consumers' Resolution of Credit Card Problems and Exit Behaviors," *Journal of Services Marketing*, Vol. 18, Iss. 1, pp.19-25

11 Richard Oliver (2009), *Satisfaction: A Behavioral Perspective on the Consumer*. New York: McGraw-Hill; Richard Oliver (1980), "A Cognitive Model of the Antecedents and Consequences of Satisfaction Decisions," *Journal of Marketing Research*, Vol. 17, Iss. 4, pp. 460-469.

12 A. Parasuraman, V. Zeithaml and L. Berry (1988), "SERVQUAL: A Multiple-Item Scale for Measuring Consumer Perceptions of Service Quality", *Journal of Retailing*, Vol. 64 Spring, pp. 12-40; A. Parasuraman, A., L. Berry, and V. Zeithaml (1991), "Refinement and Reassessment of the SERVQUAL scale", *Journal of Retailing*, Vol. 67, pp. 420-50.

13 Karin Newman (2011), "Interrogating SERVQUAL: A Critical Assessment of Service Quality Measurement in a High Street Retail Bank," *International Journal of Bank Marketing*, Vol. 19, Iss. 3, pp. 126-139; W. Lassar, C. Manolis, and R. Winsor (2000), "Service Quality Perspectives and Satisfaction in Private Banking," *Journal of Services Marketing*, Vol. 14, Iss. 3, pp. 244-253; R.F. Blanchard and R.L. Galloway (1994), "Quality in Retail Banking," *International Journal of Service Industry Management*, Vol. 5, Iss. 4, pp. 5-23.

14 A. Parasuraman, V. Zeithaml and L. Berry (1988), "SERVQUAL: A Multiple-Item Scale for Measuring Consumer Perceptions of Service Quality", *Journal of Retailing*, Vol. 64 Spring, pp. 12-40; For relevant examples of the application of the SERVQUAL scale to financial services, consult the following sources: Karin Newman (2001), "Interrogating SERVQUAL: A Critical Assessment of Service Quality Measurement in a High Street Retail Bank," *International Journal of Bank Marketing*, Vol. 19, Iss. 3, pp. 126-139; G. Leblanc and N. Nguyen (1988), "Customer Perceptions of Service Quality in Financial Institutions," *International Journal of Bank Marketing*, Vol. 6, Iss. 4, pp. 7-18; W. Kwan and T. Lee (1994), "Measuring Service Quality in Singapore's Retail Banking," *Singapore Management Review*, Vol. 6, No. 4, pp. 7-18; G. Sureshchandar, C. Rajendran, and R. Anantharam, "Determinants of

Customer-Perceived Service Quality: A Confirmatory Factor Analysis Approach," *Journal of Services Marketing*, Vol. 16, Iss. 1, pp. 9-33.

15 V. Zeithaml (2009), *Delivering Quality Service*. New York: Free Press; A. Parasuraman, V. Zeithaml and L. Berry (1988), "SERVQUAL: A multiple-item scale for measuring consumer perceptions of service quality", *Journal of Retailing*, Vol. 64 Spring, pp. 12-40.

16 K. Waite, T. Harrison and G. Hunter (2011), "Exploring Bank Website Expectations Across Two Task Scenarios," *Journal of Financial Services Marketing*, Vol. 16, Iss. 1, pp. 76-85; Interested readers should also consult the details of the quality improvement process outlined in V. Zeithaml (2009), *Delivering Quality Service*. New York: Free Press.

17 U. Yavas and E. Babakus (2010), "Relationships Between Organizational Support, Customer Orientation, and Work Outcomes: A Study of Frontline Bank Employees," *International Journal of Bank Marketing*, Vol. 28, Iss. 3, pp. 222-238;Dyan Haugen and Arthur Hill (1999), "Scheduling to Improve Field Service Quality," *Decision Sciences*, Vol. 30, Iss. 3, pp. 783-804; Robert Ford, Cherrill Heaton, and Stephen Brown (2001), "Delivering Excellent Service: Lessons From the Best Firms," *California Management Review*, Vol. 44, Iss. 1, pp. 39-56.

18 T. Keiningham, L. Aksoy and L. Williams (2010), *Why Loyalty Matters*. Dallas: BenBella Books.; *The Loyalty Effect: The Hidden Force Behind Growth, Profits, and Lasting Value*. Cambridge, MA: Harvard Business School Press; Roland Rust and Anthony Zahorik (1994), *Return On Quality: Measuring the Financial Impact of Your Company's Quest for Quality*. Burr Ridge, IL: Irwin; G. Easton and S. Jarrell (1998), "The Effects of Total Quality Management on Corporate Performance: An Empirical Investigation," *Journal of Business*, Vol. 71, Iss. 2, pp.253-307; James Heskett, Thomas Jones, Gary Loveman, W. Sasser Jr., and L. Schlesinger (1994), "Putting the Service Profit Chain to Work," *Harvard Business Review*, 73 (November-December), 88-99; James Heskett and W.E. Sasser, and L. Schlesinger (1997), *The Service Profit Chain*. New York: The Free Press.

19 Gary Loveman (1998), "Employee Satisfaction, Customer Loyalty, and Financial Performance: An Examination of the Service Profit Chain in Retail Banking," *Journal of Service Research*, Vol. 1, Iss. 1, pp. 18-31; Hooman Estelami and Robert F. Hurley (2004), *Does Employee Turnover Predict Customer Satisfaction*, Marketing Science Institute: Cambridge, MA; R. Bruce Money (2000), "Word-of-Mouth Referral Sources for Buyers of International Corporate

Financial Services," *Journal of World Business*, Vol. 35, Iss. 3, pp. 314-321; K. File and R. Prince(1992), "Positive Wordof-Mouth: Customer Satisfaction and Buyer Behavior", *International Journal of Bank Marketing*, Vol. 10 No. 1, pp. 25-9; Richard Oliver (2009), *Satisfaction: A Behavioral Perspective on the Consumer*. New York: McGraw-Hill.

20 Richard Oliver (2009), *Satisfaction: A Behavioral Perspective on the Consumer*. New York: McGraw-Hill; *The Loyalty Effect: The Hidden Force Behind Growth, Profits, and Lasting Value*. Cambridge, MA: Harvard Business School Press; Justin Hibbard (2004), "Banks Go Beyond Toasters," *Business Week*, Dec 20, citing research by the TowerGroup.

21 C. Zuccaro and M. Savard (2010), "Hybrid Segmentation of Internet Banking Users," *International Journal of Bank Marketing*, Vol. 28, Iss. 6, pp. 448-464; A. Sunikka and J. Bragge (2009), "Promotional Messages in Multichannel Banking: Attractive or Annoying," *Journal of Financial Services Marketing*, Vol. 14, Iss. 3, pp. 245-263.

22 C. Varela-Neira, R.. Vazquez-Casielles and V. Iglesia (2010), "The Effects of Customer Age and Recovery Strategies in Service Failure Settings," *Journal of Financial Services Marketing*, Vol. 15, Iss. 1, pp. 32-48; George Moschis, Danny Bellenger and Carolyn Folkman Curasi (2003), "Financial Service Preferences and Patronage Motives of Older Consumers," *Journal of Financial Services Marketing*, Vol. 7, Iss. 4, pp.331-340.

23 Interested readers are encouraged to examine the following articles for the application of survival analysis techniques to customer relationship management in financial services: Tina Harrison and Jake Ansell (2002), "Customer Retention in the Insurance Industry: Using Survival Analysis to Predict Cross-Selling Opportunities," *Journal of Financial Services Marketing*, Vol. 6, Iss. 3, pp. 229-239; T. Tang, L. Thomas and J. Bozzetto (2007), "It's the Economy Stupid: Modeling Financial Product Purchases," *International Journal of Bank Marketing*, Vol. 25, Iss. 1, pp. 22-38; E. Steffes, B. Murthi and R. Rao (2008), "Acquisition, Affinity and Rewards: Do they Stay or do they Go?," *Journal of Financial Services Marketing*, Vol. 13, Iss. 3, pp. 221-233.

CHAPTER TEN

Regulations Governing Financial Services Marketing

WHY REGULATE?

The financial services industry in the United States is arguably one of the most heavily regulated industries worldwide. This is especially apparent if one considers the number of regulations in place and the number of companies and consumers that are impacted by these regulations. It is also noteworthy that the number of these regulations has grown over the years due to increased public concerns about consumer protection issues and conflicts of interest which often characterize many financial services transactions. It is therefore important to have an adequate level of knowledge about regulations that impact the activities of financial services marketers. In this chapter, we will review the key regulatory measures that govern the practice of financial services marketing.

There are many reasons for regulating the marketing activities of financial services organizations. Financial services have a direct effect on the social, emotional, and economic wellbeing of most individuals who use these services.[1] Regulations provide the means for protecting consumers' financial wellbeing by establishing standards for the quality of the financial products and services offered in the marketplace. Regulating financial services marketing activities is important due to the elusive nature of quality in financial services. Unlike manufactured goods, for which quality can be objectively measured using scientific instruments, the quality of a financial service is difficult to quantify. For example, the future investment returns expected from a mutual fund, or the payout behavior of an insurance company, is unknown prior to the purchase of these financial products and may not be evident for years after the purchase. It is therefore critical that regulators ensure that delivering quality service, however it may be defined, is a primary objective of financial services organizations. This concern is further compounded by the fact that many financial transactions, such as purchases of investment and insurance products, are irreversible in nature, placing consumers at significant financial risk.

Additionally, consumers are vulnerable to information asymmetry that may exist in financial services markets. Information asymmetry arises since most financial services organizations have access to an abundance of data on their customers' personal information. The personal information available to financial services marketers may provide them with a great deal of power in determining what products and services to promote to consumers, and how best to pitch them. While this may be a very helpful aspect of conducing financial services marketing activities, it may also facilitate deceptive marketing practices which can become of concern to consumer protection authorities and regulators. Financial services marketers could for example, choose to use consumers' personal information to pitch products that are not in the best interest of consumers, price them noncompetitively, or provide consumers with products and services that lack the basic elements of quality. A relevant example can be found in the financial disasters that followed the growth of sub-prime mortgages issued to homebuyers with weak credit histories during the past decade. As evident by this example, by attempting to expand their customer base, companies may be tempted to make financial products and services available to individuals who are not qualified or are incapable of handling the required financial responsibilities. These individuals may be unqualified due to their past credit history, low income, or lack of financial resources and may eventually experience considerable financial hardship resulting from their use of these products and services.[2] Such marketing practices not only damage the individual's credit records, but also may result in bankruptcy and loss of financial control and independence.

CONSUMER VULNERABILITY

The extent of consumer vulnerability in financial services markets is evident in the types of products and services that have been promoted to consumers over the years. The explosive growth in consumer credit card debt during the last decade has been associated with consumers' inability to comprehend the amount of financial responsibility that they are undertaking and the aggressive marketing campaigns used by credit card companies to acquire new customers. For example, many consumers fail to recognize that, by paying the minimum monthly payment, they may spend decades paying off a seemingly small credit card bill. For example, a $1000 balance on a credit card with a

17% rate of annual interest will take approximately two decades to pay off if the cardholder makes the minimum monthly payments.[3] Many consumers fail to recognize this dramatic trade-off and often engage in excessive use of credit cards for discretionary expenditures, which eventually results in massive accumulation of high-interest debt. This has been one of the driving forces behind regulatory measures that have mandated clear disclosure of the length of financial obligations resulting from credit card usage.

Another example is what many tax return firms offer their clients. After completing a client's taxes, the tax accountant may offer the client immediate access to his or her refund. This option is made available to the client, as the alternative for the client would be to wait the usual four-to-eight weeks that it takes the tax authorities to process a tax return. If the client agrees, he or she would receive payment instantly, less certain administrative fees. Many clients choose to accept the accelerated return since immediate access to a refund is desirable. This pattern of consumer preference relates to the notion of asymmetric discounting discussed in Chapter 2, whereby immediate access to funds is generally preferred by consumers, to an extent where the discount rates that would apply may far exceed prevailing interest rates in the financial markets. In fact, when considering the administrative fees compared to the net refund received, the interest rate implied by the transaction, typically translates into extremely high levels, often far exceeding what credit card companies might charge for making equivalent amount of funds available to their customers. Clearly, the client might have been far better off borrowing these funds through a credit card, even at the relatively high interest rates that may be charged by some credit card companies, than to use the offered service. Nevertheless, millions of taxpayers use such services every year. A similar practice is that of personalized blank checks which are often enclosed with the bills that credit card companies and other financial institutions mail out to consumers. These checks give consumers the impression that they have a personal bank account from which they can write checks. However, the interest rates that are associated with the use of such funds, as well as the additional fees such as late payment fees and transaction charges are not only considered by many to be excessive, but are also typically not clearly communicated to consumers. Some observers have argued that these marketing practices may not only be harmful to consumers, but they can also pose a threat to the financial services industry, which is often observed and scrutinized by regulators.[4]

The harmful impact of questionable marketing practices on consumers is disturbing. For example, over the past two decades there has been an overall growth in consumer bankruptcy filings.[5] Similar patterns are observed with respect to delinquency rates for mortgages and credit cards, especially among specific segments of the population, such as the senior citizens.[6] In addition, studies that have examined the general population's view of financial services professionals have shown that the public has great concerns about the ethical and moral standards of the industry. A classic study by the Gallup Organization, for example, found that only one third of the population rated bankers to be "very high" or "high" in their ethical standards.[7] It is no surprise that the avalanche of regulations that has hit the industry over the years may be motivated by consumer protection initiatives as well as political forces capitalizing on these public concerns.

OBJECTIVES OF REGULATING FINANCIAL SERVICES MARKETERS

The underlying motivation behind regulatory measures in financial services can be summarized by three general objectives:

1. Protecting consumers against misleading marketing practices. Many of the regulations in place are intended to ensure that consumers are not deceived by deceptive and misleading financial services offers.

2. Fostering healthy competition in financial services markets. Regulatory bodies have a fundamental obligation to the financial services industry as well as to the general public to facilitate a market environment in which consumers have an array of competing offers to choose from. Specific regulations have therefore been created to encourage competition among financial services providers and to prevent monopolistic and predatory behavior by competitors.

3. Ensuring that all consumers have access to essential financial services. Individuals depend on financial services such as insurance, home mortgages, and consumer credit to maintain their financial security and to prosper economically. It is therefore critical for consumers to have access to essential financial services at reasonable costs. Regulations ensure that financial services providers make their services available to all segments of the population and that discrimination, price gouging and unfair denial of services are not practiced.

The financial services industry is guided by regulations, some of which are specific to financial services providers and others that influence all industries. Among the regulations with wide impact across industries is the *Clayton Act of 1914*, which helped establish the *Federal Trade Commission*. According to the Clayton Act, price-fixing, which is the pre-meditated coordination of prices among different competitors in the marketplace, is illegal.[8] Therefore, insurance companies or mortgage providers cannot discuss and adjust their prices in harmony. Such coordination among competitors is likely to result in higher prices for the consumer and would be considered anti-competitive. Various forms of antitrust laws have since been put in place to control the extent to which different financial institutions could merge and consolidate. These antitrust laws, which are often enforced by the *Federal Trade Commission*, apply not only to financial services, but also to other industries in which ensuring a healthy level of competition is a primary concern. Among the regulations that are specific to the financial services industry, is the *Truth in Lending Act of 1968* which focuses on the amount of information that is disclosed by banking institutions when lending funds to borrowers. According to this regulation, lenders are required to state clearly the terms and conditions governing the loan arrangement, such as the interest rate and administrative fees charged.

It is important to note that different regulations and different regulatory bodies apply to different segments of the financial services industry. For example, some of the regulations and organizations that monitor banks are different from those that influence the insurance industry or the securities trading business. Moreover, regulations governing financial services markets systematically evolve, and an up-to-date knowledge of recent developments is important for the formulation of educated marketing strategies. It is therefore critical for financial services marketers not only to be well-trained in the specific regulations that influence their markets, but also to have access to the latest and most skilled professional and legal advice.

THE REGULATORY BODIES

There are many regulatory bodies and regulations that influence the activities of financial services marketers. Arguably, these regulations make the job of marketing financial services more difficult by restricting creative marketing tactics and by upholding stringent requirements that make the task of marketing communications less innovative and more mechanical. It is therefore critical for financial services marketers to study closely the regulations that have been filed at the *Federal Register* (*www.gpoaccess.gov*) and to consult an attorney and other relevant resources in order to ensure compliance with established laws. Having access to the latest information and the most qualified legal advice is critical since regulations, especially those governing financial services marketing activities, are in a state of flux. These regulations are updated and changed at a relatively quick pace, and maintaining current knowledge of their detailed requirements is critical to the marketing practice. The material presented in this chapter is intended to provide an overview of the topic, and readers active in marketing of financial services are encouraged to consult specialized legal professionals to ensure compliance with regulatory requirements.

The process by which regulations are formed varies from product to product. Different regulatory bodies are assigned the task of monitoring and enforcing these regulations. Below, we will discuss the mandates of regulatory bodies most relevant to financial services marketing. Interested readers are recommended to consult relevant sources for additional details on the functions of these regulatory bodies.[9]

Department of Commerce (www.commerce.gov): Was established in its current organizational structure in 1913. The Secretary of Commerce, who is appointed by the U.S. President, heads the Department. The primary responsibilities of the Department of Commerce are to facilitate international trade, monitor the export and import of goods and services, monitor economic affairs (including the operations of the Census Bureau), as well as to overlook the use of natural resources and the development of the tourism industry in the United States.

Justice Department (www.usdoj.gov): Established in 1870, the Justice Department is headed by the Attorney General, who is appointed by the U.S. President. The Justice Department focuses on a variety of legal matters central to the American population, covering issues related to criminal justice, civil rights, land and natural resource use, taxation, and consumer protection. The department also advises the President and other U.S. government offices on the development of legal policies and specific legal matters. The Antitrust Division of the Justice Department is of unique interest to many industries, including financial services, because its main task is to encourage healthy competition by enforcing antitrust laws. These laws are designed to avoid monopolies and to facilitate healthy competition by preventing anticompetitive behavior. Antitrust laws, for example, might restrict the extent of mergers among banks, insurance companies, and brokerage firms in order to prevent the monopolization of those markets by a small number of powerful competitors. The Justice Department's Antitrust Division often works closely with the Federal Trade Commission to establish and prosecute cases of anticompetitive behavior.

Federal Trade Commission (www.ftc.gov): Motivated by the Sherman act of 1890, the Federal Trade Commission was established in 1914 as an entity for overlooking the implementation of antitrust laws. The FTC therefore works very closely with the Antitrust Division of the Justice Department. The scope of FTC's activities include protecting consumers against misleading advertisements, monitoring the labeling and packaging of products to prevent deceptive communications, controlling the amount and extent of mergers among competitors, and ensuring that price discrimination does not occur in the marketplace. The FTC also provides guidelines for companies in order to help them better understand antitrust regulations.

U.S. Treasury (www.ustreas.gov): Established in 1789, the Treasury Department is responsible for developing the national monetary policy and the supply of money in the economy. The Treasury is also responsible for producing coins and paper currency. Issues of concern to the Treasury include taxation, international financial policy, and currency stability. The Treasury also overlooks the national banks, which is a task primarily conducted through its *Office of the Comptroller of Currency (OCC)*. The OCC, which was established in 1863, reports directly to the U.S. Congress and has the primary task of monitoring the activities of national banks in order to ensure that they are solvent, well managed, and properly organized. The OCC has regulatory authority for federal thrifts and may also need to be consulted when national banks set up new branches or cross state lines. The Treasury Department is also the home of the *Federal Insurance Office (FIO)* established in 2010 with the role of consolidating and disseminating information on state-level regulations in the insurance industry.

Securities and Exchange Commission (www.sec.gov): Appropriate disclosure of financial information in securities markets is critical to the healthy operation of a capitalist economy. The Securities and Exchange Commission (SEC) was established in 1934 as an authority responsible for overlooking the trading activities for securities. The SEC is responsible for monitoring the activities of securities brokers, as well as the exchanges in which securities are traded. The monitoring is done in order to ensure that manipulation and misrepresentation of securities information in these markets do not take place. The SEC also requires publicly traded companies to disclose their financial status and company officers to report their own holdings of their company's securities. Stockbrokers and dealers are also required to register with the SEC, which also has monitoring authority over the major stock exchanges such as the American Stock Exchange, the Boston Stock Exchange, the Chicago Board of Options, the New York Stock Exchange, as well as other major exchanges. The SEC is able to enforce regulations on brokers through self-regulating bodies such as the Financial Industry Regulatory Authority (FINRA), as well as legal prosecution through the Department of Justice.

Financial Industry Regulatory Authority (www.finra.org): Established in 1938 (previously called National Association of Securities Dealers) as a result of an amendment made to the Securities and Exchange Act that required the organization of securities dealers into self-regulating associations. FINRA is a national network of securities dealers aimed at regulating the over-the-counter market for securities (securities that are not traded on the major stock exchanges). FINRA has a series of codes of conduct, closely developed with the SEC. These codes of conduct must be closely followed by FINRA member brokers. Code violations such as fraudulent and unethical practices by members may result in punitive measures such as fines by the FINRA, and in certain cases, the SEC may also request FINRA to expel members or request the Department of Justice to proceed with legal prosecution of violators.

National Association for Insurance Commissioners (www.naic.org): The insurance industry in the United States is not regulated at the federal level. Instead, each state's *Department of Insurance* or *Insurance Commissioner* is responsible for regulating the activities of companies that sell insurance products within the state's borders. The state insurance department will monitor the financial well-being of these companies and serve as an appeal mechanism for consumers who have complaints about specific insurance companies. In order to ensure that the various states follow similar guidelines on how insurance companies operate, the NAIC provides a framework for insurance company operations as well as general codes of conduct which the individual states' regulators may choose to enforce on insurers operating in their state. The NAIC works closely with the *Federal Insurance Office* (a division of the Treasury Department) whose goal is to collect and disseminate information on state-level insurance regulations.

Federal Reserve Board (www.federalreserve.gov): The Federal Reserve Board was established in 1913 with the objective of overlooking the activities of the 12 regional Federal Reserve banks. Subsequently, the Federal Reserve Board was given the responsibility of regulating all bank holding companies. The board regulates the reserve requirements of state banks and facilitates transactions between the banks by operating clearing houses at various locations throughout the country. The Federal Reserve Board has a central role in the implementation of national monetary policy because it specifies the reserve requirements that banks must honor. These reserve requirements determine the total amount of loans that banks could issue as a multiple of reserves on transaction account deposits such as cash in the bank's vaults, checking account balances, and savings account deposits. These requirements are designed to provide liquidity in the banking system by ensuring the ability of the banks to pay off their liabilities to the public. In addition to specifying reserve requirements, the Federal Reserve Board has over two-dozen regulations, many of which control the interface between banking institutions and their customers. These regulations for example dictate the terms by which credit information is to be disclosed to consumers applying for credit products and specify the procedures for handling consumer complaints. Federal Reserve regulations for protecting consumers against discriminatory denial of credit also exist. The Federal Reserve regulations also govern the logistical aspects of information exchange, by for example, specifying the conditions and procedures for operating electronic fund transfers. In addition, the Federal Reserve regulations specify the conditions that constitute incomplete and deceptive advertising for credit products. One of the agencies of the Federal Reserve, established in 2010, is the *Consumer Financial Protection Bureau (CFPB)* which is responsible for supervising compliance with financial laws in consumer financial markets such as those of credit cards, mortgages and student loans.

Two other important governmental organizations also need to be recognized. The first is the *General Accounting Office (GAO)*, which was established in 1921 by the U.S. Congress. The objective of the GAO is to overlook the financial transactions of the Federal Government and its associated organizations. The GAO conducts non-partisan and unbiased accounting audits of U.S. federal organizations. The second organization that is noteworthy is the *Financial Accounting Standards Board (FASB)*. Established in 1973, the FASB is responsible for developing the standards by which companies account and report their financial results. The recommendations of this office and the advice that it provides to the accounting community sometimes have significant impact on the realized and expected profits of financial services companies.

REGULATIONS GOVERNING FINANCIAL SERVICES MARKETING

In this section, we will review specific regulations that apply to various types of financial services. Focus will be given on marketing regulations in banking, insurance, and the securities trading businesses. In addition, regulations related to consumer privacy and marketing communications that apply to all forms of financial services will be discussed. Readers are encouraged to examine the *Federal Register* for a list of current regulations and to consult the appropriate regulatory bodies and specialized legal professionals in order to develop an informed interpretation of regulations relevant to their own practice.

Bank Regulations

National banks – those that operate across state lines – are regulated by the Office of the Comptroller of Currency (OCC). State banks, which are banks that operate within a single state, are regulated by the Federal Reserve Board bank district to which their state is assigned. To regulate the operation of bank branches, regulators issue bank charters, which allow banks to open bank branches, collect deposits, and issue loans. In addition, banks would be able to cross-sell products to their customers, creating additional sources of revenue. Research has long established that the majority of bank customers have a tendency not to switch banks once they have opened an account except for geographic and logistical reasons.[10] Therefore, bank branches often experience high levels of customer retention and a relatively stable base of customers for attracting deposits, issuing loans, and generating revenues from transaction and service fees.

In the past two decades, there have been a notable number of mergers and consolidations taking place in the banking sector. During this period, the total number of deposit-taking financial institutions has dropped from over 15,000 to less than 10,000. This trend is partially attributed to the desire of banking institutions to achieve economies of scale by consolidating and operating on a larger scale. The trend is also attributed to the deregulation of the financial services industry at the turn of the century, which allowed financial institutions from a diverse range of backgrounds to merge. The result has been a smaller number of banks, each operating a much larger number of bank branches.

The foundation of the modern banking system relies on the ability of banks to issue loans based on the amount of deposits that the public has placed in their deposit accounts. The issuing of these loans enables businesses and individual consumers to borrow funds in order to purchase goods and to engage in economic activity. The Federal Reserve Board has specific regulations that govern the extent to which banks could issue loans as a function of the total amount of deposits placed in the bank's own vaults, checking account deposits, and savings account balances. In addition, *Regulation D* of the Federal Reserve requires commercial banks to obtain insurance from the *Federal Deposit Insurance Corporation (FDIC)*. The FDIC was set up in 1933 in response to a series of catastrophic bank failures. These bank failures were largely due to commercial banks overextending loans and participating in high-risk investment banking activities. This resulted in a general lack of confidence in the banking sector by the public and lead to the establishment of the FDIC. FDIC insurance protects the first $250,000 of deposits placed by a customer into a deposit account, such as a checking or savings account or a certificate of deposit. Regulation D also requires savings and loans associations as well as mutual and stock savings banks to purchase deposit insurance from the Federal Savings and Loan Insurance Corporation, which serves a similar role as the FDIC. Regulation D also specifies the reporting requirements according to which member banks should disclose the details of their operations to the Federal Reserve.

In addition to Regulation D, several other Federal Reserve regulations govern the interactions that banking institutions have with their customers. *Regulation A* is primarily concerned with the complaint-filing procedure for bank customers. It establishes the steps for investigating allegations of misleading communications by member banks and specifies disclosures that should be included in consumer credit agreements. *Regulation B* is focused on ensuring equal access to credit for all consumers. This regulation makes it illegal to deny applicants credit, based on the applicant's race, national origin, age, gender, religion, and certain other demographic variables. According to this regulation, if a bank denies an applicant credit, a written notice must be provided, and the applicant can request an explanation of the justification used for the denial decision.

Regulation E of the Federal Reserve is related to the procedures governing electronic fund transfers. This regulation specifies the rights of parties involved in the electronic transfer of funds. The regulation is aimed at protecting consumers in electronic fund transfer transactions by specifying limits on consumer liabilities in cases of unauthorized access to funds. It also requires banks to disclose specific information on their fund transfer procedures and to document meticulously electronic transfer activities. Amendments to Regulation E were made in 2010 through the *Dodd-Frank Wall Street Reform and Consumer Protection Act*. They require that bank accountholders must opt-in to obtain overdraft coverage and cannot be forced by the bank to use overdraft services. *Regulation M* is focused on consumer leases. This regulation specifies the disclosure requirements for leasing contracts. The requirements state that, in a leasing contract, the lending institution must specify the cost of the lease as reflected in the monthly payments, maintenance fees, registration and taxes, security deposits, as well as any end-of-lease balloon payments that might apply. In addition, warranties and service responsibilities as well as wear-and-tear restrictions need to be specified in written form and communicated clearly to the consumer.

Two other regulations of the Federal Reserve Board are noteworthy in a marketing context, especially as they relate to competition and antitrust concerns. The first is *Regulation L*, which is concerned with encouraging competition in the retail-banking environment. According to this regulation, top officials in a deposit-taking financial institution are prohibited from holding official positions in other deposit-taking institutions if it is established that the two institutions are not related and that they compete with one another in certain markets. Clearly, this regulation is aimed at securing sufficient competition and preventing competitors from colluding in their marketing activities. *Regulation R* attempts to achieve the same objectives by limiting the relationships that exist between securities dealers and banks.

One of the most influential regulations of the Federal Reserve is *Regulation Z*, otherwise known as the *Truth in Lending Act*. It governs the disclosure requirements for credit contracts by specifying what needs to be communicated regarding the cost of credit. The regulation also establishes the methods for determining the cost of credit. In addition, procedures and timelines for correcting errors in credit transactions and the required responses to consumer complaints are spelled out. Regulation Z also requires that lenders communicate the information in written form, quantify the cost of credit in the form of an annual percentage rate (APR), and inform credit applicants of their rights in credit transactions. According to this regulation, interest rates must be stated for a twelve-month period. When lending funds, such costs as service charges, origination fees, application fees, and other related loan expenses must also be clearly stated in the contract.

The *Truth in Savings Act* attempts to achieve similar objectives as the Truth in Lending Act. It focuses on deposit accounts maintained by depository institutions such as commercial banks and savings and loans institutions. The regulation requires that these institutions provide the necessary details related to these deposit accounts to their customers. Terms such as the rate of interest, applicable fees, and conditions of the deposit contract such as the minimum length of time required prior to withdrawal of the funds need to be clearly communicated. The Act also specifies the procedures that depository institutions need to undertake in order to comply with the regulation and methods for demonstrating compliance.

The *Homeowners Equity Protection Act* is an expansion of the Truth in Lending Act that focuses on the specific category of home equity loans. Home equity loans are a closed-end form of credit that requires regular payments of principal and interest and the repayment of the total principal by a pre-specified point in time. The loans are secured by the real estate property owned by the borrower. The Act is intended to protect borrowers from predatory marketing activities that might be carried out by some lending institutions. It protects consumers in conditions where the annual percentage rate charged exceeds the yield on Treasury securities by a certain percentage, or if the upfront fees charged such as application and brokerage fees exceed certain pre-determined amounts. In addition, the Act prohibits the provider of home equity loans from extending credit to unqualified applicants. Lenders are also prohibited from enforcing prepayment penalties, or creating debt repayment conditions that may be deemed impossible for a borrower to comply with, resulting in the loan's default.

Other regulations that govern the banking sector have evolved over the years. For example, the *Glass-Steagall Act* of 1933 prevented commercial banks from participating in investment banking activities. This act went into effect during a period when the confidence of the public in the banking sector was at a low point. This was because the catastrophic bank failures of the late 1920s were largely attributed to the high-risk investments that many banks had taken on at the time, using the public's savings deposits as the source of the invested funds. The failure of these investments had resulted in an avalanche of consumers approaching their bank branches to withdraw their deposits, leading them to the disappointing realization that no funds were available for withdrawal. The end effect was the failure of the banking system and a loss of confidence in the integrity of the banking sector altogether. By separating the operations of banks into either commercial or investment banking, the Glass-Steagall Act was intended to protect consumers' deposits in their bank accounts from the high-risk game of investment banking. The *Bank Holding Act* of 1956 further restricted bank holding companies (parent companies of banks) from owning businesses that are not closely related to banking, as judged by the Federal Reserve Board. This was done in order to ensure that banks do not diversify into high-risk businesses, which would place the deposits and savings of the public at risk. In addition, regulations were put in place to limit the amount of excess deposits that banks could invest in any single project. Banks are also required to report regularly their financial statements to regulatory bodies and to have accounting audits of their transactions conducted periodically.

The Glass-Steagall Act was repealed in 1999, when the *Financial Services*

Modernization Act (also known as the Gramm-Leach-Bliely Act) went into effect. This deregulatory measure broke down many of the boundaries that prevented financial services organizations from diversifying the portfolio of their offerings to consumers. It also allowed a single institution to carry out both investment and commercial banking operations, which Glass-Steagall had prohibited. The Financial Services Modernization Act enabled the creation of financial supermarkets in which consumers are able to have a wide range of their financial needs served by a single provider. Financial services organizations no longer had to be limited to a narrow range of products and services. For example, a bank could provide deposit account services such as checking and savings accounts, participate in brokerage and investment services, sell and underwrite insurance, and issue mortgages to homebuyers.

One of the original assumptions behind the repeal of Glass-Steagall was that operational efficiencies would eventually be gained by consolidating bank operations under one single umbrella and, as a result, cost savings will be passed on to customers. However, the validity of this assumption has been challenged and research has shown that allowing large-scale mergers does not necessarily translate into increased competition or better service.[11] The consolidations and mergers that have resulted from this Act have in fact produced larger harmonious organizations and, in certain cases, may have reduced competition and the variety of choices available to consumers. A more significant result was the financial crisis which came to a head at the end of the last decade. It is argued that the increased complexity of financial services organizations resulting from deregulation created a market environment in which regulatory oversight was difficult to achieve. Business activities which were made possible due to deregulation resulted in marketing and investment practices that put customers at great financial risk, and helped create a depressed economic environment similar to that of the 1930s. These practices included liberal lending standards which resulted in massive volume of sub-prime lending in credit markets and excessive risk taking by financial institutions in their investment activities.

Lack of coordination among regulatory bodies compounded the harmful effect of such practices, leading to the enactment of additional regulations and the establishment of new regulatory bodies. In 2009, the *Credit Card Accountability, Responsibility and Disclosure (CARD) Act* went into effect. It eliminated unfair rate increases and fees on credit cards, and required specific language and disclosures to be used on credit card statements to clarify the nature of financial obligations to accountholders. In addition, it increased the level of accountability for issuers and provided specific protections for students and young people. In 2010, the *Dodd-Frank Wall Street Reform and Consumer Protection Act* was signed into law. It limited the activities and ownership of hedge funds and prevented banks from engaging in proprietary trading. It also established the *Federal Insurance Office (FIO)* and the *Financial Stability Oversight Council (FSOC)* under the Treasury Department. The FSOC has the objective of identifying and informing other governmental bodies regarding specific forms of financial and economic risks and the FIO has the goal of consolidating and disseminating information on state-level insurance regulations. Some of the elements of this Act, such as the separation of hedge fund and private equity operations from commercial and investment banking activities, represented a degree of reversal from deregulatory measures put in place at the turn of the century. The Act also resulted in the establishment of the *Consumer Financial Protection Bureau* as an agency of the Federal Reserve Board, with the goal of supervising and regulating consumer financial laws. One of the aspects of the Act with direct implications on commercial banking activities was amendments made to Regulation E of the Federal Reserve, in relation to overdraft lines of credit for bank accounts. According to this change, accountholders must opt-in to obtain overdraft coverage, whereas in the past all bank accountholders were provided this form of coverage often with very high fees and could avoid those fees and the implied service only if they opt-out.

Significant efficiencies in the banking industry were realized through the implementation of the *Check Clearing Act for the 21st Century*, otherwise known as *Check 21*, which went into effect in 2004. For over a century, the process by which checks were written and associated funds transferred between banks was a physical and logistical challenge. Traditionally, when an individual wrote a check to a recipient, the recipient would pass on the check to his or her own bank, which would then have to forward the paper check to a clearinghouse operated by the Federal Reserve. The clearinghouse would then have to forward the check to the payer's bank at which time funds would be electronically transferred through the Federal Reserve System to the payee's bank account. This involved a tremendous amount of logistics of physical paper, resulting in expensive and slow processing of payments made using checks. According to *Check 21*, electronic scans made of a written check have an equal legal footing as the original paper check. Therefore, banks would no longer have to logistically handle paper checks through clearing houses. Simple electronic image transfers of checks would serve equally well, speeding up the processing and reducing associated costs by orders of magnitude.[12]

Insurance Regulations

The marketing activities of insurance companies are primarily regulated at the state level. The Insurance Commissioner or Department of Insurance in each state is responsible for regulating and monitoring the activities of insurance companies that sell insurance products in the state. The individual control of states over insurance companies is attributed to the 1945 *McCarron-Ferguson Act*, which exempted insurance companies from federal regulation. The states' insurance regulators, however, adopt guidelines that are nationally developed by the *National Association of Insurance Commissioners (NAIC)* in collaboration with the *Federal Insurance Office (FIO)*.

In order to operate an insurance company, the company must demonstrate its financial capability to sell insurance products and serve insurance claims made by policyholders. Insurance regulations, which may vary from state to state, specify minimum capital requirements needed to start an insurance company. The state's insurance regulator would also need to conduct background checks on company officers and investors. In addition, a formal business plan outlining the financial projections of the company and a demonstrated ability to meet claims requirements would need to be submitted to regulators. Once established, insurance companies have regular reporting requirements that mandate the periodic communications of their financial statements and the reporting of their reserves status. In addition, they must demonstrate to their state's insurance regulator that the asset allocation of the company does not place policyholders at risk.

Selling and advertising activities in insurance markets are also regulated. Individuals that sell insurance products must complete specific licensing courses and be issued a license by regulators. In addition, the forms used to sign insurance contracts are required to be standardized in terms of their minimum content requirements. The language used to advertise insurance products is also highly restricted. It is critical that an individual of "average intelligence" be able to make the correct inferences when examining an insurance advertisement.[13] While it is difficult to establish what constitutes "average intelligence" the objective of this restriction is to prevent misleading and deceptive advertisements. In legal cases, surveys using random samples of consumers are sometimes used to establish the inferences made from an advertisement and to validate or refute claims of misleading advertising. In addition, exaggerating outcomes of accidents, disasters, or catastrophes is not allowed in insurance advertising. This restriction has been established in order to prevent consumers from making emotional decisions driven by unfounded fear, in the process of purchasing insurance policies. Regulations also prohibit the display of currency or checks in insurance advertising.[14] This restriction is designed to prevent consumers from implicitly or explicitly assuming that the insurance product translates into cash benefit payouts. The choice of terminology used in insurance advertising is also restricted. Highly technical terms that are clear to financial services professionals only and not to the average consumer are not to be used. In addition, terminology that implies cost savings or a high propensity for the insurance company to pay out claims is to be avoided. For example terms such as "low," "low cost," "extra," "special," "liberal," and "generous," are typically not allowed in insurance advertising in most states.[15] Regulations also exist to prevent anti-competitive selling practices by insurance brokers and agents. For example, an insurance agent might be tempted to lure a potential customer into purchasing a policy by providing the customer with a rebate funded from his own commissions. According to insurance regulations, insurance sales associated with such "rebates" that are passed on to the consumer and are funded using the sales commission are not allowed. It is believed that such a practice not only forces consumers to make rushed decisions when purchasing insurance products, but it also creates an uneven playing field among competitors.

The fundamental principle behind regulating insurance prices is to prevent price fixing and excessive rates. Since insurance is a typically captive product that many consumers are required to have, price-fixing can be a significant threat to consumer welfare. Price-fixing, which is illegal, constitutes of competitors' colluding on how they will set prices, which may often result in price increases that are not substantiated by costs. Excessively high premiums in the insurance industry may in fact result in interference by regulators and the enforcement of rebates, which the insurance companies would then have to translate into rate cuts or rebate checks that are passed on to policyholders. State insurance regulators are also responsible for monitoring and responding to consumer complaints about insurance companies operating in their state. Most state regulators operate complaint hotlines, which consumers may call or email, in order to initiate a complaint process against an insurance company. The frequency by which these complaints are filed for any given insurance company is often translated into a commonly comparable scale. This is done by computing the frequency rates on the basis of the number of policies sold or the total dollar amount of assets insured by the insurance company. This figure is sometimes reported by state insurance regulators for the public to inspect.

Brokerage and Investment Services Regulations

Brokerage and investment services cover a wide array of service offerings to consumers. These include the activities of financial advisers, stockbrokers, mutual fund companies, and fund managers. The details of all the regulations that apply to these individuals are beyond the scope of this book. However, some of the key elements of regulatory constraints that apply to these professions will be discussed below. It is critical for practitioners in these fields to complete the appropriate licensing requirements and to seek advice and training continuously as new regulations are frequently introduced in this category of financial services.

An investment adviser is any individual who, for a paid fee, provides advice to others on the purchase and sale of securities and investments. From a consumer perspective, it is critical that investment advisers have the best interest of their clients in mind, and are sufficiently trained to provide the informed advice that would meet the unique investment objectives of their clients. To ensure these characteristics, the *Investment Advisers Act of 1940* was established. Investment advisers are required to register with the Securities and Exchange Commission (SEC). State and federal regulations as well as guidelines provided by the SEC govern the actions of an investment adviser. These regulations guide the contents of advertisements as well as the contents of advisory contracts signed with clients. In addition, investment advisers have regular reporting requirements to the SEC. The objective of these regulations is to ensure that advisers provide accurate representation of investment options to their clients, provide clients with educated and financially sound advice, and do not engage in fraudulent activities. The SEC is the primary regulating body for investment advisers with more than $25 million of assets under their management. Investment advisers, with less than $25 million under their management, are often regulated by the state in which they operate.

Stockbrokers have been exempt from the requirements of the Investment Advisers Act. Unlike investment advisers, whose goal is to focus on the best interest of their client in return for a paid fee, brokers are allowed to earn commissions on trades and transactions that they may recommend to their clients. Brokers might benefit from encouraging their clients to buy certain products due to the high commissions associated with those products, or they may encourage clients to trade securities more frequently than needed in order for the broker to receive higher trading commissions. As a result, there is a recognized underlying conflict of interest that can complicate the motivations of a broker. The Securities and Exchange Commission is responsible for the examination of the activities of securities brokers functioning at the major securities exchanges. Violations of securities laws or any SEC guidelines by a broker may result in various forms of punitive actions: the loss of the brokerage license, loss of membership from the exchange, or civil and criminal prosecution that the SEC might request the Justice Department to pursue.

Brokers that conduct over-the-counter securities trades through the NASDAQ, for example, are subject to FINRA licensing requirements. Upon completing the training requirements of FINRA, the broker would receive the appropriate certification status. The training programs are designed to equip brokers with an understanding of the relevant regulations, restrictions, and procedures that they must comply with in the conduct of their brokerage business. One of the central guidelines of FINRA relates to so called "suitability" standards, which mandate that member brokers of FINRA should assess the suitability of investment decisions in the context of each client's specific financial circumstance. This standard imposes a degree of responsibility upon the broker to ensure that he is well aware of the client's financial needs before committing their assets to decisions that may eventually not be in the clients' best interests. It is important to note that the FINRA is a private regulatory body with no governmental or legal punitive authority. Its members choose to follow its rules in return for maintaining their membership status as a FINRA broker. FINRA's punitive measures might for example involve the inability to conduct trades for a pre-specified period of time, monetary penalties, or loss of the membership status.

When communicating various investment choices to clients, great care must be taken not to overstate the potential returns of an investment. Regulations limit what an investment adviser, stockbroker, or investment company may choose to communicate about the prospects of various promoted investment options. Whether communicated orally or in writing, it is critical that the communication clarifies that there are no guarantees with securities purchases due to the risks and volatility involved. When advertising mutual funds, potential prospects must be encouraged to examine the prospectus of the fund, and the required contact information must be provided in the advertisement. Once mutual fund shares have been purchased, a prospectus must be sent out to the investor. The prospectus is a formal document outlining the details of the fund's investment strategy and its performance history. The prospectus is not only required so that the investor may obtain a complete picture of the investment product, but it also serves as a baseline for the items of information that may need to be communicated in promotional material related to the fund.

The regulations that govern the activities of investment advisers and brokers have become more complex over the years due to the increased risk of terrorism following the tragic events of 9/11. The *U.S. Patriot Act* (2002), which has had great influence on how the United States copes with threats facing its national security, has also had an influence on the activities of investment professionals. According to this act, securities brokers and dealers are required to report financial transactions exceeding $5,000 for clients whose activities they might consider to be suspicious and possibly related to terrorism or other forms of crime.[16] Another regulation that has influenced how initial public offerings (IPOs) are made by companies seeking to raise funds in the securities markets is called a *Regulation Fair Disclosure*, otherwise known as "Reg FD." According to this regulation, companies that are seeking to raise funds through issuing securities are prohibited from disclosing investment details only to a select inside group of investors or analysts. The details of their investment offer and performance related information about such investments must be publicly disclosed.[17] This regulation was put in place to prevent situations in which a select group of individuals gain privileged access to valuable information from which they are able to realize profits, potentially at the loss of the average investor who lacks access to the privileged information. In 2010, the *Dodd-Frank Wall Street Reform and Consumer Protection Act* was signed into law. It prohibited the investment activities of banks, as related to proprietary trading whereby a bank's own assets are used in its own investment activities in securities markets. It also created restrictions for hedge funds and forced a separation between hedge private equity operations and commercial banking activities.

Consumer Privacy Regulations

The Federal Trade Commission provides guidelines for the means by which businesses are allowed to interact with consumers and exchange consumer-related information. Many of these guidelines focus on protecting consumer privacy. The *Fair Credit Reporting Act* (1970) focuses on information about consumers that is made available through consumer credit reporting agencies. It requires that, for consumer credit information to be disclosed to private or governmental bodies, specific conditions need to be established. In addition, it allows consumers to limit the amount of personal information passed on to credit reporting agencies by their own financial services providers. The objectives of the Act are to prevent consumers from publicly providing unnecessary amounts of personal information and to protect individuals' civil rights where governmental organizations with potentially excessive powers may be involved. This act was amended in 2003 with the *Fair and Accurate Transaction Act*, which enforces conditions for improving the quality and accuracy of credit information reported by the credit reporting agencies. The 2003 act also requires that financial services providers demonstrate sufficient effort to obtain the most accurate credit information prior to arriving at credit decisions on applicants. It also facilitates mechanisms for fraud detection and the prevention of identity theft.

The *Fair Credit Billing Act* (1974) applies to consumer credit obtained through open-ended credit products such as credit cards and revolving lines of credit. Its focus is on establishing procedures and guidelines for cases in which billing errors or fraudulent charges are made to customer accounts. Billing errors might occur due to clerical mistakes by the financial services provider, for example by double-billing an item on a credit card, or through fraudulent use of the credit card information by a criminal. The act establishes specific procedures that consumers must follow in order to file billing-related complaints with a financial services provider. It also specifies the actions that the financial services provider must undertake to deal with consumer complaints.

The *Fair Debt Collection Practices Act* (1974) provides guidelines for debt collectors on procedures used for the collection of past-due debt obligations from consumers. The Act was put in place because of abusive and excessive actions that were observed in the debt collection business and the recognized need to protect consumers in such situations. The Act identifies the means by which debt collectors are allowed to communicate with consumers for the collection of debt. It also specifies conditions that constitute harassment, abuse, and misrepresentation, and also spells out the civil penalties that apply to violators. While the primary objective of the Act is to protect consumers against abusive debt collection practices, it also serves as a mechanism to ensure that law-abiding debt collection businesses are not placed in an uncompetitive position by their competitors who may choose to treat consumers abusively in the debt collection process.

The *Identity Theft Protection Act* (1998) was established in response to the explosive growth of identity theft cases. Identity theft occurs when an individual takes on the identity of a victim in order to obtain credit or to misrepresent himself when dealing with law enforcement authorities. The growing incidents of identity theft, along with its devastating effects on consumers' credit records, pose a serious concern to the financial wellbeing of the victims as well as the economic functioning of society. The Act was put in place to establish the conditions that constitute identity theft. It also specifies punitive measures such as fines and imprisonment terms that apply to various levels of identity theft. While prosecution of identity theft cases is often carried out by the Justice Department, identity theft cases may be investigated by a number of governmental agencies such as the FBI, the Secret Service, and the U.S. Postal Inspection Service. The Act also requires the Federal Trade Commission to operate a central database in order to collect all identity theft complaints.

Regulations Governing Communications with Consumers

In the past decade, several additional regulations have been established, focusing on the communications modes and informational content used in the marketing of financial services and other types of products and services. The *Federal Communications Commission (FCC)*, which overlooks how individuals and organizations communicate with one another, is the primary regulatory body involved in many such matters. In 1992, the *Federal Telephone Consumer Protection Act* went into effect. The Act aimed at controlling the activities of telemarketers and protecting consumers in their interactions with telemarketing organizations. For example, it limits the time in which telemarketing calls can be made between the hours of 8 am and 9 pm. It also requires that telemarketing organizations train their staff on proper calling procedures when making outbound calls. In addition, the Act required that companies maintain a "do not call" list and that consumers who inform a company of their lack of desire to be called must be omitted from all of the company's calling lists. Violators can be sued by the individual consumer filing the complaint or by the state on behalf of a group of consumers. The Federal Communications Commission is assigned the task of being the central recipient of these consumer complaints.

Nearly a decade later, the *Telemarketing Act of 2003* widened the scope of the "do not call" list. Prior to this act, individual companies or states were required to maintain a do-not-call list, which would have to be consulted in order to purge telemarketing call lists. This was a highly decentralized and poorly coordinated system, and the 2003 Act required the establishment of a nationwide do-not-call registry to consolidate all lists. Consumers are able to sign up on the registry maintained by the FCC and telemarketers are not allowed to call those on the registry. All outbound telemarketing call lists must therefore be regularly updated to exclude those individuals who are on the national do-not-call list. Names on the registry are kept for a period of five years, after which individual consumers have to renew their registration. Specific penalties for telemarketers who violate the restrictions are also established by the act. It is important to note that the restrictions imposed on telemarketers by both the 1992 and 2003 acts make the task of marketing financial services more difficult. Individuals who choose not to be called become more difficult to reach due to these regulations. Similar regulations related to unsolicited email exist and are often enforced at the state level. It is also important to note that the regulations do not apply to circumstances in which a pre-existing relationship between the consumer and the company might exist. For example, banks may be able to call on their existing customers to promote new products. In addition, calls may be allowed if an incomplete transaction, perhaps due to missing or incomplete information, needs to be completed by the company.

CONCLUDING POINTS

Regulatory compliance is one of the most challenging tasks facing financial services marketers today. For financial services marketers, having confidence in the correctness of their marketing tactics requires an additional overlay of regulatory checklists and legal advice. This can easily transform the typically creative tasks of marketing, advertising, and communicating into highly mechanical and restricted exercises. Nevertheless, financial services marketers should take great care to understand fully the scope and details of regulations applied to their practice. Legal advice from qualified professionals as well as compliance departments within the larger financial services organizations is critical to protecting the organization from punitive measures imposed by regulators. The challenge facing all financial services marketers today is to communicate effectively the unique benefits of their products and services, while complying with the numerous restrictions placed on them by existing regulations.

CHAPTER QUESTIONS

1. What differentiates the responsibilities of an investment adviser from that of a stockbroker?

2. What specific regulatory requirements need to be met when communicating investment choices to consumers?

3. What trends in the marketplace may suggest a need for further regulation of the activities of financial services marketers?

4. What specific regulations influence the marketing activities in the following categories of financial services:
    (a) Brokerage and investment services
    (b) Insurance
    (c) Banking

5. What are some reasons for regulating financial services marketing? What reasons do you believe suggest that the industry is already over-regulated?

6. Which federal agency operates a central database for all identity theft cases throughout the country?

7. What are the responsibilities of the following organizations?
    (a) Federal Insurance Office
    (b) Federal Trade Commission
    (c) Office of the Comptroller of the Currency
    (d) Financial Stability Oversight Council
    (e) Securities and Exchange Commission
    (f) National Association of Securities Dealers
    (g) Consumer Financial Protection Bureau
    (h) National Association of Insurance Commissioners
    (i) Federal Reserve Board
    (j) Federal Deposit Insurance Corporation

8. Describe the following:
   - (a) Information asymmetry
   - (b) Clayton Act
   - (c) Truth in Lending Act
   - (d) Federal Register
   - (e) Financial Services Modernization Act
   - (f) Regulation A of the Federal Reserve
   - (g) Regulation B of the Federal Reserve
   - (h) Regulation E of the Federal Reserve
   - (i) Regulation M of the Federal Reserve
   - (j) Regulation Z of the Federal Reserve
   - (k) Glass-Steagall Act
   - (l) McCarron-Ferguson Act
   - (m) Investment Advisors Act
   - (n) Fair Credit Reporting Act
   - (o) Fair and Accurate Transaction Act
   - (p) Fair Credit Billing Act
   - (q) Check 21
   - (r) Credit Card Accountability, Responsibility and Disclosure Act
   - (s) Dodd-Frank Wall Street Reform and Consumer Protection Act

9. Which federal agency maintains the national "do not call" list?

CONTACT INFROMATION FOR GOVERNMENTAL AND REGUALTORY ORGANIZATIONS

Department of Commerce
1401 Constitution Ave.,
N.W. Washington, DC
20230
www.commerce.gov

Federal Communications Commission
445 12^t_h Street, S.W.
Washington, DC 20554
(888)225-5322
www.fcc.gov

Federal Trade Commission
600 Pennsylvania Ave.,
N.W Washington, DC
20580 www.ftc.gov

National Association of Insurance Commissioners
Executive Headquarters
2301 McGee Street, Suite 800
Kansas City, MO 64108-2662
(816)842-3600

Financial Industry Regulatory Authority
1735 K Street, N.W.
Washington, DC 20006
(301)590-6500
www.finra.org

Securities and Exchange Commission
100 F Street, N.E.
Washington, DC 20549
(202)551-6551
www.sec.gov

ENDNOTES

1 P. Bone (2008), "Toward a General Model of Consumer Empowerment and Welfare in Financial Markets with an Application to Mortgage Services," *Journal of Consumer Affairs*, Vol. 42, Iss. 2, pp. 165-188; Elizabeth Warren and Amelia Warren Tyagi (2003), *The Two Income Trap: Why Middle Class Mothers and Fathers Are Going Broke*. Chicago: Basic Books; Robert Blackburn (1999), "Understanding Social Inequality," *The International Journal of Sociology and Social Policy*, Vol. 19, Iss. 9-11, pp. 1-21; A. Carswell (2009), "Does Housing Counseling Change Consumer Financial Behavior?" *Journal of Family and Economic Issues*, Vol. 30, Iss. 4, pp. 339-356.

2 R. Gupta, H. Sharma and C. Mitchem (2010), "The Home Mortgage Disclosure Act and Subprime Lending," *Journal of Applied Business Research*, Vol. 26, Iss. 5, pp. 97-107; Jim Barmlett, and Dave Kaytes (2004),"Credit

Disconnect," *Credit Card Management*, Vol. 17, Iss. 1, pp. 54-57.

3 I. Livshits, J. MacGee and M. Tertilt (2010), "Accounting for the Rise in Consumer Bankruptcies," *American Economic Journal*, Vol. 2, Iss. 2, pp. 165-193.

4 F. Akinbami (2011), "Financial Services and Consumer Protection After the Crisis," *International Journal of Bank Marketing*, Vol. 29, Iss. 2, pp. 134-147; Hooman Estelami (2003), "The Strategic Implication of a Multi-Dimensional Pricing Environment," *Journal of Product and Brand Management*, Vol. 12, Iss. 4, pp. 322-334.; Jonathan Edwards (2003), "Individual and Corporate Compliance Competence: An Ethical Approach," *Journal of Financial Regulation and Compliance*," Vol. 11, Iss. 3, pp. 225-234.

5 M. White (2007), "Bankruptcy Reform and Credit Cards," *Journal of Economic Perspectives*, Vol. 21, Iss. 4, pp. 175-199; I. Livshits, J. MacGee and M. Tertilt (2010), "Accounting for the Rise in Consumer Bankruptcies," *American Economic Journal*, Vol. 2, Iss. 2, pp. 165-193; James Mehring (2004), "No Shame in Bankruptcy?," *Business Week*, June 28, Iss. 3889, p. 36.

6 D. Immergluck (2009), "The Foreclosure Crisis, Foreclosed Properties, and Federal Policy," *Journal of the American Planning Association*, Vol. 75, Iss. 4, pp. 406-423;Linda Punch (2004), "Older Debtors, New Problems," *Credit Card Management*, Vol. 17, Iss. 5, pp 26-29.

7 C. Kendric Fergeson (2004), "Ethical Banking," *ABA Banking Journal*, Vol. 96, Iss. 6, p. 14, citing a survey conducted by the Gallup Organization.

8 N. Bevans (2011), *Consumer Law & Protection*. Charleston: Carolina Academic Press; Gene A. Marsh (1999), *Consumer Protection Law in a Nutshell*. St. Paul, MN: West Group, Chapter 2.

9 Encyclopedia of Banking and Finance. Chicago: Probus Professional Publications; Gene A. Marsh (1999), *Consumer Protection Law in a Nutshell*. St. Paul, MN: West Group; The Federal Register: http://www.gpoaccess.gov/fr

10 T. Frischmann and S. Gensler (2011), "Influence of Perceptual Metrics on Customer Profitability: The Mediating Effect of Behavioral Metrics," *Journal of Financial Services Marketing*, Vol. 16, Iss. 1, pp. 14-26; Ron Garland (2002), "Estimating Customer Defection in Personal Retail Banking," *The International Journal of Bank Marketing*, Vol. 20, Iss. 7, pp. 317-324; Bill Orr (2003), "Are NSF Fees on the Way Out?," *ABA Banking Journal*, Vol. 95, Iss. 5, p. 55; Justin Hibbard (2004), "Banks Go Beyond Toasters," *Business Week*, Dec 20, citing research by the TowerGroup.

11 D. Bush (2010), "Too Big to Bail: The Role of Antitrust in Distressed Industries," *Antitrust Law Journal*, Vol. 77, Iss. 1, pp. 277-312; Michelle Higgins and Rachel Emma Silverman (2004), "Should You Bank with the Big Boys?," *Wall Street Journal*, Jan 20, p. D1; Ken Smith and Eliza O'Neil (2003), "Bank-to-Bank Deals Seldom Add Value," *ABA Banking Journal*, Vol. 95, Iss. 12, pp.7-9, citing SECOR Consulting.

12 Lauren Bielski (2004), "A New Era Begins: Making The Transition to a Revised Check Processing Scheme," *ABA Banking Journal*, Vol. 96, Iss. 6, p. 51.

13 M. Barrett (2008), *Financial Services Advertising: Law and Regulation*. Dublin: Clarus Press; Alec Benn (1986), *Advertising Financial Products and Services*. Quorum Books: New York, pp. 175-180.

14 James Cain and John Fahey (2000), "Banks and Insurance Companies - Together in the New Millennium," *The Business Lawyer*, Vol. 55, Iss. 3, pp. 1409-1425; Alec Benn (1986), *Advertising Financial Products and Services*. Quorum Books: New York; Peter Lencsis (1997), *Insurance Regulation in the United States*. Quorum Books; Alec Benn (1986), *Advertising Financial Products and Services*. Quorum Books: New York, pp.175-177.

15 Alec Benn (1986), *Advertising Financial Products and Services*. Quorum Books: New York, pp.175-177; *Insurance Regulation in the United States*. New York: Quorum Books; Interested readers should also consult the department of insurance in individual states and the *National Association of Insurance Commissioners* (www.naic.org) for further details; H. Estelami and Peter DeMaeyer (2010), "An Exploratory Study of Divided Pricing Effects on Financial Service Quality Expectations," *Journal of Financial Services Marketing*, Vol. 15, Iss. 1, pp. 19-31.

16 A. Tellechea (2011), "Economic Crimes in the Capital Markets," *Journal of Financial Crime*, Vol. 15, Iss. 2, pp. 214-222; Mara Der Hovanesian (2003), "Still Drowning in Dirty Money," *Business Week*, Iss. 3860, p.102.

17 A. Hovakimian and E. Saenyasiri (2010), "Conflicts of Interest and Analyst Behavior: Evidence from Recent Changes in Regulation," *Financial Analyst Journal*, Vol. 66, Iss. 4, pp. 96-107.

CHAPTER ELEVEN

Strategic Market Planning in Financial Services

WHAT IS "STRATEGY"?

The term "strategy" is often used to describe a variety of actions and behaviors exhibited by individuals, groups, and organizations in business, politics, and other social and competitive settings. However, most people do not fully appreciate the formal definition of this rather powerful term, and most are unaware of its roots. The term strategy consists of two parts: "Stratos," which in Greek means "army," and "Agien," which means "to lead." The classical definition of the term would equate to the science for directing and planning military operations.[1] Therefore, the foundation of the concept of strategy is in fact based in military science. However, in modern terms, the concept of strategy is more closely linked to the management skills needed to plan and organize activities of individuals and organizations.

Nevertheless, the fact that the roots of strategy are based in military thinking has had a profound effect on the practice of strategic market planning. Many of the terms that are commonly used to describe marketing strategies in both financial and non-financial markets are based on terminology used in military science. For example, one may describe "field" tests for the introduction of a new service or a "field sales force," similar to a military general's reference to the battlefield. Similarly, one may talk about an advertising "campaign" when describing an extended commitment of large advertising budgets, just as a military general may use the term "campaign" to describe large deployment of forces on the battle front.

Over the years, many individuals have contributed to the understanding of strategy in both military and business contexts. One of the most recognized contributors to this area was a Prussian general named Carl von Clausewitz, who wrote a book titled *On War*, published in 1832.[2] In writing this book, Clausewitz asked himself a very simple, yet revealing question: what are good strategies to follow in military confrontations? In the process of addressing this question, he examined records of all documented battles over the years in order to determine what conditions created winning scenarios for an army. To do this, Clausewitz had to rely on battle records, historical documents, and other sources that had accumulated through nearly 2,500 years of recorded history. One interesting but disturbing finding was that, in almost every year in the 2,500 years of recorded history that he consulted, there were multiple military campaigns at different locations around the world. While sadly this indicated that the human race rarely takes a break from the act of warfare, it also provided an abundance of data for Clausewitz to work with.

His study of these battles revealed two general categories of strategies: *offensive* and *defensive*. Offensive strategies, as can be inferred from the term, are those in which one army attacks another, while defensive strategies reflect the mirror image of this: an army defends its grounds against the marching enemy. He further dissected each of these two types of strategies into several subcategories.[3] For example, an offensive strategy might be a frontal attack in which an army marches forward, head-on against its enemy's frontlines. His study of frontal attacks showed that, despite popular belief about their effectiveness, less than one in twenty cases using such a strategy would result in victory. His prescription to military strategists was therefore to avoid direct confrontations unless a significant (3-to-1) advantage in military power is held by the attacking army. Clausewitz also observed other patterns of victory, which helped him identify strategies that are more likely to succeed than others. Encirclement—a strategy in which the attacking army surrounds the enemy—was found to be highly successful. Encirclement cuts off the supply line of the enemy and forces it to surrender because of its inability to gain access to basic supplies such as food and ammunition. Flanker strategies, in which pockets of weakness in the front lines of the enemy are identified and penetrated, through overwhelming force, were also found to have high success rates. As a result of these systematic and scientific observations, Cluasewitz was able to establish categories of strategies that are most likely to succeed as well as those that are likely to result in failure.

On War has since become a classic book in military science. Many military academies both in the United States and abroad require a thorough study of the book as a standard part of their curriculum for officers in training. The work has also had a profound impact on modern thinking in marketing strategy. Numerous books have been written based on its framework, and the terminology and thought processes associated with it have found their way into executive boardrooms and strategic discussions of marketing campaigns in almost every industry. As a result, traditional concepts of military science have for decades found parallel applications in the marketing of competitive and unregulated markets such as those for consumer packaged goods, durables, consumer services, and industrial products.[4] Consistent with the approach taken by Clausewitz, in this chapter, we will discuss the emerging views on the various categories of financial services marketing strategies, and identify those strategies that have proven successful in the emerging market environment.

THE NEED FOR FINANCIAL SERVICES MARKETING STRATEGIES

There are many reasons why financial services organizations should proactively develop and implement well-defined marketing strategies. The first is that research evidence suggests that financial services providers that systematically follow strategic plans tend to outperform those that do not.[5] An additional reason for organizing financial services marketing activities into strategic plans is that financial services organizational structures are primarily dominated by human activities. The mobilization of a larger number of skilled employees requires a clear statement of the direction and long-term objectives of the organization. Failure to spell out one's strategy not only causes loss of organizational morale, but will also likely result in notable levels of inefficiency and organizational disarray.

The extended nature of financial service engagements with individual customers, which may span the years, requires a financial services institution to ensure its own long-term stability. For example, customers who have life insurance policies or pension plans with a particular financial services provider expect it to be around for many years. Business failure in such contexts can translate into significant inconveniences and potentially catastrophic financial results for the customer. It is therefore essential that financial services organizations comply with customer desire for stability by developing and implementing strategic plans that assure the long-term health of the business.

The importance of strategic market planning in financial services is further amplified by the quickly changing environment in which financial services companies operate today. As discussed in Chapter 1, the economic and technological environments of the recent years have already begun to impact how financial services are delivered to consumers. Failure to recognize the impact of economic forces and emerging technologies on organizational change can translate into an inability to match customers' rapidly changing needs, resulting in the loss of ground to the more agile competitors. Overall, companies that are better able to gauge their environment and are capable of redirecting their efforts in a responsive and well-planned manner perform significantly better than those that fail to do so.[6] Such a response can only be achieved through strategic thinking and the development of strategic marketing plans designed to guide marketing activities in such volatile times.

What is rather interesting about strategic market planning is that financial services providers have yet to recognize fully the critical importance of the role of market planning on the long-term survival of their businesses. Many financial services organizations have only begun to adopt strategic marketing plans into their standard management processes. Surveys of bank executives have for example found that a significant proportion of banks do not have detailed marketing plans guiding their marketing acitivites.[7]

STRATEGIC CHALLENGES IN FINANCIAL SERVICES MARKETING

One of the primary reasons why formal strategic marketing plans are needed in financial services organizations is the unique challenges that face marketers in this area. The complexity of issues with which financial services marketers must contend typically far exceed those influencing marketing activities in other goods or services markets. One of these challenges, as discussed at several points throughout this book, is the fact that financial services are generally highly complex. For example, the price of a financial service such as an automobile lease does not consist of single number (for example, $19,995), but it rather consists of multiple numbers (for example, "$149/month for 24 months, $1,295 down"), which the consumer must be able to quantify and integrate into an overall evaluation. The mental process that is used by the consumer to determine the attractiveness of such lease offers has a significant impact on the consumer's overall impression of the lease. As a result, the marketer would need to possess an accurate understanding of what dimensions of a lease are most influential on consumer decisions. This is clearly a far more difficult task than understanding consumer responses in most other contexts where price often consists of a single number.

The marketing of financial services is further complicated by the fact that financial services and products are generally non-emotional. Rarely would an individual find the purchase of a financial service to be associated with the same level of interest and excitement experienced from the purchase of automobiles, consumer electronics, fashion clothing, or other popular consumer goods. Therefore, financial services marketers are challenged daily with how to communicate their services in a way that would create excitement and interest in consumers. The communication of the specific benefits of a financial service is further complicated by the highly intangible nature of financial service quality. For example, the quality of an insurance policy or the wisdom of investment advice provided by a broker may not be evident for a long time, if ever. Financial services providers therefore need to undertake additional effort to make information related to the quality of their products and services clearer to consumers, especially in cases where the level of quality exceeds that of competitors' offers. The marketing of financial services is also affected by the extent to which financial products and services are affected by general economic forces. The impact that the economic indicators such as interest rates, exchange-rate shifts, and stock market performance have on the attractiveness of a financial product can be far more profound, as for example, the attractiveness of most investment products cannot be evaluated without knowledge of interest rates and expected trends in the stock market.

Effective marketing of financial services is also challenged by the large number of regulations that control financial services marketing activities. These regulations may for example, impact the types of financial services one could market, the prices charged for them, and the information that must be disclosed to customers when promoting the services. Regulatory bodies such as *FINRA*, the *SEC*, and the insurance departments of the individual states have great influence on how financial services marketers practice their trade. Furthermore, regulations require marketing professionals to complete specific licensing requirements in order to be active in a given market. For example, investment brokers, insurance agents, and financial advisers must complete rigorous licensing curricula, most of which focus on training these individuals on regulations that govern their profession.

The activities of financial services marketers are further complicated by the fact that the employees serving customers can significantly help or hinder the customers' overall impression of the company. The manner by which these employees interact with customers has a direct influence on the customer experience. The personal connection between a customer and his broker, agent, or bank teller may help create a sense of trust that may outweigh many of the other aspects of the service. Since the financial services provider is intrinsically inseparable from the overall customer service experience – for example, a bank teller is part of the customer service encounter in a bank – it is essential to monitor service encounters in financial services closely, and to provide quality control mechanisms that ensure customer satisfaction.

Strategic marketing of financial services is further complicated by the difficulty of quantifying costs associated with an individual customer in many financial services categories. For example, in the commercial banking business, while customers are the purchasers of the bank's numerous services, they can also be suppliers of the "raw material" used to run the bank. This is because customers with checking or savings accounts supply the deposits that the bank needs in order to issue loans to borrowers. The fact that customers are also suppliers of the funds used to run a banking institution is a unique aspect of financial services that is rarely found in other marketing contexts.[8] While certain bank customers may be quite demanding because they engage the bank in numerous costly transactions, their large deposits and the associated interest earned by the bank in transforming these deposits into loans may far outweigh the costs that the customer may present to the bank. Nevertheless, the difficulty of quantifying the profits associated with individual customers makes a mass-market approach to the marketing of financial services highly impractical. Use of individual-level customer data associated with segmentation techniques is therefore critical to appropriately assessing individual customers' profitability levels.

The segment-based approach to marketing financial services is a practical and realistic way to develop successful marketing strategies. In many organizations, this is fundamentally driven by the extensive use of technology and the abundance of individual level data that is both internally and externally available. From a strategic planning perspective, this translates into a need for close collaboration between trained technology professionals and marketing practitioners. The need for technology training of marketing staff is further amplified due to the growth in internal data warehouses as well as the increasingly precise targeting capabilities of externally supplied segmentation data. When conducting market segmentation and target marketing, it is important to acknowledge that technology is also finding its way into how consumers communicate with financial services providers. The use of the Internet, mobile phone and versatile ATM devices capable of providing customized and detailed financial information have transformed the delivery systems for financial services. Consumers' use of these technologies help them make decisions that are better informed than decisions a decade earlier when the use of these technologies was not as widespread. Information disseminated through these means regarding the objective performance and quality of financial services providers is becoming increasingly accessible to the masses. A customer's experience with a particular financial services provider can be logged and reported through Internet forums, user reviews and other forms of social media, influencing other consumers in their own financial services decisions.

THE DIAMOND FRAMEWORK FOR FINANCIAL SERVICES MARKETING

In this section, we will discuss a framework used to describe successful strategies in financial services The deregulation of the financial services sector at the turn of the century had a profound impact on the structure of competition within the industry and on what strategies are most likely to be successful in this new competitive landscape. Prior to deregulation, markets. competition within the industry had been partitioned due to the Glass-Steagall Act, which went into effect in 1933. Glass-Steagall was a response to a series of catastrophic bank failures, which were attributed to the ability of banks at that time to participate in both investment banking and commercial banking activities. This

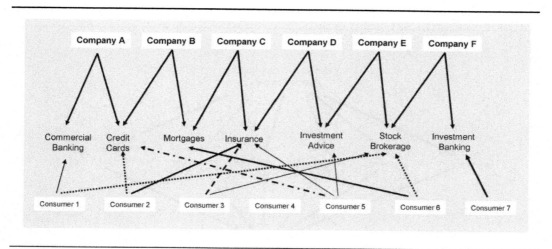

Exhibit 11.1: Financial Services Marketing Prior to Deregulation

had resulted in millions of Americans losing their savings held by the failing banks. Glass-Steagall was put in place in order to separate investment banking activities, which are typically high risk, from commercial banking activities, which involve accepting and safekeeping of deposits from the public.[9] As a result of Glass-Steagall and subsequent regulations, financial services organizations were for decades restricted in the kinds of products and services that they could provide their customers.

Exhibit 11.1 provides an abstract visual representation of how financial services marketers competed prior to deregulation. As a result of the regulations, the industry was highly fragmented, and companies were restricted in terms of the range of markets they could function in. Different financial services providers were protected from competition with one another, but had to compete within their own smaller sub-markets. Therefore, commercial banks were separated from investment banks. In addition, commercial banks could not underwrite their own insurance products and were restricted in their level of participation in the wider array of financial services. Similar restrictions limited other financial services providers from cross-category participation. As a result, different companies (for example, companies A and E in Exhibit 11.1) were isolated from direct competition with each other. In this environment an individual consumer would have to approach multiple companies to gain access to the full range of basic financial services needed on a regular basis. For example consumer 5 in Exhibit 11.1 would have to come into individual contact with three different companies in order to obtain a credit card (from company A), purchase an insurance policy (from company C)

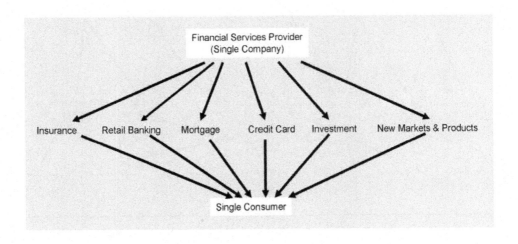

Exhibit 11.2: The DIAMOND Framework

and seek investment advice (from company D).

Exhibit 11.2 shows the emerging framework that depicts the evolving nature of market competition. The repeal of the Glass-Steagall Act broke down many of the cross-category barriers and opened up most financial services markets to open-market competition. The new framework, which visually resembles a diamond, is one in which a single financial services provider is now able to provide a wide array of financial services to its customers. This was made possible because the repeal of the Glass-Steagall Act enabled financial services providers to supply a diverse range of financial products and services and to participate in new categories of services from which they were previously prohibited.

The abbreviation "DIAMOND," which will be used to describe successful emerging strategies, refers to the fundamental drivers of marketing strategy in financial services markets. These are: *D*iversification, *I*ntegration of resources, *A*cquisitions, *M*ergers, *O*rganizational restructuring, *N*ew products, and *D*eregulatory aspirations. These will be discussed below:

Diversification: The Bank Modernization Act which repealed Glass-Steagall was instituted in order to allow more efficient and profitable operations in financial services markets. It has allowed for greater participation by competitors in a variety of financial services categories, enabling them to tap into new profitable markets, by providing other types of financial services to existing and new customers. As a result, financial institutions are able to pursue emerging marketing opportunities and can diversify their scope of operations. The ability to diversify not only provides access to new markets and new products, but it also reduces the risks that would otherwise be associated with running a business that is solely focused on a narrow range of the market.

One of the interesting aspects about diversification strategies is that companies that fail to exercise diversification tend to perform poorly. For example, Washington Mutual, which had traditionally been a leading mortgage provider, remained primarily active in the business of mortgages for years following industry deregulation. Even following industry deregulation, it decided to limit its exposure to the wider array of financial services. As a result of the highly competitive state of the mortgage business and the risks associated with maintaining a limited range of products and services, the company's lack of diversification had direct influence on its financial performance and eventual downfall.[10]

Integration of Resources: In addition to diversifying into new businesses, financial services organizations may choose to combine resources in order to gain cost efficiencies. For example, the merger of J.P. Morgan-Chase and Bank One in the previous decade allowed for a unique integration of the resources and capabilities of the two institutions. Bank One brought to J.P. Morgan-Chase a highly advanced information technology infrastructure, while J.P. Morgan-Chase's contribution was its immense resources and retail banking customer base.[11]

Acquisitions and Mergers: A financial services provider may decide to acquire or to merge with another company in order to gain access to markets that it had traditionally not been able to reach. For example, the 2003 merger of Bank of America and Fleet Boston was attributed by some observers to Bank of America's desire to reach higher end clients through Fleet, and to expand its geographical presence by gaining access to Fleet's branch locations.[12]

Organizational Restructuring: The rapidly changing picture of the financial services marketplace requires organizational flexibility. Flexible financial services organizations are necessary to match the emerging offerings of competitors and the shifting needs of customers, which can be served by the introduction of innovative technologies and services. As a result, in the emerging competitive environment flexibility is essential, and financial organizations that are able to quickly adapt are more likely to be successful than inflexible organizations. This can be achieved either by drawing from existing infrastructures of recently acquired organizations or, as stated above, by merging with companies that have developed specialization in specific areas of marketing or operations. In addition, the use of technologies that allow for flexible delivery of services is critical to this venture. For example, technologies such as smart ATM devices and mobile applications, facilitate drastic cost-reductions for commercial banking operations compared to the traditional means of serving customers through branch operations.

An additional aspect of organizational restructuring relates to the realization that face-to-face contacts in financial services interactions are generally on a decline. For example, customer inquiries using tellers at bank branch locations have given way to the use of the Internet, banking by phone, and ATM transactions.[13] As a result, organizations that have adapted to these trends more quickly have benefited from the associated cost efficiencies that accompany them. Offshore outsourcing of service operations is also associated with flexible organizational restructuring. Many financial services customer interactions delivered over the telephone are carried out using call centers located abroad, thousands of miles away. The lower cost of labor as well as the drop in the cost of telephony due to the use of voice over IP technology have made offshore outsourcing an attractive option for the restructuring of financial services organizations.[14] Offshore outsourcing of customer service operations provide significant cost advantages over similar operations located in the United States.

New Products and Markets: Financial services markets have over the years witnessed the introduction of new innovative products with great consumer demand. For example, in the insurance business, identity theft insurance experienced growth driven by consumer insecurity over the growing incidence of identity theft cases. The unique needs of high-risk skiers gave rise to a specific class of travel insurance, "wipeout insurance," which can provide medical and financial coverage in case a skier is injured on the slopes. The introduction of these new products and the creation of new markets for existing ones bring great profit potential to companies that introduce them.

Deregulatory Aspirations: The relaxation of government regulations can intensify competition and may result in more efficient market conditions. In financial services markets, the Bank Modernization Act, which repealed Glass-Steagall, attempted to achieve this very objective, with mixed results. By allowing financial services providers from a variety of backgrounds to participate in a wide array of services, competition became more dynamic. Similarly, the Check Clearing Act for the 21st Century (Check 21), resulted in monumental efficiency gains in the banking sector. It allowed electronic scans of a written check to be legally treated as equivalent to the original written check. The resulting efficiency gains have not only translated into increased profits for the banks, but also resulted in consumer conveniences through the faster processing of bank transactions. The formation of new regulations and the relaxation of existing ones may enable financial services providers to better position themselves in meeting society's evolving financial needs, and to pursue new opportunities which may have been ignored or untapped by the industry altogether. Despite this, the forces of regulation often counter deregulatory aspirations. For example, public concerns following the financial crisis of 2008 resulted in the enactment of new regulations and the establishment of new regulatory bodies to curb irresponsible and risky actions by financial services providers. Public outcry about lack of sufficient oversight on the activities of financial services organizations following the repeal of Glass-Steagall resulted in new regulations being signed into law. These include the *Credit Card Accountability and Disclosure (CARD) Act of 2009* and the *Dodd-Frank Wall Street Reform and Consumer Protection Act* which was signed into law in 2010, and were discussed in the previous chapter.

THE TEN GUIDING PRINCIPLES OF FINANCIAL SERVICES MARKETING

Success in marketing financial services is typically affected by a series of principles that help determine effective marketing strategies. These principles, which are listed below, have been true both prior to industry deregulation and following it and therefore have a persistent effect on marketing success:

Principle 1 – Quantify Quality: As discussed in detail throughout this book, the notion of quality in financial services is built on three fundamental factors: (a) objective financial performance of the product or service, (b) the quality of human contacts with the customer, and (c) the image of the company. However, as discussed in detail in chapters 2 and 9, the objective performance of a financial product or service can be very difficult for consumers to quantify. Therefore, in financial services, human contacts as well as the image associated with the company seem to have a much greater impact on consumer perceptions. This highlights the critical importance of managing and monitoring employee interactions with customers in order to ensure high quality service experiences. In addition, careful execution of advertising content and appropriate pre-testing of corporate communications is necessary to implement effective brand-building strategies.

Principle 2 – Focus on the Life-time Value of the Customer: An additional principle that has guided financial services marketing for decades states that the profit that a financial services organization generates is a function of two factors: (a) the profit generated from the average customer, and (b) the total number of customers. Profitability can therefore be enhanced by increasing either of these two measures. While it may be challenging to gain new customers in a competitive and saturated market, profits per customer may be more readily increased through cross-selling other products and services, and extending the length of time that a customer stays with the company. This is especially important in the years following deregulation as cross-selling of a wide range of financial products and services to existing customers has opened new paths for profit growth.

Principle 3 – Pioneering Advantage: A principle that has influenced the marketing practice both within and outside financial services is what is often referred to as the *pioneering advantage*. The pioneer, which is the company that first introduces a product to the marketplace, has been empirically shown to have a significant strategic advantage over competitors that follow it.[15] This is especially true in the context of financial services where customer defection rates are generally low. Therefore, the acquisition of a customer early in the customer's life-stage is likely to generate a long stream of business transactions and a high level of profitability. Despite an increase in the switching behavior of customers, which has been noted in recent years, customers' tendency to stay with their current financial services provider helps validate the strategic importance of first-time customer acquisitions. It is therefore no surprise that mergers and customer portfolio acquisitions have been so common among financial services providers. The high value of an established customer base often translates into pricey acquisitions of companies that have a strong and stable portfolio of customers.

Principle 4 – Company Image May Drive Consumer Evaluations: An additional guiding principle states that consumer perceptions of a financial services provider may greatly influence their decisions to transact with the company. Perceptions of the financial strength of an insurance company as communicated through advertising, the company image conveyed by employees in a service encounter, or the physical atmosphere and cleanliness of a bank's branch location, can generate powerful inferences in the customer's mind, which may have a great influence on her overall perceptions of quality. This may be somewhat of a disturbing fact since a financial services provider that may lack the less critical aspects of service quality (for example, cleanliness of the branch office) but provides high-quality financial products (for example, superior performing investments) may be devalued by consumers. It is therefore critical for financial services organizations to identify how consumer perceptions are formed and to ensure that they do not fall short of customer expectations with respect to image-driven aspects of their service. Financial services organizations that fail to understand the decision process of their customers are likely to limit their own profit potential.

Principle 5 – Avoid Adverse Selection: The harmful effects that adverse selection may have on company profitability cannot be ignored in most financial services settings. Adverse selection is reflected by a company's acquisition of a customer that is high-risk and unprofitable. For example, in the insurance business, a policy applicant who intentionally misinforms an insurance agent by presenting himself as a low-risk individual, places the company at financial risk due to the potential costs he may present to the company in the future. Use of segmentation technology as well as information sources that help to identify high-risk applicants is critical to preventing profit depletion. This is not to say that financial services organizations should steer away from serving high-risk customers, as such measures may not only be unethical, but are also often challenged by the regulators. However, it is important that the pricing of a financial service reflect the true risk profile of the customer as accurately as possible. The appropriate use of segmentation techniques and the use of pre-screening technologies and databases are the primary means to achieving this objective.

Principle 6 – Avoid a Diluted Focus: Despite the favorable effects that diversification may have on financial services organizations, excessive levels of diversification can be harmful. Evidence from consumer markets has testified that brand names can be extended into new product categories only up to a certain limit. Consumer psychology, the human brain's categorization process, and the notion of brand identity limit a company's ability to extend into new categories. Examples of this in the consumer packaged goods markets include the introduction of bottled water by Coors and the introduction of baby food by Heinz, both of which did not experience significant market success.[16] While these are extreme examples of brand over-extensions, it is important for financial service marketers to conduct the necessary market research to establish the attractiveness of extending their core brand beyond their traditional services. The challenges faced by many discount brokers to move up-market by providing offerings such as private investment services and financial advice testify to this fact.

Principle 7 – Customer Defections Can be Very Costly in the Long Run: The harmful effects of a customer's loss through defection to a competitor must also be quantified and closely monitored by marketing managers. While defection rates in financial services have traditionally been low compared to other markets, they have increased in recent years due to intensified competition and the lower level of brand loyalty exhibited by the younger generations.[17] Not only are defection rates likely to increase, but also the word-of-mouth effect associated with dissatisfactory customer experiences is likely to continue to be more quickly disseminated within consumer populations through the use of social media. Internet forums, consumer review sites, and other means of exchanging information on service experiences can result in a greater impact associated with the loss of a single customer. While in the past financial services marketers may not have placed great weight on avoiding customer defections to competitors, the impact that these defections might have on the future competitive dynamics of the industry may be significant.

Principle 8 – Establish A Unique Selling Proposition: The importance of having a unique selling proposition was discussed in Chapter 5. A financial services organization must be uniquely proficient in at least one important attribute in order to be able to attract customers. Failure to possess a unique selling proposition creates difficulties when customers attempt to differentiate the company from its competitors, and makes the task of selling the company's products and services considerably more challenging. Most successful financial services organizations have a unique selling proposition. For example, GEICO's unique selling proposition is its low prices. The company emphasizes this point through massive advertising campaigns, most of which communicate the same consistent point of cost savings. To be able to deliver these savings, the company has developed a distribution system that eliminates the traditional insurance agent who is responsible for selling insurance products.[18] State Farm Insurance, on the other hand, focuses on the agent organization and emphasizes the personal care and service that its agents provide the customer.

Principle 9 – Regulatory Alertness: A principle that continuously influences financial services organizations and successful marketing strategies is the emergence of new regulations that will directly impact marketing activities. New regulations on disclosure requirements as well as consumer communications and advertising content have greatly influenced the practice of marketing financial services. The introduction of new regulations is likely to continue in the coming years. At the same time, the emergence of new technologies and industry pressure to utilize these technologies may force the relaxation of certain existing restrictions. Flexible organizational structures and active scanning of market conditions and political forces are therefore critical to ensuring a quick response to both regulatory and deregulatory forces. Certainly, the financial services marketplace in the United States is one of the most heavily regulated industries worldwide, and the ability of individual companies and the coalition of the industry to adjust to these regulations is essential for the long-term stability of the sector.

Principle 10 – Business Integrity and Consumer Trust: Similar to other fields such as health care, legal services, and dentistry, consumer trust in the service provider is often a primary determinant of the consumer's eventual decisions with respect to financial services. Trusting that a financial advisor is providing the most educated advice, or that an insurance company will protect its policyholders in times of need are driving forces behind an individual's transaction decisions. It is therefore essential for financial services providers to focus on the best interests of their customers, demonstrate their commitment to customers, and conduct their business with a high degree of integrity. Not only is this good business practice, but it would also help strengthen consumer confidence in the company's products and services. Companies that fail to follow this path tend to suffer in the long-run as the public's perceptions of the quality of their products and services can greatly suffer.

DEVELOPING A MARKETING PLAN

As highlighted earlier in this chapter, the development of formal marketing plans is vital to the long-term health of a financial services organization. Nevertheless, many financial services providers do not regularly develop sufficiently detailed marketing plans, and most operate without any formal strategy. In this section, we will discuss an overall structure for strategic market plans for financial services organizations. The steps that are involved in developing a marketing plan for a financial services organization are the following:

1. Understanding the Market Environment: The first step in the market planning process is for the marketing managers to obtain an accurate understanding of the environment in which the business operates. It is critical to recognize emerging trends that have affected the business in the past and those that will influence its future. This analysis requires one to examine the demographics of potential and existing customers, to understand emerging technologies that may influence the process of selling and servicing financial products and services, and to recognize the economic forces that can affect the business. In addition, it is important in this step to gain an appreciation for the potential impact of regulations on the business and to understand trends that may influence the attractiveness of the company's offerings to customers. Furthermore, a study of the competitive spectrum and actions and capabilities of competitors in the marketplace is essential. The end objective of this phase is to provide the necessary inputs needed for the next step of opportunity identification.

2. Opportunity Identification: Once the environment of the financial services organization has been closely examined, the management must be able to identify opportunities for improvement and growth. In this step, both the potential opportunities in the marketplace, as well as potential threats that may limit the company's growth need to be assessed, and the strengths and weaknesses of the company when contending with these forces need to be explicitly identified. The objective of this phase is to ensure that the strengths of the business match the opportunities upon which it will capitalize.

3. Setting Goals: In this step, the management should begin to set specific goals for the planning horizon. These goals should reflect the company's capabilities as well as the customers' needs and requirements for the offered services. The number of goals identified should be limited, to avoid a loss of focus and the inability to prioritize marketing activities. Goals can be prioritized as either primary or secondary. Primary goals would include such targets as the number of new policies generated, year-over-year revenue growth rates, and return on investment levels desired, which are measures of significant importance to most financial services organizations. Goals may also be categorized as secondary when they are of lesser significance, such as the number of applications or inquiries generated from an advertising campaign, the level of customer satisfaction, and the extent of the company's brand awareness in the marketplace. These secondary goals typically have an indirect long-term effect on the achievement of the primary goals either during the planning cycle, or in subsequent planning periods. It is important that, while the goals are set at high levels, they reflect realistic and achievable objectives so that the organization as a whole can place faith on the contents of the marketing plan and the overall mission it will guide. Typically, the goals are set for time horizons ranging from six months to three years.

4. Specifying an Overall Strategy: Once the goals have been identified it is critical to specify the overall strategy that would help achieve them. The strategy should be based on the various capabilities of the business that would have been identified in Step 2 (opportunity identification). For example, the strategy could be based on competitive pricing, through which price reductions result in higher levels of new customer acquisitions. The strategy can also focus on image-building advertising campaigns, cost reduction measures, or the use of referral-based marketing programs to capitalize on networks of customers. The marketing strategy could also incorporate partnerships with other organizations that may improve the competitive position of the company.

5. Determining the Expected Financial Results of the Marketing Plan: The next step in the market planning process is to quantify the results that may be expected as a result of implementing the plan. In this phase, the effects on three vital signs of business performance need to be quantified: (a) profits, (2) return on investment, and (3) revenues. Financial models and spreadsheets that help to quantify revenue and cost streams need to be deployed and a financial forecast needs to be generated. In fact, in many marketing plans, permutations of the results are generated to provide a full picture of three possible outcomes: (a) the optimistic scenario, (b) the pessimistic scenario, and (c) the most likely scenario. Doing so provides a full picture of the range of possible outcomes for a given marketing strategy, and is a very important part of the process, as the estimated results may be closely examined and questioned by higher levels of management and potential investors.

6. Specifying Actions and Timing: The final step in the market planning process is to explicitly outline and detail the activities that will take place throughout the planning period. In doing so, it is important to develop a chronological order to specify when the various aspects of marketing a financial service will be carried out. It is often good practice to develop timelines for the various activities such as price changes, the introduction of new advertising campaigns, and other marketing tasks related to distribution and delivery of services.

Readers interested in a more formal discussion of the market planning process are encouraged to consult specialized books on this topic.[19] Based on careful examination of the facts and an accurate understanding of the environment in which the business is operating, financial services marketers can align their organizations to capitalize on emerging opportunities. The years ahead will be enriched with both challenges and opportunities, and the development and implementation of well-informed and calculated marketing plans is an essential requirement for achieving strategic success in the competitive environment facing financial services marketers.

CHAPTER QUESTIONS

1. Define the term "strategy".

2. What specific advantages are gained by developing formal strategies for financial services organizations?

3. What connections exist in strategic concepts used in warfare and those used in marketing?

4. Of the ten principles of financial services marketing strategy discussed in this chapter, which do you feel are the most relevant to recent market activities you have observed in financial services markets?

5. What role do the following factors have in ensuring effective marketing strategies for financial services providers?
    (a) Deregulation
    (b) Mergers and acquisitions
    (c) Diversification
    (d) Resource integration
    (e) New product development
    (f) Organizational restructuring

6. Applying the overall framework for market planning, develop a series of templates and tables to formalize the process outlined in this chapter.

ENDNOTES

1 *Merriam-Webster Online Dictionary: www.m-w.com*

2 Clausewitz, Carl von (1832), *On War*. London: Penguin Books.

3 For more in-depth analysis of the classification of various strategies and their relationship to modern business strategy, interested readers are encouraged to consult the following sources: A. Dixit and B. Nalebuff (1993), *Thinking Strategically: The Competitive Edge in Business*, Politics, and Everyday Life. New York: W.W. Norton and Company; D. Aaker (2001), *Developing Business Strategies*. New York: Wiley.

4 Al Ries and Jack Trout (2009), *The 22 Immutable Laws of Marketing*. New York: McGraw-Hill. Al Ries and Steve Rivkin (2009), *Repositioning: Marketing in an Era of Competition, Change and Crisis*. New York: McGraw-Hill.

5 A. Ghobadian, N. O'Regan, H. Thomas and J. Liu (2008), "Formal Strategic Planning, Operating Environment, Size, Sector and Performance," *Journal of General Management*, Vol. 34, Iss. 2, pp. 1-15; L.. Moutinho and P.A. Phillips (2002),

"The Impact of Strategic Planning on the Competitiveness, Performance, and Effectiveness of Bank Branches: A Neural Network Analysis," *The International Journal of Bank Marketing,* Vol. 20, Iss. 2/3, pp. 102-110; W.E. Hopkins and S.A. Hopkins (1997), "Strategic Planning-Financial Performance Relationships in Banks: A Causal Examination," *Strategic Management Journal,* Vol. 18, No. 8, pp. 635-652; R. Robinson and J. Pearce (1983), "The Impact of Formalized Strategic Planning on Financial Performance of Small Organizations," *Strategic Management Journal,* Vol. 4, pp. 197-207.

6 R. Smith and A. Vibhakar (2007), "Strategic Marketing Guidelines for Financial Professionals," *Services Marketing Quarterly,* Vol. 28, Iss. 4, pp. 1-12; M.R. Young (1999), "Market Structure Analysis: A Foundation for Developing and Assessing Bank Strategy," *International Journal of Bank Marketing,* Vol. 17, No. 1, pp. 20-25; C. Ennew, M.Wright, and D. Thwaites (1993), "Strategic Marketing in Financial Services: Retrospect and Prospect," *The International Journal of Bank Marketing,* Vol. 11, No. 6, pp. 12-18.

7 Steve Cocheo and Kaisha Harris (2004), "Community Bank CEO Census: How Do You Compare to Your Fellow CEOs?" *ABA Banking Journal,* Vol. 96, Iss. 2, pp. 41-46.

8 A. Saunders (2010), *Financial Institutions Management: A Risk Management Approach.* New York: McGraw-Hill; J. Kimball Dietrich (1996), *Financial Services and Financial Institutions.* Upper Saddle River, NJ: Prentice Hall.

9 "Shattering Glass-Steagall," *Wall Street Journal,* June 22, 1998, p. 1.

10 D. Fitzpatrick (2011), "FDIC Poised to Sue WaMu Executives," *Wall Street Journal,* Feb. 22, p. 1; M. Hill (2008), "Positive, Negative Conclusions with Failure of WaMu," *McClatchy-Tribune Business News,* Sept. 27.

11 Emily Thornton (2004), "Banks: Desperately Seeking Stability," *Business Week,* February 2, Iss. 3868, p. 68; Charles Forelle (2004), "J.P. Morgan Ends Accord with IBM – Technology Will Return to Being Done In-House," *Wall Street Journal,* Sep 16, p. A3.

12 Dean Foust (2003), "Bank of America Heads Back to Main Street," *Business Week,* November 10, Iss. 3857, p, 41; Ben Wright (2001), "Acquire or be Damned," *Global Investor,* Feb. 2001, Iss. 139, p. 36.

13 David Gousnell (2004), "Hard-Core Enthusiasm for High-Tech ATMs," *Credit Card Management,* Vol. 16, Iss. 11, p. 16.

14 R. Kennedy and A. Sharma (2009), *The Services Shift: Seizing the Ultimate Offshore Opportunity.* London: FT Press. Manjit Kirpalani (2003), "The Rise of India," *Business Week,* Dec. 8, Iss. 3861, p. 66-74; Pete Engardio, Josey Puliyenthuruthel, and Manjeet Kripalani (2004), "Fortress India?", *Business Week,* Aug. 16, Iss. 3896, pp. 42-43; Robinson, M., and R. Kalakota, (2004), *Offshore Outsourcing: Business Models, ROI and Best Practices.* Chicago: Mivar Press; M.F. Greaver (1999), *Strategic Outsourcing: A Structured Approach to Outsourcing Decisions and Initiatives.* American Management Association: New York.

15 G. Carpenter and K. Nakamoto (1989), "Consumer Preference Formation and Pioneering Advantage," *Journal of Marketing Research,* Vol. 26, Iss. 3, pp. 285-298.

16 Al Ries and Jack Trout (2009), *The 22 Immutable Laws of Marketing.* Harper Collins: New York.

17 J. Mylonakis (2007), "A Bank Customer Analysis and Mortgage Service Evaluation: Implications for Market Segmentation Policies," *Banks and Bank Systems,* Vol. 2, Iss. 3, p. 157; Melanie Hardwood (2002), "Talking to the Generations: How to Market to Different Age Groups," *Community Banker,* Vol. 11, Iss. 7, pp. 28-33.

18 S. Miller (2007), "Leapin' Lizards," *Brandweek,* Vol. 48, Iss. 36, pp. 10-12; K. Krebsbach (2007), "With 'Caveman', GEICO Hones its Brand Instincts," *US Banker,* Vol. 117, Iss. 10, p. 24.

19 R. Michaeli (2011), *Competitive Intelligence: Competitive Advantage through Analysis of Competition, Markets and Technologies.* Springer; Donald Lehmann (2008), *Analysis for Marketing Planning.* New York: McGraw-Hill/Irwin.

CHAPTER TWELVE

Cases

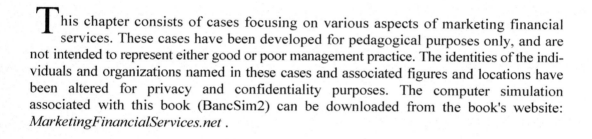

This chapter consists of cases focusing on various aspects of marketing financial services. These cases have been developed for pedagogical purposes only, and are not intended to represent either good or poor management practice. The identities of the individuals and organizations named in these cases and associated figures and locations have been altered for privacy and confidentiality purposes. The computer simulation associated with this book (BancSim2) can be downloaded from the book's website: *MarketingFinancialServices.net* .

LIBERTY ASSET FINANCING

In early 2011 during a staff meeting, Donna Sanchez, the marketing manager for Liberty Asset Financing (LAF), expressed her many concerns about the future of the business and the potential downfalls that it would face if innovation was not actively pursued by her staff. She oversaw a payroll of nearly 80 employees including both administrative staff located in their head office in Bethesda, Maryland, and sales specialists located across the country. While business may have been too slow to even discuss growth, the mandate given by LAF's Board of Directors to all of its senior managers was to focus on growth and to counter the recessionary trends of the time by building long-term capabilities and establishing new footholds in markets where LAF operated.

Liberty Asset Financing was established in 1990 to provide customized financial services to small and medium sized industrial companies as well as to distributors who carry their products. For example, when a furniture manufacturer would sell a large volume of products to a retailer or distributor, LAF would take on the task of providing credit for the transaction and financing the sale. This not only helped the manufacturer to focus on its core strength – manufacturing – but it also brought large volumes of financing business for LAF. The close relationship between manufacturers, distributors and LAF enabled it to generate large profit streams during good economic times. LAF had grown from financing only $7 million of business in 1991 to a peak of $346 million in 2008. However, recent figures, shown in Exhibit 12.1, seemed to indicate a disturbing drop in business volume.

Exhibit 12.1: LAF Financing Volume (2004-2010)

Year	Volume ($ mil.)	Yearly Growth
2004	$218	15.1%
2005	$254	16.5%
2006	$302	18.9%
2007	$329	8.9%
2008	$346	5.2%
2009	$289	-16.5%
2010	$165	-42.9%

LAF's Target Markets

LAF's marketing focus was primarily on companies that accumulated large volumes of inventory either because they themselves manufactured the products in large volume, or because they served as the middleman in distributing large volumes of manufactured goods from the manufacturers to retailers. These companies often needed to facilitate sales to their own customers through credit products and financial solutions such as short-term loans and leases. LAF was the provider of such financing to over 2,500 such companies nationwide, and had a considerable market position, specifically in the home furnishing business and specialized gift shops. Within these two markets, it was estimated that about one in every five such businesses use LAF's financial solutions in handling their transactions.

While the concentrated focus of LAF in these two markets helped reinforce a strong brand name customer loyalty toward the company, it also made the business vulnerable to market downturns that could affect these markets. This was very much the case at that time. Following the economic slowdown and the crash of the stock market in 2008, the volume of consumer spending, especially for durable non-essential goods significantly dropped. Both furniture sales and the purchase volume of gifts through gift shops collapsed as consumers curbed much of their non-essential spending and tightened their belts for what seemed to be rough economic times ahead. LAF's drop in business volume in the years following the 2008 crash largely reflected the hard economic times. This drastic drop in business volume, while shared by most of LAF's national competitors was a cause for concern at LAF headquarters in Bethesda and for Sanchez, who had to find a way out of this grave scenario.

LAFIN: Liberty Asset Financing Inventory Neutralization

The products that Sanchez was responsible for were marketed under the umbrella name of LAF Inventory Neutralization, or *LAFIN*. LAFIN products consisted of two general families:

> *Sales Financing (SF):* Loans or leases provided to buyers (such as retail chains) to facilitate sales by manufacturers or distributors. Typically LAF's customers who

were manufacturers or distributors would promote LAF's Sales Financing products to their own customers in order to speed up the selling process and to increase the probability of a sale.

Inventory Financing (IF): Short-term loans issued to manufacturers or distributors for large volumes of inventory which have built up in their warehouses due to a slowdown in sales. Since these businesses typically have a long history of market presence and the warehouses are in established locations, issuing short-term loans for such a purpose was generally deemed by LAF as a low-risk business, especially during stable economic times. Manufacturers and distributors often had to rely on such loans in order to manage their short-term cash flow needs and to cover regular business expenses such as payroll costs, utilities, and rent.

Sanchez did not believe that LAF could do much to improve volume in the Sales Financing category. However she had much higher hopes for Inventory Financing (IF). The slowdown of markets had increased the volume of unsold inventory in the warehouses of many US-based manufacturers and distributors. Based on industry reports that she had studies, Sanchez and her marketing team had recognized that the inventory volume of the businesses which they served through IF products had significantly grown over the second half of 2010. An industry report indicated that by the end of 2010, the volume of inventory by furniture manufacturers that had been stored in a warehouse for more than 6 months had grown by nearly 38%. This growth is what Sanchez was hoping to capitalize on.

To capitalize on this growth, Sanchez had to reexamine LAFIN's pricing. She believe that while having a dominant position in the specific market of home furnishing and gift shops may have helped LAF during good times, the pressing market conditions had intensified the competition. As result, she and some of her sales managers were of the belief that LAF financial solutions had become overpriced compared to the competition and that the LAF brand name was no longer valued as strongly by customers as it was during better economic times. Customers were now looking for more competitive prices and better value. She therefore decided to commission an extensive pricing study.

The Pricing Study

Price Analytics Research Corp (PARC), an international marketing research firm specialized in optimizing corporate pricing practices was hired to conduct the study.

PARC conducted an extensive survey to assess the level of price sensitivity of customers for Inventory Financing (IF) products. A total of 63 randomly selected operations managers of furniture manufacturers and distributors were recruited for this study. These individuals were identified using publically available information as well trade and industry association membership lists. The respondents were pre-screened to ensure that they have in the past dealt with LAF and three of its major competitors and therefore have the necessary knowledge to accurately respond to the survey questions. Survey administration was conducted online and the respondents were paid $150 for participation.

The pricing of most Inventory Financing (IF) products is driven by two price dimensions. One dimension is the application fee associated with applying for financing. This fee may be waived in rare occasions but in some cases may be as high as $125 per application. LAFIN typically charges an application processing fee of $75. The second pricing dimension is the interest rate associated with the loan. This rate was often based on the 'spread', which is the percentage increment over the prime interest rate. This increment typically ranged from 0.5% to as high as 7.5% over the prime rate, depending on the level of risk LAF assumed to exist in the transaction. For example if at the time of issuing the loan the prime rate is 3% a spread of 2% would result in an interest rate of 5% being charged. Since the prime rate varies from time to time, the spread was often used as the measure of the price competitiveness of an IF product as far as the interest rate is concerned. The combination of the spread and the application fee determines the overall price for inventory financing.

To determine the price competitiveness of LAFIN, a questionnaire consisting of three parts was developed by PARC. The first part of the questionnaire measured the respondent's thresholds to variations in price. The second part of the questionnaire consisted of a conjoint analysis study, whereby the respondent was shown variations of *IF* products and asked to rate each of them. The final part of the questionnaire asked the respondent to rate LAF and three of its major competitors on various price and service quality attributes. The objective of this part of the questionnaire was to develop a visual map which would aid Sanchez and her staff to determine the price competitiveness of LAFIN in the IF category. The structure of the questionnaire is outlined below.

Part 1: Price Thresholds

A set of standard questions were used to probe a respondent's views on what price levels are deemed to be acceptable. The specific questions asked were:

1. *At what price would you consider this [application fee/spread] to be a good value?*
2. *At what price would you say the [application fee/spread] is beginning to get expensive, but you would still consider moving forward with the transaction?*

Since IF products have two price dimensions, the above set of questions were asked once for the application fee and once for the spread. Exhibit 12.2 provides a summary of the results.

Exhibit 12.2: Summary Results for Price Thresholds

	"At what price would you consider this [application fee/spread] to be a good value?"		"At what price would you say the [application fee/spread] is beginning to get expensive, but you would still consider moving forward with the transaction?"	
Application Fee ($)	$0	17 respondents	$0	0 respondent
	$10	11 respondents	$10	3 respondents
	$25	9 respondents	$25	6 respondents
	$50	15 respondents	$50	7 respondents
	$65	7 respondents	$65	16 respondents
	$75	2 respondents	$75	13 respondents
	$100	2 respondents	$100	18 respondents
Spread (%)	0.5%	23 respondents	0.5%	0 respondent
	1.0%	13 respondents	1.0%	2 respondents
	2.5%	16 respondents	2.5%	4 respondents
	5.0%	5 respondents	5.0%	26 respondents
	6.5%	4 respondents	6.5%	16 respondents
	7.5%	1 respondent	7.5%	8 respondents
	10.0%	1 respondent	10.0%	7 respondents

Part 2: Conjoint Analysis

The second part of the questionnaire developed by PARC consisted of a conjoint task. Subjects were told that they would be evaluating a series of Inventory Financing price offers and asked to rate them. The conjoint task systematically varied the two pricing components (application fee and spread). Application fee was varied at four levels: Free,

$25, $50, and $75. The spread was also varied at four levels: 0.5%, 2.5%, 5%, and 7.5%. This resulted in sixteen possible combinations (4 levels of application fees × 4 levels of spread).

Each of these combinations was shown to the respondent on a computer screen and at the bottom of the screen the respondent was asked to rate his/her preference for the price presented on a scale of 1 ("not interested at all") to 7 ("extremely interested"). The order of presentation of the various profiles was randomly changed for each respondent in order to avoid any possible order or carryover effects. The summary results for the 63 respondents are provided in Exhibit 12.3.

Exhibit 12.3: Conjoint Analysis Summary Results
(Average Ratings on 1-to-7 Scale for Each Profile)

Application Fee \ Spread	0.5%	2.5%	5.0%	7.5%
Free	6.7	6.5	6.3	3.4
$25	6.1	5.8	5.3	2.8
$50	5.9	5.3	2.8	2.4
$75	2.8	2.2	2.3	2.1

Part 3: Rating of LAF and its Competitors

The final section of the questionnaire administered by PARC consisted of a series of questions which measured LAF's Inventory Financing products and comparable products offered by three of its major national competitors. This section of the questionnaire focused on the following measures:

(a) Rating of the prices offered by LAF and its competitors
(b) Rating of the quality of service provided by LAF and its competitors
(c) Importance of various price and service attributes in general

In addition the respondents were asked about the importance of price versus quality in their financial decisions. When asked whether a low price or high service quality was important to them, 81% of the respondents chose low price and 19% chose service quality. The summary of this section of the survey is provided in Exhibits 12.4 and 12.5 and can be downloaded from MarketingFinancialServices.net .

The Decision Facing Sanchez

Having waited the first two months of 2011 for the collection of the pricing surveys and having incurred a consulting fee nearing $50,000, Sanchez had to determine if LAFIN products are properly positioned in the marketplace. The first quarter of 2011 was about to come to a close, and with the time pressure put on her by the Board of Directors, the challenging market conditions of the time, and the 43% drop in LAF's business the previous year, pricing of LAFIN was of central concern

Case Question

Based on the presented research, what do you believe should be the price of LAFIN, in terms of the application fee and the spread?

Exhibit 12.4: Importance of Price and Service Quality
(Obtained as Percentage Weights)

Questions Asked	Importance Weight
IMPORTANCE OF PRICE ATTRIBUTES:	
Importance of having a low application fee	28%
Importance of having a low spread	72%
IMPORTANCE OF SERVICE QUALITY:	
Importance of speedy processing	58%
Importance of personal care by salesperson	42%

Exhibit 12.5: Average Ratings of LAFIN Products and Three National
Competitors on Price and Service Quality*

	LAFIN	Competitor A	Competitor B	Competitor C
PRICE-RELATED ATTRIBUTES				
Has a low application fee	3.52	5.42	2.91	6.31
Has a low spread	4.23	5.91	3.41	2.35
SERVICE-RELATED ATTRIBUTES				
Speedy processing of the application	6.34	4.52	3.21	5.89
Salesperson exhibits high degree of personal care	5.44	3.82	4.16	6.19

* Note that the names of competitors A, B and C are disguised in order to protect the confidentiality of the survey. The reported figures are averages on 1 to 7 scales with 7 being the positive end of the scale. Market shares for these competitors based on 2009 figures were estimated to be as follows: LAFIN (16%), Competitor A (49%), Competitor B (27%), Competitor C (8%)

FARMERS BANK OF VIRGINIA

Company Background

It was late November 2003. At a Friday afternoon board meeting of the top executives of Farmers Bank of Virginia (FBV) in Richmond, VA, an atmosphere of confusion and frustration could be sensed. The board meeting, which was scheduled for two hours, had gone over time and was well into its fourth hour of heated deliberations. At stake was the future identity of a bank that for decades had been a trusted name among all the Virginian communities it served. Farmers Bank of Virginia was established in 1924 by George Capaccio. Capaccio, an Italian immigrant that had volunteered to serve with the American forces in World War I, was a strong believer in traditional values and the importance of keeping a strong foundation in every element of his life, including the many successful businesses he helped launch and manage. For example, in the 1920s, many competing banks participated in both commercial and investment banking activities. Capaccio, however, believed that the deposits made by his customers were not to be played with in the high-stakes game of investment banking. He therefore persuaded the bank's board of directors to steer most of the bank's assets away from investment banking and to engage only in investments that were deemed safe. "We should treat customer deposits with the respect we'd give our own families' life savings, and make sure we do one thing and do it damn well," he mentioned at the 1927 annual meeting with the bank's employees.

As a result of Capaccio's traditional approach, FBV was considered one of the strongest and most stable community banks in the east coast, especially during the late 1920s and early 1930s, when many competing banks began to fold. The stability and discipline that Capaccio brought to the bank was always appreciated by the bank's customers, many of whom stayed with the bank through their entire lives. Most of their children and future generations also became loyal bank customers, creating an image of tradition and strength for FBV. The bank eventually grew from a single branch in Richmond to 32 branches throughout various locations in Virginia. By 2003 FBV was praised by many for providing the best personalized service in the retail banking business. Small-town values and the personal touch were key driving forces in the marketing efforts of the bank, and the bank prided itself on the relationships with its customers developed over the years. In 2003, the bank employed nearly 500 people. Approximately 124,000 FBV customers primarily used it for checking and savings purposes, and the bank was largely viewed by the communities it served as a safe place to deposit funds.

Emerging Trends

Despite the strong traditions and loyal customers that had characterized FBV's experience over the years, change was sensed everywhere. Only three years earlier, the banking industry was deregulated. The emerging picture for all banks in the US, and especially for small community banks such as FBV, was that competition from all sources could be expected, and innovation and creativity were in short supply. Anne Bagozzi, the Vice President of Marketing, had been assigned by the board of directors to identify the bank's overall marketing strategy for the next several years. Bagozzi, who was the granddaughter of Capaccio, felt a strong sense of responsibility to make sure that Capaccio's principles would be a core part of the bank's future strategy. As an ex-medic who had served in Vietnam, she knew the demands of a quickly changing environment and the need for rapid response. Yet her three decades of service with the bank had typically been far from the experiences of the battlefields of Vietnam, and she questioned at times the bank's ability to mobilize in new and untested territories.

To reinvent itself, the bank had taken on some new directions since the year 2000. A new ad campaign was designed to communicate the core values of the company and its long history and tradition of customer care. Slogans such as "The bank you can trust ..." and "Old time values ..." were featured in both print and broadcast ads. Between the years 2000 and 2002, FBV had spent nearly a half million dollars on these ads. In addition, an outside consulting firm was hired to develop the specs for moving the bank into the online platform. As of mid-2003, the online facilities of the bank were not yet operational, but the launch of the web site was expected to be completed by the end of that year. FBV also expanded its automated teller machine (ATM) network by providing additional ATM devices in its 32 bank branches. It was mandated by the top management that all bank branches have at least two operational ATM devices. Fifteen (15) of these branches also had an additional drive-through ATM for use by motorists.

Reflecting on the bank's current situation, Bagozzi noted, "even credit card companies and insurance agents are fighting for our business ... it's ridiculous who we have to deal with ... the next thing you know, we'll have to compete with the local convenience store." In addition to the new competitors springing up, an additional concern of Bagozzi was the changing picture of the typical customer:

> "Up until the mid 1990s, we had a very good feel for who we were serving. Most of our customers had their parents and grandparents banking with us as well. In fact, in 1997 when we conducted a series of focus groups, we had found that some of our older customers even remembered their grandparents talking about what my great grandfather had done to ensure the safety and security of their life savings. The strength of the bank and its traditions were with us, decades after the fact. But today, I'm not sure who the customers are. The older customers are getting older and doing less of the types of transactions we'd like them to do.

> Many have retired and even moved down south, and we now have a new breed of customers, younger and affluent, but different from those we served less than a decade ago"

	1990 Census	2000 Census
Average household income (in 2000 dollars)	$38,820	$51,259
Average age	36.5	34.7
Percent of population over the age of 65	35%	31%
Percent of population with college degrees	19%	27%

Exhibit 12.6 Target Market Demographics

To better understand the trends, Bagozzi referred to demographic data and how the population had changed for the census tracks within a 3-mile radius of the bank's 32 branch locations (Exhibit 12.6). This form of analysis would provide a general feel for the way in which the population base in the surrounding areas of the branches had evolved.

Bagozzi conceded that FBV's understanding of who the customers are and what they want is somewhat limited. "Its fuzzy science right now, and I hope we can quickly get a feel for where we should be going ... we don't know who they are and what they want now, let alone five years from now," she said. Nevertheless, the board of directors had given her a mandate to develop a 5-year strategy for the bank and to do so before the end of the year – a tough task, even for a former war-time medic.

In July of 2003, Bagozzi hired Jill Banner as her assistant in charge of strategic marketing. Banner, 29, had worked for five years as a marketing manager for an upstart online broker in Washington, DC before the company folded in late 2001. Banner then completed her MBA with a concentration in marketing and joined FBV shortly after graduation. As one of six people reporting directly to Bagozzi, Banner would be responsible for all elements of market research, business planning, and overall administration needed to design and implement the new face of the bank.

Having been on the job for less than a month, Banner had commented in a weekly meeting with Bagozzi that the general image of the bank needed to be shifted:

"I know the bank has its traditions and values, but the general direction of the bank is simply not appealing to me and people in my age bracket. I mean even the name of the bank with "farmers" being part of it. When was the last time you

saw a farmer walking in Richmond, or see one go into one of our branches?"

In fact, Banner believed that, not only did the bank have to change its products and services, but that it should also change its name and do a complete rebuilding of its image. She wanted to build a new bank from the ground up. Bagozzi, despite her enthusiasm over hiring a young energetic executive, was uncomfortable about the drastic changes she proposed. Bagozzi's gut feeling was that the bank should capitalize on the segment of its customers that was affluent, move up-market, and engage in higher margin activities such as investment services and financial advising. She was reluctant to move the bank away from its traditional strengths and to abandon her great grandfather's principle, which for decades had guided the bank through rough waters. She therefore asked Banner to arrange a series of market research studies to help both of them better understand their customers and to use this information in order to strategize their next steps.

Secondary Market Research

Banner's first step was to conduct a thorough examination of secondary data sources. She also consulted various national organizations and regulatory bodies who normally collect useful data and monitor bank activities, such as the Federal Deposit Insurance Corporation (FDIC) and the Federal Reserve. Many of the points that Bagozzi had mentioned to her turned out to be true. For example, Banner found that a decade earlier, 18 banks competed with FBV in its top three markets. The number had since dropped to 7 due to the consolidations and mergers that had been commonplace among banks in Virginia, especially in the previous three years. She also found that five of these seven banks offered free checking accounts to new customers, while FBV still offered a series of fee-based checking account choices. Banner's study of the bank's own records also showed some disturbing trends that she found surprising, especially since no one, not even Bagozzi, had been aware of them. For example, the number of customers that the bank served had consistently dropped in the past 5 years, but a notable decline was evident in the very last year for which complete data were available (Exhibit 12.7). Moreover, this trend did not seem to be true of FBV's leading competitors.

Year	1997	1998	1999	2000	2001	2002
Number of Customers *	137,932	141,395	138,943	138,289	137,902	123,850

* Customer counts as of January 1st of each year

Exhibit 12.7 Yearly Customer Base Trends

While this was probably not a sufficiently large decline to sound any major alarms, it was unclear why such a dramatic drop in the number of customer accounts had occurred. Banner had also noted that, out of the seven competing banks, six provided online banking and, out of these six, only one charged additional fees for this service.

Banner also sent out several mystery shoppers to understand the flavor of the competing banks' offerings. The mystery shoppers were mostly her college friends who were doing this work for her as a favor. They spent considerable time going to branches of each of the seven competing banks. In their observations, they noted that most of the competing branches offered customer service that was much less personalized and less accessible than what FBV offered. Long teller lines and relatively cold teller interactions were typical of these banks, and the prices charged for relatively standard services were somewhat confusing. In fact, when looking at the prices for the competing banks' services, it seemed that, while checking services were offered for free, some of the banks might charge special fees for visiting a bank teller or calling the bank's customer service phone lines. This was true of three of the seven banks. They did, however, notice that these competing banks offered a much wider array of financial services to their customers. For example, almost all offered some form of insurance product and prominently featured them in brochures available at the branches. Two of these banks had also set up investment service offices at their branch locations.

Primary Market Research

Unconvinced that the available research would provide the full scope of information needed to make the necessary strategic decisions, Bagozzi and Banner contacted Financial Research Associated Solutions (FRAS), a market research company specialized in financial services marketing, to conduct two waves of primary research studies. The first wave consisted of eight focus groups with both customers and non-customers of the bank. The focus groups were designed by FRAS to help develop a better understanding of what the perceptions of the bank were and what needs customers had that were not currently being served by FBV. The second wave of research by FRAS used consumer surveys conducted at several shopping malls in the vicinity of several FBV branch locations. The surveys were intended to help test and quantify some of the observations made through the focus groups.

Focus Group Findings

A total of eight focus groups were conducted in September and October of 2003. The focus groups were held in two central locations where FRAS operated specialized focus group facilities. Half of the focus groups were with existing FBV customers and the other half were with non-customers. The focus group sessions were further split by age. Half of the focus groups were conducted with individuals below the age of 45 and the other half were conducted with individuals 45 and older. As a result, a total of four categories of focus group sessions were carried out, with each category consisting of two focus group sessions. The focus groups were moderated by a consumer research specialist at FRAS who had conducted qualitative research on bank marketing for over a decade. The moderator discussed several issues related to the customers' views of FBV, specifically related to the image of the bank, its perceived strengths and weaknesses, and new services which they thought might best meet their needs. These responses were then categorized and tabulated by the moderator and two assistant researchers at FRAS, and the most frequently mentioned responses are shown in Exhibit 12.8.

Consumer Surveys

Following the focus group sessions, a series of surveys were administered in shopping malls at various locations in the vicinity of several key FBV branches. These locations were chosen based on the belief that the shopping public would be representative of the customer profiles that each bank branch attempts to attract. The survey did not focus on FBV in particular but probed individual consumers' views of the kinds of services that they believed to be important in the operations of a bank branch. Importance ratings were obtained using a 1-to-5 scale, with 1 being "not important" and 5 being "very important."

A total of 368 surveys were administered during early November 2003. The results were subsequently tabulated, analyzed using statistical software, and dissected into two groups of consumers, those below the age of 45, and those that are 45 and older. Exhibit 12.9 reports the results. The reported figures are top-box percentages, which reflect the percentage of respondents in each age category who believed the item to be "very important" by rating it a 5 on the 1-to-5 importance scale.

The Decision

Bagozzi and Banner began preparing for their presentation of a 5-year strategic plan. Having spent nearly $170,000 on marketing research, the quality of their advice would not only be important to the future of their own professional status within the bank, but also to the long-term survival of FBV.

	Below the age of 45	45 years old and older
FBV Customers	Image of FBV: - Family oriented - Old - Slow Strength: - Name I can trust - Security - Orderly Weakness: - Technology - Slow service - Narrow range of products Additional Services Needed: - Insurance - Investment services - More flexible loan policy	Image of FBV: - Family oriented - Traditional - Trustworthy Strength: - Name I can trust - Orderly - Security Weakness: - Narrow range of products - Limited parking space - No weekend hours Additional Services Needed: - Investment services - Financial advice - Wider choice of home loans
Non-Customers	Image of FBV: - Old - Slow - Archaic Strength: - Traditional - Security - Name I can trust Weakness: - No online facility - Technology - Need to use tellers Additional Services Needed: - Online banking - Insurance - Auto loans	Image of FBV: - Trustworthy - Family oriented - Old Strength: - Security - Name I can trust - Stable business Weakness: - Old systems - No weekend hours - Slow service Additional Services Needed: - Financial advice - Home mortgages - Investment services

Exhibit 12.8 Summary of Focus Group Findings

	Below 45 years old	45 years and older
Weekend operations	35%	54%
Availability of online banking	67%	34%
Friendly teller service	43%	68%
Wide ATM network	71%	57%
Convenient branch locations	23%	63%
Availability of parking	37%	68%
Well-lit parking and branch location	32%	71%
Well-decorated branches	18%	21%
Knowledgeable staff	39%	57%
Availability of investment services	15%	71%
Availability of insurance products and services	57%	52%
Availability of mortgages	24%	53%
Free checking	79%	77%

Exhibit 12.9 Top-Box Percentages

Case Questions

(1) What objectives do you think should be included in the 5-year strategic plan for FBV?

(2) Provide a timeline of the activities needed to achieve the objectives you have identified.

ASSETSGUARD

It was a Friday evening in late December of 2001. At the headquarters of *InsuOn.com* in White Plains, New York, most of the company's 85 employees were getting ready for the Christmas season, which was just around the corner. Many had been spending part of their time shopping for gifts and organizing a big office Christmas party to be held later that night, to celebrate the company's 3rd Christmas. However, the spirit of Christmas had not yet found its way to the cubicle of Christopher Winer, the Executive Vice President of Marketing. Winer had the challenging task of making several key decisions over the weekend that could affect the entire future of InsuOn and all of its employees.

Winer's challenge was to decide on the company's strategy to introduce an identity theft insurance policy called AssetsGuard. This was a considerable deviation from InsuOn's traditional insurance product lines, which primarily consisted of term life insurance and traveler's insurance policies. Nevertheless, the opportunity to move into what seemed to be a fast-growing market was difficult to ignore. Identity theft occurs when an individual obtains access to personal information such as a person's credit card number or social security number, and uses this information to either obtain access to credit or to misidentify himself. Three forms of identity theft are known to occur frequently. The first is criminal identity theft, which occurs when a criminal that has been confronted by law enforcement authorities does not provide them with his own real name, but proceeds to provide another individual's name. As a result, criminal records and arrest warrants would be issued to the name of the individual that was named, rather than the individual apprehended by law enforcement.

A somewhat similar form of identity theft is referred to as identity cloning; this involves the use of an individual's personal information by a criminal to establish for himself a completely new identity. This act involves the use of the individual's name and personal information to obtain a social security number, driver's license, or other critical documents that identify an individual in modern day society. The third form of identity theft is referred to as financial identity theft (FIT). FIT involves the use of a victim's name or social security number by the criminal in order to obtain access to credit from a financial institution. For example, using such personal information, the criminal could apply for a credit card and use the card for personal purchases. The victim would be footed with the bill, unless an appeal was made to the credit card company. While most credit card companies had their own protection plans to cover potential losses due to FIT, the growing occurrence of FIT had begun to cause considerable alarm among consumers and regulators. For example, the Federal Trade Commission (FTC) estimated that incidents of identity theft were doubling every year, and hundreds of thousands of consumers would eventually be affected by it. Some estimated that, in 2002 alone, of the approximately 180 million adults in the United States with active credit records, well over 5 million would be affected by identity theft, and that the cost of reversing the damaging effects of FIT, in terms of legal fees, lost wages, and administrative expenses would typically range between $500 and $1,500 per case. AssetsGuard was InsuOn's response to the explosive growth in financial identity theft cases.

Company Background

InsuOn (short for Insurance Online) was founded in 1997 by Joseph Wilson, a 32-year-old millionaire. Wilson, who as a young adult never had the financial resources to attend college, joined a Fortune 500 information technology company after graduating from high school. He worked his way up from mailroom clerk to computer programmer. His technical skills combined with his outgoing personality eventually helped him move up the ranks; at the age of 28, he was one of the top 15 managers in the company. At around that time, Wilson decided to leave the corporate world; capitalizing on the Internet boom experienced at that time, he set up his own company—InsuOn.com. InsuOn started off as a distributor of term-life insurance products to teachers, university professors, scientists, and educators in New York, New Jersey, and Connecticut. In the first year of its operations, the company sold nearly 12,000 policies, far exceeding even the most aggressive projections. By 2001 this figure had nearly tripled to 34,500 policyholders.

The fast growth of the company, which led to the issuance of an IPO (initial public offering) in late 1999, created an infusion of funds needed to support the company's growth. InsuOn quickly moved to the business of providing traveler's insurance, which was primarily sold online through travel agencies as well as directly to individual consumers. The company also expanded its Internet offering of term-life insurance beyond teachers and educators and expanded coverage to five additional states, mostly on the east coast. Within three years, a company that had started off with seven employees now employed nearly ten times that number.

Wilson's philosophy on running a successful business was largely based in his own personal values and life beliefs. He believed that, in many business transactions, the middleman does not add any value to the customer experience, but is primarily there to take away cash from both the seller and the buyer. He often cited examples such as GEICO, a direct marketer of property and casualty insurance that, by skipping the middleman, has been able to challenge the traditional models by which insurance companies had operated for decades; however, it also provides good service and attractive prices to its customers. According to Wilson, many insurance markets were becoming commoditized, and the true differences between the various brands were diluting. Automotive insurance, term life insurance, homeowners insurance, and travelers insurance were, in his opinion, the types of products that do not need personal selling and can be sold with little or no human interaction. "All you need is a good web site and nice people on the customer service phone line," he once told Winer. Wilson was also a strong believer in breaking down barriers within his own organization. For example, he believed that top executives in the company should not be treated differently from other employees; they too should have cubicles, not their own offices, and park in the regular employee parking lot rather than in reserved parking spots. As a result, on the floor where InsuOn operated in White Plains, no one, including Wilson and Winer, had their own personal office. Wilson believed that, by following such an organizational model, one not only broke down the barriers that separate management from the rest of the company, but one also created a much more communicative and efficient work environment.

AssetsGuard

While Wilson's philosophy of cost efficiencies was crucial to the company's early successes with term life and travelers insurance markets, the competitive nature of these markets had limited InsuOn's contribution margin to about 38%. Wilson was under considerable pressure from InsuOn investors and industry analysts to move the margins up, and the goal was to secure margins of 45% or higher for most of the company's new products. Wilson's new idea of providing identity theft insurance may have been just the solution for this goal. AssetsGuard was a unique form of protection against financial identity theft. While identity theft insurance was beginning to be offered by some of the major property and casualty insurance companies, public awareness of the availability of this service was altogether very limited. A survey conducted by a Washington–based lobbying group in early 2001 had shown that less than 5% of the population was even aware of the existence of identity theft insurance products. Moreover, Wilson noticed that competing identity theft insurance policies offered by the major insurance companies provided very specific levels of coverage. For example, for a premium of $14.99 a month, an individual could obtain coverage for up to $20,000. This would be the maximum amount for which the insurer would protect the policyholder. The policy would cover the costs of legal fees that attorneys might charge for reversing the effects of FIT on the policyholder's financial and credit records. It would also cover up to $2,500 (as part of the maximum $20,000 coverage) of lost wages in case the policyholder had to attend court hearings related to the FIT case. Similar policies with nearly identical coverage were provided for prices in the $12.99/month to $39.99/month range by insurance agents nationally.

AssetsGuard was a considerably different type of FIT insurance. While the competing FIT insurance policies had specific amounts and conditions of coverage, it was Wilson's vision that consumers that may be in a state of distress when victimized by identity theft should not be bothered by policy limits and terms and conditions. He personally had designed the product to carry some attractive features. For example, in case of identity theft, AssetsGuard would cover the policyholder for up to $40,000, which was a much higher coverage level than what the majority of competing policies offered. In addition, the entire face value of $40,000 would be available to the policyholder to retain the services of a pre-defined network of attorneys specialized in FIT with whom InsuOn had established relationships. As a result, the policyholder would neither have to pay an attorney out of pocket, nor subsequently have to file for, and await, claim payments. The availability of a specialized network of attorneys also helped ease possible policyholder anxieties related to finding the right attorney with the necessary background and specialization. AssetsGuard also conducted regular monthly checks of policyholder credit reports to monitor potential cases of FIT and to alert the policyholder. This was a truly unique feature of the product that, in combination with the generous and well-organized structure of the policy, would relieve most concerns and anxieties an individual might have regarding financial identity theft.

Similar to InsuOn's other insurance products, AssetsGuard would be sold through the company's web site. Wilson also envisioned promoting the product to financial advisors, who would in turn recommend it to their clients. The expected launch date for AssetsGuard was March 2002, giving Winer less than 100 days to plan the launch and to set up the infrastructure and marketing programs needed to support it. Winer estimated that the incremental cost of expanding the web site and hiring additional staff to support AssetsGuard would be approximately $650,000 a year; an additional $400,000 a year would be needed for the first two years to fund related advertising campaigns. Having been in the business of selling insurance for nearly two decades, and being 12 years senior to Wilson, Winer was not fully convinced that Wilson's idea would be well received by the market.

Consumer Research

Only 6 weeks ago, in early November, Winer had attended three focus groups on AssetsGuard commissioned by the company. The focus groups, which were held in Boston, were attended by panels of consumers. The attendees were pre-screened to be heads of households with annual household incomes in the $100,000-$249,999 range who owned their residential property. Winer believed this to be a representative target group for those who might be interested in purchasing FIT insurance policies. The focus groups were moderated and conducted by a research company specializing in insurance marketing. The sessions were designed such that, at the beginning, participants were queried on their general knowledge of identity theft and companies they know that provide identity theft insurance or might provide it in the future. They were then given the description for AssetsGuard and asked for their opinions. Open-ended conversations then followed and, at the end, their recall of the AssetsGuard name, its policy description, and price expectations were measured using a short questionnaire. Each participant was paid $75 for attending.

The consumer research results revealed that most of the participants in all three focus group sessions were unaware that identity theft insurance policies even existed. Of the 27 individuals who participated in the focus group sessions, only five claimed to have known that such insurance policies exist. When asked which companies they believed would be good providers of such insurance policies, the most frequently mentioned companies were established insurers that had agent organizations and were active in both property and casualty, and life insurance markets. The second most frequently mentioned group of companies were the major commercial banks. Finally, some participants believed that their mortgage companies might also be trustworthy providers of identity theft insurance. In the second phase of each focus group session, participants were engaged in open-ended conversations about the value they saw in the features of the AssetsGuard policy. These discussions revealed that the focus group participants found the benefits to be highly attractive and beneficial to their peace of mind. An unrelated task followed in order to distract the participants for approximately 10 minutes, following which recall measures and price estimates were obtained (this is common practice in consumer research to help measure consumer memory).

After the distraction task, participants were given a short questionnaire that asked them to recall the name of the insurance policy that had been presented to them earlier and to provide an estimate of the monthly premiums that they think would be reasonable. Of the 27 participants, only 14 could remember the exact name of AssetsGuard. Other names mentioned were "AssetCard", "AssGuard" and "LastGuard". As for the question on monthly premiums, the average for the 27 participants was $28.32, but the figure ranged from a low of $18 to a high of $48. Half of the participants did not see sufficient need for purchasing such an insurance policy. The questionnaire concluded with an open-ended question that asked the participants to point out any reservations they had about buying a policy such as AssetsGuard. The most frequently mentioned concern was the need to purchase identity theft insurance. The second most frequently mentioned concern was that the existing insurance policies that the person has such as homeowners insurance might already cover FIT. Finally, some participants were concerned with using the Internet to purchase identity theft insurance. This is especially a concern as a significant amount of identity theft takes place over the Internet. Many of these participants were also concerned about the process of the online sale of a policy such as AssetsGuard, which would involve no face-to-face contact, and questioned the trustworthiness of such a transaction.

Though the focus group results provided Winer with a first-hand feel for market response to the AssetGuard concept, he requested additional information from the research provider with respect to the expected cost of various media he could use to advertise and promote AssetsGuard, and the resulting conversion rate, which reflects the probability that a given consumer targeted with the ad would sign up for the policy. While the research provider was not able to provide exact estimates, general ball-park figures were provided (Exhibit 12.10). In addition, the research company conducted a survey of 60 competitors in various regions profiling their prices for policies with coverage similar to AssetsGuard. Based on filings with state insurance commissioners and a statistical model, the research company produced a table of conversion rates, reflecting their estimates of the percentage of customers targeted with the insurance product at a given price are likely to subscribe (Exhibit 12.11; detailed data can be downloaded from *MarketingFinancialServices.net*).

Winer's Decision

Winer's time for committing to decisions had arrived. He not only had to make a strategic decision on whether to launch AssetsGuard or not but also if a launch decision were to be made, the details of the pricing and promotion plan had to be determined. While Wilson questioned the product's potential, he also wondered about the brand name and its fit to what the product was truly intended to represent. His traditional training as an economist conflicted with the inspirations and pragmatic style of Wilson, who seemed keen on InsuOn's venture into this little known territory of the insurance world.

Case Question

Should AssetsGuard be launched?

Exhibit 12.10: Media Costs and Expected Conversion Rates

Target Audience	Medium	CPM*	Conversion Rate **
Non-customers	Direct mail	$25-$35	0.020%-0.050%
Non-customers	Radio advertising	$32-$47	0.050%-0.075%
Non-customers	Cable TV advertising	$68-$91	0.115%-0.145%
Existing customers	Direct mail	$25-$35	0.190%-0.350%
Existing customers	Telemarketing	$98-$125	2.25%-3.15%

* CPM reflects the cost of reaching out to a target audience of one thousand individuals
** Conversion rate reflects the probability that an individual who has observed the ad will purchase the promoted product.

Exhibit 12.11: Penetration Rates of 60 Competing Policies*

Competitor	Price	Coverage Level	Conversion Rate	Competitor	Price	Coverage Level	Conversion Rate	Competitor	Price	Coverage Level	Conversion Rate
1	$19.95	$5,000	1.8%	21	$19.95	$1,500	1.7%	41	$29.95	$750	0.2%
2	$14.95	$2,000	9.9%	22	$12.95	$2,500	6.9%	42	$29.95	$1,500	0.2%
3	$19.95	$1,500	1.7%	23	$10.95	$750	9.7%	43	$12.95	$5,000	7.2%
4	$29.95	$2,500	0.2%	24	$29.95	$2,500	0.2%	44	$12.95	$1,500	6.8%
5	$29.95	$1,500	0.2%	25	$9.95	$10,000	13.7%	45	$9.95	$1,500	11.8%
6	$10.95	$750	9.7%	26	$29.95	$2,500	0.2%	46	$9.95	$5,000	12.6%
7	$10.95	$5,000	9.5%	27	$41.95	$2,500	0.0%	47	$9.95	$2,500	12.0%
8	$10.95	$2,500	10.0%	28	$12.95	$2,500	6.9%	48	$29.95	$1,500	0.2%
9	$10.95	$1,500	9.8%	29	$10.95	$1,500	9.8%	49	$10.95	$2,500	10.0%
10	$54.95	$1,500	0.1%	30	$10.95	$1,500	9.8%	50	$12.95	$5,000	7.2%
11	$54.95	$2,000	0.2%	31	$19.95	$2,500	1.7%	51	$12.95	$2,500	6.9%
12	$12.95	$5,000	7.2%	32	$29.95	$2,500	0.2%	52	$19.95	$1,500	1.7%
13	$10.95	$2,500	10.0%	33	$19.95	$1,500	1.7%	53	$10.95	$10,000	9.5%
14	$29.95	$1,500	0.2%	34	$10.95	$5,000	9.1%	54	$41.95	$1,500	0.0%
15	$29.95	$2,500	0.2%	35	$9.95	$10,000	10.7%	55	$19.95	$750	1.7%
16	$41.95	$5,000	0.0%	36	$41.95	$3,000	0.1%	56	$29.95	$10,000	0.3%
17	$54.95	$750	0.1%	37	$29.95	$5,000	0.2%	57	$19.95	$750	1.7%
18	$10.95	$1,500	9.8%	38	$10.95	$1,500	9.8%	58	$10.95	$5,000	8.5%
19	$19.95	$1,500	1.7%	39	$9.95	$1,500	11.8%	59	$10.95	$1,500	9.8%
20	$54.95	$5,000	0.2%	40	$19.95	$2,500	1.7%	60	$13.95	$3,000	7.2%

* Data set can be downloaded from *MarketingFinancialServices.net*
** Conversion rate reflects the probability estimates produced by the research company, that an individual who is presented with the insurance product at a given price and coverage level by the identified competitor will subscribe to it

HOME ENDORSERS INC.

Home Endorsers Inc (HEI) is a small mortgage broker located in Wayne, NY. HEI was established in 1993 by Janet McIntyre and George Mavis, two business school graduates from a private university in upstate New York. After its inception, the company gradually grew in both mortgage volume and client base; it employed 12 staff members by 1999. HEI witnessed considerable growth at the end of the 1990s because of the housing boom at the time and growing consumer interest in purchasing real estate properties. By 2001, three new branches had opened in other cities in New York State and plans for expanding beyond state lines were being considered.

HEI often had repeat customers, and positive customer experience created considerable word-of-mouth advertising for the company; friends and relatives of many previous homebuyers applied for their mortgages through HEI. At the end of 2001, despite contentment with their own success and the notable growth of HEI's mortgage volume, McIntyre and Mavis decided to objectively examine the company's performance by carefully studying some of their competitors in local markets. A market research firm was hired to document the mortgage origination volume of HEI's competitors and to compare and contrast their business practices with those of HEI.

The market research report, which was delivered to McIntyre and Mavis in April of 2002, caused considerable alarm. The numbers suggested that HEI was performing at considerably lower levels than its competition. For example, notable differences were observed in the mortgage origination volume of these competitors and that of HEI. Between 1998 and 2001, the mortgage origination volume of HEI had grown by 78%. While this number may seem impressive at first glance, it was disappointing when compared to some of its direct competitors who, on average, experienced a 115% growth rate. Furthermore, the market research firm, through an examination of the mortgage records filed at local government offices, estimated that the competitors' revenues from administrative fees and additional charges was at least twice that of HEI.

Mavis and McIntyre were alarmed by these numbers because they hinted at the possibility that HEI was leaving considerable amounts of profit on the table and was not realizing all revenue potential in its dealings with homebuyers. In fact, the financial burdens of growth and the costs of establishing new branch offices seemed to require them to find additional sources of revenue. They asked the market research firm to probe further the activities of some of the competing mortgage brokers. The consulting team decided to utilize two specific sources of data. The first source was focus groups conducted with recent homebuyers who had purchased their homes with mortgages supplied by these competitors. These individuals could be easily identified through property records and mortgage documents made publicly available at local government offices. The second source of data was consumer complaint records filed with regulatory bodies and consumer protection agencies, which might provide insights on the business practices of some of these competitors.

Focus Groups

In May of 2002, three focus group sessions were held with recent homebuyers who had used the mortgage products of some of HEI's competitors. The focus groups were designed to help the researchers understand the mortgage selection process of homebuyers and the application procedures of competitors. It was also important to identify good and bad business practices used by the competing mortgage brokers through the focus group discussions. Each focus group was attended by six to ten individuals, and the conversations were recorded and transcribed for subsequent analysis.

The results of the focus groups indicated that homebuyers in general do not have a great deal of knowledge about the various companies and mortgage brokers in their local areas. Most could only name three other mortgage brokers that they were aware of, or had come into contact with, in their neighborhoods. Their choice of a mortgage company was often affected by recommendations made by the real estate agent. Focus group participants also indicated that they were often attracted to a particular broker through advertising in print or on cable TV in which low interest rates were mentioned. One-on-one contact with the mortgage broker and the personal attention given to the mortgage applicant were also considered important in their decisions.

Several focus group participants mentioned that, while the low advertised mortgage rates were the primary attraction, they were surprised at the hidden fees and 'closing costs' that appeared last-minute at the time of closing the contract. The homebuyers believed they were not made fully aware of the fees ahead of time, but could not dispute them since they were informed within a very short time—typically two days or less—of the purchase date of the house. Disputing these charges would require delaying the closing date or the termination of the purchase contract, which is often associated with stiff penalties such as the loss of the down-payment made on the property.

Consumer Complaint Records

The consulting team also examined public information related to the selected companies that was made available through consumer protection agencies, local government offices, and court documents. A series of questionable business practices were revealed through such analysis. In particular, the following cases were found to be frequently experienced by homebuyers who had obtained their mortgages through some of these companies:

Bait-and-Switch: Mortgages advertised with attractive interest rates. Without disclosing such information in the ad, the rate only applied to applicants with unusually high credit scores. Most homebuyers who proceeded to contact the broker found upon the completion of their mortgage application that the interest rate they would be charged exceeded the advertised rate.

Step-Up-Pricing: Mortgage applicants were faced with last-minute fees that they were not clearly informed about until shortly before the closing date. Often, this resulted in the payment of thousands of dollars of additional fees by the homebuyer. Homebuyers rarely disputed these fees due to the time constraints placed on them and the financial penalties of backing out from the purchase of the property.

Affiliated-Providers: Mortgage companies explicitly or implicitly required the homebuyer to obtain homeowners insurance from affiliated insurance companies or to conduct the property inspection from a list of pre-approved inspectors. The rates charged by some of these affiliates were found to be higher than prevailing market rates. Furthermore, in certain cases, a commission structure was in place to compensate the mortgage company for channeling business to the affiliates.

These practices were found to take place across different residential markets ranging from small apartments to luxury homes. They were often associated with the mortgage brokers being charged fines for violating specific regulations. However, these punitive measures only occurred in the rare cases in which homebuyers made the effort to report the case or pursued legal action against the mortgage company. In the majority of cases, homebuyers seemed to move on with their lives without legally confronting their mortgage providers, leaving few, if any, public records of their experience.

Decision Facing McIntyre and Mavis

HEI's future, as well as its ability to maintain its financial health and to grow, largely depended on the ability of Mavis and McIntyre to find new sources of income. Given the questionable approaches used by their competitors to boost their own revenue streams, the two former college classmates were faced with ethical dilemmas which they never had to confront as college students.

Case Questions

1. What ethical issues do you find relevant to the practices of HEI's competitors?

2. How should McIntyre and Mavis respond to these practices?

3. What examples of marketing practices similar to those used by HEI's competitors have you seen profiled in the press?

LEXZMMAR INVESTMENTS

Company Background

Located in Seattle, WA, Lexzmmar Investments is a fund management firm with a history of nearly eight decades of managing an array of successful mutual funds. Founded by Joseph Lexzmmar in 1933, the company's investment products have traditionally been among the most innovative in the industry. Lexzmmar was a Finnish immigrant who came to the U.S. in 1927 to complete a Ph.D. in economics. While completing his Ph.D., he managed to publish several scientific articles that have since become classics in economic theory and finance. Upon the completion of his Ph.D. in 1931, he was offered several top academic positions in leading universities in the U.S. and Europe. However, Joseph Lexzmmar always had a preference for practicality that manifested itself in a passionate interest in the complexities of everyday decisions facing investors rather than the theoretical abstractions that characterized the work he was expected to carry out as an academician. As a result, he joined one of the leading banks on the West Coast as an economist upon graduation. He rose quickly through the ranks and was promoted to the status of Chief Investment Officer within five years.

In the early 1930s, the banking sector in the U.S. experienced considerable turmoil. Due to the inadequate banking regulations of the time, many banks had actively engaged their customers' deposits in high-risk investments; the economic depression of the time gave the majority of consumers a reason to withdraw their funds from the banks. Without sufficient deposits in their vaults, and with poor investment returns, many banks began to collapse and a series of catastrophic bank failures followed. These failures resulted in a state of economic turmoil, increased regulations, and the elimination of many management positions within the banking sector. Soon, people like Joseph Lexzmmar found themselves unemployed in a distressed and unstable industry. In 1935, having been relieved of his duties by his former employer, Joseph Lexzmmar set out to establish his own investment company. Lexzmmar believed that many individuals like himself were wrongfully deprived of their professional lives due to an industry's poor management style and failing regulations.

Management Philosophy

In 1935, Joseph Lexzmmar set out on a mission to build a company in which his visions of investment strategy could be combined with scientific models of financial markets. This combination would produce innovative financial products that could help the masses. One of the guiding principles in Lexzmmar's management style was the central importance of the client. He made a point of spending at least one third of his own time with clients of all wealth levels. Lexzmmar's hands-on style was unique; despite being one of the wealthiest bankers on the West Coast, he typically logged nearly one thousand hours of one-on-one time with Lexzmmar clients every year.

One of the other guiding principles that Joseph Lexzmmar established in his company was the importance of innovation. He believed that clients often appreciate products that resolve their investment constraints, and he encouraged his managers to spend considerable time sharing their observations with one another in order to understand clients' needs. He believed this to be a fruitful way to design and develop new investment products. The result of this approach to innovation was the introduction of new breeds of mutual funds. These were found to be highly attractive not only to Lexzmmar's own clients, but also to competing fund companies, many of whom eventually became distributors of some of Lexzmmar's investment products for their own client base. In a 1941 interview with a financial reporter, Joseph Lexzmmar was quoted as saying, "customers are the lifeblood of this business ... we need to listen to them to see what we should do tomorrow ... without them there would be no tomorrow for us."

The result of this approach to business was a consistent and impressive path of growth. Between 1935 and 1940, the number of clients grew from 50 to well over 500. The total assets under management grew from $2.1 million to $130 million. One of the contributing factors of this growth was the unique approach used to compensate Lexzmmar employees. Nearly half of the salaries of employees with client contact (for example, investment professionals, customer service employees, and fund managers) were linked to the financial performance of the client portfolios and the results of client satisfaction surveys. This approach was considered revolutionary at that time because the typical broker's compensation was based on the number of securities trades made by clients; brokers in competing firms were rarely held accountable for clients' account performance or client satisfaction. In 1957, the explosive growth of the client base led the company to impose a stop-growth policy limiting new account issuance. This decision was based on Joseph Lexzmmar's driving principle of maintaining high levels of customer care and individualized attention. However, to support growth, Lexzmmar gradually developed a branch infrastructure and expanded its workforce; by the year 2010, the company had nearly 11,000 clients and operated 17 branch offices in eight major cities in the states of Washington, California, and Arizona. Many of the company's mutual fund products are sold today through other fund companies, brokers, advisors, and even a select group of commercial banks.

Performance Protected Products

Joseph Lexzmmar passed away in the summer of 2010. However, his approach to running a successful investment business remained with the company. In early 2011,

Randall Weinstein was hired as the company's CEO. Weinstein, 48, had a long history of running several successful investment banks in New York and was a well-respected individual in the industry having authored numerous landmark business articles and two best-selling books on investment strategy. His business philosophy and credentials, which in many ways resembled those of the company's founder, were the primary reasons he was hired for the job. Nevertheless, Weinstein was challenged by many forces at that time. The poor performance of the stock market in the last few years had made many Lexzmmar clients unhappy with their investment results. Furthermore, the competitive environment of fund management companies was quickly changing. The emergence of online trading, the aggressive pursuit of the market by discount brokers, and the unease caused by uncertainty about interest rates vastly complicated the decisions that Weinstein would have to make.

One of the decisions facing Weinstein at that time was the possible launch of what the company's investment strategists had named Performance Protected Products (PPPs). These short-term investment products provide market-linked returns such as stock market indexed mutual funds which follow the general trends in particular stock markets. However, they protect investors from potential downturns in investment value. When a client purchases a PPP, she agrees to invest in the product and not to withdraw the invested amounts for a pre-specified period of time. At the end of the time-period, the investor is then able to collect the originally deposited funds plus any applicable investment returns. The attractive characteristic of the PPP was that Lexzmmar would guarantee the product against downward movement in asset value upon maturity. Therefore, the originally invested amount would be protected, and clients' potential investment losses would be eliminated if the market were to go down. The eventual investment returns of PPPs were linked to the returns on the major exchanges and established stock indexes.

Lexzmmar investment strategists had developed three versions of PPPs: one linked to the S&P 500 Index, the other linked to the NASDAQ, and the last linked to the Toronto Stock Exchange (TSE). It was believed that these investment products would be attractive to investors at that time since they allowed active participation in some of the major investment markets while providing protection against downward drops in investment value. To participate in PPPs, clients were charged 2.5% of the total investment amount on a yearly basis. Weinstein, however, believed that, while the 2.5% upfront cost may detract some clients from investing, levels as high as 5% to 10% might be needed to provide some "insurance" against possible downward trends in the stock market. Given the poor stock market results in recent years, this became a central question for the product team.

Despite his reservations, Weinstein's discussions with the PPP product team and his understanding of the company's guiding principles suggested to him that this product may fit many of Joseph Lexzmmar's guiding principles. PPPs provided Lexzmmar's existing clients with a broader range of investment choices. The product was innovative and would enable these clients to remain active in the stock market even in volatile times.

Furthermore, PPPs provided other brokers, investment advisors, and third parties the ability to introduce their own customers to a new approach to investing in the stock market while limiting any downward movements in investment value.

Market Research

Having only been at Lexzmmar for less than a month, Weinstein was hesitant to undertake any major product launches without some form of scientific market research. To help understand clients' possible responses to Performance Protected Products, Weinstein asked the PPP product team to commission a market research study designed to determine the product's optimal marketing strategy. Several marketing issues were to be investigated. The first was the effects of the upfront costs on client interest. The second concern was the receptiveness of the clients to direct mail information about the product. These two factors constituted the primary marketing tools available to Lexzmmar at that time to market PPPs to the client base.

The market research firm designed a systematic experiment in which different groups of clients received product brochures by mail. Subsequently, the number of inquiries generated were tabulated and quantified. The experiment engaged a total of 900 clients who were split into six equally sized groups of 150 clients. Each group was mailed direct mail pieces with detailed descriptions of the PPP products including the upfront investment fees. The number of direct mail pieces sent to each group varied from two to six (in increments of two), and the upfront fees varied at two levels: 2.5% and 5%. The number of customer inquiries was tracked by recording the tracking number included in the direct mail brochures sent out to each customer from those clients who called Lexzmmar's Client Care line to request additional information. The direct mail brochures were sent out in March of 2011. Exhibit 12.12 summarizes the results as reflected by the number of clients who responded to the direct mail pieces by making a follow-up inquiry and requesting additional product information within fifteen days of the mailing. It was expected that one in every ten clients who respond to the brochure would eventually purchase a PPP product from Lexzmmar.

Number of Direct Mail Pieces Sent Out	Upfront Fee at 2.5%	Upfront Fee at 5%
2	11 out of 150	6 out of 150
4	21 out of 150	9 out of 150
6	35 out of 150	11 out of 150

Exhibit 12.12 Number of Clients Responding

It was estimated that the cost of a single mailing is $1.50. Furthermore, the incremental yearly administrative costs of launching PPP products and servicing the client base were estimated at $450,000. Furthermore, using statistical models and several financial assumptions, the product team estimated that one in ten clients to whom the product is promoted would purchase it. In order to estimate the incremental life-time profit estimates associated with clients who were pitched PPP products at the 2.5% and 5% fee levels were produced by the Finance department at Lexzmmar and are provided in the Exhibit 12.13 (detailed data can be downloaded from MarketingFinancialServices.net). In the initial three years following product introduction, Weinstein envisioned selling the product only to Lexzmmar's existing clients because he anticipated regulatory hurdles that would limit access to other brokers, advisors, banks, and remaining channels.

Exhibit 12.13: Expected Incremental Profit Figures Based on Customers Who Purchased PPP Products in the Market Experiment[*]

Number of Direct Mail Pieces Sent	Upfront Fee at 2.5%	Upfront Fee at 5%
2	$4,124	$6,394
4	$4,359	$6,596
6	$4,284	$3,897

[*] Figures represent the incremental life-time profits expected from the client due to the purchase of the PPP product. Figures are estimates produced by a financial model

Case Questions

1. What is the optimal launch strategy for Lexzmmar's Performance Protected Products?

2. Develop a marketing plan including a chronology of activities that Lexzmmar should undertake during the first 3 years of product introduction.

PIONEER ACCELERATED MORTGAGE

On a Wednesday afternoon in late October 2005, Hillary Walters received a surprising phone call from one of the leading consumer protection agencies in the state of Maryland. Walters, the Marketing Vice President for Pioneer Accelerated Mortgage Inc. (PAM), was informed of a number of consumer complaints filed by individuals who had applied for mortgages through the company's web site. A total of eight complainants had accused PAM of misleading advertising practices. They claimed the company stated in its Internet banner ads that their customers' mortgage applications would be processed and approved in less than 24 hours. In all eight cases, the applicants were emailed a "preliminary approval" within hours of filing their applications. However, within two days, they had all been contacted by PAM and informed that their mortgage application was subsequently denied. Walters was told that the agency might pursue a class action law suit against PAM on behalf of the complainants on the grounds of deceptive advertising, and that federal and state regulators would also be informed.

PAM's Marketing Strategy

Pioneer Accelerated Mortgage Inc. was an online mortgage provider based in Bethesda, Maryland. The company was established in 1997 as a broker of mortgage products and subsequently became the primary issuer of mortgages. Most of PAM's business was conducted online and, with the growth of the Internet and the boom in the real estate market, the company experienced significant growth in its mortgage volume. Between 1997 and 2004, the annual volume of the company's issued mortgages grew from $15 million to over $200 million. By mid-2005, PAM employed 46 individuals across a variety of marketing, legal, administrative, and sales functions.

PAM's primary customer acquisition strategy was intense banner advertising on the Internet. In addition, the company established partnerships with real estate search web sites and online credit search engines. Once a homebuyer clicked through PAM's links, the application process was completed online. The banner ads and Internet links promoted the company's quick application processing and competitive mortgage rates. The ads also emphasized its commitment to a 24 hour turnaround time on mortgage application decisions, which was guaranteed by a $200 deduction in closing fees in case this failed to occur. The aggressive positioning of the company seemed to create considerable consumer interest and, as a result, the click-through rates for PAM's Internet ads were considerably higher than the average for the industry.

The Application Process

The mortgage application process at PAM had five stages. The first stage consisted of collecting background information on the homebuyer through the PAM web site. The collected information included items such as the individual's name, social security number, date of birth, place of employment, annual income, existing assets, and other relevant personal and financial information. Once this information was collected, the second stage of application processing was conducted by using the applicant's personal information to access credit records and to obtain the individual's credit score. This information, along with data on the property being purchased, was then used to arrive at the "preliminary decision." The third stage of the application process consisted of informing the applicant of the preliminary decision, usually via email. PAM had a 24 hour turnaround commitment to mortgage applicants for completing Stage Three of the process. The fourth stage of the application process consisted of conducting detailed background research on each application. For example, verification of the place of employment, income validation, and criminal background checks were conducted during this stage. Stage Four often took between one and three days to complete. The final stage of the process consisted of confirming application approval or denial decisions. Applicants for whom insufficient or unfavorable background information was revealed in Stage Four were sent out a "denial of mortgage application" (DMA) email. Those whose mortgage application had been approved were sent confirmation emails and were requested to initiate the processing of legal paperwork, if applicable. Exhibit 12.14 is a flowchart of the application processing procedures used by PAM.

Despite the streamlined approach to application processing, the entire process was a costly and, at times, labor-intensive activity. For example, in order to attract applicants through banner advertising, a large number of Internet impressions were needed. It was estimated that the banner advertising cost associated with a single applicant's click-through to the application page (Stage One) was about $38. Conducting the required credit checks and communicating the decision to the applicant via email (Stages Two and Three) was estimated to cost $26. Stages Four and Five, which required more labor-intensive activities, detailed decision-making, and often resulted in one-on-one phone conversations between applicants and customer service staff, cost PAM approximately $85 per application. This brought the total cost of processing a single completed application to well over $100.

To better understand the claims made against PAM by the consumer protection agency, Walters asked one of her mangers to obtain data related to the company's mortgage applications for the first half of 2005. In particular, data on the number of mortgages that completed Stages Three and Five of the process were needed. In addition, Walters wanted to examine the applicant pool in more detail by separately studying the numbers for different mortgage amounts. Exhibit 12.15 provides a summary of the findings for applications filed between January and June of 2005.

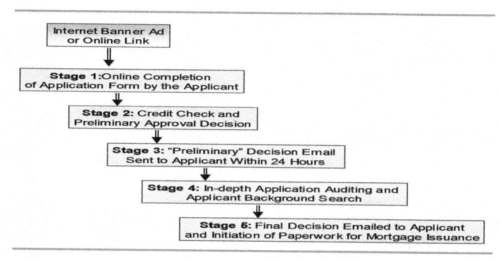

Exhibit 12.14 PAM's Application Procedures

While the 2005 numbers indicated a significant number of Stage Five application rejections, Walters was unclear of the reason why the numbers were so high. Stage Five rejections were the primary source of consumer complaints, and understanding their nature was essential to developing an educated strategy in response to the crisis. Discussion with the administrative staff regarding these applications and subsequent analysis revealed that, in nearly every case, the applicants had provided inaccurate or misleading information on their background. For example, an applicant may have reported an income level higher than their true earnings, over-stated their assets or understated their existing credit obligations. In some cases, individuals listed as references in the application were contacted by phone and provided inconsistent or unfavorable information about the applicant. This was good news for Walters because it suggested that Stage Five application rejections could most likely be defended based on applicants' misrepresentation of personal information. While this was reassuring to Walters, the numbers revealed in this exercise prompted her and other senior management at PAM to question the company's overall promotional policies. The numbers implied the lack of a segment-based approach to marketing the company's products as well as the need for a better understanding of applicants' thought processes.

	Mortgage Amount Under $100,000	Mortgage Amount $100,000- $249,999	Mortgage Amount $250,000- $499,999	Mortgage Amount $500,000 and higher
Number of Applications	83	138	110	78
Number Approved Same Day (Stage 3)	61	103	84	53
Number Denied in Stage 5	7	4	4	8

Exhibit 12.15 Mortgage Processing Statistics

Market Research

To answer some of these emerging questions, Walters commissioned Hanzen Intelligence and Research Enterprise (HIRE) in December of 2005, to conduct a survey of recent mortgage applicants. The study's primary objective was to reveal the rate of applicant misinformation and some of the factors contributing to application inaccuracies among PAM mortgage applicants. While the subject of this line of questioning was PAM's current applicant pool, regulations and company policy restricted surveying this group. As a result, it was necessary to conduct primary market research using a sample of the population to arrive at estimates of overall misinformation rates and related attitudinal measures. HIRE's access to a large market research panel of Internet users was a valuable asset because most of PAM's applicants were also Internet users. An analysis of HIRE panel member demographics revealed similarities with PAM's applicant pool, making the group relevant to a market survey.

Emails were sent out by HIRE to its panel members who had recently reported purchasing a residential property. A total of 1,287 panel members who had purchased a home in the past twelve months were contacted, and 318 individuals responded to the survey. Each panel member was given a monetary incentive and the opportunity to win small home electronics products through a lottery. The survey consisted of 38 questions administered through an Internet questionnaire distribution web site. Respondents were asked an array of questions related to their finances, including their perceptions of mortgage companies and information needs when applying for mortgages. In order to prevent bias in the responses of participants, eighteen of the 38 questions used were unrelated to mortgages. However, two specific mortgage-related questions were of particular interest to Walters: "Mortgage companies request excessive amounts of unnecessary personal information," and "Mortgage companies do not have the right to ask for too much personal information." Respondents were asked to respond either "yes" or "no" to these two questions. In addition, the questionnaire asked respondents to state their total mortgage amount for their recent home purchase. Exhibit 12.16 summarizes the results.

	Mortgage Amount Under $100,000	Mortgage Amount $100,000- $249,999	Mortgage Amount $250,000- $499,999	Mortgage Amount $500,000 and higher
Number of Respondents	95	143	48	32
Number Agreeing with the statement ... "Mortgage companies request excessive amounts of unnecessary personal information"	52	55	17	19
Number Agreeing with the statement ... "Mortgage companies do not have the right to ask for too much personal information"	40	59	18	24

Exhibit 12.16 Summary of Survey Results

Case Questions

1. How should PAM adjust its marketing programs in order to focus its promotions on specific segments of the market?

2. What percentage of PAM's mortgage applicants believe that mortgage companies require excessive amounts of personal information?

GEORGIA SUPPLEMENTAL

Georgia Supplemental Insurance (GSI) was a regional provider of supplemental insurance policies in the states of Georgia, South Carolina, and North Carolina. The company prided itself on offering the best value to its customers through supplemental policies for dental, vision, and travel coverage. Georgia (short for Georgia Supplemental Insurance) sold its policies primarily through employers in these three states. Employers in turn promoted the policies to their employees, who could choose to participate in the offered supplemental insurance plans. Employee participation was typically voluntary and associated with regular monthly premiums, which would be paid directly to Georgia by the employee. Employers who chose to make Georgia's policies available to their employees profited from the ability to bring additional benefits to their workers without having to pay for these added benefits themselves.

Georgia Supplemental was founded in 1973 by Samuel Adler. Adler, who at that time was a dental technician with several years of experience, had noted that the majority of his dental patients had little or no dental insurance coverage. He recognized that, while many of the better employers offered health insurance to their workers, rarely was dental coverage a standard part of their benefits package. After being laid off in early 1973, he invested his life savings into building a company that would tap into this need. The company was incorporated by the end of that year, and a small office was set up in Atlanta. Georgia's mission was to become a leading provider of supplemental dental insurance coverage for employers in the state of Georgia. In 1975, the company expanded its operations into South Carolina; in 1980, employers in North Carolina were also being pitched Georgia's offerings. By 1987, the company had expanded its product array to include supplemental vision; in 1993, travel insurance was also added to its offerings.

Traditionally, Georgia had focused on employers with 50 to 250 employees. Adler believed that companies with smaller operations are often financially strapped and may not be able to convince their workers about the benefits of obtaining supplemental insurance. In addition, it was believed that larger insurance companies that provide group medical plans often penetrate the market for companies that have 250 or more employees either through their own products or through partnerships with third parties. Past experience also seemed to suggest that the most receptive group to Georgia's sales pitches were typically employing anywhere between 50 to 250 employees.

In the spring of 2004, Adler was faced with a potentially costly decision to expand Georgia's geographic range while opening up new channels of profitability for the company. Adler had set a personal goal for himself and for Georgia to expand its operations into Florida, where he believed great profit potential existed. Nevertheless, the decision to move into Florida may prove to be costlier, though more promising, than any of the other expansions that the company had undertaken in its three-decade history.

The Selling of Supplemental Insurance

In the insurance business, most policies have exclusion terms and conditions that limit the amount of benefits for the policyholder. The existence of these exclusions creates a demand for increased coverage either through paying higher premiums to the insurance company or by purchasing supplemental insurance. Supplemental insurance coverage provides benefits that traditional insurance policies may not provide in a cost-effective manner. For example, while a health insurance plan offered by an employer may cover the majority of the costs of a medical procedure, not all costs are covered. These policies, for example, do not cover any yearly deductibles or co-pays for which the policyholder is responsible. Furthermore, indirect costs related to the medical treatment, such as the cost of lost wages due to missing work or out of pocket expenses such as the cost of transportation to a medical facility, are typically not covered by employee-sponsored health plans. Supplemental health insurance could provide coverage for some of these additional items. Similarly, supplemental dental insurance may cover portions of dental bills and supplemental vision plans may cover some of the costs of eye exams and eyewear for individuals who may not have coverage through their employers. Supplemental insurance plans therefore provide a potentially attractive way to control these commonly occurring expenditures. In addition to the financial protection that supplemental insurance policies provide to policyholders, they also represent attractive profit opportunities to the insurance companies selling them. Adler estimated that the average contribution margin for each individual enrolled in a supplemental health plan is $108. For a supplemental dental plan, the estimated margin was $65 and for supplemental travel and vision, it was estimated to be $37 and $45 respectively for each insured individual.

Supplemental policies can be directly purchased by individuals from an insurance company or its agents; they may also be purchased through employers who make them available to their workers. Georgia Supplemental primarily sold its policies through employers. Until the late 1990s, before the growing use of the Internet, the company did not have the infrastructure necessary to sell directly to consumers, and it never functioned through an agent organization. Georgia's sales staff personally made sales calls to the human resources administrators or benefits officers at major employers' headquarters. The sales process often consisted of presenting these individuals with a background of the company and its insurance programs, discussing relevant questions, and presenting the various plans and associated prices. Adler estimated that, out of every twenty sales calls or visits made to new prospects, at least one employer would choose to sign up with Georgia. The sales force also revisited existing accounts two to three times a year to secure repeated business and to pitch new products and plans. On a weekly basis, the average salesperson was on the road about four days of the week, making a total of 28 sales visits. The demanding tasks of the sales force were well compensated, and in

2003 the average salary (base, commissions, and bonuses) for Georgia's 21 sales people was $94,750. Adler estimated that an additional $45,000 had to be spent on transportation and benefits for each sales person.

Expansion Plans

The current sales force covered the states of Georgia and the Carolinas, and over the years these states had helped the company develop 720 loyal accounts (employers), through which 93,560 individual policyholders had obtained supplemental insurance policies from Georgia. The expansion into Florida seemed inevitable to Adler, who often cited state and national statistics to support his long-held beliefs. By his estimates, moving into Florida could double the size of the business in less than five years. Several features of the state were deemed attractive. He also believed that human resources administrators and benefits officers in the state of Florida would be more receptive to Georgia Supplemental and its products. This was based on his own interactions with these individuals in a benefits conference held in Tampa, through informal discussions with his own sales staff, and partially motivated by Florida being his native state.

A primary source of opportunity was the demographics of Florida, which were quickly changing. While there was a significant population of retired individuals who had moved into Florida to spend their retirement years, there was also an influx of young families. These families found the low cost of housing, the warmer climate, and good employment opportunities to be attractive reasons to move into the state. It was this younger market segment that formed the basis for Adler's interest in expanding into Florida. He estimated the size of this segment of the population to grow by an average of 6-7% annually over the next decade. The need that these families had for supplemental insurance coverage combined with the promising economic picture of the state would make Florida a natural point for expansion.

What further sparked Adler's interest was the limited amount of coverage that employers in Florida typically offered with their standard employee benefit plans. A survey conducted by Benefits Research Inc (BRI) in 2003 showed that the average family had to spend $480 in out of pocket expenses to cover dental expenses, of which only $139 was for preventive care. BRI also found that, in Florida, only 17% of employers provided vision coverage as part of their standard health plans, whereas nearly half of the population needed some form of vision care every year. The survey also found that most employers did not participate in travel insurance programs, and that only 6% of employers offered some form of travel insurance policy to their workers. BRI estimated that the total potential market in Florida that would meet Georgia Supplemental's criteria is 3,580 employers, with a total of about half a million employees, each of whom may have several family members in need of supplemental policies.

Adler's Decision

It is April, and Adler would have to arrive at his decision by the middle of May. The strategy to move into Florida could prove to be a costly one. Adler has devised a plan to lead a newly hired sales force into Florida by first sending personalized direct mail letters to the human resources managers in the 3,580 companies identified by BRI (Exhibit 12.17), costing the company nearly $75,000 (production, mailing, list acquisition). The mailing would be conducted by Georgia's marketing department in Atlanta and would be followed up with sales calls and visits by a newly formed Florida sales force that would be in full force by the start of 2005. The yearly overhead cost of setting up a branch office in Tampa was estimated at about $250,000. For a CEO who had been at the helm for over three decades, and for a company that had not launched into a new market for over a decade, this could prove to be a more challenging decision than anyone had originally expected.

Case Questions

1. Should Georgia launch into Florida?

2. What is your assessment of the proposed direct mail campaign and the promotional letter?

James Winterz
Georgia Supplemental Insurance
391 Brook Street, Suite 9A
Tampa, FL

Wilfred Lampelle
Human Resources Manager
APCO Electronics
Miami, FL

Dear Mr. Lampelle,

Please allow me to introduce my company, Georgia Supplemental Insurance (GSI) and myself. GSI is a provider of supplemental insurance policies to employers throughout Florida, Georgia, and the Carolinas. We have been in business for over three decades and provide supplemental health insurance to nearly 100,000 happy employees. GSI provides companies like yours with the ability to provide an array of attractive supplemental insurance policies, from which your employees are very likely to benefit. Our dental plan provides employees and their families with two yearly exams and a 75% discount on major dental procedures[1]. Our vision plan provides a yearly exam for all family members and a 50% discount on eyewear1. We also provide a travel insurance plan and will soon be providing our policyholders with a supplemental health plan[2].

Customer satisfaction and quality service to our policyholders is a founding belief at GSI. We believe that our generous treatment of the customer and liberal and quick processing of claims is the driving force behind why so many companies like yours have chosen to provide our services to their employees.

In the next few weeks, I will be contacting you to see if it is possible to meet briefly and discuss together the details of GSI's plans, which I believe will be very beneficial to APCCO employees. In the meantime, please do not hesitate to call me or my secretary Robert Gains at (217)xxx-xxxx. I look forward to speaking with you shortly.

Sincerely,

James Winterz
Sales Manager
Georgia Supplemental Insurance

---

1. At participating dental offices
2. Subject to state approval

Exhibit 12.17 Sample Letter to be Mailed Out to Human Resources Managers

TIRE INSURANCE PROGRAM

Norvest Banc, located in Seattle Washington was a strong regional competitor, providing a variety of financial solutions in the states of Washington, Oregon, Montana and Idaho. Having been established in 1962, Norvest provided this market with a range of credit and insurance products for both individual and business customers, and operated over 130 bank branches in the four states. In early 2012, the potential for growth for institutions such as Norvest seemed somewhat limited. The financial climate of the time had contributed to inactivity in most financial services categories. Consumer spending was on a decline, the housing market was experiencing price drops, and access to credit was limited due to increased lender sensitivity to risk.

The collapse of the mortgage-backed securities market had further made the business climate unfavorable for lending institutions and new regulatory measures were being implemented to enforce higher standards for lending practices. In this environment, consumers' sense of insecurity about their financial future encouraged them to save more, thereby increasing their savings deposits. However, consumers no longer took out the volume of loans they did in years earlier. As a result, products such as home equity loans, lines of credit, and mortgages witnessed historic drops in application volume and issuance rates for Norvest and its competitors. The low interest environment of the time further limited Norvest Banc's profits, making drastic measures to pursue profit growth a primary focus for the management.

The Norvest Banc Mission

Norvest Banc's CEO, John Dawes along with the Chief Marketing Office, Nancy Hawthorne, had discussed the need for a niche-driven approach to growth in this challenging environment. Discussing this potential in the annual meeting with branch managers during the summer of 2011, Dawes had pointed out that "the traditional markets we serve are bound to shrink next year and the only way to sustain our current size is to find untapped pockets of potential in the market." He then charged Hawthorne with the task of finding these pockets and to initiate actions that will help Norvest to capitalize on them.

Hawthorne's task was a challenging one. As a former technology specialist with a major software developer, she appreciated the need for embracing change and realigning the organization to capitalize on new opportunities. She cited that while in 2007 only three banks in the United States had folded, in 2010 the figure was close two hundred. While she did not consider Norvest to be among those likely to fail in the near future, the pressures of the environment, and the demands of senior management required quick and successful execution of creative marketing campaigns for innovative products.

What most concerned Hawthorne was that in this environment many failing banks and their branch operations would be acquired by larger competitors, increasing the power of the few national players in Norvest's regional markets, and inhibiting the bank's ability to compete based on its recognized brand name and its efficient cost structure. Recent trends of bank mergers and acquisitions both at the national and regional levels indicated that they generate cost efficiencies and produce new organizations that may be far more aggressive in taking over the market. This was a story which she was very familiar with in her previous career in the software industry, and did not want to see repeated in the case of Norvest.

Growth Opportunities

Unlike the bigger national banks with great resources, expansion of its retail presence by opening or acquiring new branches was not an option for Norvest Banc due to its financial constraints. However, Hawthorne and Dawes began discussing specific steps Norvest could take in order to combat the evident market pressures. Some of the ideas emerging from these discussions soon took on the shape of specific marketing campaigns and products which could be launched within a very short time period. For example, more aggressive marketing campaigns were deployed to promote the bank's credit card products to existing customers. Also short-term credit products began to be systematically promoted to business customers by the bank branches' loan officers. Some of these steps were dramatic shifts in Norvest's marketing philosophy. For example, traditionally Norvest did not promote credit card products to its existing customers since Dawes was previously under the belief that credit card marketing is a mass-market operation and should not be undertaken by regional banks. As a result Norvest came to recognize the need to further push this product line late in the game, especially compared to many of its local competitors. As a result more aggressive promotion programs through direct mail to existing customers were put in place. This included the inclusion of promotional material in monthly bank statements as well as more visible advertising for various credit card options available to online banking customers through the bank's web site.

A second initiative that developed from the conversations between Dawes and Hawthorne was to expand the number of Automatic Teller Machines (ATMs) operated by Norvest. The goal was to identify strategic locations that have little presence of competing ATM machines, but experience high volume of pedestrian traffic. A total of 68 locations in the four states were identified, and ATM machines were leased and installed in these locations. The ATM fees generated from these machines were projected to create a profitable return, with a projected ROI of approximately 16%.

The third initiative discussed between Hawthorne and Dawes was to expand the company's insurance business into very specialized categories of insurance. The deregulation of the financial services industry in 1999 had long made this a possibility for banking institutions such as Norvest. In 1999 the repeal of the Glass-Steagall Act which had been put in place in 1933 made it possible again for financial institutions to become active in a wide range of financial markets. Glass-Steagall, having been made into law following a series of catastrophic bank failures in the late 1920s and early 1930s prohibited banks from actively underwriting insurance products and participating in many related marketing activities. Its repeal in 1999 opened new opportunities for banks to become active participants in the insurance business – a potential that only a limited number of banking institutions effectively capitalized on.

The Tire Insurance Program (TIP)

The inspiration behind Hawthorne's insurance product came out of a minor driving incident she had experienced in the summer of 2007. While driving on one of the major highways north of Seattle, her car ran over debris that had fallen from a construction truck ahead. She momentarily lost control of the vehicle but managed to avoid collision with other vehicles and successfully slowed her vehicle down to a stop. When she stepped out of her car she realized that one of the front tires had been punctured by a sharp piece of metal, beyond the point of repair. Being an avid sports car driver she knew that to replace this high-performance tire she would be spending nearly $350, and that her automobile insurance policy did not cover such expenses.

This incident sparked Hawthorne's interest in developing an insurance product for Norvest Banc called TIP. TIP, which stands for "Tire Insurance Program", would consist of tire insurance coverage to protect car owners when facing situations similar to what Hawthorne had experienced. If the tire becomes damaged for any reason beyond a point of a simple repair, TIP would pay the full replacement cost of the tire, including installation costs. Such products are widely promoted by national chains of tire distributors. However, Hawthorne's market research revealed that the majority of independent service stations and repair shops, while accounting for over 30% of all tires sold in the country, do not have such a product offered to those customers who purchase tires from them. To Hawthorne, this represented the "pockets of potential" that Dawes had tasked her to look for. In addition such incidents were often not covered by automobile insurance companies since the associated costs fell below the typical deductible level of $500 associated with auto insurance policies.

TIP could therefore represent a good option for many car owners as well as service stations that may benefit from its availability to their customers. Market research indicated that tires on most vehicles last about 38,000 miles allowing for a driving period of 32 months. Replacement costs for all four tires vary from car to car, and depend on the tire size and performance characteristics. Tire size (e.g., "225/50/16") is quantified by three measures : (a) the width of the tire (e.g., 225 millimeters), (b) side wall aspect ratio representing the size of the sidewall height compared to the radius of the tire (e.g., 50 would mean 50%), and (c) the wheel diameter in inches (e.g., 16 inches). In addition, factors such as the speed rating of the tire (how fast the vehicle could be driven), the weight rating (what load the tire could carry) and the material used to construct the tire affected its value to buyers. Exhibit 12.18 provides a sampling of tire prices. Market research by industry associations and expert estimates indicated significant variation in replacement costs ranging from a low of about $250 for four tires to a high of over $2,000 for high performance tires.

However, research also indicated that the primary cause of tire replacement is the natural wear and tear on the tire, poor wheel alignment, or faulty suspension systems on the vehicle. Tire punctures due to nails resulting in tire deflation were often easily repaired at an average cost of $23, and catastrophic tire failures due to large objects – like the one experienced by Hawthorne resulting in the need for total replacement of the tire – were very rare. Less than half of one percent of all tires replaced were assumed to be due to such catastrophic failures. However, consumers tend to overestimate the likelihood of such events, and given the high price for replacing the tire often opt to purchase the additional tire protection polices from chains of tire retailers that offer them. This represents a great profit opportunity for these retailers and insurers who underwrite the policies. Similar patterns had been observed in home electronics retailing, whereby major retail chains were able to reap unprecedented profits by selling supplemental warranties for major appliances and electronic products. While these warranties provided customers with peace of mind, the low incident of product failures during the term of the coverage, transformed extended warranties to a source of profits which at times exceeded the profit margins for the majority of electronic products sold by these retailers. Hawthorne wondered if the same profit opportunity may await Norvest if TIP were to be launched.

Tire Size	Replacement Cost
195/65/15	$60-$115
205/60/16	$75-$125
215/60/16	$80-$125
215/65/17	$95-$155
225/65/17	$120-$180
235/55/18	$110-$210
245/65/17	$115-$395
275/65/18	$135-$525

Exhibit 12.18: Range of Replacement Costs of a
Single Tire Depending on Size

However, research also indicated that the primary cause of tire replacement is the natural wear and tear on the tire, poor wheel alignment, or faulty suspension systems on the vehicle. Tire punctures due to nails resulting in tire deflation were often easily repaired at an average cost of $23, and catastrophic tire failures due to large objects – like the one experienced by Hawthorne resulting in the need for total replacement of the tire – were very rare. Less than half of one percent of all tires replaced were assumed to be due to such catastrophic failures. However, consumers tend to overestimate the likelihood of such events, and given the high price for replacing the tire often opt to purchase the additional tire protection polices from chains of tire retailers that offer them. This represents a great profit opportunity for these retailers and insurers who underwrite the policies. Similar patterns had been observed in home electronics retailing, whereby major retail chains were able to reap unprecedented profits by selling supplemental warranties for major appliances and electronic products. While these warranties provided customers with peace of mind, the low incident of product failures during the term of the coverage, transformed extended warranties to a source of profits which at times exceeded the profit margins for the majority of electronic products sold by these retailers. Hawthorne wondered if the same profit opportunity may await Norvest if TIP were to be launched.

Distribution System for Automobile Tires

Tire protection policies had been sold for well over a decade by national and regional chains of tire retailers. While tires can be expensive and tend to account for a large portion of the cost of maintaining a vehicle, the increased level of competition over the years reduced the ability of tire retailers to realize high margins on the sale of tires alone. Price competition and the publicizing and advertising of prices have become common practice in this business, creating downward pressure on prices. In order to counter the resulting margin depletion, tire retailers have developed new approaches to generate profits. Often the advertised prices do not include the cost of installation, nor are the costs of disposal of the old tires explicitly mentioned in the ads. While consumers may be drawn to a particular retailer due to its low advertised price for the tire, they may not pay sufficient attention to these additional costs. However these additional costs represent lucrative sources of profits for the retailer, especially when a large volume of tires is sold.

An additional source of profits for chains of tire retailers has been supplemental tire protection policies, which represent little costs and can significantly boost the profits associated with the individual sale of tires. When pitched effectively to customers who are about to spend hundreds of dollars replacing their old tires, tire protection policies represent a small fraction of the overall expenditure, yet they create a sense of security in the customer's mind and as a result have a high acceptance rate among consumers. Some estimated that about 21% of all tires sold in 2010 by those retailers that offer them were sold in conjunction with such a policy. However, the infrequent occurrence of catastrophic tire failures made the costs of providing such insurance protection very low, and estimates were that while a supplemental coverage for a single tire may cost the customer as much as $15 per tire, the cost of providing such coverage could be less than 50¢ to the insurer.

Hawthorne's desire to launch TIP was consistent with the general direction that Norvest Banc had taken in advancing its position in the insurance markets in the four states it was active in. A central part of Norvest's marketing strategy was to establish itself in insurance markets that experienced low incident rates for policyholder claims yet were considered to be experiencing stable growth in policy sales. Tire protection certainly fit these two criteria and following discussions with Dawes and the legal team at Norvest, Hawthorne sought and obtained regulatory permission to launch TIP. Hawthorne, recognizing that the national and regional chains of tire retailers already have tire replacement programs in place, decided to no approach them, and to instead focus Norvest's efforts on independent service stations. These service stations often consist of a gas station which may carry fuel from major oil companies, a convenience store, and a repair shop. Due to their independent nature, the tires sold by these stations to their customers are often not pitched to customers with the added option of tire protection – a feature heavily promoted by competing chains of tire retailers.

The independent service stations are often family-operated businesses and provide repair service to the population in the immediate vicinity of the station. As a result they tend to be stable businesses that have long-established customer relationships, and many of the station operators have had bank accounts or other financial transactions with Norvest bank branches located near them. This, Hawthorne believed, creates the pocket of opportunity: "We know these folks, and they know us, and the sense of trust they have with us can make this venture work, as long as we put enough resources behind it, and price TIP properly". She estimated that in the four states where Norvest has bank branches, there are over 3,600 service stations that can be pitched with TIP.

Testing the Waters

In order to test the waters, Hawthorne decided to launch the product concept in Idaho first. If the Idaho results turn out to be favorable, she would then launch TIP in the other three states. The Idaho launch would also enable her to examine the market acceptance rate and degree of price sensitivity associated with TIP. As a result, following regulatory approval obtained in mid 2011, TIP was launched in Idaho in October of 2011. Each Norvest bank branch was asked to assign one staff member to approach a target group of service stations in its immediate vicinity. The use of existing bank staff for this incremental effort was partially motivated by Hawthorne's view that existing employees should be retained as much as possible, despite the slowdown in business and reallocation of some employees to new marketing activities would help prevent the need for employee layoffs. To further motivate branch staff assigned with this task, a $50 commission for every service station that signs up with TIP would be paid to the employee.

To enable a flexible selling process, the employee would be able to set the retail price of TIP (price paid by the customer to the service station) anywhere between $5 a tire to $15 per tire. Furthermore, the salesperson would be able to vary the retail margins from 40% to 75%. For example, having set the retail price at $10 and a 40% margin, the customer would pay $10 per tire to obtain the protection by TIP, and the service station would pass on $6 to Norvest Banc and keep the remaining $4. The exact terms would be negotiated between the bank employee and each service station operator and could therefore vary from one service station to the next. The cost of underwriting TIP to Norvest, as reflected by the actuarial cost of replacing a damaged tire was estimated to be 54¢ (this cost takes into account both the probability of catastrophic tire failure and the replacement cost of the tire). However this figure ranged from a low of 37¢ for smaller tires to a high of $3.45 for high-performance tires.

An internal debate within the Norvest marketing group was regarding whether the prices should be tiered so that coverage for the more expensive high-performance tires would be priced at higher levels. However Dawes believed in launching a simple pricing scheme and ideally a universal program that could be implemented in an identical form across all states. No agreement on a tiered price structure was reached by the January launch date in Idaho. It was therefore decided to launch the product in Idaho at a single price regardless of tire size and type. This decision was made considering that the industry norm – as exercised by the chain tire retailers – was to charge a single price for all sizes and types of tires being protected by the policy. However, to allow some flexibility in the selling process, the bank staff making the pitch to the service station operators could offer the operators a gift card valued anywhere between $10 to $25. To prevent cases of abuse, half of the value of this card would be funded from the $50 commission paid to the employee. Therefore, if a service station signs up for TIP and is offered a $10 gift card, the bank employee would only receive $45 (i.e., $50 less $10×½).

The selling of TIP was a relatively systematic process. Each Norvest bank branch manager received a list of service stations in the branch's surrounding area and was asked to assign one branch employee to visit these stations. In order to ensure a proper sales approach, the selected employee would have to have had previous selling experience and would conduct background checks on the list of service stations provided by the Norvest head office in order to prioritize selling efforts on the larger and more established businesses. About 19% of businesses were eliminated from further processing either due to their unfavorable financial standing or questionable status as judged by the bank branch manager. The remaining 81% of service stations on the list were then approached for the pitch through a personal visit by the bank employee.

Three main selling points were emphasized in such visits. One was the established brand name of Norvest Banc in the neighborhood which would make it easy for the service station to pitch the product to its customers. The second benefit pitched was the ability of the service station to introduce a new benefit to its customers, and the third benefit – perhaps the most important – was the incremental profits that the service station could realize from promoting TIP to those customers who buy tires. These visits resulted in a success rate of 22%, with the service station operator signing up to offer TIP to its customers, during the sales visit. Follow-up calls to the service station operator boosted this success rate to 37%. As a result of the 238 service stations approached over the months of October to December of 2011, a total of 88 service stations signed up for TIP. To enable tracking, the service station was required through the signed agreement to disclose the total number of tires it sells every month, regardless of whether or not TIP was sold alongside the tire. This would enable Norvest head office analysts to examine TIP's market penetration and observe the potential effects of its pricing and promotion campaigns.

Data from the Idaho Launch

The 238 stations approached between October and December of 2011 represented 31% of all service stations registered in the five mile radius of the Norvest branches in Idaho. To document the effectiveness of the selling process, data from the bank employees was consolidated. The resulting data set captured the characteristics of each individual sales visit, including information on the TIP price pitched by the employee, the value of the gift card offered (if any), the retail margin pitched, and whether or not the retailer signed for TIP. In order to allow time for service station operators to familiarize themselves and their customers with TIP, sales figures for the immediate months following the adoption of TIP by the service station were not used and instead figures for the month of March (2012) were compiled for further analysis. It was believed that by that time the service station operators have developed enough knowledge of the product to promote it to their customers and therefore the March 2012 figures would be a good basis for analyzing their customers' reactions to TIP. Exhibit 12.19 provides a summary of this information (detailed data can be downloaded from MarketingFinancialServices.net) .

Hawthorne's Challenge

Given the results of the Idaho launch, Nancy Hawthorne needed to consider the expansion of TIP to Oregon, Montana and Washington, in addition to further penetration of the Idaho market. In her assessment the cost of the staff reaching out to service station operators was already captured by each bank branch's infrastructure expenses and did not represent incremental expenses to Norvest. This assessment was a reflection of the direction given by the Board of Directors of Norvest to mobilize underutilized bank staff for such projects. However, many other issues remained to be assessed regarding pricing and promotion campaigns. Specifically, Hawthorne had been asked by Dawes and the Board to develop a universal marketing program based on the Idaho experience. Dawes had suggested to her that keeping the price and promotion (e.g., gift cards) flexible can make the program very difficult to manage and cause considerable confusion among customers and branch employees. It also introduces potential sources of tension if service station operators and their customers from neighboring areas realize that they have been offered different prices for the exact same coverage levels, and can therefore potentially compromise their trust and confidence in Norvest – something that Dawes wanted to avoid given the sense of public distrust that had developed toward the financial services sector at that time.

Exhibit 12.19: Average Figures for TIP (March 2012)

Number of tires sold per station	27.6
Number of tires sold with TIP per station	8.1
Retail price of TIP	$9.39
Retail margin	54.9%
Value of gift card given to the service station	$9.56

Hawthorne was therefore charged with the task of determining the optimal price and promotion program for TIP, based on the data collected from Idaho. The base program being considered was to offer a TIP price per tire of $10, a $10 gift card to the station operators and a 50% retail margin. These figures closely resembled the numbers which evolved out of Idaho. However four other options also had to be evaluated by Hawthorne:

(A) The same program as the base program being considered, however at a TIP price per tire of $5 (i.e., price: $5, gift card: $10, retail margin: 50%).
(B) The same program as the base program being considered, however at a TIP price per tire of $15 (i.e., price: $15, gift card: $10, retail margin: 50%).
(C) The same program as the base program (TIP price per tire of $10 and 50% retail margin), however without any gift cards being given to the service stations (i.e., price: $10, gift card: $0, retail margin: 50%).
(D) The same program as the base program, however with the retail margin boosted to 75% (i.e., price: $10, gift card: $10, retail margin: 75%).

Dawes believed that option D would be the best since it provides a great incentive for the station operators to adopt TIP. However he also recognized the fact that many of the station operators making decisions on such matters may not have long-term perspective on such decisions and not consider the retail margin heavily in their decisions. Perhaps for this reason and ethical concerns he favored option C as well. Dawes viewed the gift card a form of bribe which the station operators may be offended to accept. Given the abundance of data collected from the Idaho test, interpretations of such type no longer needed to be a matter of personal opinions, and an issue that had to be settled through scientific analysis by Hawthorne and her staff.

Case Question

What is the optimal price for launching TIP?

BANCSIM2

Purpose of the Simulation

BancSim2 is a marketing simulation program that trains managers to utilize market research data and make marketing decisions to manage a community bank with multiple branches. It can be downloaded from *MarketingFinancialServices.net*. Marketing research data ranging from qualitative information to highly quantitative information, using both secondary and primary data sources, will be used in this simulation. The simulation can be run individually or in teams. During the simulation the user(s) will make a sequence of decisions managing the bank's marketing activities over a two year (eight quarter) time period.

Company Background

In BancSim2 you will be managing a bank named BankCentral, which operates multiple branches in the town of Waterloo. This is a small town of roughly 300,000 people, and BankCentral has been operating in this market for nearly four decades. The population of Waterloo is divided by marketers into two general segments (A and B), which vary in terms of their characteristics, banking needs, preference patterns and resources.

Management Decisions

For each quarter, the following decisions have to be made by you – the bank's marketing management team – for each of the two segments:

1. **The number of staff in the bank branch servicing the customers.** This figure can range from a low of two to a high of 10 for each segment. In each quarter you can choose to add or drop staff as needed, subject to the aforementioned limits.

2. **The amount of money spent on advertising and promoting the bank's services.** This amount can range from a low of $1,000 per quarter to a high of $100,000 per quarter, for each segment.

3. **The nature of advertising content delivered.** You will be given various choices of advertising, ranging from mass media advertising to direct mail and telemarketing. You can also choose to delegate advertising decisions to your ad agency.

4. **The unique selling proposition (USP).** This reflects the one phrase you think would be most effective in communicating BankCentral's appeal to its target market. You would not need to specify this phrase if you choose to delegate the selection of the USP and media to the ad agency (item 3 above).

5. **Price.** This reflects the pricing structure of your banking fees and service charges to new customers, which are spelled out in the contracts customers sign when opening an account at BankCentral. The price you set for each quarter can range from a low of $10 per quarter (i.e., approximately $3.29/month) to a high of $150 per quarter (i.e., approximately $49.99/month).

6. **Buy and sell decisions for bank branches.** You will have the opportunity to either buy or sell a portfolio of customers by acquiring or selling branches, if you consider such a choice to be a good one. You cannot conduct a buy and a sell in the same time period. You can also choose not to engage in any buying or selling of customer portfolios.

The Exhibit 12.20 shows the layout of the *Decision Input Screen*.

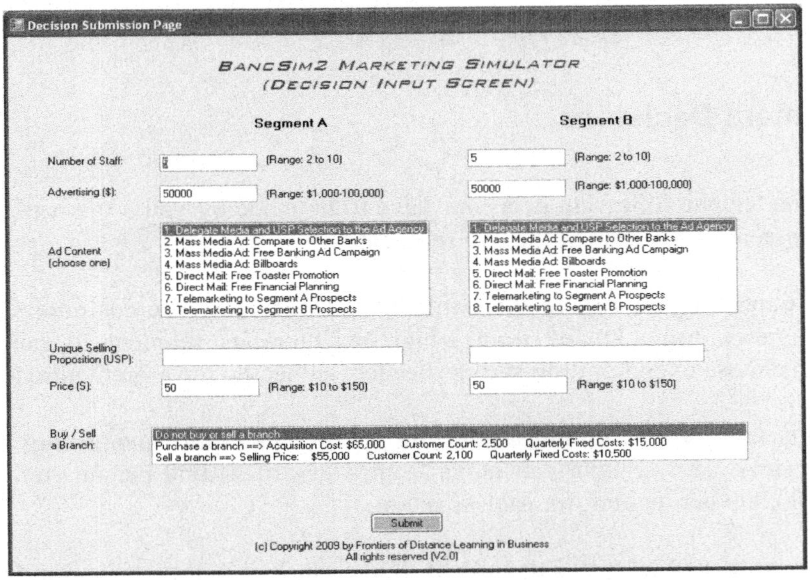

Exhibit 12.20 Decision Input Screen

Running BancSim2

In order to start BancSim2, you must first go to ***MarketingFinancialServices.net.*** You should locate the icon for running BancSim2, and then click on the button. You may be prompted several times for various add-on software downloads and prerequisites which are required to run the simulation. The installation process may take several minutes (as long as 10 minutes) to complete. Having responded to these prompts you will then be able to enter the simulation's main page. Please enter your name (and any team members' names) and then click the Next button. Entering this information is optional and is only for purposes generating a final report which allows your instructor to learn about the experience of each student or team. Once you have pressed "Next", the Main Menu will appear (Exhibit 12.21). Also, please note that if you are using a Mac computer, you would need to install additional software to emulate the Windows operating system. This information and helpful links can be found at *MarketingFinancialServices.net.*

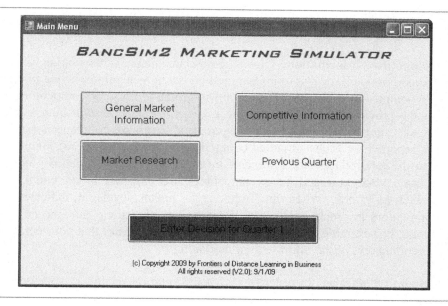

Exhibit 12.21 Main Menu

Sources of Market Information

In order to make well-informed decisions, you are able to obtain access to various forms of market information:

Market Research Reports: Each quarter you will be able to obtain access to market research reports produced for the marketing management team of BankCentral. These reports vary in format and content from one quarter to the next. They can include qualitative studies, analysis of secondary data, survey findings, conjoint analysis and other forms of primary and secondary market research studies. Make sure to use the *Market Research* button in the Main Menu of the simulation.

General Market Information: Each quarter you will be provided with general information on how the nature of competition and the marketplace in Waterloo may be changing. This information is typically not based on formal market research, but rather on information provided by the bank managers, regulatory bodies, the local municipality and other relevant sources.

Competitive Information: Given the regulated nature of the market, you (and your competitors) have access to information regarding general marketing practices of all competitors. You can therefore obtain information on your competitors' decisions for the previous quarter through the *Competitive Information* button in the Main Menu. Competitors' decisions are aggregated across all competitors (and therefore not reported for each individual competitor). These decisions are summarized in a measure referred to as the *Competitive Index*. When the Competitive Index is 1.0, it indicates that you and your competitors are engaged in an equal amount of marketing efforts. When the Index is at higher levels, it indicates that your competitors are more active than you in marketing their banking services to the public. For example, a Competitive Index of 2.0 indicates that your competitors are expending double the effort in their marketing.

Previous Quarter: In order to revisit information related to your decisions and financial results for BankCentral in the most recent quarter, you can utilize the *Previous Quarter* button from the Main Menu.

Output of the Results

The output generated for each decision outlines the results for each of the two segments, as well as overall measures of profitability and company performance. Exhibit 12.22 provides a sample of the output generated.

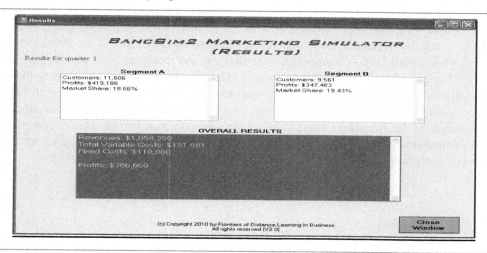

Exhibit 12.22 Sample Output

In addition, at the very end of the simulation (after completing 8 quarterly decisions), a summary screen will appear which will report your overall results (cumulative profits, market share, etc.) for the entire simulation. You should make a copy the contents of the report for your records by cutting and pasting the contents into a text file or an email message. You should also email a copy to the simulation instructor. The entire box from the very top to the very bottom needs to be copies as it contains the necessary diagnostic information for you and your simulation instructor.

Tracking Your Decisions and Performance

In order to record your thought process and sequence of decisions, the *Decision Information Tables* provided on MarketingFinancialServices.net must be used. For each quarter, please keep a log of your decisions, your team's underlying motivation behind these decisions, and record the relevant results of the decisions. The resulting information will help you and your team develop a coherent presentation reflecting your thought process and your use of the market research information.

Accessing BancSim2

BancSim2 can be accessed from *MarketingFinancialServices.net*. You should ensure to have the Microsoft .NET framework installed on the computer on which you will be running BancSim2. Please consult your systems administrator to ensure the .NET framework is installed or that you have administrator-level access for the computer you will be running the simulation on, that would enable software updates and .NET prerequisites to be installed. BancSim2 is designed to run on PC-based computers. If Apple computers are used, they must have the appropriate software overlay to emulate the Windows operating system.

Index

CPSIA information can be obtained at www.ICGtesting.com
Printed in the USA
BVOW09s0820120916

461858BV00009B/90/P